Using WordPerfect 2.1 for the Mac

David Reiser

Holly J. Morris

Using WordPerfect 2.1 for the Mac

Copyright © 1992 by Que® Corporation

All rights reserved. Printed in the United States of America. No part of this book may be used or reproduced in any form or by any means, or stored in a database or retrieval system, without prior written permission of the publisher except in the case of brief quotations embodied in critical articles and reviews. Making copies of any part of this book for any purpose other than your own personal use is a violation of United States copyright laws. For information, address Que Corporation, 11711 N. College Ave., Carmel, IN 46032.

Library of Congress Catalog No.: 91-66624

ISBN: 0-88022-739-7

This book is sold *as is*, without warranty of any kind, either express or implied, respecting the contents of this book, including but not limited to implied warranties for the book's quality, performance, merchantability, or fitness for any particular purpose. Neither Que Corporation nor its dealers or distributors shall be liable to the purchaser or any other person or entity with respect to any liability, loss, or damage caused or alleged to be caused directly or indirectly by this book.

94 93 92   4 3 2

Interpretation of the printing code: the rightmost double-digit number is the year of the book's printing; the rightmost single-digit number, the number of the book's printing. For example, a printing code of 92-1 shows that the first printing of the book occurred in 1992.

Screens reproduced in this book were created using Capture! by Mainstay Software Corp.

This book is based on WordPerfect for the Macintosh, Version 2.1.

Publisher: Lloyd J. Short

Associate Publisher: Rick Ranucci

Product Development Manager: Thomas H. Bennett

Book Designer: Scott Cook

Production Team: Jeff Baker, Claudia Bell, Michelle Cleary, Christine Cook, Mark Enochs, Dennis Clay Hager, Audra Hershman, Betty Kish, Phil Kitchel, Laurie Lee, Jay Lesandrini, Linda Quigley, Linda Seifert, Kevin Spear, Suzanne Tully, Christine Young

Product Director
Shelley O'Hara

Production Editor
Tracy L. Barr

Editors
Louise Lambert
Anne P. Root
Susan M. Shaw
Brad Sullivan
Micci Swick-Volk

Acquisitions Editor
Tim Ryan

Technical Editor
Robert Raleigh

Composed in ITC Garamond and MCPdigital by Que Corporation

Dedication

Each to the other for making this book possible
Both to Jennifer for reminding us of what is truly important

About the Authors

David Reiser holds a Ph.D. in chemical engineering from the University of Illinois and is currently a corrosion engineer at Air Products and Chemicals, Inc. After battling rust all day, he enjoys working on the Macintosh and playing soccer. Dave has been involved in personal computing since buying a Kaypro II in 1983, and his conversion to the Macintosh way occurred with the purchase of a Mac Plus in 1986. Even before the release of Version 1.0, he has been using WordPerfect for the Macintosh. He has been married to Holly Morris for 10 years.

Holly J. Morris has an M.S. in anatomy from the University of Pennsylvania and is an assistant professor of biology at Lehigh County Community College. She has been using WordPerfect for the Mac since the release of Version 1.0. Holly and Dave share computer time with their five-year-old daughter, Jennifer.

Trademark Acknowledgments

Que Corporation has made every effort to supply trademark information about company names, products, and services mentioned in this book. Trademarks indicated below were derived from various sources. Que Corporation cannot attest to the accuracy of this information.

Adobe Type Manager is a trademark and PostScript is a registered trademark of Adobe Systems Incorporated.

Claris is a registered trademark of Claris Corporation.

CompuServe Information Service is a registered trademark of CompuServe Incorporated and H&R Block, Inc.

DataVis is a trademark and MacLink Plus is a registered trademark of Datavue Corporation.

DeskWriter is a registered trademark of Hewlett-Packard Co.

Microsoft and Microsoft Word are registered trademarks of Microsoft Corporation.

NEC is a registered trademark of NEC Information Systems, Inc.

On Technology On Location is a trademark of Oldurai Corporation.

PageMaker is a registered trademark of Aldus Corporation.

QMS is a registered trademark of QMS, Inc.

TrueType is a trademark and Apple, ImageWriter, LaserWriter, Macintosh, and MultiFinder are registered trademarks of Apple Computer, Inc.

UNIX is a registered trademark of AT&T.

WordPerfect is a registered trademark of WordPerfect Corporation.

Trademarks of other products mentioned in this book are held by the companies producing them.

Acknowledgments

We would like to thank the following people:

Family and friends for their support and encouragement.

Ed Watts and Ed Stevens of WordPerfect Corporation for their patience, help, and enthusiasm during testing of WordPerfect for the Macintosh Version 2.

Tracy Barr, Jeannine Freudenberger, Shelley O'Hara, and the editorial crew at Que for helping to make this a better book.

Contents at a Glance

Introduction 1

Part I: Getting Started

1	Quick Start: Creating a Business Letter	9
2	An Overview of WordPerfect 2.1	29
3	Editing a Document	57
4	Formatting a Document	91
5	Using the WordPerfect Speller and Thesaurus	161
6	Printing a Document	189

Part II: Refining Documents

7	Managing Files and Documents	219
8	Formatting with Styles	249
9	Using Columns and Text Boxes	275
10	Creating Outlines and Lists	311
11	Using the Drawing Window	353

Part III: Using Advanced Features

12	Merging Documents	397
13	Sorting Text	417
14	Using Macros	439
15	Customizing WordPerfect	475
16	Taking Advantage of System 7	511
A	Installing WordPerfect	527
	Index	537

Table of Contents

Introduction 1
    What's New in Versions 2.0 and 2.1? 1
    Who Should Use This Book? 2
    What's In This Book? 3
    How To Use This Book 5
    Program Versions Covered by This Book 6
    To the User 6

I Getting Started

1 Quick Start: Creating a Business Letter 9
    Starting WordPerfect 10
    Getting Help 10
    Creating a Document 12
        Changing the Screen Display 13
        Typing Text 15
        Setting Tabs 19
    Editing a Document 20
        Selecting Text 21
        Inserting and Deleting Text 21
        Cutting and Pasting 22
        Using Right and Left Alignment 22
    Saving a Document 23
    Using the Speller 25
    Printing a Document 27
    Quitting WordPerfect 2 27
    Chapter Summary 28

2 An Overview of WordPerfect 2.1 29
    Starting WordPerfect 30
    Reviewing the Screen Display 31
        The Status Bar 32
        The Scroll Bars 36
        The Mouse Pointers 36
    Accessing Menu Commands 37
        Using the Mouse 37
        Using the Keyboard 38
        Understanding Types of Menu Commands 39
            Direct Menu Commands 39
            Hierarchical Menu Commands 40
            Commands that Open Dialog Boxes 40

  Using Command-Key Shortcuts 41
 Getting Help 42
 Creating a Document 44
 Moving around in the Document 45
  Using the Scroll Bars 45
  Using the Arrow Keys 46
  Using the Repeat Function 46
  Using Page Up, Page Down, Home, and End 48
  Using the Numeric Keypad in Command Mode 48
  Using the Go To Command 50
 Working with Text 51
  Inserting Text 51
  Selecting Text 51
   Using the Mouse 51
   Using the Keyboard 52
  Deleting Text 53
  Using Typeover Mode 53
 Saving a Document 53
 Exiting WordPerfect 54
 Chapter Summary 55

3 Editing a Document 57

 Opening a Document 58
  Opening a Document from the Finder 58
  Opening a File from within WordPerfect 59
   Navigating the Macintosh File Lists 60
   Controlling the File List 61
  Opening More Than One Document 62
  Creating a New Document 62
 Working with Text 62
  Cutting Text 65
  Copying Text 65
  Pasting Text 66
  Appending Text 67
  Deleting Selected Text 69
  Using Undo 70
 Changing Text Styles 70
  Using Boldface, Italic, and Underline 71
  Removing Text Attributes 72
  Using the Plain Text Command 72
 Understanding Hidden Codes 73
  Showing Hidden Codes 73
  Resizing the Code Window 74
  Scrolling through Codes 74
 Using the Search Menu 74
  Finding Text 76
  Replacing Text 77

Understanding the Find Dialog Box 79
   The Direction Menu 79
   The Where Menu 80
   The Match Menu 81
   The Affect Menu 82
   The Action Menu 84
   The Insert Menu 85
Using Find Next and Find Previous 87
Finding Codes 88
Chapter Summary 89

4 Formatting a Document ... 91

Choosing a Formatting Method 92
   Menus and Keyboard Shortcuts 92
   The Ruler 93
      Displaying the Ruler 93
      Using the Zoom Pop-Up Menu 94
      Copying and Pasting the Ruler 97
Formatting Characters 98
   Changing the Font 98
   Changing the Font Size 100
   Using Relative Character Sizes 101
   Using the Character Map 103
   Changing Text Styles 105
   Using Subscripts and Superscripts 107
   Using Redline and Strikeout 109
   Setting Underline Styles 111
   Using Small Caps 112
   Changing Case 112
   Kerning Text 113
   Using Color with Text 115
Formatting Lines of Text 116
   Applying Formatting Changes 116
   Using Tabs 117
      Understanding Tab Types 117
      Specifying Relative and Absolute Tabs 121
      Setting Tabs with the Tabs Dialog Box 122
      Clearing Tabs 124
   Aligning Text 124
      Alignment Settings 124
      Center Line and Flush Right 126
   Setting Line Spacing, Line Height, and Leading 127
      Line Spacing 128
      Line Height and Leading 129
   Numbering Lines 129
   Using Hyphenation 131
      Turning Hyphenation On and Off 131
      Inserting Soft Hyphens 132

  Understanding the Hyphenation Zone 133
  Using the Hard Space and Nonbreaking Hyphen 133
 Using Subtitles 134
Formatting Paragraphs 136
 Setting Left and Right Margins 136
 Indenting Text 137
  First-Line Indent 137
  Paragraph Indent 138
  Hanging Indent 138
 Adding Space between Paragraphs 140
Formatting Pages 140
 Setting Top and Bottom Margins 140
 Inserting a Hard Page Break 142
 Adding Page Numbers 142
 Adding Headers and Footers 144
 Using Watermarks 148
 Suppressing Page Format Elements 150
 Keeping Text Together 151
 Centering Text Vertically 153
Adding Page, Paragraph, and Character Borders 153
 Page Borders 155
 Paragraph and Character Borders 157
 Filled Regions 158
 Border Location 159
Chapter Summary 160

5 Using the WordPerfect Speller and Thesaurus 161

Using the Speller 162
 Selecting Text To Spell-Check 162
  Spell-Checking an Entire Document 163
  Spell-Checking a Part of a Document 164
  Spell-Checking from the Insertion Point to the End 164
 Using Other Check Menu Options 165
  Checking Words with Numbers 165
  Checking for Duplicate Words 166
  Controlling the Search for Phonetic Suggestions 166
 Running the Speller 167
  Replacing Misspelled Words 167
  Adding Words to the User Dictionary 167
  Skipping Words 168
 Practicing with the Speller 168
 Looking Up a Word Not in the Document 171
  Entering the Word 171
  Using Wild Cards 171
 Using Set Language To Limit Spell-Checking 173
 Selecting Alternate-Language Dictionaries 174

Using the Thesaurus 175
   Looking Up a Word 175
   Extending a Document Word Search 177
   Displaying a Search History 177
   Clearing a Column 178
   Looking Up a Nondocument Word 178
Using ST Utility 179
   Modifying Existing Dictionaries 179
   Deleting Words from a Dictionary 183
   Creating New Dictionaries 183
   Using ST Utility with Thesaurus Files 185
   Counting Words in a Dictionary 186
Chapter Summary 187

6 Printing a Document 189

Choosing a Printer 189
Using Page Setup 193
   Paper Size 195
   Reduce or Enlarge 196
   Orientation 197
   Options Added by WordPerfect 197
      Binding Width 198
      Fractional Character Widths 199
   Printer Effects 200
      Font Substitution 200
      Text Smoothing 201
      Graphics Smoothing 201
      Faster Bitmap Printing 201
   Additional Options 201
      Flip Horizontal and Flip Vertical 202
      Invert Image 202
      Precision Bitmap Alignment 203
      Larger Print Area 203
      Unlimited Downloadable Fonts 203
   Help 204
Previewing Your Document 204
Using the Print Dialog Box 208
   Printing Part of the Document 208
   Specifying the Number of Copies 209
   Using Other Print Options 209
      Cover Page 209
      Paper Source 209
      Print Color 210
      Destination 210
      Every Other Page 210
      Print Overlay Layer 210
      Print Backwards 211

Printing a Document 211
Printing Envelopes 211
    Center-Fed Envelopes with No Return Address 212
    Center-Fed Envelopes with a Return Address 213
    Edge-Fed Envelopes with a Return Address 215
Chapter Summary 215

II Refining Documents

7 Managing Files and Documents 219

Understanding the File Manager Dialog Box 219
    Finding a File in the File List 220
        Navigating the File List 221
        Using the Show Menu 222
        Using the Retain Menu 223
    Using the File Manager Menus 225
        The File Menu 226
        The Folder Menu 228
        The Search Menu 230
Working with Multiple Documents 233
    Arranging Windows On-Screen 233
    Using Two Windows with a Single Document 235
    Changing the Active Window 237
    Combining Two Files 238
Converting File Formats 239
    Reviewing File Conversion Filters 239
        RTF Documents 240
        The XTND Conversion Utility 240
    Importing Files 240
    Exporting Files 242
        Exporting in Other Word Processing Formats 242
        Exporting Text Files 245
    Using WordPerfect Special Format Files 245
        Stationary Files 246
        Compressed Files 246
Chapter Summary 246

8 Formatting with Styles 249

Understanding Styles 250
    Default Styles 250
    Style Definitions 251
    Style Precedence 252
        Document Styles 252
        Private and Common Library Styles 252
Creating Styles 253
    Defining a Style 253
        Preserving Attributes 254

- Preserving Attributes and Formatting 256
  - Preserving Formatting 258
  - Preserving Nothing 258
- Applying a Style 258
- Editing a Style 260
  - Adding a Style to the Styles Submenu 262
  - Assigning a Keystroke Command 263
  - Updating a Style 265
- Using Text in a Style Definition 265
- Removing a Style from Text 268
- Using Advanced Style Features 268
  - Linking Styles 268
  - Basing One Style on Another 270
- Deleting a Style 271
- Avoiding Common Problems 272
  - Retaining Style Formatting 272
  - Retaining Manual Formatting 273
- Chapter Summary 274

9 Using Columns and Text Boxes 275

- Defining Types of Columns 276
  - Adding and Adjusting Columns 277
  - Choosing the Column Type 281
    - Newspaper 281
    - Parallel 281
    - Extended 283
- Adding Column Borders 283
  - Designing the Border 284
  - Adding Fill Styles 287
  - Changing the Spacing 288
- Creating a Text Box 289
  - Entering Text 290
  - Editing a Text Box 291
  - Resizing a Text Box 292
  - Changing Margins 293
  - Using Columns in Text Boxes 294
- Setting Text Box Options 294
  - Anchoring a Text Box 296
    - Anchoring As a Character 296
    - Anchoring to a Page 296
    - Anchoring to a Paragraph 297
  - Changing the Label Type 298
  - Changing the Horizontal Position 299
    - Absolute 299
    - Margin 299
    - Column 301
  - Changing the Vertical Position 301

Absolute	301
Relative To	302
Wrapping Text around a Box	302
Hiding the Contents of a Text Box	304
Changing Box Size	304
Moving a Box	304
Adding a Caption	305
Creating a Caption	305
Editing a Caption	306
Creating Frames	306
Adding a Frame	307
Adding a Fill	307
Changing the Spacing	308
Changing the Caption Position	308
Chapter Summary	310

10 Creating Outlines and Lists ... 311

Creating an Outline	312
Selecting Number Options	313
Selecting an Outline Style	315
Customizing a Style	318
Editing an Outline	319
Creating Endnotes	320
Editing an Endnote	321
Viewing Endnotes	322
Deleting an Endnote	323
Changing Endnote Options	323
Creating Footnotes	325
Editing a Footnote	326
Deleting a Footnote	327
Changing Footnote Options	328
Changing the Footnote Label	329
Changing Spacing	329
Changing Footnote Position	330
Creating Generated Lists	330
Creating Indexes	331
Marking Index Entries	332
Defining the Index Format	335
Generating an Index	336
Creating a Table of Contents	337
Marking Table of Contents Entries	337
Defining the Table of Contents Format	338
Generating a Table of Contents	341
Creating a Table of Authorities	341
Marking Citations	341
Defining Table of Authorities Section Formats	343

Editing a Full Form of a Citation 344
Generating a Table of Authorities 345
Creating Custom Lists 345
Creating Lists of Boxes 345
Creating Other Lists 346
Creating Cross-References 347
Marking Targets 349
Generating Cross-References 350
Chapter Summary 351

11 Using the Drawing Window 353

Defining WordPerfect Graphics 354
Figure Boxes 355
Graphic Overlays 355
Watermarks 356
Using the Graphics Tools 357
The Pointer Tool 359
The Rotation Tool 359
The Text Tool 361
The Line Tool 361
The Rectangle Tool 362
The Rounded Rectangle Tool 363
The Arc Tool 363
The Oval Tool 365
The Polygon Tool 366
The Curve Tool 367
The Pen Tool 369
The Fill Tool 370
The Pen Pattern and Fill Pattern Tools 371
The Pen and Fill Color Tools 374
The Pen Size Tool 375
The Zoom Tool 377
Using the Grid 377
Changing the Grid 377
Changing the Grid Size 378
Changing the Grid Color and Lines 378
Using the Grid Snap Feature 379
Editing a Graphic 379
Selecting Objects to Edit 380
Grouping Objects 380
Duplicating and Replicating an Object 382
Duplicating Objects 382
Replicating Objects 382
Flipping an Object 386
Editing Patterns and Colors 387
Editing Colors 387
Editing Patterns 388

Changing Graphic Options 390
    Box Size 391
    Graphic 391
Importing Graphics from Other Programs 392
Chapter Summary 394

III   Using Advanced Features

12 Merging Documents 397

Understanding Merge Codes 398
Creating a Secondary File 401
Creating a Primary File 406
Performing the Merge 408
    Merging without a Secondary File 410
    Inserting Messages 411
    Merging to the Printer 414
Chapter Summary 415

13 Sorting Text 417

Understanding Sort Options 417
    Sort Items 418
    Sort Keys 419
Sorting a List 419
    Sorting an Address List by Company Name 420
    Sorting Addresses by State and Company Name 423
    Sorting Tabbed Text 425
    Sorting Addresses by ZIP Code 427
    Sorting Merge Secondary Files 428
    Using Files for Sort Input and Output 430
Using Filters 432
    Setting Filter Keys and Criteria 432
    Understanding Filter Operators 434
    Using Multiple Filter Criteria 435
    Using KeyG to Search a Sort Item 436
Combining Sorting and Filtering 437
Chapter Summary 438

14 Using Macros 439

Using the Predefined Macros 440
    Running a Predefined Macro 440
    Installing Predefined Macros 443
Recording Macros 445
    Creating a Macro To Enter Repetitive Text 445
    Converting Tabbed Text to Merge Records 447
Editing a Macro 451

Preparing to Edit a Macro 452
    Excluding a Macro from the Macro Menu 452
    Defining a Macro Keystroke 453
    Modifying the Macro Description 454
Using the Macro Editor Window 454
    Changing a Recorded Macro 456
    Using On-Line Help 456
Editing a Macro Being Recorded 458
Using the Macro Options Menu 459
    The Save As Option 459
    Macro Text Files 460
    The Pause/Resume Toggle 461
    The Continue Command 461
Creating Macros with Programmable Commands 462
    Using Variables in Macros 462
        Read/Write Variables 463
        Read-Only Variables 463
        Operators 466
    Including User Input 467
        The Get Commands 467
        The Prompt Command 467
        The Menu Command 468
    Adding Loops to Macros 469
    Nesting and Chaining Macros 472
Creating Graphics Macros 473
Chapter Summary 474

15 Customizing WordPerfect 475

Differentiating Preferences and Styles 476
Setting Preferences 477
    Environment 478
        Automatic Backups 478
        Screen Colors 480
        The Format Menu 480
        The Options Menu 482
        The Windows Menu 484
        The Ruler Menu 486
        The Graphics Menu 487
        The Units Menu 488
        The Language Menu 488
    Default Folders 489
        The Default Document Folder 490
        The Dictionary/Thesaurus and Help Files Path 491
        The Common Library and Private Library Folders 491
    Keyboards 492
        Using Another Keyboard Definition 493
        Modifying Keyboard Definitions 493

   Creating Your Own Keyboard Definitions 496
   Printing a List of Keyboard Commands 496
 Setting a Custom Date and Time Format 497
 Controlling the Normal Style 499
  Modifying the Normal Style 500
  Using the Normal Style in Shared Documents 502
 Using the Librarian 502
  Understanding Librarian Resources 503
   Styles 503
   Macros 503
   Character Maps 504
   Conversion Filters 504
   Keyboards 504
  Comparing the Private and Common Libraries 504
  Moving a Resource 505
  Deleting a Resource 508
 Chapter Summary 509

16 Taking Advantage of System 7   511

 Using Publish and Subscribe 511
  Creating a Publisher 512
  Creating a Subscriber 514
  Choosing a Subscriber Format 517
  Setting Publisher Options 519
  Setting Subscriber Options 520
  Canceling a Publisher or a Subscriber 521
 Using Movies in Documents 522
  Inserting a Movie 522
  Playing a Movie 524
  Changing Movie Settings 524
  Changing Frames, Captions, and Options 526
 Chapter Summary 526

A Installing WordPerfect   527

 Preparation 527
 Easy Installation 528
 Custom Installation 532
 File Organization 534

Index   537

Introduction

The high end of the Macintosh word processing market has become much more crowded recently. The Macintosh has become more accepted as a business computer, and the Mac word processing market has benefitted greatly from the software vendors' ability to complete bigger and better programs. Version 2.1 of WordPerfect for the Macintosh is a major step forward in an already powerful word processor. The new version offers the most powerful combination of flexibility and features of any word processor available for the Mac.

What's New in Versions 2.0 and 2.1?

The major enhancements made by WordPerfect in Version 2.0 include the following:

- A significantly redesigned interface. Extensive consultation by WordPerfect with both their customers and Apple Computer personnel has resulted in a program that meets even the most ardent Mac enthusiast's definition of Mac-like, while also providing ease of use for the features most important to the largest population of users.

- A completely integrated graphics editing environment, including the capability to import and edit graphics from other computer platforms.

- The addition of draw overlay and watermark graphics to extend the flexibility of mixing text and graphics.
- Complete macro editing capabilities. Now, not only can you record and run macros as you could in many earlier applications, but you also can edit the macros to correct mistakes, add messages for the user, and control the macro execution. The Macro Editor even indicates whether the commands you enter are valid.
- Style sheet management at the document, computer, or network level.
- Text and figure box management that makes page layout programs unnecessary for many tasks.
- A sorting utility that enables you to sort almost anything.

In Version 2.1, WordPerfect added the following:

- Full support for Macintosh System 7, including Publish and Subscribe, Apple Events, Balloon Help, and QuickTime movies.
- A substantial speed improvement over Version 2.0.

The preceding lists just *some* of the improvements made to WordPerfect for the Macintosh. The goal of this book is to help users understand the program so that they easily can make use of the features WordPerfect provides in daily word processing tasks.

Who Should Use This Book?

This book is intended for both beginning and intermediate users. As much as possible, this book is arranged to follow a normal cycle of creating, editing, printing, and modifying documents. Each new task is presented simply at first, and additional options are presented later; the more advanced features appear in the last chapters of the book.

This book, which explains all the elementary features of WordPerfect and many of the advanced features, assumes that you have some familiarity with the Macintosh computer. The guided tour disk and tutorial manual supplied by Apple are excellent for gaining familiarity with Macintosh basics. In addition, directions and tips covering this basic material are included throughout the book, especially for operations that may be hard to remember as you learn the Mac.

Introduction
Using WordPerfect 2.1 for the Mac

For the intermediate user, the logical progression within each chapter, as well as from chapter to chapter, enables you to easily locate your present level of understanding and then go beyond it.

No one learns WordPerfect Version 2.1 overnight. For each new feature you tackle, you may experience confusion associated with incorporating the new feature into your everyday collection of word processing tools. This book can help you expand your collection.

What's In This Book?

Using WordPerfect 2.1 for the Mac consists of three parts and 16 chapters that are roughly organized by level of complexity. Beginners may benefit most by reading the chapters sequentially; intermediate and advanced users, on the other hand, may discover that their needs are best met by jumping to chapters of particular interest. The following paragraphs describe briefly the content of this book.

Part I, "Getting Started," includes basic information you need to produce nicely finished documents. Creating documents, editing text, formatting text and documents, checking spelling, and printing are covered in Part I.

Chapter 1, "Quick Start: Creating a Business Letter," is designed to explain the fundamentals of using WordPerfect by enabling you to create a standard business letter. In creating the sample letter, you learn not only how to create, edit, save, and print a document, but also how to access the Help file and use the Speller and Thesaurus.

Chapter 2, "An Overview of WordPerfect 2.1," provides more detailed information of standard WordPerfect techniques, such as choosing menu commands, using the mouse and keyboard, and accessing dialog boxes. In addition, you learn about the different types of menu commands, how to enter text and navigate around the document window, and how to save a document.

Chapter 3, "Editing a Document," describes the many ways that you can edit a document. You learn how to use the Clipboard to cut, copy, paste, and append text and how to apply text attributes such as boldface and italic. This chapter also explains how to use the Search menu to find and replace text and how to reveal and use hidden codes.

Chapter 4, "Formatting a Document," focuses on formatting techniques. In this chapter, you learn how to use menus, keyboard shortcuts, and the ruler to format your document. You learn how to format characters, lines, paragraphs, and pages. In addition, you learn how to create borders around pages, paragraphs, and characters and how to fill the background of these objects with colors and patterns.

Chapter 5, "Using the WordPerfect Speller and Thesaurus," explains the Speller and Thesaurus features. You learn how to spell check entire documents or portions of documents and how to use the various dictionaries that WordPerfect provides. This chapter also explains how to use the Thesaurus to add variety to your document text.

Chapter 6, "Printing a Document," discusses how to select a printer, specify the page setup requirements, and print a document. This chapter also explains how to preview your document prior to printing.

Part II, "Refining Documents," explains the more advanced WordPerfect formatting features. Using styles, managing documents, using columns, and creating lists, as well as using text and graphics boxes, are included in Part II. Part II also describes editing graphics.

Chapter 7, "Managing Files and Documents," describes how to use the File Manager to manage your files. This chapter also provides a discussion of how to manage multiple open documents. You learn how to convert file formats, export and import files, and use WordPerfect's special format files.

Chapter 8, "Formatting with Styles," explains WordPerfect styles and describes how to create and apply styles that meet the requirements of your document. In this chapter, you also learn how to edit, link, and delete styles.

Chapter 9, "Using Columns and Text Boxes," discusses the types of columns and explains how to select column types and enhance columns with borders and fills. You also learn how to create text boxes and specify text box options. This chapter also describes how to create captions.

Chapter 10, "Creating Outlines and Lists," explains how to create outlines, endnotes and footnotes, indexes, tables of contents, tables of authorities, and cross references.

Chapter 11, "Using the Drawing Window," describes how to use the many graphics tools that WordPerfect provides. In this chapter, you learn how to create various types of objects and edit graphics.

Part III, "Using Advanced Features," contains instructions on using the merge feature, sorting text, creating and running macros, customizing your WordPerfect environment, and using System 7 features.

Introduction
Using WordPerfect 2.1 for the Mac

Chapter 12, "Merging Documents," uses an example of a form letter to explain how to merge documents by using merge codes and primary and secondary files.

Chapter 13, "Sorting Text," explains the sort options, items, and keys, in addition to explaining how to sort various types of lists. This chapter also explains how to use filters, either alone or with the sort option, to limit the output to items that meet specified criteria.

Chapter 14, "Using Macros," explains how to use predefined macros and how to create and edit macros. This chapter also explains using the Macro Editor and creating macros with programmable commands.

Chapter 15, "Customizing WordPerfect," explains how you can change the system preferences of the WordPerfect environment. This chapter also explains how to use the Librarian.

Chapter 16, "Taking Advantage of System 7," explains how to use the Publish and Subscribe feature and QuickTime movies in your documents.

Appendix A, "Installing WordPerfect," covers the entire installation procedure.

Tips and *Cautions* are inserted throughout the text to call attention to alternate methods of performing a task or to warn you of unexpected results. (WordPerfect does a good job tracking down bugs, and features design changes for maintenance upgrades. If your version of the program is more recent than 2.1, the cautions may not apply.) In the tutorial sections of this book, information that the user should type is in *italic* type.

How To Use This Book

If you're new to word processing, reading sequentially through the book may be most beneficial for you. Part I includes basic information required to successfully manage working on a Mac. When you are familiar with the basic functions and program capabilities, you can proceed to Parts II and III to expand your expertise.

If you are comfortable using other word processors for the Macintosh but have never used WordPerfect for the Macintosh, you may want to cover the information in Part I fairly closely. (You probably can safely skip Chapter 1, however.) Your familiarity with the Macintosh should enable you to cover Part I quickly and dive into Parts II and III.

Introduction
Using WordPerfect 2.1 for the Mac

If you're familiar with WordPerfect for the Macintosh, skim through the information in Part I, paying particular attention to the Tips and Cautions. With so many ways to accomplish the same task, some of this information is bound to be new to you. You may discover a quicker way to do a common editing task, for example. Use the Table of Contents, which gives you an overview of the book's organization, as a guide to the rest of the book. You also can use the index to locate specific topics.

One chapter you may not want to wait to read is Chapter 15, "Customizing WordPerfect." The level of detail involved in describing the customizing process made this chapter too distracting to include earlier, yet by customizing the way WordPerfect displays windows, menus, formatting features, and command dialogs, you can improve the ease with which you produce documents. If you're getting tired of setting a particular option for every document you create, look at Chapter 15 to see if you can turn the option on once and for all (or at least until you change your mind).

Program Versions Covered by This Book

This book was written about WordPerfect Version 2.1, running under Apples System 6.0.5 or newer (including System 7.0). If you have an earlier version, you can upgrade to the current version for a reasonable fee by calling WordPerfect's customer service 800 number, which you can find in the program documentation. If you have Version 2.0, ask about the disk-only upgrade. The disk-only upgrade can save you the cost of the Version 2.1 manuals, which contain much of the same information as the 2.0 manuals.

To the User

We'd like to thank you for buying our book and hope you find it easy to use. If you find errors or have suggestions for future editions, please write to us in care of the publisher. If you have a CompuServe account, you can send us email via Dave's account, user ID 72510,205.

David Reiser and Holly J. Morris

Allentown, Pennsylvania

Introduction
Using WordPerfect 2.1 for the Mac

PART I

Getting Started

Includes

Quick Start: Creating a Business Letter

An Overview of WordPerfect 2.1

Editing a Document

Formatting a Document

Using the WordPerfect Speller and Thesaurus

Printing a Document

CHAPTER 1

Quick Start: Creating a Business Letter

This chapter—geared to users who want to start quickly on a document—introduces you to the basics of creating, editing, and printing a one-page business letter. Keep in mind, though, that these instructions are elementary. Complete information about WordPerfect features appears in chapters that follow.

This chapter covers the following:

- Starting WordPerfect
- Typing and basic formatting
- Simple editing, including cutting and pasting
- Saving a document
- Checking for misspelled words
- Printing a document
- Quitting WordPerfect

Starting WordPerfect

The following steps enable you to launch WordPerfect and open a new document window. If you have not installed WordPerfect on your hard disk, see Appendix A for information on installing the program.

To start WordPerfect, follow these steps:

1. Open the WordPerfect 2.1 folder by double-clicking it.

2. Double-click the WordPerfect icon (see fig. 1.1). A new document window opens for your first document.

Fig. 1.1
Opening WordPerfect.

Getting Help

If you are not sure what a WordPerfect command does, you can look up the command in the Help file, which you installed with the rest of the WordPerfect program. The Help file briefly describes WordPerfect features and commands, tells you which menu to access to find a particular feature, and lists related features.

To use WordPerfect's Help feature, follow these steps:

1. Choose Help from the Apple menu by placing the pointer on the Apple icon in the upper left corner of the screen. Press and hold down the mouse button; a menu appears. At the top of the menu are the headings About WordPerfect and Help.

2. Drag the pointer to Help and release the mouse button (see fig. 1.2).

   Note: You use this technique to choose any command from a menu.

Part I

Getting Started

Fig. 1.2
Choosing Help from the Apple menu.

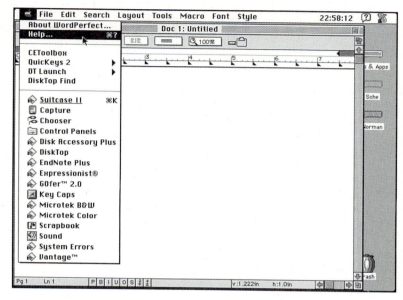

Another way to display the Help screen is to press ⌘-?, or, if you have an extended keyboard, the Help key to the right of the Delete key.

Your Apple menu may look different than the menu shown in figure 1.2, depending on the software that is installed on your Macintosh.

When you choose Help, the Help dialog box appears (see fig. 1.3).

Fig. 1.3
The Help dialog box.

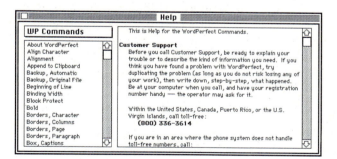

Chapter 1
Quick Start: Creating a Business Letter

> **Tip**
>
> If the Help dialog box does not appear, you probably did not install the WP Help file. See Appendix A or your installation manual for instructions.

The Help dialog box is divided into two sections. WordPerfect commands appear on the left side of the dialog box and information about the commands appears on the right. You can use the *scroll bars*, narrow vertical columns with arrows at both ends, to scroll through the available information.

3. To look up a command, place the mouse pointer on the downward arrow of the WP Commands scroll bar. Press the mouse button to scroll through the list of commands. Release the button when you see the command in which you are interested.

   Alternatively, you can estimate where a specific command may be on the list and drag the scroll box within the scroll bar to that relative location. Suppose that you want to look up Line Format. The letter *L* is about half way through the alphabet. Drag the scroll box half way down the scroll bar. You see the entry Line Format. Click Line Format to highlight it. An explanation for Line Format appears in the right-hand portion of the Help screen (see fig. 1.4).

Fig. 1.4
Choosing Line Format from the Help scroll list.

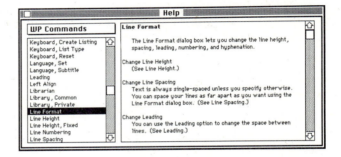

If the explanation for the command does not fit on one screen, you can use the scroll bars on this box to view the rest of the entry.

4. To return to your document, click the close box in the upper left corner of the window.

Creating a Document

After you start WordPerfect, an empty document window appears (see fig. 1.5). At the top center of the screen, you see `Doc 1: Untitled`. All documents begin as Untitled until you save them. Saving a document is covered later in this chapter.

Part I

Getting Started

Fig. 1.5
The untitled document window.

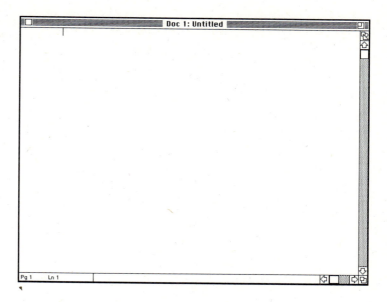

Along the bottom of the document window you see the status bar, which tells you what page and line you are working on. When you open a new document, for example, the message on the status bar (Pg 1 Ln 1) indicates that you are one the first line of the first page.

Changing the Screen Display

By adding features to the status bar, you can add another level of flexibility to your work. You can add style buttons, for example, that enable you to choose text styles, such as boldface, underline, or superscript. The Show Position feature shows you the location of the insertion point at any given time.

To add or change status bar features, follow these steps:

1. Choose Preferences from the File menu (see fig. 1.6).

2. Slide the pointer to Environment and release the mouse button. The Environment dialog box appears (see fig. 1.7).

3. Click the Windows menu in the dialog box to see a list of choices (see fig. 1.8).

4. Drag the pointer to Show Position and release the mouse button. A check mark appears beside Show Position to indicate that this feature is active.

Chapter 1
Quick Start: Creating a Business Letter

Fig. 1.6
Choosing Preferences from the File menu.

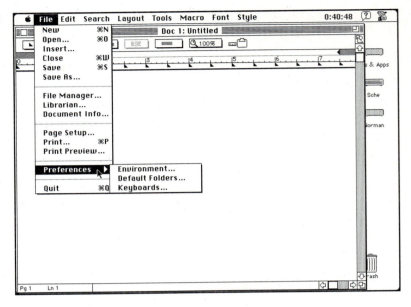

Fig. 1.7
The Environment dialog box.

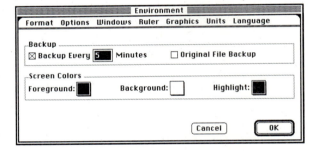

Fig. 1.8
Choosing Windows from the Environment dialog box.

Part I

Getting Started

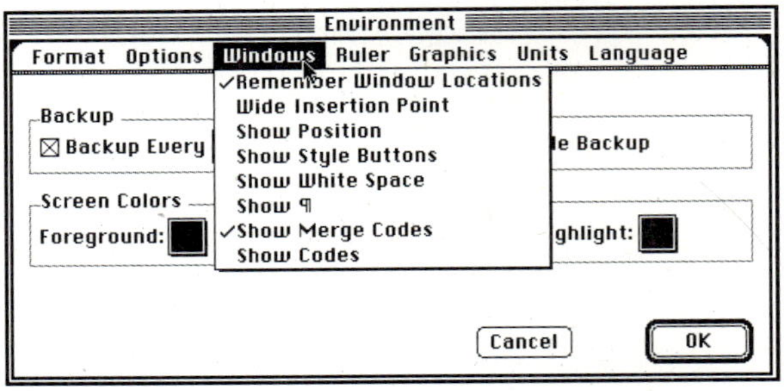

5. Choose Windows again, drag the pointer to Show Style Buttons, and release the mouse button. A check mark appears beside the feature.

6. Click OK.

The style buttons and the position of the insertion point appear in the status bar to the right of the line number (see fig. 1.9).

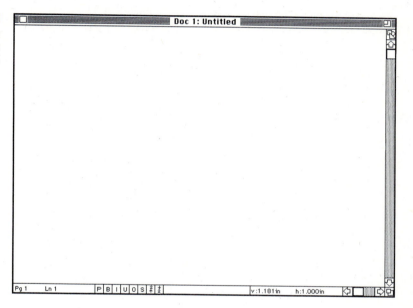

Fig. 1.9
The status bar showing the style buttons and insertion point position.

The letters on the style buttons represent the available text styles. Clicking a button activates that text style. Clicking the button a second time turns off the style. By clicking B, for example, you activate the boldface text style; by clicking P (plain text), you turn off all styles. You also can activate text styles from the Style menu; using the Style menu is discussed later in this chapter.

The position of the insertion point appears to the right of the style buttons. This display tells you how many inches from the top (v:) and the left side (h:) of a sheet of paper the insertion point is located.

Typing Text

Word processing programs use a technique called *word wrap*, meaning that at the end of a line, the text automatically wraps to the next line;

Chapter 1
Quick Start: Creating a Business Letter

pressing Return when you reach the end of a line is not necessary. You press Return only to end a paragraph or to insert a blank line.

To type a sample business letter, follow these steps:

1. Choose Show Ruler from the Layout menu or press ⌘-R. A ruler, with margins and tab settings, appears across the top of the window (see fig. 1.10).

   The ruler is not a default feature; it does not appear unless you indicate in the Environment dialog box or in the file (as done in step 1) that the ruler should be displayed.

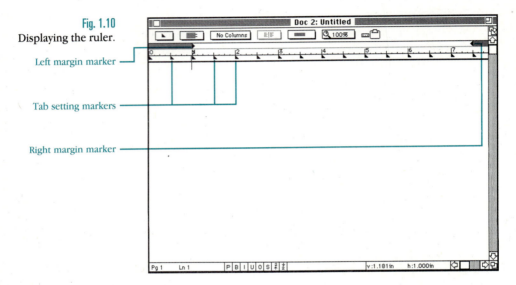

Fig. 1.10
Displaying the ruler.

Left margin marker

Tab setting markers

Right margin marker

   The black right triangles every half inch represent tab settings, which you can adjust. You also can change margins by dragging the triangles above the numbers to the left or right. For this document, leave the tab settings as they are.

2. Move the insertion point down approximately 2 1/2 inches by pressing Return. (Notice the vertical position (v:) in the status bar.) This spacing leaves room for a letterhead on your stationery.

3. To enter the date, choose Text from the Date/Time submenu, which you access through the Tools menu (see fig. 1.11).

Tip

Changing the font alters the vertical spacing. You can set an absolute 2 1/2-inch space by setting the top margin. Setting absolute margins is covered in Chapter 4, "Formatting a Document."

Part I
Getting Started

Fig. 1.11
Choosing Text from the Date/Time submenu.

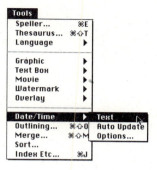

4. Press Return twice and type the following, pressing Return after each line:

   Dr. Suzanne Moore
   Orefield Community College
   Orefield, PA 18069

   So far, your document should look like fig. 1.12.

5. Press Return to leave a blank line, and type

   Dear Dr. Moore,

6. Press Return twice to end the paragraph and leave a blank line.

7. Type the following exactly as shown—errors and all:

   As we have discussed, I have done a study to determine your college's microscope needs, and I want to thank you for your inquiry to Mid Atlantic Microscope Distributors. Our curent stock of medium-priced educational microscopes should be more than enough to meet your needs. I have enclosed an estimate that I am sure will please you and I would like to meet with you to discuss these figures further. May I hear from you at your eariest convenience to discuss your needs.

8. Press Return twice. Type

   I have enclosed a copy of the book that you requested,

9. The rest of the sentence begun in step 8 uses the underline text style. To activate the underline text style, choose Underline from the Style menu (see fig. 1.13). Alternatively, click U on the status bar.

Regardless of how you choose underlining, a line appears under the U in the status bar until you turn underlining off.

Chapter 1
Quick Start: Creating a Business Letter

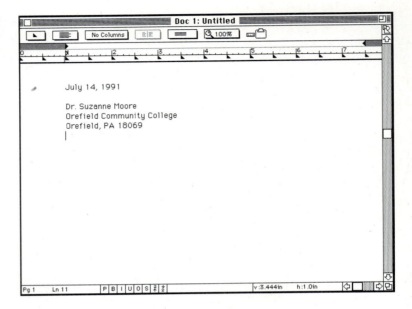

Fig. 1.12
The date and inside address on a business letter.

Fig. 1.13
Choosing Underline from the Style menu.

10. Type the name of the book:

> Microscope Care, Getting the Most Out of Your Student Microscopes

Part I

Getting Started

11. Turn off underlining by choosing Underline again from the Style menu. Then type a period at the end of the sentence.

12. Press Return twice.

Setting Tabs

The closing of your letter appears at the right side of the document. To place the closing in this location, you can press Tab eight times or adjust the tab settings.

To adjust tab settings, follow these steps:

1. Click the Tabs pop-up menu (the box with the black triangle in the ruler, that is just below the close box).

2. Choose Clear Tabs from the pop-up menu (see fig. 1.14). All tab markers disappear.

Fig. 1.14
Clearing the tab settings.

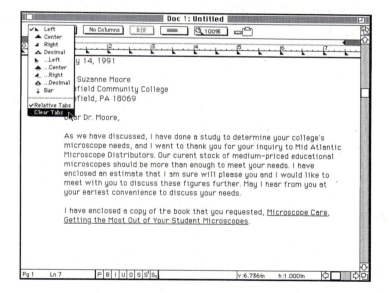

3. Choose Left from the Tabs pop-up menu.

4. Click below the vertical line marked 5 on the ruler. WordPerfect inserts a triangle representing a left tab setting.

Chapter 1
Quick Start: Creating a Business Letter

5. To continue your letter, press Tab once (the insertion point moves to the tab you just set) and type

    Very truly yours,

6. Press Return three times, press Tab, and type

    Fred Smith

7. Press Return once, press Tab once, and type

    Sales Representative

   Your document should resemble figure 1.15. (The ruler has been removed from the screen in this figure to show the entire letter.)

Fig. 1.15
The first draft of the business letter.

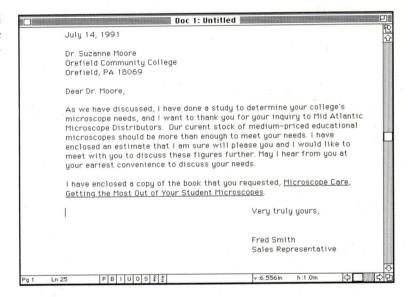

Editing a Document

After you type the letter, you can make changes. You may want to move, delete, or insert text, for instance. You also can change the text style of existing text—apply boldface or italic to text, for example. In this section, you edit the letter that you created in the preceding exercise.

Part I
Getting Started

Selecting Text

To make many kinds of changes, you first select the text you want to modify. A simple way to select text is to place the insertion point at the beginning of the text you want to modify, click and hold the mouse button, and drag the mouse pointer to the end of the text to be modified. Use this technique to select *I want to thank you for your inquiry to Mid Atlantic Microscope Distributors*. WordPerfect highlights the selected text (see fig. 1.16).

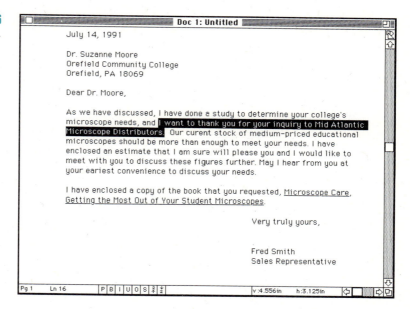

Fig. 1.16
Selected text.

If you select the wrong text or you change your mind, you can remove the highlighting by clicking elsewhere on-screen.

Inserting and Deleting Text

To add text, move the I-beam pointer to where you plan to insert the new text. Click to display the blinking insertion point, and then start typing. The text to the right of the insertion point moves to accommodate the new text. In the letter, for example, click in front of the word *medium-priced* and type *low and*.

Chapter 1
Quick Start: Creating a Business Letter

To delete a single character, place the I-beam pointer to the character's right or left and click. If the insertion point is to the right of the character, press the Delete key. If the insertion point is to the left of the character to be deleted, press the Delete Right key (the decimal point on the numeric keypad or the extended keyboard).

To delete several characters, select the text to be deleted and press the Delete key. All the selected text disappears. In the letter, select *to discuss your needs* (do not include the period) at the end of the first paragraph and press Delete. The text and space in front of it disappears.

You also can delete and insert at the same time. Select *May I hear from you*. Leaving the text selected, type *Please call me*. The text *May I hear from you* is replaced by *Please call me*.

Cutting and Pasting

Suppose that you have the right words but put them in the wrong place. You can cut words or phrases from one location and paste them to another location.

To cut and paste, follow these steps:

1. Select *I want to thank you for your inquiry to Mid Atlantic Microscope Distributors*.
2. Choose Cut from the Edit menu. The selected text disappears.
3. Move the insertion point to precede the first word of the letter (*As*).
4. Choose Paste from the Edit menu. The cut text reappears in the new location, and a space appears between the pasted text and the word *As*.
5. Select *and* and the comma at the end of the second sentence, and type a period.

Using Right and Left Alignment

You can align text with the left or right margin. The date on the letter you created is currently aligned against the left margin. To move the date to the right margin, you can place the insertion point in front of the date and press Tab several times, or you can choose Right Alignment.

To align the date with the right margin, follow these steps:

Part I
Getting Started

1. Select the date.
2. Click the Alignment pop-up menu (the second box from the left in the ruler). The available alignment styles appear.
3. Choose Right to right align the date (see fig. 1.17). The selected text moves to the right margin (see fig. 1.18).

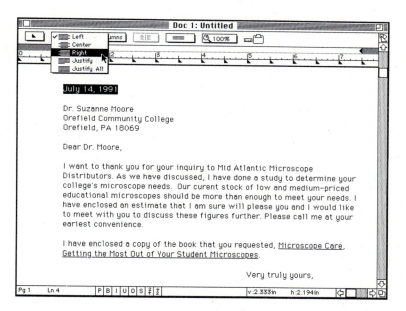

Fig. 1.17
Choosing Right Alignment from the Alignment pop-up menu.

Saving a Document

Saving your work often is important. Computers can crash for inexplicable reasons and usually seem to do so at the worst possible time. If your system crashes, everything that you saved to disk is intact; only the work entered since the last save is lost.

To save a document, follow these steps:

1. Choose Save from the File menu (see fig. 1.19).

   When you choose the Save command to save a document for the first time, the Save As dialog box appears. You type the document's file name in the Save Document As text box. The file name can consist of as many as 31 characters and use any character except a colon.

Chapter 1
Quick Start: Creating a Business Letter

Fig. 1.18
The edited letter.

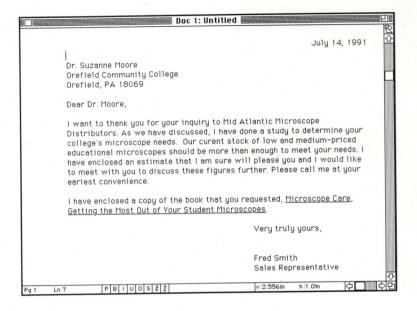

Fig. 1.19
The File menu.

Tip

You should save your document not only as you enter text, but also before you use the Speller or print. These two features tend to increase the risk of a crash.

2. Type *Microscope Letter* as the file name (see fig. 1.20).

3. Click the Save button.

WordPerfect saves the document to the folder listed above the scroll box (in this figure, `WordPerfect Files`) and returns you to your document.

Part I
Getting Started

Fig. 1.20
Saving the document as Microscope Letter.

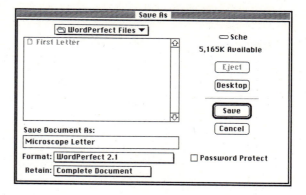

Using the Speller

Checking your document for spelling errors is a good idea. (Before you use the Speller, however, save your document.) When you use the Speller, WordPerfect checks the entire document; the insertion point can be anywhere within the document.

To check spelling, follow these steps:

1. Choose Speller from the Tools menu, or press ⌘-E. The Speller dialog box appears (see fig. 1.21).

Fig. 1.21
The Speller dialog box.

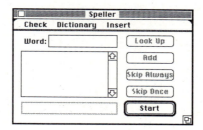

2. Click Start.

   Because proper names, such as Moore and Orefield, may not be in the Speller dictionary, the program flags proper names as possible misspelled words. If you click Skip Once, the Speller ignores that occurrence of the word but stops if the word appears later in your document. If you click Skip Always, the Speller ignores that word for the rest of the session.

Chapter 1
Quick Start: Creating a Business Letter

3. Click Skip Once each time the Speller stops at a proper name, but check the spelling in each case (see fig. 1.22).

Fig. 1.22
A proper name not in the Speller dictionary.

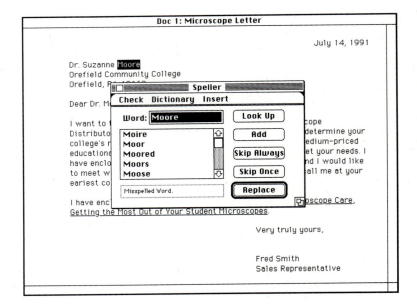

The first real misspelled word is *curent*, which is highlighted in the document and appears in the Word text box in the Speller dialog box. Four possible spelling alternatives, including the correct spelling *current*, appear in the window below the Word box.

4. Click *current*. *Current* replaces *curent* in the Word Text box, but not in the document. To accept this alternative spelling, click the Replace button. *Current* replaces *curent* in your document.

The next misspelled word is *eariest*.

5. Replace that word with *earliest*.

After the Speller checks the entire document, the computer beeps.

6. Return to your document by clicking the Speller's close box.

Because you made some changes to the document text, be sure to save your document again. This time when you choose Save, the Save As dialog box does not appear. WordPerfect saves the document, using the same file name and folder you specified earlier in the Save As dialog box.

Part I
Getting Started

Printing a Document

After saving your letter, you are ready to print it. To print the document, follow these steps:

1. Choose Print from the File menu.

   The Print dialog box appears (see fig. 1.23).

Fig. 1.23
The Print dialog box.

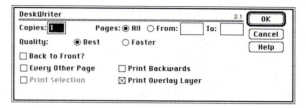

The default settings for printing are as follows:

- A single copy of the document is printed.
- The entire document is printed.
- The document is printed in best quality.

2. Click OK to accept the default settings and print the letter.

Your letter prints (assuming your printer is on and is connected properly).

Quitting WordPerfect 2

After you save and print your document, you can quit WordPerfect. *Do not turn off the computer to quit.* If you turn off the computer without quitting WordPerfect, you lose all unsaved changes. Although WordPerfect has an automatic backup system (see Chapter 15, "Customizing WordPerfect"), you still can lose quite a bit of work if you turn off your computer rather than quit WordPerfect and shut down normally.

To quit WordPerfect, follow these steps:

1. Choose Quit from the File menu.

   If you edited your document since you last saved it, WordPerfect displays a message box asking whether you want to save changes (see fig. 1.24).

Chapter 1
Quick Start: Creating a Business Letter

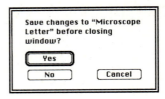

Fig. 1.24
Saving changes to a file before exiting.

2. Click Yes to save your changes and quit WordPerfect; click No to quit WordPerfect without saving your changes. (To return to the document, click Cancel.)

    WordPerfect returns you to the Macintosh desktop. You now can safely shut down your Macintosh.

Chapter Summary

In this chapter, you have learned how to do the following:

- Start WordPerfect
- Get Help
- Enhance the status bar
- Enter text
- Use text styles
- Edit text
- Save a document
- Use the Speller
- Print a document
- Exit WordPerfect

Each function is covered in more detail in later chapters.

Part I
Getting Started

CHAPTER 2

An Overview of WordPerfect 2.1

In this chapter, you find an overview of the basic operations of WordPerfect 2.1, such as creating, navigating through, and editing a document. The features of WordPerfect's main editing window also are explained in relation to these basic operations. You learn about editing in more detail in Chapter 3, "Editing a Document."

After you complete this chapter, you will be able to do the following:

- Start WordPerfect
- Navigate the WordPerfect document window
- Choose a menu command
- Use a dialog box
- Use WordPerfect's Help feature
- Enter text
- Move around in a document
- Insert or delete text in a document
- Use hidden codes
- Save a document
- Exit the program

Don't be afraid to explore the many available features. In WordPerfect, few situations exist that you cannot get out of again by clicking the Cancel button or close box or choosing Undo from the Edit menu. Any of these techniques usually return you to safer and more familiar ground.

Starting WordPerfect

If you have not installed WordPerfect 2.1 onto your hard disk, consult Appendix A or the instructions that come with the software for the installation procedure. After you install WordPerfect, you can start the program by following these steps:

1. Turn on your computer.

2. If a window showing the contents of your hard disk is not open, double-click the hard disk icon in the upper right corner. The folders and software applications contained on the hard disk appear.

3. Double-click the WordPerfect 2.1 folder to open it. The WordPerfect 2.1 window displays the files installed in the WordPerfect folder (see fig. 2.1).

Fig. 2.1
The files in the WordPerfect folder.

4. Double-click the WordPerfect icon.

5. If you are running the program for the first time, a window appears in which you must type your name and registration number. Enter your name in the Name text box.

6. To move to the Number text box, press Tab or click the box. Type the registration number, which appears on the customer registration card that comes with your software. Although you can type *any* six-digit (or longer) number, this location is a convenient place to store the registration number. To receive assistance from WordPerfect Corporation, you must use this number.

7. After you type the appropriate name and number, click OK. A new document window opens.

Before beginning a document, you must familiarize yourself with the WordPerfect screen, mouse pointer, and basic procedures and techniques.

Reviewing the Screen Display

The WordPerfect document window is similar to the main screens of other Macintosh applications. This similarity of design is part of what makes the Mac easy to use. If you are new to the Mac, you may learn a trick or two about document windows that can help you in other applications.

When you first start WordPerfect, an Untitled Document window appears (see fig. 2.2).

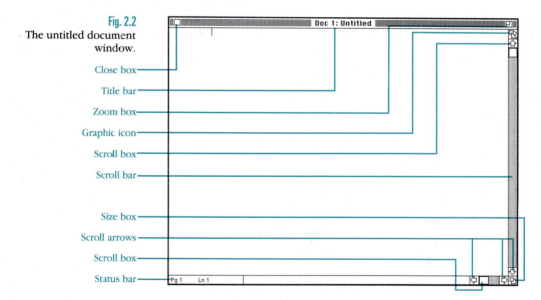

Fig. 2.2
The untitled document window.

Close box
Title bar
Zoom box
Graphic icon
Scroll box
Scroll bar

Size box
Scroll arrows
Scroll box
Status bar

The features of the document window are explained in the following list and sections:

■ *Title bar*. The document name, which is *Untitled* until you save the document, appears in the title bar. The title bar of the active window is striped.

- *Close box.* Click this box, which appears in the upper left corner of the window, to close the window; WordPerfect prompts you to save your work, if necessary.

- *Zoom box.* This box, which resembles a box within a box, appears in the upper right corner of the window and enables you to change the window size. When you click the Zoom box, the window size changes to nearly full-screen; click the Zoom box again, and the window reverts to the preceding size.

- *Graphic icon.* By clicking the Graphic icon, you open the Graphics Editor, which is covered in Chapter 11, "Using the Drawing Window."

- *Size box.* You use the Size box, which appears in the lower right corner of the window, to change the dimensions of the window. Place the mouse pointer over the Size box, press and hold the mouse button, and drag the mouse pointer to a new location. This technique, more commonly referred to as *dragging the Size box*, enables you to change the right and bottom margins of the window. The top and left margins remain fixed.

The ruler, shown in figure 2.3, appears across the top of the document window and provides a convenient way to make many line-formatting changes, such as adjusting tabs, line spacing, or alignment. You can display the ruler (covered in more detail in Chapter 4, "Formatting a Document") by choosing Show Ruler from the Layout menu or pressing ⌘-R.

The Status Bar

The status bar appears along the bottom of your screen. At the left end of the status bar, you can see the location (page and line) of the insertion point. When you first open a document, the status bar displays Pg 1 Ln 1, indicating that the insertion point is on the first line of the first page. If you press Return a few times, the line number (Ln) advances. By pressing ⌘-Return, you advance to page 2.

You can add two other options to the status bar as additions to the *environment* (settings used all the time). You can add style buttons, which enable you to add text styles such as boldface, italic, and underlining. The other option provides information about the location of the insertion point in inches from the top and the left side of a sheet of paper.

Part I

Getting Started

Fig. 2.3
A document window with the ruler displayed.

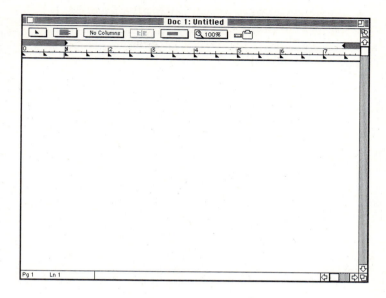

To add these features for the current work session, follow these steps:

1. Choose Preferences from the File menu (see fig. 2.4).

Fig. 2.4
Choosing Preferences from the File menu.

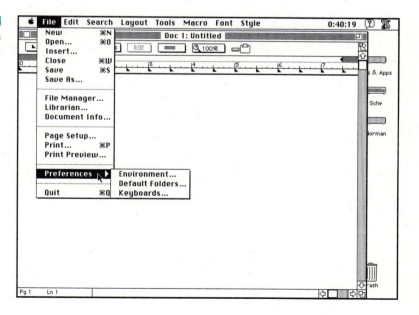

Chapter 2
An Overview of WordPerfect 2.1

2. Holding down the mouse button, move the pointer to Environment and release the mouse button. The Environment dialog box appears (see fig. 2.5).

Fig. 2.5
The Environment dialog box.

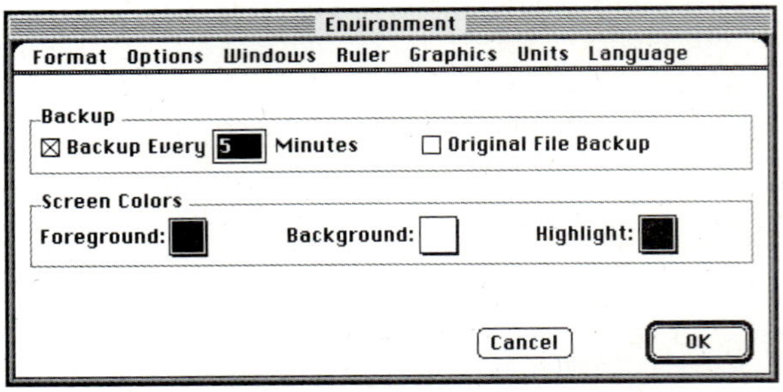

3. Place the pointer on the word Windows in the dialog box; then press and hold the mouse button. The Windows menu appears (see fig. 2.6). (This action is commonly called *pulling down the menu*.)

Fig. 2.6
Pulling down the Windows menu in the Environment dialog box.

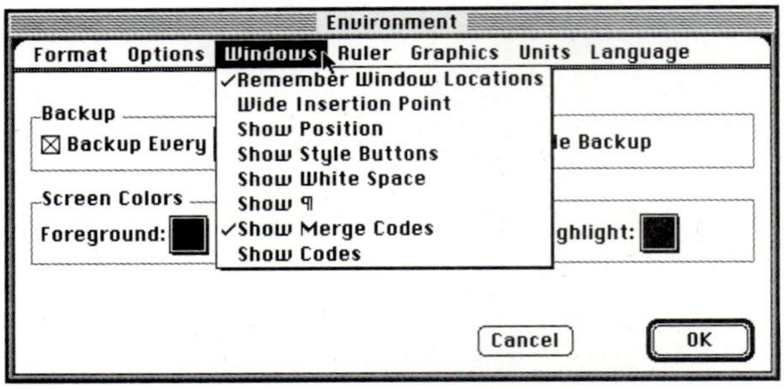

4. Drag the pointer to Show Position and release. A check mark appears beside Show Position to indicate that this option is now active.

5. Pull down the Windows menu again and drag the pointer to Show Style Buttons and release the mouse button. A check mark appears beside Show Style Buttons.

6. Click OK.

The style buttons appear on the status bar (see fig. 2.7).

Part I
Getting Started

Fig. 2.7
The enhanced status bar.

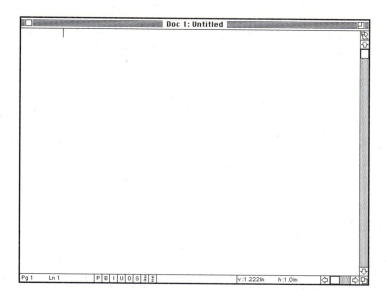

The letters represent the following text styles:

P   plain text

B   **boldface text**

I   *italic*

U   underline

O   outline

S   **shadow**

S^1 super script

S_1 sub script

Clicking a style button activates that text style. Clicking the button a second time, or clicking P, turns off the style. You also can activate text styles from the Style menu. (See Chapter 4, "Formatting a Document," for more information on text styles.)

The insertion point position appears to the right of the style buttons (refer to fig. 2.7). This display indicates how many inches from the top (v:) and how many inches from the left side (h:) of a sheet of paper the insertion point is located.

Chapter 2
An Overview of WordPerfect 2.1

In the preceding exercise, you added these features to the current status bar. To add style buttons and position markers to all status bars, however, you must change the default settings. Changing the defaults is covered in Chapter 15, "Customizing WordPerfect."

In addition to the features you can add, the status bar also displays temporary information. If you place the mouse pointer on a tab marker and hold down the mouse button, for instance, the marker's position appears on the status bar. As you drag the marker, WordPerfect displays the new position. When you release the button, the position display disappears (see Chapter 4, "Formatting a Document" for more information on this feature.) If you applied a style to the paragraph containing the insertion point, paragraph style names also appear on the status bar (see Chapter 8, "Formatting with Styles").

The Scroll Bars

Your screen displays two scroll bars: one to the right of the document screen and the other at the lower right of the document window. The scroll bars enable you to move (or scroll) through a document. See the section "Moving around in the Document" in this chapter for more information.

The Mouse Pointers

As you move around in and out of your document, the mouse pointer changes shape. When the pointer is outside the document window, the pointer resembles an arrow. Inside the document window, the pointer resembles an I-beam. The *insertion point*, which indicates the location of your next action (such as inserting text), appears as a blinking vertical line.

Keep in mind that, although you can move the I-beam pointer throughout your document, the location of the insertion point does not change. To move the location of the insertion point, you must place the I-beam pointer in the location you want the insertion point to be and click. The insertion point appears at the I-beam location. The other way to change the location of the insertion point is to move through the window by some means other than scrolling. You can use the arrow keys to move the insertion point, for example.

Accessing Menu Commands

With a Macintosh, you choose commands from menus that appear across the top of the screen. You can choose menu commands with the mouse, the keyboard, or function keys. Learning alternative ways to perform every task may seem like too much; however, you really need to remember only one or two—the ones that are most comfortable for you. The choices add flexibility to your use of the program.

As you become more familiar with WordPerfect, you can learn the keyboard commands for functions that you frequently use. Although the keyboard commands are faster, menus provide more help for seldom-used commands.

Using the Mouse

Because you can use the mouse to access any menu command, the device is especially handy if you have not memorized command keystrokes. To choose a menu command by using the mouse, follow these steps:

1. Move the mouse pointer to one of the menus at the top of the screen—for example, Layout—and press and hold the mouse button. The Layout menu appears (see fig. 2.8).

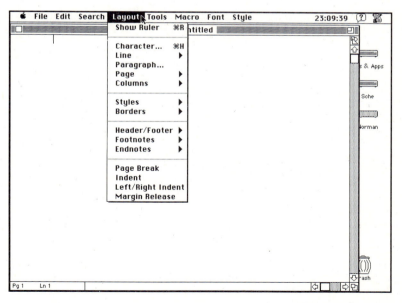

Fig. 2.8
The Layout menu.

Chapter 2
An Overview of WordPerfect 2.1

2. While you hold down the mouse button, drag the pointer to one of the commands in the menu, for example, Character; then release the mouse button. The Character Format dialog box appears.

3. Click the Cancel button or OK to close the dialog box.

Using the Keyboard

You can use the keyboard or the function keys to choose most commands. Most of these keyboard shortcuts use the *Command key* (⌘) and a letter, for example, ⌘-R. Other commands may use one or more of the following:

- ⌘ key plus the Shift key
- ⌘ key plus a function key
- Shift key plus a function key
- Option key plus a letter

Using the keyboard or function keys to choose menu commands saves time. Table 2.1 lists some of the commonly used keyboard shortcuts.

Table 2.1 Keyboard Shortcuts

Command	Keystrokes
Center Align	⌘-Shift-C
Close Window	⌘-W
Codes Show/Hide	⌘-Shift Option-F2
Copy	⌘-C F3
Cut	⌘-X F2
Cycle Windows	⌘-Shift-W
Date/Time	⌘-Shift-D
Find Next	⌘-Shift-N
Find Previous	⌘-Shift-B
Go To Dialog	⌘-Shift-G

Part I
Getting Started

Command	Keystrokes
Help	⌘-?
	⌘-Shift-?
	Help
Indent	⌘-Shift-I
	F5
Italics Toggle	⌘-I
Num Lock	Shift-Esc
	Shift-Clear
Open	⌘-O
Paste	⌘-V
	F4
Print	⌘-P
Print Preview	⌘-Shift-P
Quit	⌘-Q
Record Macro	⌘-F9
Run Macro	⌘-Shift-X
	F9
Save	⌘-S
Save As	⌘-Shift-S
Speller	⌘-E
Undo	⌘-Z
	F1

Tip
Practice choosing commands with the ⌘ key or function keys rather than with the mouse; otherwise, you may find yourself automatically reaching for the mouse and slowing yourself down.

Understanding Types of Menu Commands

WordPerfect has three types of menu commands: direct commands, hierarchical commands, and commands that access dialog boxes. When you choose a direct command, WordPerfect executes the command immediately. Hierarchical commands display an additional menu. Other commands display a dialog box.

Direct Menu Commands

Direct menu commands do not require additional information to carry out a function. You do not need to make more selections or decisions.

Chapter 2
An Overview of WordPerfect 2.1

You choose these commands, which are not followed by an ellipsis or triangle, from a menu (see fig. 2.9). All the commands from the Style menu, except Remove, are direct commands.

Fig. 2.9
Examples of direct menu commands.

Hierarchical Menu Commands

You also access hierarchical commands from a menu. Unlike direct commands, however, hierarchical commands are followed by a triangle. This triangle indicates that another menu containing additional commands opens when you choose one of these commands. The Line command, in addition to several other commands in the Layout menu, is a hierarchical command (see fig. 2.10).

Commands that Open Dialog Boxes

Some commands—such as Format, Tabs, and Kerning on the Line submenu—are followed by an ellipsis (...). An ellipsis indicates that a dialog box appears when you choose one of these commands. If you choose Format from the Line command, for example, the Line Format dialog box appears (see fig. 2.11). In the dialog box, you can make more choices.

You can move through the options in a dialog box in two ways: by clicking the mouse button or pressing Tab. When you use Tab to move through the dialog box, WordPerfect highlights each option or text box in sequence. You can replace the current setting in the highlighted option by typing the new setting. If you click an option with the mouse, you choose that option. To add text in dialog box options, double-click the setting and type a new value. Dialog boxes also contain pop-up menus. Pop-up menus, which are outlined by a drop shadow, usually contain additional options or commands.

Part I
Getting Started

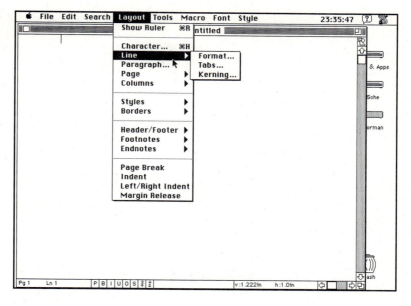

Fig. 2.10
Hierarchical menu commands.

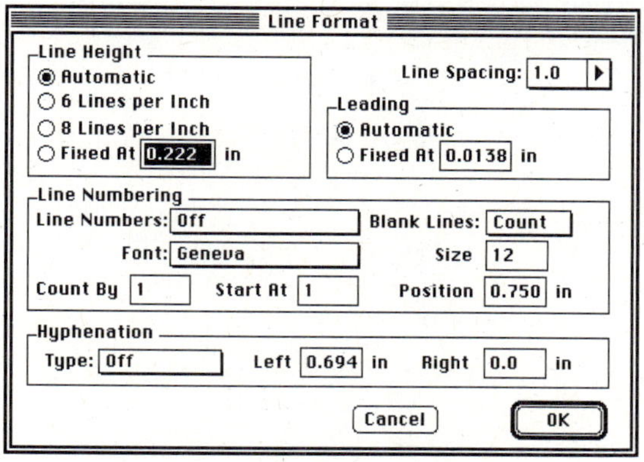

Fig. 2.11
The Line Format dialog box.

Using Command-Key Shortcuts

A quick way to change options in a dialog box is to use the Command key (⌘). To see the command-key shortcuts in a dialog box, press and hold down the ⌘ key. Command-key shortcuts appear next to several options. If you press the ⌘ key while the mouse pointer is in the Line Format dialog box, for example, Command-key shortcuts appear next to several options (see fig. 2.12). To use a command-key shortcut to choose an option, press the ⌘ key and the appropriate letter or letters.

Chapter 2
An Overview of WordPerfect 2.1

Fig. 2.12
Command-key shortcuts in dialog boxes.

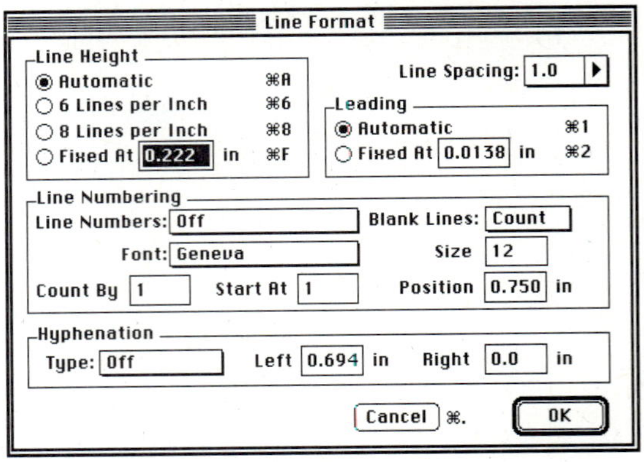

The Command-key shortcuts in dialog boxes are an extension of the Macintosh method of enabling you to use keyboard shortcuts rather than the mouse to access commands and options. You also find Command-key shortcuts in most of the pull-down menus.

Getting Help

If you are not sure what a WordPerfect command does, you can look it up in Help. The Help feature provides a brief description and cross-references for most of WordPerfect's features and commands.

Version 2.1 also has a new feature called Balloon Help, but this feature is available only if you use System 7. When Balloon Help is active, a Help balloon appears next to features that you point to in your document window (see fig. 2.13).

To activate Balloon Help, choose Show Balloons from the Balloon Help menu. (This menu, which resembles a cartoon bubble containing a question mark, is located in the upper right corner of the screen, beside the WordPerfect icon.) Be sure to choose Hide Balloons from the Balloon Help menu when you no longer need help. Because a Help balloon appears for every option that the mouse pointer points to, leaving Balloon Help on while you work can be distracting.

To display the Help dialog box, pull down the Apple menu, drag the pointer to the Help command and release the mouse button. You also can display the Help screen by pressing ⌘-?, pressing the Help key to the right of the main keys (if you have an extended keyboard), or

Part I
Getting Started

choosing WordPerfect Help from the Balloon Help pull-down menu. When you choose Help, the Help dialog box appears (see fig. 2.14).

Fig. 2.13
Balloon Help revealing a shortcut to the Environment dialog box.

Balloon Help icon

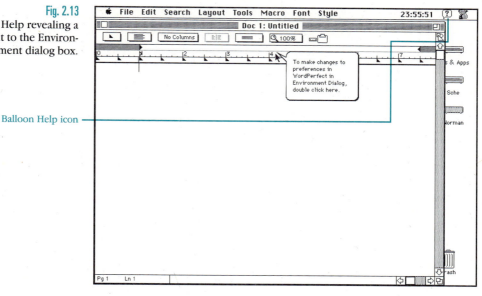

Fig. 2.14
The Help dialog box.

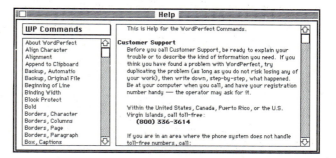

> **Tip**
>
> If the Help dialog box does not appear, you probably did not install the WP Help file. See the WordPerfect installation manual for instructions.

The Help dialog box contains two list boxes. The left list box contains WordPerfect commands. The right list box displays explanations about the commands. To find a command, scroll through the list of commands (place the pointer on a scroll arrow and press the mouse button). Release the button when you see the command you are interested in. You also can type the first few letters of a command to move directly to that command.

Chapter 2
An Overview of WordPerfect 2.1

Alternatively, you can estimate where a specific command may be within the list and drag the scroll box to that location. Suppose, for example, that you want to look up *Watermarks*. The letter *W* is near the end of the alphabet. Click the scroll box and pull it to the bottom of the scroll bar to see the entry *Watermarks*. If you click *Watermarks*, an explanation of that command appears in the explanation list box of the Help screen (see fig. 2.15).

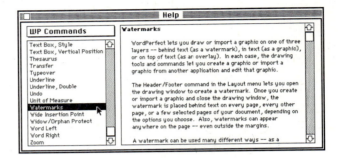

Fig. 2.15
Choosing Watermarks from the list of commands.

If the explanation for the command does not fit on one screen, you can scroll through the explanation to see the rest of the entry.

To return to your document, click the close box in the upper left corner of the Help dialog box.

Creating a Document

To enter text, you just begin typing in a document window. Unlike a typewriter, pressing Return (or Enter) at the end of each line is not necessary when you use a word processor. When you reach the end of one line, the words automatically wrap to the next line. You press Return only to end a paragraph or insert a blank line.

Pressing the Tab key indents the first line of a paragraph. Pressing the Backspace (or Delete) key deletes the character to the left of the insertion point.

To insert text, place the insertion point at the location where you want to add the new text and type. To accommodate the new text, WordPerfect moves the existing text to the right of the insertion point.

The Show ¶ command enables you to see where you placed spaces, tabs, and returns. You also can see where you marked text for a list, table of contents, index, table of authorities, or cross-reference. These formatting

Part I
Getting Started

marks do not show when you print the document. You can click Show ¶ from the Edit menu or press Option-F1 to show the hidden codes. Figure 2.16 shows a document with the symbols displayed.

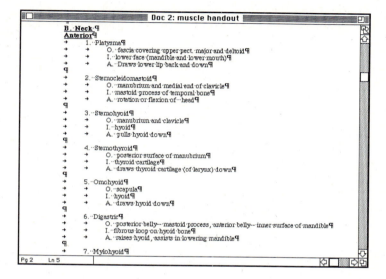

Fig. 2.16
Using Show ¶ in a document.

Moving around in the Document

WordPerfect provides several ways that you can move around in a document. If you have a favorite method from another word processing program, chances are you can use that method in WordPerfect. If you don't have a favorite method for moving through a document, try several of the techniques explained here, and pick one or two that work best for you.

One of the most common techniques for moving from one location in your document to another is to place the I-beam pointer in the desired location and click the mouse button. The disadvantage of using this technique when you are typing is that you must take one hand off the keyboard to use the mouse.

Using the Scroll Bars

To browse through a document, you can use the scroll bars, which offer a convenient way to move quickly through the document. The document window has two scroll bars: one located along the right of the screen, the other located at the bottom of the screen. The right scroll bar enables you to move up or down through a document. You can move line-by-line by clicking the arrows at the top or bottom of the scroll bar (holding the mouse button down repeats the line-by-line function). To move more quickly through your document, click the box inside the scroll bar and drag it up or down.

You use the scroll bar at the bottom of the screen to move document text left or right. This scroll bar is useful if the width of your text exceeds the width of the screen. For most documents, however, your text probably stays within the confines of the screen.

Using the scroll bars enables you to see other parts of the document but does not reposition the insertion point. Click somewhere in the text to move the insertion point to the current viewing location.

When you scroll through a document, be sure to move your insertion point to the appropriate location before you activate a command. WordPerfect sometimes jumps back to the insertion point before carrying out the command.

Using the Arrow Keys

The arrow keys are located to the right of the main keyboard. They move the insertion point one character or line in the direction of the arrow. To move a few characters or lines only, this method may be the fastest way to go.

You also can use the arrow keys with the ⌘ and Option keys to move the insertion point quickly, as explained in the following list:

- To move to the end or beginning of the current line, press ⌘-→ or ⌘-←, respectively.
- To move to the top or bottom of the current screen, press ⌘-↑ or ⌘-↓, respectively.
- To move to the right or left one word at a time, press Option-→ or Option-←, respectively. (Pressing Option-↑ or Option-↓ has the same effect as pressing the up or down arrow alone.)

Using the Repeat Function

To consecutively repeat a character or function, you can press the same keystroke once and use WordPerfect's repeat function. By using Repeat

Part I

Getting Started

Count, the character or keystroke repeats the number of times you indicate. You can use the Repeat Count feature, for example, to repeat a macro, any character, tabs, the movement of the insertion point, or text deletion.

You access the Repeat feature by pressing ⌘-Esc. This command displays the Repeat dialog box, in which you indicate how many times WordPerfect should repeat your next entry. The default number for the Repeat feature is eight. If you invoke this feature and then press an arrow key, for example, the insertion point moves eight lines or characters, as if you had pressed the arrow key eight times. To change the number of repetitions, you must access the Set Repeat Count dialog box (see fig. 2.17).

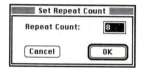

Fig. 2.17
The Set Repeat Count dialog box.

To change the Repeat Count value, follow these steps:

1. Press ⌘-Shift-Esc.

   The Set Repeat Count dialog box appears.

2. Type a new number in the text box. (You can choose any number from 1 to 32,767.)

3. Click OK.

When you access the Repeat dialog box now, the number you entered in the Set Repeat Count dialog box is displayed. The new repeat count remains until you change it or quit WordPerfect.

Suppose, for example, that you want pound signs (#) to appear across the page. In the Set Repeat Count dialog box, set the repeat count to something like 55 and click OK. Access the Repeat dialog box (the repeat count should be 55) and press the pound sign. WordPerfect enters 55 pound signs across the page.

If you decide to test this function by changing the count to 32,767 and pressing the down arrow, for instance, but have only 100 lines in your document, the insertion point goes as far as possible; then, the computer stalls while it tries to complete the remaining 32,667 repetitions. To cancel the Repeat operation, press the Esc (Escape) key or ⌘-period (.).

Chapter 2
An Overview of WordPerfect 2.1

Using Page Up, Page Down, Home, and End

If you have an extended keyboard, you can move up and down one page at a time with the Page Up and Page Down keys. (You can find Page Up and Page Down keys on the numeric keypad.) You also can move to the beginning or end of the document in one keystroke by pressing the Home or End key, respectively.

Using the Numeric Keypad in Command Mode

The default condition for the numeric keypad is the Command mode. In Command mode, you cannot use the numbers on the numeric keypad. When you press the 4 or the 6, for example, the number doesn't appear; instead, the insertion point moves one character to the left or to the right.

To enter numbers from the numeric keypad, turn on number lock by pressing Shift-Clear. (The Clear button is on the upper left of the numeric keypad.) If your number pad has only numbers written on the keys, refer to table 2.2 to see what each key does in Command mode:

Table 2.2
Number Keys in Command Mode

Key	Command Mode Function
1	No command mode function
2	Down arrow
3	Page Down
4	Left arrow
5	Gold key
6	Right arrow
7	Gold key
8	Up arrow
9	Page Up

The 5 and the 7 keys are Gold keys. A *Gold* key (which works the same way that the Home key in the PC version of WordPerfect works) is a modifier for the arrow keys. Pressing a Gold key once or twice before pressing an arrow key moves the insertion point much farther through the document than pressing an arrow key by itself. The following list explains the arrow key/Gold key combinations.

Part I
Getting Started

- Gold ← or Gold → moves the insertion point to the beginning or end, respectively, of that line or screen (whichever is shorter).
- Gold ↑ or Gold ↓ moves the insertion point to the beginning or end of that screen.
- Gold, Gold ↑ or Gold, Gold ↓ moves the insertion point to the beginning or end of the document.
- Gold, Gold → or Gold, Gold ← moves the insertion point to the end or beginning of a line.

Table 2.3 lists some of the most common keyboard commands for moving the insertion point.

Table 2.3 Common Keyboard Commands

Keyboard Command	Result
→ or ←	Moves insertion point right or left one character
↑ or ↓	Moves insertion point up or down one line
Option-→ or Option-←	Moves insertion point right or left one word at a time
⌘-→ or ⌘-←	Moves insertion point to end or beginning of current line
Page Up (9 on keypad)	Moves insertion point to top of page
Page Down (3 on keypad)	Moves insertion point to bottom of page
Screen Up (– on keypad)	Moves insertion point to top of window
Screen Down (+ on keypad)	Moves insertion point to bottom of window
Home (on extended keyboard)	Moves insertion point to beginning of document
End (on extended keyboard)	Moves insertion point to end of document
Gold ← or Gold →	Moves insertion point to beginning or end of current line
Gold ↑ or Gold ↓	Moves insertion point to top or bottom of screen
Gold, Gold ↑ or Gold, Gold ↓	Moves insertion point to beginning or end of document

Chapter 2
An Overview of WordPerfect 2.1

Using the Go To Command

The Go To command enables you to go to any page within your document and choose a location within the page. To use the Go To command, follow these steps:

1. Choose Go To from the Search menu.

   Alternatively, press Option-F13 or ⌘-Shift-G.

   The Go To dialog box appears (see fig. 2.18).

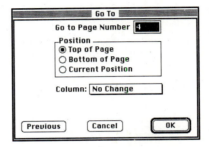

Fig. 2.18
The Go To dialog box.

2. In the Go to Page Number text box, type the number of the page to which you want to go. (The default page number is the page you are on.)

3. Select the top or bottom of that page by clicking the appropriate button, or—if you prefer—set the insertion point at the desired location within your current page and go to that same location on the new page.

4. Click OK.

   WordPerfect moves the insertion point to the page and position you chose.

The Previous button in the Go To dialog box enables you to return to the location of the insertion point before you changed the insertion point location.

If you know which page (or approximately which page) you want to go to, the Go To command is a convenient way to move through large documents.

Part I
Getting Started

Working with Text

After you enter text, you may want to change it. You may discover, for instance, that adding words, deleting sentences, or rearranging entire paragraphs is necessary. An advantage of using WordPerfect is that editing is easy. You can select and modify any amount of text, often with just a few keystrokes.

Editing text is covered in detail in Chapter 3, "Editing a Document," but many of the basics—including several ways to insert, select, and delete text—are covered here. Typeover mode is discussed at the end of this section.

Inserting Text

Inserting text is one of the easiest tasks you can do in a word processor. Just move the insertion point to the location where you want the new text and type. (You can position the insertion point by clicking the new location or using the arrow keys.) Text to the right of the insertion point makes room for the text you enter.

Selecting Text

Almost all editing on the Macintosh is done by first *selecting* text. After you select text, you can type over it, delete it, cut it (to be pasted elsewhere), copy it, or use it in a Find function. Most of these uses are covered in other chapters, but the way you select the text remains the same. You can use the mouse, the keyboard, or a mouse-keyboard combination to select text.

Using the Mouse

To select text with the mouse, place the pointer at one end of the text and click; then, drag the pointer to the other end of the text. You can go forward or backward. WordPerfect highlights the selected text (see fig. 2.19).

Another way to select text is to use the mouse and keyboard together. Place the insertion point at one end of the desired text and press the Shift key; then place the insertion point, using the mouse, at the other end of the text to be selected. Again, whether you go forward or backward doesn't matter. The entire text between the first location of the insertion point and the second location is selected.

Chapter 2
An Overview of WordPerfect 2.1

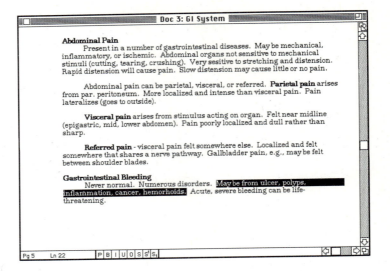

Fig. 2.19
Selected text.

If you change your mind, you can unselect the text by clicking the mouse elsewhere in the document window.

Using the Keyboard

To select text with the keyboard, you can press the Shift key while you use any of the cursor-movement keyboard combinations; you select the text between the current insertion point location and the end of the move operation. For example, place the insertion point at the beginning of a line and hold down the Shift key; then, press ⌘-→. The entire line is selected.

You also can select defined units of text, such as a word, sentence, paragraph, or entire document, as explained in the following list:

- ■ To select a word, place the I-beam pointer within the word and double-click.

- ■ To select a sentence, place the I-beam pointer anywhere within the sentence and press ⌘-Shift-U or F6.

- ■ To select a paragraph, place the I-beam pointer anywhere within the paragraph; then press ⌘-Shift-Y, ⌘-F6, or triple-click.

- ■ To select an entire document, choose Select All from the Edit menu or press ⌘-A.

- ■ To unselect text, you can press Esc or an arrow key.

Deleting Text

You can delete any amount of text—as little as one character or as much as an entire document. When you delete characters, the remaining text "follows" the insertion point, removing the space that the deleted character occupied. Rather than leave "blank paper" when deleting text, the program also removes the space.

You can delete text one letter at a time by pressing the Delete key. (Older Macintosh keyboards and some third-party keyboards label this key Backspace.) Delete is located in the upper right corner of the main section of the keyboard. Pressing Delete deletes one character to the left of the insertion point. You can press the key many times to delete several characters, or you can hold down the key; WordPerfect deletes characters until you release the key.

To delete characters to the right of the insertion point, use the period (.) key in the numeric keypad. Again, the auto repeat function enables you to delete many characters by holding down the keypad period key.

To delete several words, lines, or paragraphs, select the text, using one of the selection methods described earlier. When the text is highlighted, press Delete. All the selected text disappears.

> **Tip**
> If you delete the wrong text or change your mind, you can restore the deleted text by choosing Undo from the Edit menu or by pressing ⌘-Z. The Undo command undoes only the last change, however. If you perform another task after the deletion, you cannot restore the deleted text by choosing Undo or pressing ⌘-Z.

Using Typeover Mode

When you are in *Typeover mode*, WordPerfect replaces a character for each character you type. If you are at the end of the document, Typeover inserts the new characters at the end of the document.

Typeover is available but inconvenient to set up for use. You can turn on Typeover mode only by assigning your own keyboard shortcut to the Typeover command. Assigning your own keyboard commands is covered in Chapter 15, "Customizing WordPerfect."

Saving a Document

You must save your document often. WordPerfect periodically backs up your file automatically (if you haven't changed that particular default setting). In case of a crash, however, you lose any text that you wrote between the last automatic backup and the crash.

To save a document in which you are working, follow these steps:

1. Choose Save from the File menu or press ⌘-S.

The Save As dialog box appears.

You must name the file. On a Macintosh, the file name can contain as many as 31 characters and use any character except a colon.

2. Type the name of your file in the Save Document As text box (see fig. 2.20).

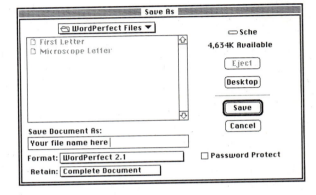

Fig. 2.20
The Save As dialog box.

Tip
Before you try an unfamiliar command and before you print or spell-check your document, protect your work by saving the document.

3. Click the Save button.

WordPerfect saves the document to the folder or disk shown above the list window of the Save As dialog box and returns you to your document.

For information about how to change the time period between automatic backups, see Chapter 15, "Customizing WordPerfect."

Exiting WordPerfect

Make sure that you exit WordPerfect before you turn off your Macintosh. To exit, follow these steps:

1. Choose Quit from the File menu or press ⌘-Q.

   If you edited your file since you last saved it, WordPerfect displays a message box asking whether you want to save changes (see fig. 2.21).

2. Choose Yes to save your changes; choose No to exit WordPerfect without saving the changes. To return to the document, choose Cancel.

Part I
Getting Started

Fig. 2.21
The message box that appears when you have unsaved changes.

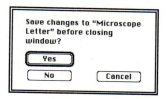

You return to the Macintosh desktop. You now can turn off the computer or enter another application.

If you do not exit WordPerfect before turning off your Macintosh, you can lose any unsaved text, and rebooting may take longer. If you turn off the computer during an automatic backup, you may lose everything on your hard disk. Although you may be able to recover the data with the appropriate software, why take the risk?

Chapter Summary

Tip

If you made changes that you don't want to save, close the document without saving your file. (Choose Close from the File menu; then click No in the message box that appears.) Then reopen the document. The document will be as it was before you made the changes. (Don't use this technique on a document that you haven't saved previously; otherwise, the entire document is lost.)

In this chapter, you learned the basics of using WordPerfect. This chapter explained how to open WordPerfect and how to use the menus and keyboard to navigate through the document execute commands. In this chapter, you also found instructions for entering text and performing simple editing tasks. This chapter ended with an explanation on how to save your document and safely exit the program.

Chapter 2
An Overview of WordPerfect 2.1

CHAPTER

Editing a Document

In the first two chapters, you got a very broad look at WordPerfect for the Macintosh. In this chapter, you learn more details about WordPerfect's powerful editing capabilities.

If you have used other Mac editors, you may find some of this information very familiar. (That familiarity is part of the appeal of the Macintosh.) Some features, however, go beyond those offered in other programs, particularly the options in the search-and-replace function.

This chapter discusses the following topics:

- Opening a document to be edited from the Finder or from within WordPerfect
- Working with selected text and using the Clipboard to move text in the document
- Changing text styles
- Using Undo to reverse editing changes
- Using Show Codes to look at WordPerfect's normally hidden formatting codes
- Using the Find/Change command to edit text
- Using the Find Code command to remove a text style

Opening a Document

ou can open a WordPerfect document for editing in two ways. You can open the file from the Finder, or you can start WordPerfect and open the file from inside the program.

Opening a Document from the Finder

> **Tip**
> To open files created in another word processor (including WordPerfect 1.0.x) from the Finder into WordPerfect 2.1, you can use a utility called Handoff II by Connectix. Make sure that a WordPerfect Version 2 conversion filter exists for the other format before you use the utility.

The *Finder* is the part of Apple system software that displays your disks, folders, applications, and files in windows. Although the utility does many other things behind the scenes, most users commonly think of the Finder as the file manager of the Mac.

The Finder, which is really *MultiFinder*, remains visible behind the other application windows. Although available with some earlier system software, the MultiFinder is required in System 7 (the latest Apple system software).

To open a WordPerfect document from the Finder, follow these steps:

1. Open the folder that contains your document.
2. Double-click the document icon (see fig. 3.1).

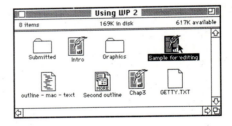

Fig. 3.1
Double-clicking a document icon in the Finder.

The system launches the WordPerfect application and opens the file.

If you have two revisions of WordPerfect Version 2 on your hard disk—for instance, you upgraded from Version 2.0, revision 2.0.3, to Version 2.1 and kept the old version—double-clicking a document icon may start the older version of the program. If you must keep both versions on your disk, use the method described in the next section to open a file in the correct release of the program.

Part I
Getting Started

Opening a File from within WordPerfect

> **Tip**
> If you are using MultiFinder and WordPerfect is already running, the system switches to WordPerfect and opens the document from within WordPerfect.

You can open a file from within WordPerfect. Before MultiFinder became available, the following method was the only way to open another file after you started an application. Using the File menu inside WordPerfect often is faster than going back to a Finder window and double-clicking a document icon.

If you started WordPerfect, you can open an existing file for editing by following these steps:

1. Choose Open from the File menu (see fig. 3.2).

    Alternatively, press ⌘-O (the letter *O*, not the number zero).

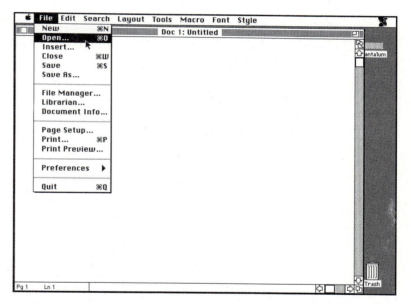

Fig. 3.2
Choosing Open from the File menu.

> **Tip**
> Using a keyboard shortcut, such as ⌘-O, is generally faster than choosing a command from a menu. If you regularly use more than one program, however, keeping track of all the shortcuts is impossible. Try to remember the shortcuts for the commands you use most often.

The Open dialog box appears (see fig. 3.3). The Open dialog box shows a list of files in the current folder. The current folder is the last one you used, unless you use default folders so that WordPerfect always opens to the same folder. (See Chapter 15 for more information on default folders.)

2. Double-click the name of the file you want to open.

    Alternatively, use the arrow keys to highlight the name of the file and then press Return, or select the file name and click the Open button on the right side of the dialog box.

Chapter 3
Editing a Document

Fig. 3.3
The Open dialog box.

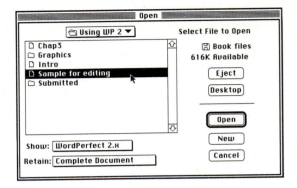

Navigating the Macintosh File Lists

The document you want to open may not be in the first file list in the Open dialog box. WordPerfect uses the standard Macintosh system file lists in the Open dialog box.

You can double-click a folder name to open that folder to see the files inside. Folders appear in the file list with a folder icon beside the file name (for example, a folder icon appears next to Graphics in fig. 3.3). To move to a higher folder level, you can click the current folder name at the top of the file list and select the new folder level you want to view (see fig. 3.4). You also can use ⌘-↑ to step back up through the file hierarchy one level at a time.

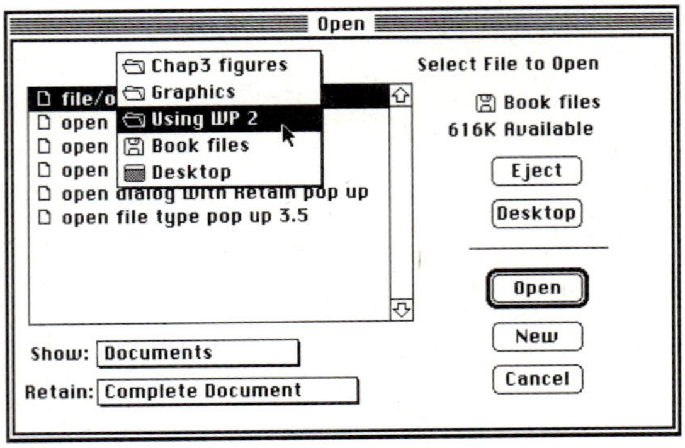

Fig. 3.4
Using the Folder pop-up list to select another folder in the file tree.

Clicking the Desktop button in the dialog box enables you to switch between the disks in the floppy drives, hard disk partitions, and network file servers. (If you are using System 6, you click the Drive button.) Clicking Desktop puts a list of active disks in the file list area.

Part I
Getting Started

> **Tip**
> Holding down the Command (⌘) key while a dialog box is open reveals the keyboard shortcuts for dialog box buttons.

The disk name, an icon indicating the type of disk (fixed drive or floppy disk drive), and the available space on the current drive are shown in the upper right portion of the Open dialog box. If the file list displayed is from a floppy disk, the Eject button is active in the Open dialog box so that you can remove the disk from the computer and insert another to search for a file.

If you change your mind about opening another file, click Cancel to return to the current file window. To open an empty document window, click New.

Controlling the File List

> **Tip**
> Pop-up menus are different than pull-down menus in that a closed pop-up menu shows the choice you made on the menu. A closed pull-down menu always shows the same menu title.

WordPerfect provides a way to shorten the Open dialog box file list so that only the documents you are most likely to want are displayed. In the lower left corner of the Open dialog box is a pop-up menu next to the word Show. (Pop-up menus are outlined by the thicker line, known as a *drop shadow*, that appears on the bottom and right sides of a box or around a word or short phrase.)

The default choice for Show is WordPerfect. With this option visible in the pop-up menu box, only WordPerfect files and folders (which may contain more WordPerfect files) appear in the file list. To change the value of the Show parameter, click the pop-up menu and choose a new option from the list that appears (see fig. 3.5).

Fig. 3.5
The Show pop-up menu in the Open dialog box.

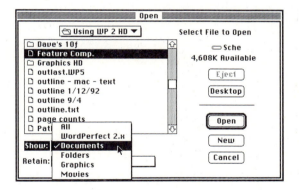

The two most frequently chosen options are WordPerfect and Documents. When you choose Documents, you see all the files except those the Macintosh recognizes internally as system files. Opening files from other word processors requires that you have the correct file conversion

Chapter 3
Editing a Document

resource installed. Chapter 7, "Managing Files and Documents," discusses in more detail opening files from other programs and understanding the options in the Show pop-up menu.

The Retain pop-up menu at the bottom of the Open dialog box affects how much of a document is included in the editing session. For the moment, leave this option on Complete Document so that everything in a document on disk remains in the document. (See Chapter 7 for a complete discussion of the Retain options.)

Opening More Than One Document

You can open several documents at the same time by repeating the Open command. You can open as many documents as the amount of memory available to WordPerfect accepts. The program performance, however, probably will slow enough to bother you before the system or the program refuses to open another file because of lack of memory.

Creating a New Document

You can open a new, blank document window any time, even while you are working on other documents in WordPerfect. Choose New from the File menu or press ⌘-N. If the Open dialog box is displayed, you can create a new document by clicking the New button on the right side of the Open dialog box.

A new window for an untitled document appears. WordPerfect arranges multiple windows so that you can see the title bars of several documents at one time (see fig. 3.6). Opening a blank document is useful for collecting copies of sections of other documents without changing the source document. You also may want to work on a new document and leave the others open for reference.

Working with Text

Enabling you to correct and revise easily is the heart of a word processor's advantage over a typewriter. You can make changes one letter at a time, as you do on a correcting typewriter, but you also can work with larger chunks of text.

The most fundamental editing operations performed on selected text are operations using the Cut, Copy, and Paste commands. The command names are fairly descriptive: Cut removes selected material (text or graphics) from a document, Copy copies selected material, and Paste inserts material at the insertion point. The Append command extends the Copy command by enabling you to copy text from multiple places without pasting each item—as is necessary without Append—before the next copy.

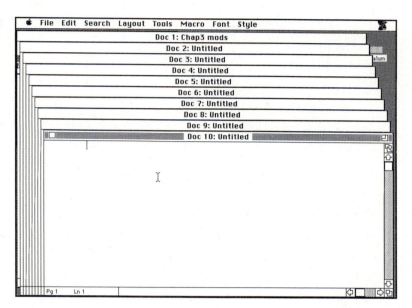

Fig. 3.6
Overlapping document windows.

The Macintosh uses a temporary storage area called the *Clipboard*. When you issue a Cut or Copy command, WordPerfect places a copy of the selected material on the Clipboard, replacing whatever was there before. If you are cutting text, WordPerfect deletes the selected text from the original document after a copy is placed in the Clipboard. Copy places the selected text on the Clipboard and leaves the original text in the document. The Paste command puts a copy of the Clipboard contents into the document at the insertion point.

As with many other commands in WordPerfect, you can issue the Cut, Copy, and Paste commands in several ways: by using Command-key shortcuts, using function keys on an extended keyboard, or choosing commands from the Edit menu. Again, use the method most convenient for your circumstances.

The following examples give a clearer idea of what happens during the Cut, Copy, and Paste operations. To set up the screen as shown in figure 3.7, follow these steps:

Chapter 3

Editing a Document

Fig. 3.7
Viewing the Clipboard and document at the same time.

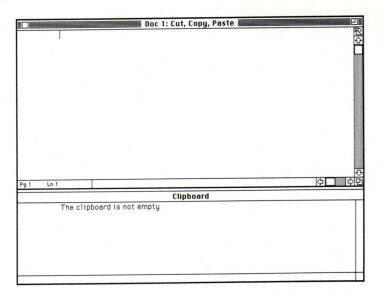

1. Open a new document and type *The Clipboard is not empty*.

2. To name the document, choose Save from the File menu. When the Save As dialog box appears, type *Cut*, *Copy*, *Paste* in the Save Document As text box, and click Save.

   The name of the document appears in the title bar.

3. Select the sentence by pressing ⌘-A for Select All.

   Although you can use many other selection techniques, pressing ⌘-A is quickest in this example.

4. Cut the sentence from the document by typing ⌘-X, pressing F2, or choosing Cut from the Edit menu.

5. Reduce the height of the main document window by clicking and dragging the size box in the lower right corner of the document window.

6. Choose Show Clipboard from the Edit menu.

7. Resize and move the Clipboard window so that it doesn't overlap the document window.

Your screen should resemble the screen shown in figure 3.7.

Part I
Getting Started

Cutting Text

Having set up the screen to view the Clipboard and the document at the same time, you can see how editing operations affect the document and the Clipboard. Before you can edit text, however, you must have some text in the document. To continue with this exercise, type the following into the document:

> Cut, Copy, and Paste provide ways to delete, move, or create multiple copies of selected text. You can paste the contents of the Clipboard anywhere in your document.
>
> The first step in Cut and Copy is to select text to be cut or copied. Both commands put a copy of the text on the Clipboard. Cut also removes the selected text from the document.

Remember that Cut and Copy only act on selected text. Chapter 2, "An Overview of WordPerfect 2.1," covers the many ways to select text in WordPerfect.

One editing operation that you may do many times is removing an entire sentence. To remove the second sentence in the text you just typed, follow these steps:

1. Place the insertion point anywhere in the sentence.
2. Press ⌘-Shift-U or press F6 to select the sentence containing the insertion point. You also can select the sentence by dragging.
3. Press ⌘-X, choose Cut from the Edit menu, or press F2. WordPerfect removes the text from the document and places it in the Clipboard. Figure 3.8 shows the results of the cut. (Notice that the contents of the Clipboard—*The clipboard is not empty*—have been replaced.)

Use Cut to delete selected text from a document or as the first step in moving text to another location in a document. Even when you are sure that you don't want to move the text somewhere else, using the Cut command rather than the Delete key provides an extra level of protection in case you change your mind.

Copying Text

When you want to leave text in place but also have a copy of the text in the Clipboard, you use the same technique explained in the preceding steps; however, instead of cutting the text by pressing ⌘-X, you copy the text by choosing Copy from the Edit menu, pressing F3, or pressing

⌘-C. When you copy text, the text remains in your document and WordPerfect places a copy of it on the Clipboard, replacing whatever was there (see fig. 3.9).

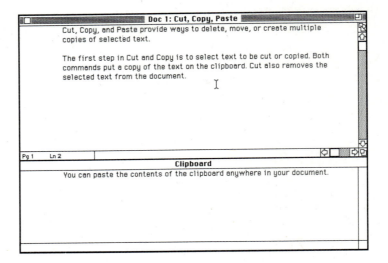

Fig. 3.8
Contents of the document and Clipboard after cutting text.

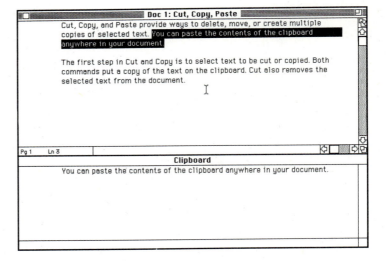

Fig. 3.9
The results of the Copy command.

> **Tip**
>
> The ⌘-X, ⌘-C, and ⌘-V shortcuts for Cut, Copy, and Paste, respectively, are excellent shortcuts to memorize. Because these shortcuts are the same in all Macintosh applications, you will use them often.

Pasting Text

After you put something in the Clipboard, you can retrieve it by using the Paste command. Follow these steps:

Part I

Getting Started

1. Using the document and Clipboard shown in figure 3.9, place the mouse pointer at the end of the last sentence and press Return twice to place the insertion point where the copy should appear.

2. Press ⌘-V, choose Paste from the Edit menu, or press the F3 function key. WordPerfect pastes the contents of the Clipboard into the document at the location of the insertion point (see fig. 3.10).

You can paste text anywhere in a document. (The pasted text in the figure has been selected to call attention to it. The paste operation does not select the text after pasting takes place.)

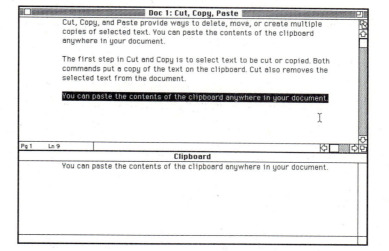

Fig. 3.10
Pasting Clipboard contents into a document.

Notice that pasting text does not remove it from the Clipboard. You can paste as many copies of the material in as many places in a document as you want. The contents of the Clipboard change only when you cut, copy, append something new, or turn off the computer.

Appending Text

WordPerfect has added an editing command to the basic Macintosh set: Append to Clipboard. Append adds the selected material to the contents of the Clipboard rather than replacing the Clipboard contents.

To append a sentence to the Clipboard, follow these steps:

1. Select the first sentence (`Cut, Copy, and Paste provide...`) by using the mouse or pressing ⌘-Shift-U or F6.
2. Press ⌘-Shift-A or choose Append from the Edit menu. WordPerfect adds the selected sentence to the contents of the Clipboard (see fig. 3.11).

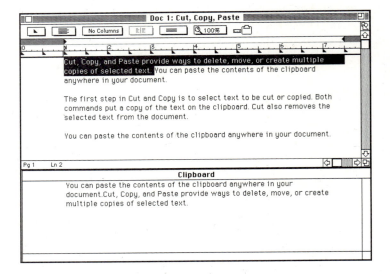

Fig. 3.11
Appending selected text.

Appending text to the Clipboard is useful when you want to copy items from several places to a new document or to rearrange several paragraphs. Because Append is like the Copy command and not the Cut command, using Append to rearrange paragraphs takes an extra step. Rearrange paragraphs by doing the following:

1. Select the material that should appear first in the rearrangement.
2. Choose Copy from the Edit menu or press ⌘-C. WordPerfect copies the selected text to the Clipboard.
3. Press Delete to delete the selected document text.
4. Select the text that should appear second in the rearrangement.
5. Choose Append from the Edit menu or press ⌘-Shift-A. WordPerfect adds the appended material to the contents on the Clipboard.
6. Delete the selected text from the document.

Part I
Getting Started

7. Repeat the Select-Append-Delete sequence until all the material to be rearranged is moved to the Clipboard. The material in the Clipboard should be in the order you want.

   If you append a great deal of material to the Clipboard, the system creates a disk file to hold the Clipboard contents instead of keeping everything in memory. WordPerfect may slow down noticeably during the Append operation if the Clipboard has much material in it.

8. Move the insertion point in the document to the destination of the rearranged text.

9. Paste the text by choosing Paste from the Edit menu, pressing ⌘-V, or pressing F4. WordPerfect copies the contents of the Clipboard—in this case the rearranged text—into your document.

Rearranging in this fashion saves time, because you place the insertion point and choose Paste only once for the entire rearrangement.

Tip
If you're doing a major rearrangement, working on a copy of a document is safer. One way to copy a document is to open your document normally, immediately choose Save As from the File menu, give the document a new name, and then click OK. By making a copy of your document, you can be sure that the original version is safe.

Deleting Selected Text

If you press the Delete key while text is selected, WordPerfect removes the selected text from the document. When you use the Delete key, WordPerfect does not place a copy of the text on the Clipboard; therefore, be careful when you delete. Deleted text is gone forever.

Because when you remove a word from the middle of a sentence, you don't want to leave the extra space, WordPerfect includes a *smart delete* feature to remove the extra space. If you select one or more whole words without selecting the spaces at either end and then delete or cut the text, for example, WordPerfect removes the extra space from the beginning of the selection.

Another way to make use of the smart delete feature is to place the insertion point within the word you are deleting by clicking the word once or using the arrow keys. Then press ⌘-Delete. WordPerfect deletes the word and one trailing space. If a punctuation mark follows the word, WordPerfect deletes the punctuation rather than the trailing space. If the insertion point is at the beginning or end of the word, ⌘-Delete deletes only the word and not the trailing space.

Finally, you also can place the insertion point at the beginning of the word to be deleted. Press Option-Shift-→ to select the word, any adjacent punctuation, and any trailing space; then you can cut or delete the entire group of characters. This method is useful if you prefer using the keyboard rather than the mouse to move through the document or select text.

Chapter 3
Editing a Document

Using Undo

You may have discovered that using Paste immediately after Cut enables you to recover from an unplanned cut operation. But what can you do when you accidentally paste something in the wrong place? Use the Undo command. Choosing Undo from the Edit menu (or pressing ⌘-Z or F1) reverses the most recent editing or formatting change you made in a document.

Undo is powerful but limited. The command reverses almost any operation, but you must use Undo before you issue another editing or formatting command. (Scrolling or moving the insertion point does not affect the Undo command.) If, for example, you delete a word, move the insertion point, and type a single letter, you lose the option of undoing the delete.

> **Tip**
> Typing many letters continuously is only one editing change. If you move the insertion point, type a paragraph, and then choose Undo, Undo removes the whole paragraph—not just the last character typed.

The Undo command is best suited for those times when you think, "Oh, no! I didn't mean to do that." If you choose Undo immediately, you almost always can return a document to the condition preceding the last action.

You even can undo an Undo operation. Issuing the second Undo command reverses the original Undo command. After the second Undo command, using the command flip-flops the two states of the document, which enables you to choose the more appropriate version for the finished document.

The Undo command doesn't restore material to the Clipboard, however. After a command has changed the Clipboard contents, the previous contents of the Clipboard are gone forever. The Undo command restores only what was (or wasn't) in the document.

Changing Text Styles

One improvement that computers and word processors have brought to individuals is the capability of using different text styles to call attention to certain words or phrases. On many typewriters, style options are limited to underlined and boldface text. With a computer, however, you have several text attribute options. In fact, the Macintosh was one of the earliest computers to use displays that show text styles almost exactly as they appear on a printed page—*almost* because the resolution of screen displays is more limited than the resolution of most printers on the market today.

Part I
Getting Started

> **Tip**
> As a practical matter, you should limit the number of different text styles you use so that a document doesn't look cluttered and confusing.

The styles used most often are boldface, italic, and underline. (Chapter 4, "Formatting a Document," covers other styles.) You can combine the styles to produce such effects as boldface italic text, for example.

Using Boldface, Italic, and Underline

You can assign a text style before or after you type the text. To use the boldface text style for text as you type, follow these steps:

1. On a blank line or in a new document, type the following:

    One of the main text styles used to emphasize text is

    Include a space after *is*.

2. Choose Bold from the Style menu or press -B (see fig. 3.12). A check mark appears beside a style to indicate that it is active.

Fig. 3.12
Choosing Bold from the Style menu.

3. Type *boldface*.

4. Choose Bold again to toggle off the boldface style; the check mark disappears.

5. Type *type*. You assigned the boldface type to the word *boldface* only (see fig. 3.13).

Many people don't like to apply text styles while they enter text, however, because the extra steps for formatting tend to slow down text entry. After you finish entering text, you easily can apply the text style to the existing text.

Fig. 3.13
Boldface text on the display.

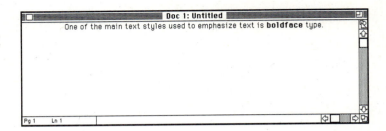

To convert existing text to boldface, perform the following steps:

1. Select the text, using the mouse or keyboard commands.

2. Choose Bold from the Style menu or press ⌘-B. WordPerfect applies the boldface text style to the selected text.

You can italicize or underline text by using the same techniques. To italicize text, press ⌘-I or choose Italic from the Style menu; to underline text, press ⌘-U or choose Underline from the Style menu.

Removing Text Attributes

After you apply a text style, you may discover that you don't like the results or that you applied the attribute to the wrong text. You easily can remove any text style from all or part of a text passage. To remove the boldface from text, perform the following steps:

1. Select the boldface text.

2. Choose Bold from the Style Menu or press ⌘-B. WordPerfect removes the style from the selected text.

You remove the other text styles by using the same technique. To remove the italic style from selected text, press ⌘-I; to remove underlining, press ⌘-U. Each text style command is a *toggle* because you use the same menu choice or keyboard command to turn the attribute on and off.

Using the Plain Text Command

By choosing the Plain Text command or pressing ⌘-T, you can remove any styles assigned to the selected text. If you have more than one style assigned to text, you can remove all styles at one time by using the Plain Text command. Select text to which you have applied a style, and then choose Plain Text from the Style menu or press ⌘-T. WordPerfect removes all text styles from the selected text.

> **Tip**
>
> Remembering the keyboard shortcuts for boldface, italic, and underline is probably worthwhile. Other Mac applications frequently use the same shortcuts. The command for Plain Text, however, varies between applications.

Part I

Getting Started

Understanding Hidden Codes

With WordPerfect, what you see on-screen is essentially what you see in print. The special formatting codes—designating text to be underlined or changing fonts, for example—are hidden. Concentrating on the text is easier without the distraction of formatting codes.

At times, however, looking at hidden codes can help you to find the cause of unexpected formatting in your document. You may need to delete a code, search for the place where you changed margins, or determine why the text does not look as expected.

You can show the formatting codes by using the Show Codes command. When you display codes in your document, the same text that appears on the top half of the screen also appears with formatting codes at the bottom of the screen.

Showing Hidden Codes

To reveal the hidden codes, choose Show Codes from the Edit menu, press Option-F2, or press -Shift-K. WordPerfect displays the coded text in the bottom window (see fig. 3.14). (Do the same to hide the codes, or click the Codes close box.)

Fig. 3.14
Revealing hidden codes.

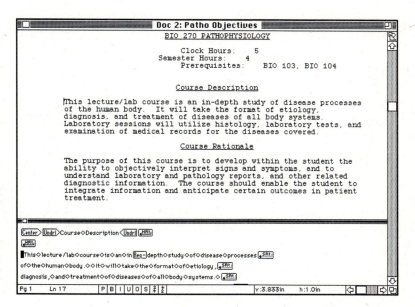

Tip

If you see a code that you don't understand, a list of code names appears with the code window symbols in the Find Code dialog box (accessed from the Search menu). Code symbols sometimes change between minor upgrades in the software, so a table may be accurate for one version of WordPerfect 2.1, but not another.

Chapter 3
Editing a Document

Formats that you apply to short sections of text—for example, underlining—have codes at the beginning and the end of the modified text (refer to fig. 3.14). These codes are called *paired codes*. The code is in a box that points to the appropriate text.

To delete a code, place the insertion point to the code's right or left. If the insertion point is to the right of the code, delete the code by pressing Delete (Backspace). If the insertion point is to the left of the code, delete the code by pressing the Delete Right key (the period/decimal point on the numeric keypad). If you delete a paired code such as underline, you must delete only one of the pair of formatting codes. WordPerfect automatically deletes the other code in the pair.

If you insert two conflicting codes in a row—for example, a left margin change to 2 inches followed by a left margin change to 3 inches—WordPerfect removes the first code and uses the remaining code to format the document.

You can change a setting in the document, however; from that point on, the format is that of the new setting. If you set the left margin to 2 inches, type one or more paragraphs, and then change the left margin to 3 inches, for example, both codes remain in the document and take effect where they are located.

Resizing the Code Window

Normally, the Show Codes window covers a little less than one-third of the lower screen. You can increase or decrease the size of the window by dragging the black band at the top of the window up or down (see fig. 3.15).

Scrolling through Codes

If you have several formatting functions in a single line of text, the text in the Show Codes window scrolls left or right, independently of the text window, in order to keep up with the insertion point in the text. The line of codes may scroll off the screen, but the codes at the same location as the insertion point in the text remain in view.

Using the Search Menu

he last editing tool covered in this chapter is the Search feature. Word processors enable you to find and change text in a document without reading the whole document to locate the text. This capability makes editing a document a relatively easy task on a word processor. Some word processors refer to this capability as *search and replace*. WordPerfect calls the process *find and change*.

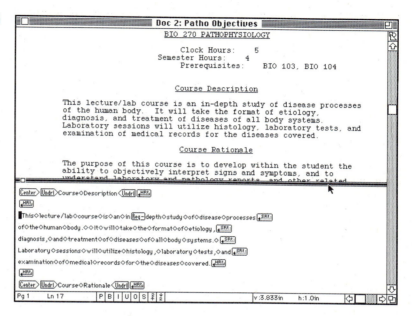

Fig. 3.15
Resizing the Code window.

The Search menu gives you access to several search functions (see fig. 3.16). The Find/Change command, for example, accesses the Find dialog box (see fig. 3.17). (The Find dialog box initially is titled Find Forward, because the default direction for searching through a document is forward.)

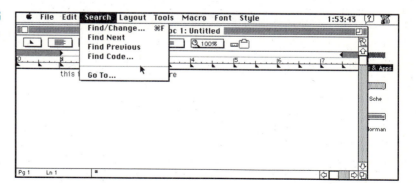

Fig. 3.16
The Search menu.

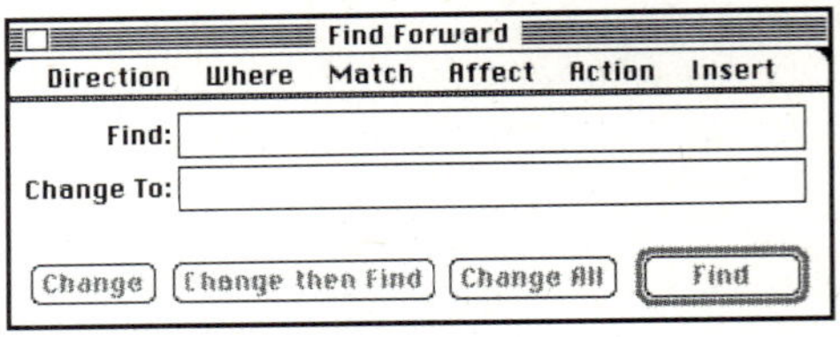

Fig. 3.17
The Find dialog box.

Changing search directions is one of the many options you can choose from the pull-down menus in the dialog box. In the Find text box, you enter text for which you are searching, and in the Change To text box, you enter the text that should replace the found text. The buttons at the bottom initiate the search or search-and-replace operation.

The other commands on the Search menu also enable you to find text. You use Find Next and Find Previous to look forward or backward for another occurrence of the text used in the last search. Find Code searches only for formatting codes. GoTo moves the insertion point to a specific page, as discussed in Chapter 2, "An Overview of WordPerfect 2.1."

Finding Text

Before the many sophisticated options and capabilities available in WordPerfect's search and replace operations are explained, step through a simple example of searching for text.

To find a specific word or phrase in a document, do the following:

1. Choose Find/Change from the Search menu or press ⌘-F. The Find dialog box appears.

2. In the Find text box, type the word or phrase you want to find. (Because the dialog box opens with the insertion point in the Find text box, you don't have to do anything except type the text.)

3. Press Return or click the Find button at the lower right of the dialog box.

WordPerfect finds the first occurrence of the specified text (see fig. 3.18). You can click the close box of the Find dialog box and begin editing, or you can click the Find button to look for the next occurrence of the text. WordPerfect stops searching when it reaches the end of the file. Changing the direction of the search is discussed in the section, "The Direction Menu."

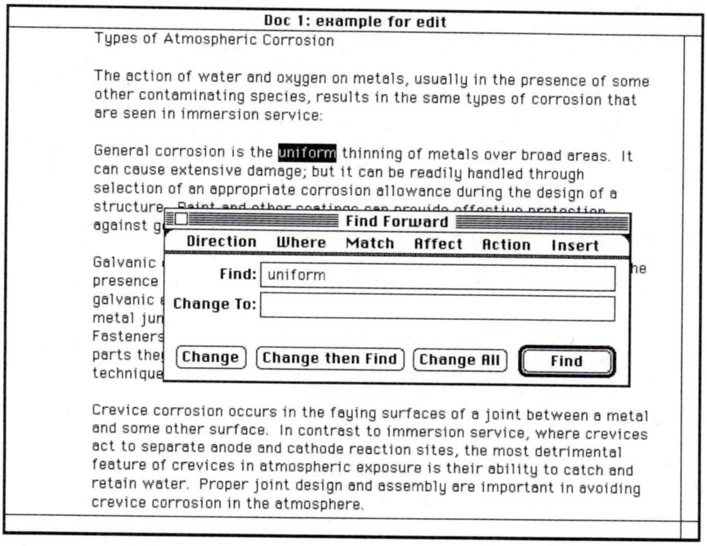

Fig. 3.18
Text found by the Search command.

Replacing Text

To change text, you can use the other half of the Find dialog box. To search for and replace text, follow these steps:

1. Open a new document window by pressing ⌘-N or choosing New from the File menu.

2. Type the following sentence:

   The weather forecaster says its going to be a fine day.

3. Move the insertion point to the beginning of the sentence and choose Find/Change from the Search menu or press ⌘-F.

   You can resize the document window and move the Find Forward dialog box so that neither window obstructs the view of the other window (see fig. 3.19).

4. Type *its* in the Find text box so that WordPerfect searches for that word.

5. Press the Tab key or click the Change To text box; type *it's*.

6. Press Return or click the Find button in the lower right of the Find dialog box.

   WordPerfect selects *its* in the document.

Chapter 3
Editing a Document

Fig. 3.19
Arranging windows to view the document and the Find dialog box.

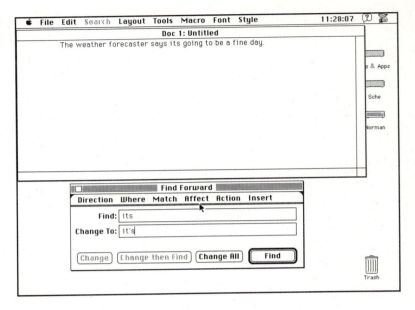

7. Click the Change button at the lower left of the Find dialog box. WordPerfect replaces the selected text (see fig. 3.20).

Fig. 3.20
The replaced text.

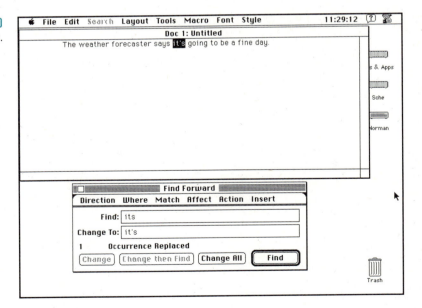

Part I

Getting Started

You can click the Change Then Find button to find and change the next occurrence.

If you are sure that you want to change all occurrences of a word, you can choose Change All in the Find dialog box. To be safe, however, always use Find to make sure that you really do want to change all occurrences.

To delete a specific word or phrase, type the word to delete in the Find text box and leave the Change To text box empty when you start a search. Anytime the Change To text box is empty, pressing the Change, Change Then Find, or Change All button deletes whatever text you typed in the Find text box.

Understanding the Find Dialog Box

When you choose Find/Change from the Search menu or press ⌘-F, the Find dialog box opens (refer to fig. 3.17). This dialog box is different from many others you have seen in WordPerfect and other Mac programs. Unlike other dialog boxes, the Find dialog box remains open until you close it by clicking the close box or pressing ⌘-W while the dialog box is the active window. (When a window is active, its title bar is striped.)

Notice also that the dialog box has its own menu bar just under the title bar and that the name of the dialog box is Find Forward. The title of the dialog box changes, depending on the option chosen on the Direction menu. To see the direction setting and many other Find settings, you must pull down the menus in the Find dialog box.

The Direction Menu

Pull down the Direction menu (see fig. 3.21). The first two options in the Direction menu are relatively straightforward. If a check mark appears beside Forward, a search begins at the insertion point and proceeds toward the end of the document.

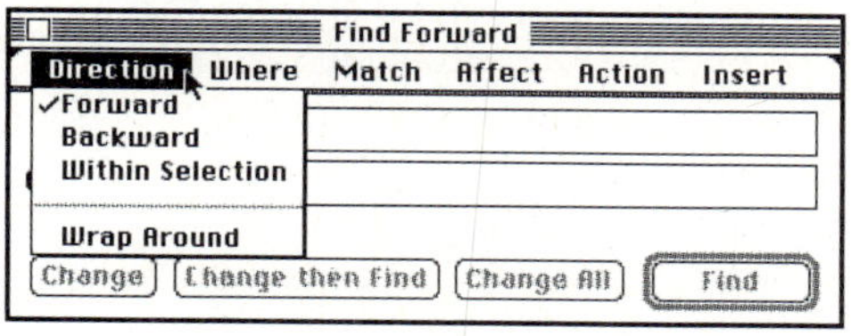

Fig. 3.21
The Direction menu in the Find dialog box.

Chapter 3
Editing a Document

When you choose Backward from the Direction menu, a check mark appears beside Backward, and the search goes from the location of the insertion point to the beginning of the document. In addition, the title of the Find dialog box also changes to Find Backward, saving you a trip to the Direction menu to see the direction of a search.

If you choose Wrap Around, WordPerfect searches the whole document, no matter where you start. You can choose Wrap Around in conjunction with Forward or Backward. If Within Selection is checked, WordPerfect limits the search to the selected text.

If you select a small amount of text before you display the Find dialog box, the selected text appears in the Find text box of the dialog box. If you select a lengthy passage and choose the Within Selection command, not all the selected text shows in the Find text box. In this case, you probably want to change the Find text anyway.

The Where Menu

WordPerfect enables you to search entire documents or *subdocuments*, which are elements such as headers, footers, endnotes, and so on. You can search subdocuments by using the Where menu, shown in figure 3.22, which lists the choices available for limiting a search. A check mark appears to the left of the option you choose.

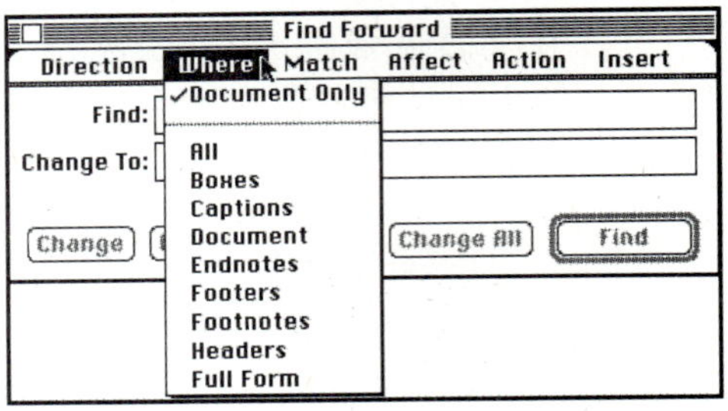

Fig. 3.22
The Where menu in the Find dialog box.

You can perform three types of searches: everything in the document (the All option), the main body of text without the subdocuments (the Document Only option), and a selection of one or more subdocuments (check marks appear next to as many options as you choose from the Where menu).

The Where menu includes Document and Document Only options. To turn off multiple subdocument selections at one time, choose the Document Only option. To search the document and a limited selection of subdocuments, choose the Document option.

Part I
Getting Started

At the bottom of the Where menu is a subdocument type called Full Form, which is a part of a table of authorities citation. See Chapter 10, "Creating Outlines and Lists," for more information on tables of authorities, which frequently are used in legal reports.

If you select a subdocument from the Where menu, perform a search, and then choose Save Defaults from Preferences under the File menu, your subdocument choice becomes the Where option default the next time you launch WordPerfect. If your Find/Change operations are not working, check the settings on the Find dialog box menus.

The Match Menu

The settings on the Match menu, shown in figure 3.23, affect what the program searches for when you enter text in the Find text box. Choosing Whole Word, for example, prevents WordPerfect from finding *itself* and *hits* as matches for *its*.

Fig. 3.23
The Match menu on the Find dialog box.

The Case option limits a match to a word that has the same upper- and lowercase text. When you choose Case, for example, and enter *Towel*, WordPerfect does not recognize *towel* as a match. If Case is unchecked, however, WordPerfect does recognize *towel* as a match. You may want to turn off the Case option so that you can find words at the beginnings of sentences (where they are capitalized) and elsewhere (where they may not be capitalized).

The Text Only option is an extension of the Case concept. Because words can be boldfaced, italicized, underlined, or formatted with other text styles, the Text Only option specifies whether the program should pay attention to text styles while performing a search.

To turn off the Text Only option, you must choose one or more of the Font, Size, and Style options. These options tell the program how much

Chapter 3
Editing a Document

of the type style information to include in the matching operation. If all three options are checked and the word *book* in boldface 12-point Geneva appears in the Find text box, WordPerfect recognizes only an occurrence of *book* in boldface 12-point Geneva as a match.

The Affect Menu

The Affect menu, shown in figure 3.24, is the flip side of the Match menu. After WordPerfect finds text, the Affect options determine how much text formatting in the Change To text box should be applied during change operations. In other words, the Match options control searches; the Affect options control replacements.

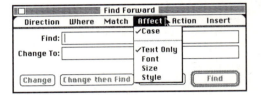

Fig. 3.24
The Affect menu on the Find dialog box.

When you choose the Text Only option from the Affect menu, the font, size, and style of the text in the Change To text box don't matter. The Change To text is inserted in the font, size, and style of the text being replaced.

To see how the Match and Affect options work, follow these steps:

1. Open a new document and type the following:

    The search utility can find and change text easily, and it can even change text styles.

2. Boldface the second *and*.

3. Move the insertion point to the beginning of the sentence and press ⌘-F or choose Find/Change from the Search menu.

4. Type *and* in the Find text box.

5. Select the *and* in the Find text box; then choose Bold from the main Style menu.

    When you apply a style to the text in the Find text box, you indicate that WordPerfect should find the word containing the same text attribute and overlook the words that don't have the attribute.

Part I
Getting Started

6. Press the Tab key to place the insertion point in the Change To text box; type *and* again.

7. Select the *and* in the Change To text box; then choose Italic from the Style menu at the top of the screen to indicate that WordPerfect should use the text attribute specified in the Change To text box (in this example, replace **and** with *and*).

   If you pull down the Match menu from the menu bar in the Find dialog box, you can see that Style is selected. Style was selected when you changed the text style of the Find text.

   If you pull down the Affect menu, you can see that Style again is selected because you changed the text style of the Change To text.

8. Click the Change All button at the bottom of the Find dialog box.

Figure 3.25 shows the results of the Change All operation. Notice that the first *and* was not changed because it was not in boldface type. The second *and* was changed, however.

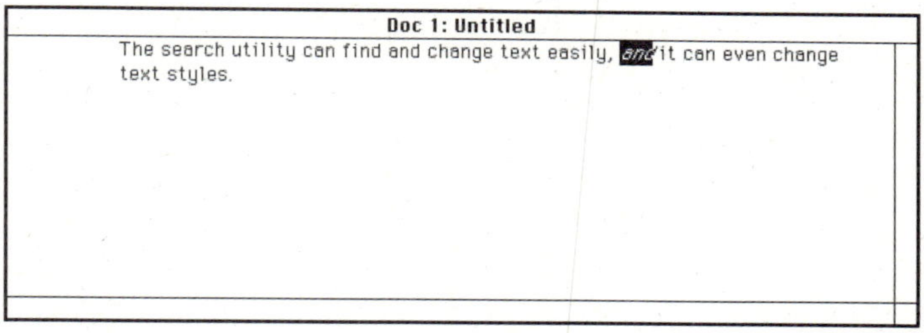

Fig. 3.25
The results of Find/Change including Text Style options.

Although the font, size, and style choices are easy to understand in a Find/Change operation, the Case options are more complex. The Case option on the Affect menu is more complicated than the Case option on the Match menu because the program makes allowances for capitalization differences in the search-and-replace operation, particularly to handle the first word in a sentence. To practice using the Case option, follow these steps:

1. In a new document, type *Her attitude was her downfall.*

2. Press ⌘-F or choose Find/Change from the Search menu.

3. Turn off the Case option on the Match menu.

4. Make sure the Case option on the Affect menu is active.

5. If Wrap Around is not active, choose Wrap Around from the Direction menu.

Chapter 3
Editing a Document

6. Type *her* (all lowercase) in the Find text box.

7. Type *his* (all lowercase) in the Change To text box.

8. Click Change All.

Her becomes *His*, and *her* becomes *his* in one operation.

The Action Menu

The options on the Action menu determine the location of the insertion point and whether anything is selected after a successful Find operation (see fig. 3.26).

Fig. 3.26
The Action menu in the Find dialog box.

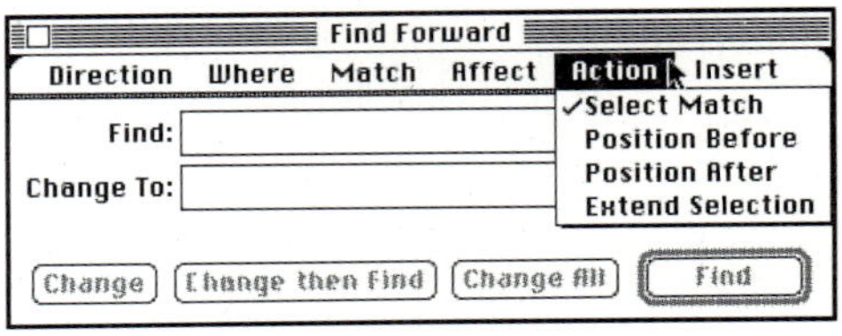

The first option on the menu, Select Match, is the standard Macintosh result. When WordPerfect matches the Find text and attributes (depending on the options selected from the Match menu) with an entry in the document, the program scrolls to the location of the match and selects the designated text. Consequently, you can edit the text for which you are searching by using the various Change buttons. You also can return to the document and type something new or choose formatting commands.

You use the next two options, Position Before and Position After, only for finding text—not for finding and changing. These options determine whether WordPerfect places the insertion point immediately preceding or following the matched text. These choices are useful if you know that you want to add text to a document without replacing anything. These options also are useful for determining where the insertion point should be located when you perform a search as part of a macro. (See Chapter 14, "Using Macros," for more information about macros.)

The Extend Selection option selects everything between the insertion point and the end of the text found by the search. Although this option probably is most useful as part of a macro, you also can use it to select a large amount of text—provided you know the ending of the text to be selected.

The Insert Menu

You cannot enter any special characters or keys, such as page breaks or returns, directly into the Find and Change To text boxes. You press Return to start the Find operation, for example, and use the Tab key to switch between the Find and Change To text boxes, but what do you do if you must search for text that includes returns or tabs? The options on the Insert menu, shown in figure 2.37, enable you to search for phrases containing special characters and to replace these phrases with text that includes the same or different special characters.

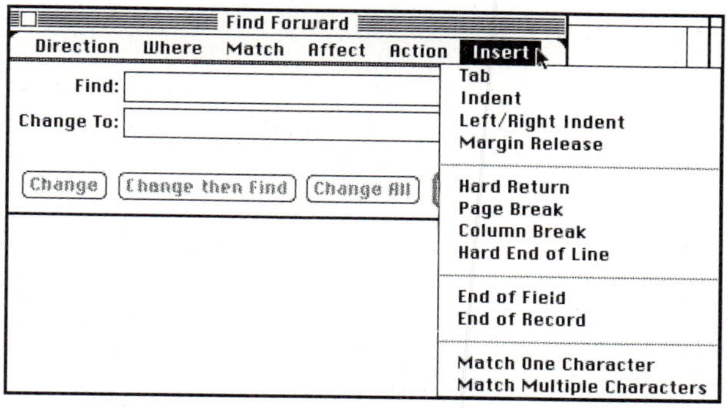

Fig. 3.27
The Insert menu in the Find dialog box.

If you're familiar with the WordPerfect Mac 1.0 series, you may remember that you can insert almost any formatting code into the search and replace dialog boxes. In the current version, you can enter only the codes listed on the Insert menu. You can use Find Code to find codes not listed, but the only way to find and replace a code not listed is to use macros.

When you choose an option from the Insert menu, WordPerfect inserts the appropriate code into the Find or Change To text box. These codes are identical to the ones you see when you show the hidden codes, as discussed earlier in this chapter. To change every Indent code to a Tab (changing paragraphs with the entire left margin indented to paragraphs with only their first lines indented), for example, do the following:

1. Make sure that the Find and Change To text boxes are empty. You can delete any text in these boxes by selecting the text and pressing Delete.

2. Click the Find text box.

Chapter 3
Editing a Document

3. Choose Indent from the Insert menu.

4. Press the Tab key or click the Change To text box.

5. Choose Tab from the Insert menu. Figure 3.28 shows the dialog box after you insert the codes.

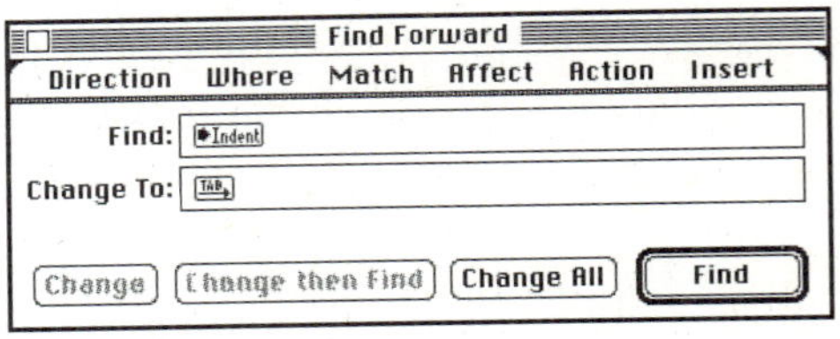

Fig. 3.28
Using formatting codes in the Find dialog box.

6. Click the Find or Change All button to start the find or change operation.

Many options on the Insert menu are self-explanatory. The Hard End of Line choice, however, is different from the others in that the option represents several other menu choices. The option searches for anything that ends a paragraph: a hard return, a hard page break, or a hard column break. If you insert the Hard End of Line choice into the Change To text box, WordPerfect inserts a hard return into the document when the change operation takes place.

The End of Field and End of Record options on the Insert menu can make some operations easy if you use the Merge feature often and must get the merge data from an external database. The most frequent use of these codes in Find/Change is to replace every tab with an end-of-field code and to replace every hard return with an end-of-record code. See Chapter 12, "Merging Documents," for more details on using these two options in creating Merge files.

The last two options on the Insert menu are *wild cards*, which enable you to look for text when you are not sure how you spelled it. The Match One Character and Match Multiple Characters options provide flexibility in finding text.

The Match One Character option enables you to find words that vary by one letter only. Type *station* in the Find text box, for example; choose Match One Character from the Insert menu; then type *ry* at the end of the Find text box. Figure 3.29 shows the Find dialog box with the wild-card character in the text string. Click the Find button or press Return. The program finds occurrences of *stationery* and *stationary*.

Part I
Getting Started

Fig. 3.29
The Match One Character code in the Find dialog box.

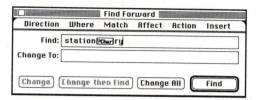

The Match Multiple Characters option works in a similar manner, except that it matches any number of characters in a word. The Find dialog box shown in figure 3.30 finds *live, lively, living*, or any other word starting with *liv*.

Fig. 3.30
The Match Multiple Character code in the Find dialog box.

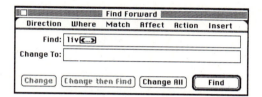

The Match Multiple Characters option works for only one word. You cannot use this option to match multiple characters over many words. You cannot use *now*<Match Multiple Characters>*time* to find *now is the time*, for example.

Using Find Next and Find Previous

Tip
If your searches don't find something you know is in the document, check the options in Find dialog box to make sure that you haven't limited the scope of the search to subdocuments, for example, or specified some other limitation.

To find the next or previous occurrence of a word or phrase, use the Find Next and Find Previous commands on the Search menu. The commands provide a convenient way to search the document. You use these commands by selecting the word or phrase; then to search forward in the document, choose Find Next from the Search menu or press ⌘-Shift-N; to search backward in the document, choose Find Previous from the Search menu or press ⌘-Shift-B.

If you don't select text before initiating Find Next or Find Previous, the program searches for the text that was last entered in the Find text box of the Find dialog box. The options set on the menus of the Find dialog box also affect Find Next and Find Previous the same way they affect a search using the Find dialog box (refer to the preceding section).

Chapter 3
Editing a Document

Finding Codes

Having limited the codes that you can enter in the Find/Change commands, WordPerfect has included another command on the Search menu—Find Code—that helps you to track down specific codes in documents. When you choose Find Code, the Find Code dialog box, which enables you to search for any code that WordPerfect inserts into your document, appears (see fig. 3.31). You do not have to issue the Show Codes command to be able to use Find Code, but you may want to open the codes window so that you can verify any changes you may make after finding a code.

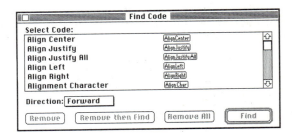

Fig. 3.31
The Find Code dialog box.

To use the Find Code feature, follow these steps:

1. Choose Find Code from the Search menu. The Find Code dialog box appears.

2. Scroll down the list until you can choose Bold On.

    Alternatively, type the first few letters of the name of the code (such as *b*, *o*). WordPerfect moves to the code that begins with these letters (or at least near enough to the code so that you can see the code in the dialog box). In this case, you must type *bold on* so that the Mac can differentiate the code from Bold Off.

3. Click the line once to select the code; then click the Find button or press Return to start the Find operation. Alternatively, double-click the line to select the code and initiate the Find operation.

After WordPerfect finds the code, the document window scrolls to the location of the code. You then can decide whether to delete the code (click the Remove button), delete the code and look for the next occurrence (the Remove Then Find button), or delete all occurrences of the code from the current location to the end or beginning of the file (the Remove All button). Remove All removes all the codes in the direction of the search until one end of the file or the other is reached.

> **Tip**
> In the Find Code dialog box, you can type the first letter of the name of a code so that the dialog box scrolls the code list to the section of the alphabet starting with the letter you typed.

A pop-up menu in the lower left of the dialog box controls the search direction for the Find Code feature. Click the box next to the word *Direction* to access the menu; then choose Forward or Backward. The Find Code search does not wrap around either end of the document; instead, it stops when it reaches the beginning or end of the document.

You cannot use Find Code to find a code and replace it with a different code. To replace a code, you must find the code, remove it, and then use normal formatting procedures to create the new code. As discussed in an earlier section, because you can include a few codes in the Find dialog box, you can do a search and replace in one step for those codes.

The Find Code dialog box is the only place where the complete names of all codes are listed next to each code's graphic representation. To find code information in the manual, you must know the name of the code as it appears in the Find Code dialog box. The code for Block Protect, for example, is shortened to *Protect* in the code window graphic.

Chapter Summary

This chapter covered the basic points you must know to edit text in a document. You first learned the methods for opening an existing document, including how to find a file in the Open dialog box. Then the basics of cutting, copying, and pasting text were covered.

The chapter discussed the use of the Undo command to reverse mistakes in editing. A brief section on using the boldface, italic, and underline text styles, in addition to displaying hidden codes, also was included.

After showing you how to find or find and replace text in a document, the chapter presented the rest of the options available in the Find dialog box. This chapter also covered the Find Code dialog box to show the complete list of formatting codes that may appear in your document and to search for and delete an unwanted code.

Chapter 3
Editing a Document

CHAPTER 4

Formatting a Document

In earlier chapters, you learned to create and edit documents. In this chapter, you learn how to adjust the file's format—the way a document looks on-screen and on a printed page. WordPerfect offers a way to adjust every appearance aspect of a document, from the space between adjoining characters (kerning) to page-by-page control of the top and bottom margins.

This chapter is organized by the size of the item being formatted: character, line, paragraph, or page. Within these categories, the following topics are covered:

- Character formatting, including font, size, and text styles; superscripts and subscripts; types of underlining; redline and strikeout markings; case; and kerning

- Line formatting, including choosing and setting nine types of tabs; aligning text; setting line spacing, line height, and leading; numbering lines; controlling hyphenation; and using subtitles

- Paragraph formatting, including setting margins; indenting text and creating hanging indents; and adding space between paragraphs

- Page formatting, including numbering pages; creating headers and footers; suppression of page format elements; using widow and orphan control; and centering items vertically on a page

- Creating page, paragraph, and character borders, including choosing border style, pattern, and fills.

Choosing a Formatting Method

You can access formatting features in three ways: using the menus, using keyboard shortcuts, and using the ruler. Using the menus or keyboard shortcuts is the primary way to format characters, paragraphs, and pages. The ruler, however, provides convenient access to most line formatting options.

Menus and Keyboard Shortcuts

You use the menus to accomplish formatting tasks or to open dialog boxes for formatting options. Place the mouse pointer over one of the menus at the top of the screen; then click and hold the mouse button. To choose an option, drag the pointer to the appropriate choice and release the button.

In this chapter, you can find most of the appropriate menu options on the Layout, Font, or Style menu. To learn keyboard shortcuts for as many commands as possible, turn on the Extra Menu ⌘ Keys option so that you can see the shortcuts each time you use the menus.

The menus are shown with the Extra Menu ⌘ Keys option enabled. If you want all your menus to show the keyboard shortcuts, follow these steps:

1. Choose Preferences from the File menu.

2. Choose Environment from the submenu. You also can press A rather than click Environment to bring up the dialog box.

3. Pull down the Options menu in the Environment dialog box and choose the Extra Menu ⌘ Keys option (see fig. 4.1).

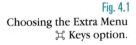

Fig. 4.1
Choosing the Extra Menu ⌘ Keys option.

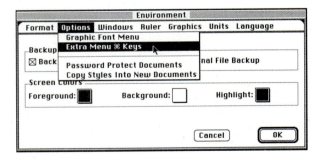

You also can choose Show Style Buttons from the Windows menu in the Environment dialog box to display the status bar style buttons for character formatting.

4. Click OK or press Return.

When you choose an option from a menu, a check mark appears on the left side of the menu. When a check mark is present, the option is on; choosing the option again turns it off, and the check mark disappears.

The Ruler

The most convenient way to make many line-formatting changes is to use the ruler. All but two of the ruler controls are also available from the menus and dialog boxes; however, adjustments made with the ruler provide visual feedback while you make the changes.

Displaying the Ruler

To display the ruler at the top of the document window, choose Show Ruler from the Layout menu or press ⌘-R.

Figure 4.2 shows the ruler and lists the ruler's components. To display the ruler in all your documents, choose Show Ruler from the Windows menu of the Environment dialog box (discussed in the preceding section).

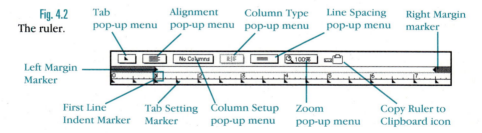

Fig. 4.2 The ruler.

Chapter 4
Formatting a Document

Table 4.1 briefly describes each item on the ruler.

Table 4.1
Formatting Controls in the Ruler

Ruler Item	Description
Tab pop-up menu	Sets the type of tab to be entered in the document
Alignment pop-up menu	Sets left, right, center, justify, or justify all alignment for paragraph margins
Column Setup pop-up menu	Turns column mode on or off and sets the number of columns to use
Column Type pop-up menu	Sets newspaper, parallel, or extended parallel column types
Line Spacing pop-up menu	Sets spacing between lines of text
Zoom pop-up menu	Sets magnification or reduction of document on-screen without affecting printed output
Copy Ruler to Clipboard icon	Copies ruler and its settings to the Clipboard so that you can transfer settings to another location in the document
Left and right margin markers	Indicates the left and right page margins
First Line Indent marker	Indicates location of the beginning of the first line of a paragraph
Tab setting markers	Indicates type and location of tab settings

Using the Zoom Pop-Up Menu

One of the two ruler features not accessible from the main menus is the view magnification capability, enabled through the Zoom pop-up menu (see fig. 4.3). The Zoom menu controls the magnification of the view. Two common uses of view magnification are editing unusually small or large text and enlarging the view to relieve eyestrain. Setting the view to 120 percent makes reading 9- or 10-point font sizes much easier, for example. You also can see an entire page layout on a 13-inch monitor by using the Zoom setting to reduce the view. (Although you can edit in reduced views, reduced text can be difficult to read unless you use a larger font size.)

Part I
Getting Started

Fig. 4.3
The Zoom pop-up menu.

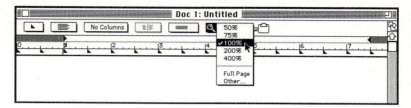

The top part of the menu, above the dotted or gray line, offers several standard magnification choices. The numbers in the menu represent percentages of normal size. A size of 100% means the view on-screen is the same size as a printed page. Smaller percentages reduce the view so that more fits on-screen. Percentages over 100 make small font sizes easier to read.

Below the dotted line the menu offers three special options. The first time you open the Zoom pop-up menu during a WordPerfect session, you see only the options Full Page and Other at the bottom of the pop-up menu (refer to fig. 4.3). After you choose Other, the View dialog box appears (see fig. 4.4). You can enter any whole number percent value between 25 and 800 in the dialog box's text box.

Fig. 4.4
The View dialog box, accessed from the Zoom menu.

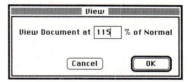

After you type a percentage magnification value into the View dialog box and click OK, the screen magnification changes to the new value, which is added to the Zoom menu (see fig. 4.5). Any time you use the Other option in the Zoom menu, WordPerfect adds the new value to the menu (and replaces the preceding special setting), enabling you to switch easily between any standard magnification and the most recent non-standard choice.

Chapter 4
Formatting a Document

Fig. 4.5
The modified Zoom pop-up menu.

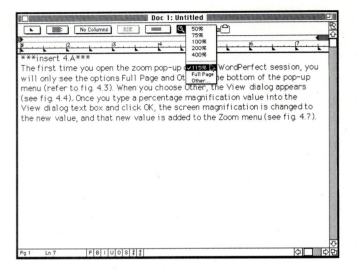

If you click the right side of the Zoom pop-up menu and immediately release the mouse button, your view shrinks to 50 percent. Be sure to move the pointer off the menu before releasing the button to retain your current view magnification.

The adjustment provided by the Full Page option is determined by the window size of the current document and the Page Setup paper size selection. When you choose Full Page, you see an image of an entire page, reduced to fit into the current window (see fig. 4.6).

Tip

You may want to use an on-screen type scaling utility, such as Adobe Type Manager or True Type, when you use 110 or 115 percent magnifications. Even with larger magnifications, some fonts are unreadable if the font rendering utility is not available.

Unlike Page Preview, which also enables you to view pages at any magnification, the ruler's Zoom menu enables you to edit reduced or expanded text. Page Preview, on the other hand, displays headers, footers, and footnotes—items that don't appear when you use Zoom from the ruler.

Notice that in Full Page (and other magnifications) the ruler marks are scaled to reflect the accurate position of the text. WordPerfect displays the value of magnification in the pop-up menu next to the magnifying glass and inserts the value into the pop-up menu just below the dotted line.

If you have an extended keyboard, you can use the function keys to switch between the 100 percent (press F13), 200 percent (press Shift-F13), and Full Page (press ⌘-F13) views.

Part I

Getting Started

Fig. 4.6
A full-page view of a document.

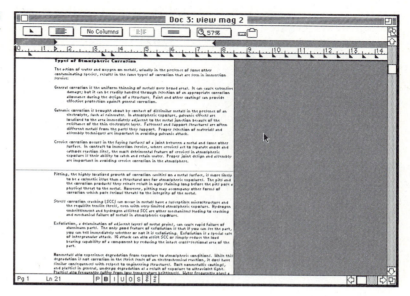

Copying and Pasting the Ruler

Another ruler function not available from menus is Copy Ruler. If you click the Copy Ruler icon in the ruler or press ⌘-F3 on an extended keyboard, WordPerfect copies all the ruler settings to the Clipboard. You then can insert the ruler settings at the new location by moving the insertion point to the appropriate location and choosing Paste from the Edit menu, pressing ⌘-V, or pressing F4. If you make many line formatting changes in a document, copying the ruler is a convenient way to duplicate settings without manually assigning each setting.

The ruler that appears at the top of the window and that is copied by the Copy Ruler command is the ruler in effect at the location of the insertion point. If you scroll to a new location but do not move the insertion point, WordPerfect copies the ruler at the insertion point's location, not the location to which you scrolled.

Chapter 4
Formatting a Document

Formatting Characters

The smallest unit of text you can format is a character. You can change the font and size of characters; change the text style; use subscripts, superscripts, redline, and strikeout; add underlining; change case; and make other changes to one or many characters.

To format a character or a group of characters, you select the characters to be formatted and issue a formatting command. You also can choose a formatting option before you type text so that the text you enter appears in the chosen option.

Although all character formatting options are available in the Character dialog box, which you access through the Layout menu, applying character formats from the Font and Style menus is common. The Character Format dialog box is covered later in this section with special font sizes, superscript and subscript options, and underline options.

Changing the Font

If, after you open WordPerfect, you do not change settings before you type, the text appears in a 12-point Geneva font. Because Geneva is guaranteed to exist on virtually every Macintosh, WordPerfect Corporation chose Geneva as its Normal Style font. Older versions of WordPerfect for the Macintosh referred to this font as the default font. Now, to distinguish between defaults that control how the program works and style elements that affect the appearance of a document, you have no default font; you have only a Normal Style font.

To change the font, choose a new font from the Font menu. When you start typing, the inserted characters appear in the selected font. To change the font of text that you typed earlier, select the text to be changed and choose the new font from the Font menu. WordPerfect applies the new font to the selected text.

If you want each font option in the Font menu to appear in its own typeface, as shown in figure 4.7, you must change the setting in the Environment dialog box. You access this dialog box by choosing Preferences from the File menu. When the Environment dialog box appears, click the Options menu and choose Graphic Font Menu. (You used the Options menu to choose Extra Menu ⌘ Keys discussed earlier in the chapter.)

Part I
Getting Started

Fig. 4.7
The Graphic Font menu.

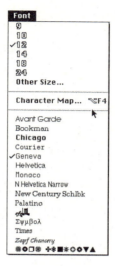

Using the Graphic Font Menu option slows the display of the Font menu. After you become familiar with the appearance of the fonts, you should turn off this option to speed the process of using the Font menu.

Depending on the fonts installed in your system, your Font menu may have more or fewer fonts than shown in figure 4.7. The fonts in the menu shown here are the minimum Mac set (Chicago, Geneva, and Monaco), a music notation font (Sonata, the musical notes following Palatino), and the fonts installed in ROM in the Apple LaserWriters and most third-party PostScript printers (the rest of the fonts).

Although possible in earlier WordPerfect versions, versions after 2.0.1 cannot apply a symbol font to existing text. For example, you cannot type *abg*, select the characters, choose Symbol font from the menu, and get the Greek alpha, beta, and gamma. WordPerfect Corporation is implementing a font-handling strategy that integrates international character sets in a way that prevents such an on-screen translation. If you need Symbol characters, choose the Symbol font first; then type letters or use the Character Map (discussed later in this chapter) to find and insert symbols.

Chapter 4
Formatting a Document

Changing the Font Size

The font sizes appear in the top portion of the Font menu (refer to fig. 4.7). Sizes that appear in outline type indicate that a screen font for that size has been installed in the system. A screen font that has been installed makes on-screen text more legible than text for which a screen font has not been installed.

Font sizes are measured in points. Each point is 1/72 of an inch. (A traditional printer's point is a fraction of a percent less than 1/72 of an inch, causing some problems when personal computers are used with traditional printing processes.) The font size is measured from the bottom of the lowest descender (*g*, for example) to the top of the highest ascender (*f*, for example) of any character in the font.

Font design is an art, however; simply measuring vertical height does not tell the whole story. You find that you can fit more words on a page in 12-point Times than in 12-point Geneva.

To change the size of existing characters, select the characters and choose a new size from the Font menu. To assign a size not shown in the menu, choose Other Size. WordPerfect displays the Other Font Sizes dialog box (see fig. 4.8). Type a value for the size in the Font Size text box of the Other Font Sizes dialog box. To get inch-high letters, for example, choose Other Size from the font menu and type *72* (an inch consists of 72 points).

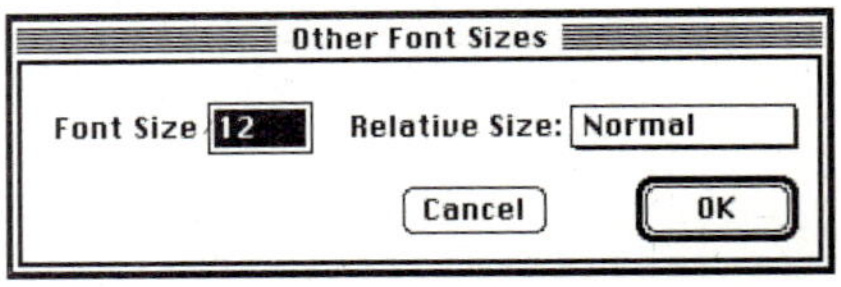

> **Tip**
> If you use fonts from Adobe Type Manager or TrueType, an installed screen font is not necessary for a legible display. With these utilities, even very large font sizes are rendered smoothly on-screen.

Fig. 4.8
The Other Font Sizes dialog box.

You can use any font size from 1 to 32,767 points in WordPerfect. Some caution is in order, though, because you cannot read 1-point type without a magnifier (even if your printer can print 1-point text reliably), and a 32,767-point character is more than 450 inches high. At 275 points in Times font, for example, the word *Sale* is 6 inches wide—which just about fills a letter-size page. Thus, you probably will not use sizes bigger than 275 points. A 6-point type is about the smallest that a 300-dpi laser printer prints legibly.

Part I
Getting Started

Some scalable fonts cannot be printed beyond certain limits. You can scale the fonts that come with the HP DeskWriter, for instance, only between 4 and 250 points. Outside these limits, the print reverts to the jagged bit maps that appear on-screen. Resolution of PostScript fonts is not limited at larger sizes, but they may look distorted at very small sizes.

Using Relative Character Sizes

You probably noticed the Relative Size pop-up menu on the right side of the Other Font Sizes dialog box (refer to fig. 4.8). The options in this menu (Fine, Small, Normal, Large, Very Large, and Extra Large) describe qualitatively sized text compared to Normal—that is, the font size in effect at the insertion point when you chose Other Size from the Font menu. The exact effect of the relative sizes is controlled in the Relative Sizes dialog box, which is discussed later in this section.

Using relative sizes instead of setting a specific point size is convenient if you make many font size changes and then decide that you must change the Normal size. If you select a block of text containing several font sizes (for example, 12, 10, and 8) and then choose a size from the Font menu, WordPerfect changes all the selected text to the new font size. If you use relative sizes, WordPerfect scales the differently sized text according to the relative font size definitions when you choose a new size.

The point size used for each relative size is controlled through the Character Format dialog box, which you access by choosing Character from the Layout menu or pressing ⌘-H (see fig. 4.9).

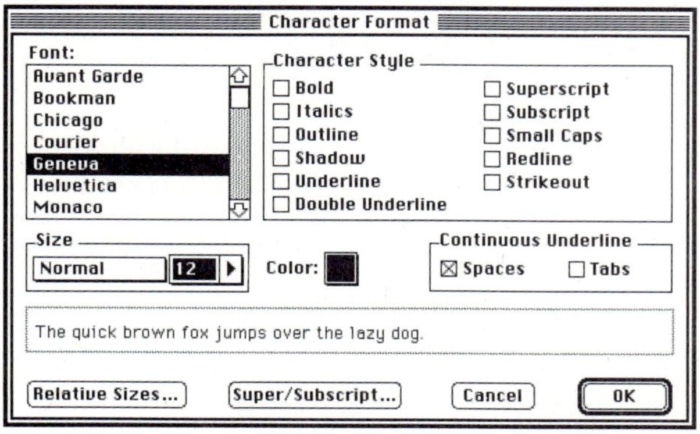

Fig. 4.9
The Character Format dialog box.

Chapter 4
Formatting a Document

Click the Relative Sizes button in the lower left corner of the dialog box to call up the Relative Sizes dialog box (see fig. 4.10).

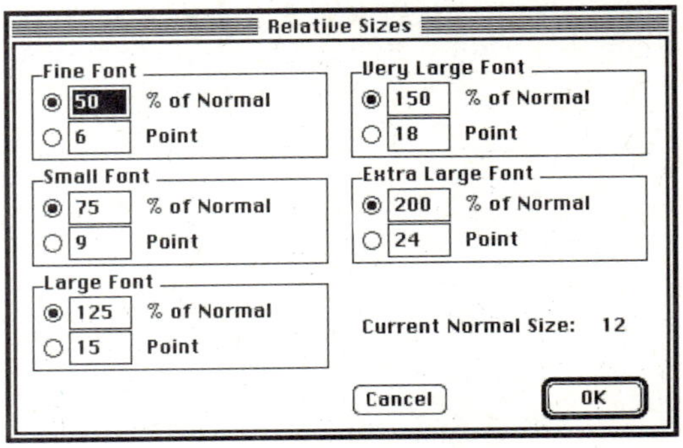

Fig. 4.10
The Relative Sizes dialog box.

The Relative Sizes dialog box contains areas in which you specify the size for the named relative sizes (except Normal) and a report of the current Normal size. Although you cannot change the Normal size in the dialog box, you can tell what the size is as you specify the other sizes.

In each font area of the dialog box, you can choose between scaling the font size as a percentage of Normal or assigning a fixed size to each relative size. The latter option doesn't make the font size relative to anything, but sometimes flexibility is more important than consistency.

The default setting for each relative size is a percentage of Normal size (refer to fig. 4.10). To change the value of the scaling factor, double-click the text box next to % of Normal and type a new value. You can enter any value in the text boxes. Unless you have some special purpose, however, the default values are sufficient for relative sizes.

To specify a fixed size in the Point text box, click the radio button next to the value box, and enter a new point value.

After you define the sizes associated with Fine, Small, Large, Very Large, and Extra Large, close the Relative Sizes dialog box by clicking OK or pressing Return. To use the relative size fonts in your document, follow these steps:

> **Tip**
> If you hold down the ⌘ key while the dialog box is displayed, you can access all the dialog box choices from the keyboard.

1. Select text to which to apply the change.

   Alternatively, you can place the insertion point where the size change should begin for subsequently typed text.

2. Choose Other Size from the Font menu. The Other Font Sizes dialog box appears.

3. Choose a size from the Relative Size pop-up menu.

4. Click OK or press Return.

WordPerfect applies the size change to the selected text or, if you did not select text, to the text you type.

Using the Character Map

You may be aware that Macintosh fonts have more printable characters than the number of keys on the keyboard. The Mac enables you to enter the extra characters from the keyboard if you hold down the Option or Option and Shift keys while you press a key from the main keyboard.

WordPerfect, on the other hand, enables you to find and enter an extended character by using the Character Map (see fig. 4.11). To access this map, choose Character Map from the Font menu or press Option-F4 on an extended keyboard. Notice that most of the extended characters are accented characters for foreign languages, but extra symbol characters also are available.

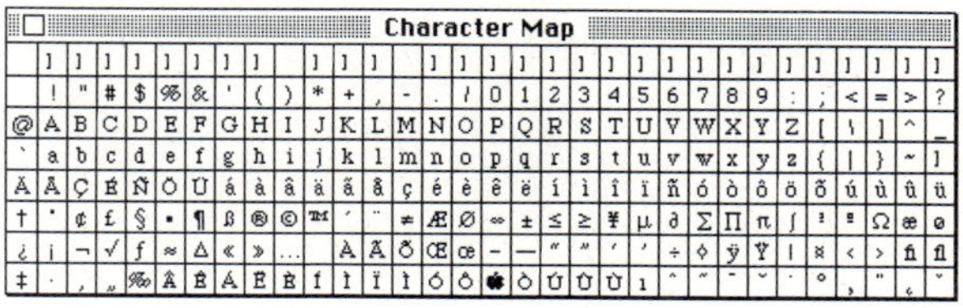

Fig. 4.11
The Character Map of the Times font.

While the Character Map is displayed, you can insert any character from the current font in your active window by clicking the character in the Character Map. If you choose a different font from the Font menu, the Character Map changes to display the characters in the new font. WordPerfect also inserts the font change in your document at the insertion point, ready for insertion of characters from the Character Map or keyboard.

Chapter 4
Formatting a Document

The top row of the Character Map of many fonts display several identical rectangular boxes as characters. If you click one of these characters, a box appears on-screen, but not on the printed page. The box indicates that the character does not have a defined shape; therefore, WordPerfect accepts the character in the document but prints nothing for it.

Notice that the title bar of the Character Map has dotted lines rather than the usual solid lines of an active window. The dotted lines indicate that the window is active for mouse clicks and that characters typed on the keyboard are inserted into the active window (designated by solid lines in the title bar). Menu commands also affect the main document as though the Character Map is not present. The only commands that affect the Character Map are a font change and clicking the close box on the Character Map. In fact, if you press ⌘-W or choose Close from the File menu, WordPerfect assumes you want to close your document window.

You cannot hide or partially hide the Character Map behind the active document window. When displayed, the Character Map appears on top of the active document window. You can resize the document window and reposition the Character Map so that both windows are visible, however. If you prefer to leave the document window full size, you can drag the Character Map out of the way by pressing and holding the mouse button while the arrow pointer is over the Character Map title bar. While you hold the mouse button down, you can drag the Character Map anywhere on-screen. Release the mouse button when the Character Map is at the desired location.

The Character Map is convenient for finding and inserting an extended character in your document or for inserting a series of characters from the Symbol font if you don't remember the keyboard mapping. Unfortunately, the Character Map doesn't help you to learn the keystrokes for any characters you are inserting.

To learn the keystrokes for extended characters or Symbol font characters, use the Key Caps desk accessory, which displays the characters on a keyboard image; to see the extended characters, however, you must hold down the Option or Option and Shift keys. The Key Caps desk accessory (available on the Apple menu if Apple's installer is on your system software) also can help you locate the right key combinations so that you can enter any specific extended character. With Key Caps, you can insert an extended character by finding the appropriate keyboard and modifier keys, returning to your document, and entering the keystroke combination. See your Macintosh manuals for more information about Key Caps.

Part I
Getting Started

Changing Text Styles

Text styles are attributes, such as boldface, italic, underline, outline, and shadow. The Mac also offers the Outline and Shadow text styles. The text styles are easy to apply, singly or in combinations. The purpose of using any text style is to add emphasis to small sections of text. (For more information on text styles, refer to Chapter 3, "Editing a Document.")

You can assign most text styles before or after you enter text; however, you can assign the Outline and Shadow text styles only to existing text. To practice assigning text to new and existing text, follow these steps:

1. Type the following sentences in a document. Press the ⌘-key combinations shown in square brackets and then press Return at the end of each line:

    This is [⌘-B] bold [⌘-B] text.

    This is [⌘-I] italic [⌘-I] text.

    This is [⌘-U] underlined [⌘-U] text.

    This is outline text.

    This is shadow text.

    And this text has all five text styles.

    In this step, you assigned all but Outline and Shadow text styles to the text as you entered it. (Remember, you must assign Outline and Shadow style to existing text.)

2. Select the word *outline* and choose Outline from the Style menu. If the style buttons are displayed in the status bar, you can click the O style button. WordPerfect outlines the selected text.

3. Select the word *shadow* and choose Shadow from the Style menu. Alternatively, click the S style button if the style buttons are displayed in the status bar. WordPerfect places a shadow around the selected text.

4. Select the word *five* and apply all styles (Boldface, Italics, Underline, Outline, and Shadow) to the word, using the Style menu or, if possible, the style buttons. Figure 4.12 illustrates the results.

Chapter 4
Formatting a Document

Fig. 4.12
An example of text styles.

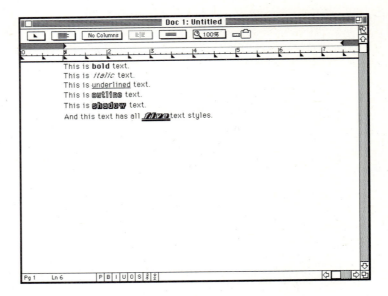

5. Select all the text; then pull down the Style menu (see fig. 4.13). A diamond rather than a check mark precedes each of the first six menu choices. The diamond indicates that some, but not all, selected text has that style.

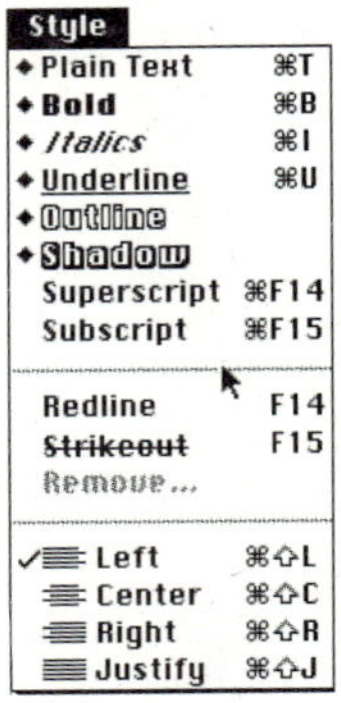

Fig. 4.13
The Style menu indicating mixed text styles.

To change text from one style to another—from bold to italic, for example—follow these steps:

1. Select the boldfaced text.

Part I

Getting Started

2. Choose Bold or Plain Text from the Style menu to turn off the boldface style.

3. Choose Italic from the Style menu, press ⌘-I, or use the I style button to apply the italic style to the selected text.

The order in which you alternate styles is unimportant. In the preceding exercise, for example, you can apply the italic style before you remove the boldface style.

To clear all character attributes, follow these steps:

1. Select the text.

2. Choose Plain Text from the Style menu, press ⌘-T, or click the P style button. WordPerfect removes the applied text styles from the selected text.

Some text styles have standard uses in business writing. Book, magazine, and journal titles usually are italicized. Headlines, section headings, and column headings in tables frequently appear in boldface type. Although underlining formerly was used to indicate titles, today the style is used primarily to emphasize text.

You should use the Shadow and Outline text styles, which are less common, with extreme caution in formal writing. If you are creating informal posters, however, these styles can call attention to the important words.

Using Subscripts and Superscripts

You use subscripts and superscripts to offset text below or above the normal line of text. Superscripts frequently are used for footnote and endnote reference numbers. Scientific writings, such as chemical formulas and mathematical expressions, commonly use superscripts and subscripts.

To insert a subscript or superscript as you type text, follow these steps:

1. Type several lines of text and leave the insertion point where you finish typing.

2. Choose Subscript from the Style menu, press ⌘-F15 on an extended keyboard, or click the Subscript style button (the button containing an arrow with a 2 beneath it). Notice that the Subscript button changes to display S_2.

Chapter 4
Formatting a Document

To produce superscript text, choose Superscript in the Style menu, press ⌘-F14, or click the Superscript style button (an arrow with a 2 above it).

3. Type the text.

4. To turn off the subscript style, choose Subscript, press ⌘-F15, or click the S_2 button again. To turn off the superscript style, choose Superscript, press ⌘-F14, or click the Superscript style button.

   (If no other text style is active, you also can choose the Plain Text option to turn off the subscript or subscript style.)

   The text you type now appears in the Normal style.

To type all the text and then change the superscripts and subscripts, select the text to be modified and issue the appropriate command once.

WordPerfect's normal superscripts may not be offset enough to break the imaginary line that skims the top of the tallest letters. These superscripts are harder to see than superscripts for which the offset is higher. You use the Superscript/Subscript Options dialog box to adjust the positions of superscripts and subscripts.

You can control the distance that the superscripts and subscripts are displaced from the normal text baseline by setting the values in the Move Up and Move Down sections of the Superscript/Subscript Options dialog box. You can enter a value for relative offset (% of Line Height) or fixed offset (Point).

To increase the superscript offset, follow these steps:

1. Make sure that the insertion point is to the left of or above any superscripts you want to change in the document.

2. Choose Character from the Layout menu or press ⌘-H. The Character Format dialog box appears.

3. Click the Super/Subscript button. WordPerfect displays the Superscript/Subscript Options dialog box (see fig. 4.14).

4. Press the Tab key twice or press ⌘-3 to highlight the % of Line Height value in the Move Up area of the Superscript Style section.

5. Type *40*. Notice that the sample text in the lower left of the dialog box shows greater offset in the superscript.

6. Press Return twice to exit the two dialog boxes.

   The program applies the modified superscript offset value to the text.

Part I

Getting Started

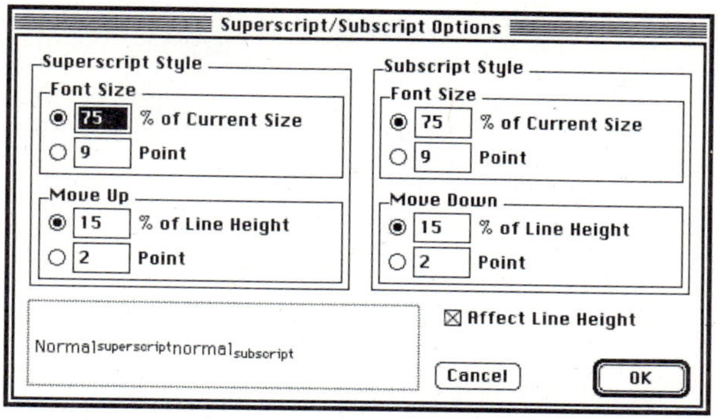

Fig. 4.14
The Superscript/Subscript Options dialog box.

You may have to experiment with the offset option to get the right effect on a printed copy.

You also can change the relative size (or specify a fixed size) for the superscript and subscript letters by choosing one of the radio button options in the Font Size sections of the Superscript/Subscript Options dialog box. If you click the radio button next to % of Current Size, the superscript or subscript appears at the percentage listed in the text box.

If you want all your superscripts and subscripts to be a specific size—regardless of the base font size—click the radio button for Point in the Font Size text box and enter the appropriate size in the Point text box. When you use many different font sizes, however, using the percentage offset is more convenient.

The Affect Line Height check box in the Superscript/Subscript Options dialog box controls whether WordPerfect inserts extra space between lines containing superscripts and subscripts to prevent the offset text from running into text on an adjoining line. Nearly the only reason to turn off Affect Line Height is when you must print with fixed-line spacing, such as on a preprinted form.

Using Redline and Strikeout

To keep track of revisions to a document, the redline and strikeout styles can help you distinguish the changed from the unchanged material. Redlining places a vertical bar in the margin to call attention to additions to a document. Strikeout crosses out text to be removed in the final version of the document.

Chapter 4
Formatting a Document

To see an example of the two kinds of text, do the following:

1. Type *This is an example of Strikeout text*.
2. Select the words *an example of*.
3. Choose Strikeout from the Style menu or press F15 on an extended keyboard. A red or black line appears through the selected text.
4. Select the sentence (press ⌘-Shift-U or ⌘-F6).
5. Choose Redline from the Style menu or press F14 on an extended keyboard. The Redline style puts a vertical bar in the left margin of any line that contains redlined text.

You normally use Redline and Strikeout when more than one person reviews and makes changes to a document. As you make several passes through the document, you can turn off Redline or Strikeout the same way you change the other text styles—by selecting the text and then toggling the style off.

To delete the strikeout text and remove the redline markings, choose Remove from the Style menu. The Redline/Strikeout dialog box appears (see fig. 4.15). Make sure that the check box next to the feature you want to remove is checked before you click OK or press Return. Remove does not give you a choice for each affected section; it removes the selected features for the entire document.

Fig. 4.15
The Redline/Strikeout dialog box for removing text and markings.

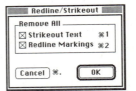

If you check Strikeout Text in the dialog box, WordPerfect deletes any strikeout text when you click OK or press Return. If you check the Redline Markings option, only vertical bars are removed when you click OK. Normally, you want to remove both features before the final printing of your document. Some technical manual revisions, however—including many mainframe computer references—are printed with the redline bars to call attention to changes from a previous version.

Part I
Getting Started

Setting Underline Styles

Using underlining has been discussed earlier in this chapter and in Chapter 3 "Editing a Document," but two other features affect the appearance of this text style. You can choose between single and double underlining, and continuous and discontinuous underlining.

Double underlining is actually separate from single underlining. You can activate double underlining by choosing the option in the Character Format dialog box (refer to fig. 4.9) or by pressing Shift-F15 on an extended keyboard. Although you can turn on single and double underlining at the same time, the single underline lines up perfectly with one of the two lines in double underlining so that the line appears to use only the double underline.

The other underlining option controlled in the Character Format dialog box is the Continuous Underline option. If neither option in the Continuous Underline section of the Character Format dialog box is checked, only visible characters are underlined. Clicking the Spaces and Tabs check boxes causes underlining to appear below spaces and tabs, respectively. Figure 4.16 shows examples of the three types of underlining.

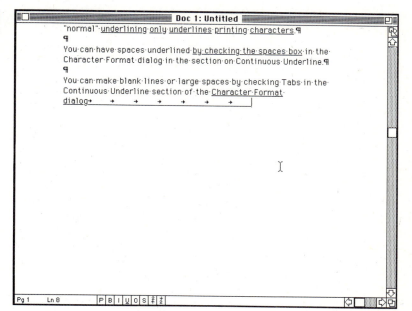

Fig. 4.16
Examples of the Underline options.

Chapter 4
Formatting a Document

You generally use underlined tabs to make blank lines in forms, for example. If you use underlined spaces to create blank lines, you often end up with uneven lines because of the irregular character widths in most fonts. By underlining tabs, however, the lines end at the tab stop, regardless of the font used for the preceding text.

Using Small Caps

The Small Caps text style prints all capital letters but prints smaller capital letters when you type lowercase letters. The following sentence shows an example of text in small caps:

    THE FIRST PRESIDENT OF THE UNITED STATES WAS GEORGE WASHINGTON.

Small caps were used commonly on typewriters, sometimes as a typeface called Orator. One use of small caps is to prepare overhead projector transparencies. At a distance, the uppercase letters make the text more legible than lowercase, without giving up the visual effects of different character heights for upper- and lowercase letters.

To enter text as small caps, follow these steps:

1. Choose Character from the Layout menu. The Character Format dialog box appears. Alternatively, press Shift-F14 on an extended keyboard. (When you press Shift-F14, the dialog box doesn't appear; you proceed to step 3.)

2. In the dialog box, click the check box next to Small Caps; then click OK or press Return.

3. Type text normally, using the Shift key for letters normally capitalized.

WordPerfect prints your text in capitals and small caps.

Changing Case

Occasionally, you may discover that you accidentally pressed the Caps Lock key and typed a sentence or two of text in capital letters. Rather than retype the sentences, you can use the Convert Case command to change the capital letters (uppercase) to small letters (lowercase). You also can convert lowercase text to uppercase, but that method is less likely unless you often use uppercase letters for emphasis.

Part I
Getting Started

In WordPerfect, because Convert Case is an editing command rather than a formatting command, you can find the Convert Case command on the Edit menu. To use the command, first select the text to be changed; then choose Convert Case from the Edit menu. The Case Convert dialog box appears (see fig. 4.17).

Fig. 4.17
The Case Convert dialog box.

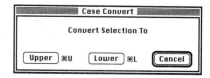

> **Tip**
> To see the dialog box keyboard shortcuts, hold down the ⌘ key while the dialog box is active.

In the Case Convert dialog box, click the Upper or Lower button. Alternatively, you can use the dialog box keyboard shortcuts: pressing ⌘-U is equivalent to clicking the Upper button, and pressing ⌘-L is equivalent to clicking Lower.

The dialog box disappears as soon as you click one of the buttons. All the selected text is converted to the case you choose. If you convert to lowercase, you must reconvert (or retype) capital letters at the beginning of sentences.

Kerning Text

When you kern text, you adjust the space between two characters. The effects of kerning are most noticeable in large point sizes, but you can kern even normal body text to improve its appearance and readability.

WordPerfect includes an example that shows the importance of kerning. To see this example, follow these steps:

1. Choose About WordPerfect from the Apple menu. Look carefully at the letter spacing between the *W* and the *o* in WordPerfect in the About WordPerfect dialog box.

2. Click the About WordPerfect dialog box anywhere to close the box.

3. With the insertion point in an empty document window, choose Times from the Font menu.

4. Choose Other Size from the Font menu, and type *92* in the text box. Click OK or press Return.

5. Type *WordPerfect*. Notice the amount of space between the *W* and the *o* compared to the logo version (see fig. 4.18).

Chapter 4
Formatting a Document

Fig. 4.18
Unkerned text.

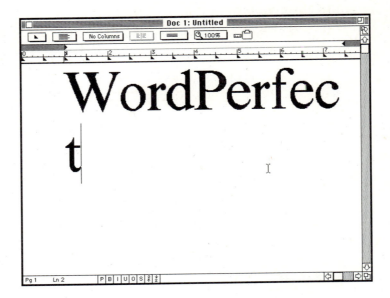

Because of the extra space between letters, the whole name does not fit on one line (unless you change the program's default margins).

6. Place the insertion point between the *W* and the *o*. Choose Line in the Layout menu and Kerning from the Line submenu. The Kerning dialog box appears.

7. Make sure that the radio button for Move Together is chosen. Type *16* in the Points text box of the Value area.

    The combination of the Type and Value options indicate the action of the command—that is, move the letters together 16 points in this example. The two characters next to the insertion point are 16 points closer (see fig. 4.19).

Fig. 4.19
The Kerning dialog box.

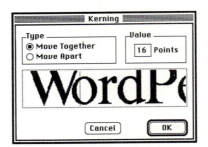

Part I
Getting Started

8. Click OK or press Return.

   If you redisplay the About WordPerfect dialog box, you can compare your typed version to the WordPerfect logo.

9. With a standard line length, WordPerfect still doesn't fit on one line. Repeat steps 6 through 8 to kern the *P* and *e* 8 points closer together and to kern the *f* and *e* 5 points closer together. When you finish, your typed text should resemble the logo.

If you have an extended keyboard, you can kern characters one point at a time by pressing Shift-F1 to move letters closer together or Shift-F2 to move letters farther apart.

In general, when curved characters such as *o* and *e* are next to vertical or angular characters such as *I* and *W*, the letter pairs look better if you move the letters together. The amount you move letters depends on the font, the size, and your personal taste. For normal-sized print in the body of a document, you probably don't want to kern text because the task requires a tremendous amount of work for a small benefit.

Using Color with Text

Color printers now are inexpensive enough that many people can consider using color printers for general documents. Although documents printed in color are still unusual, WordPerfect is ready for the inevitable increase in the use of color. In the meantime, you can use color with on-screen text (if you have a color monitor) and distribute your documents electronically.

To apply a color to any characters in your document, follow these steps:

1. Select the characters.

2. Choose Character from the Layout menu. The Character Format dialog box appears.

3. Place the arrow pointer over the square labeled Color, press and hold the mouse button, and choose the desired color from the pop-up color palette.

You also can use the standard Macintosh color wheel to pick a color for your text by double-clicking the Color square in the Character Format dialog box. Refer to your Macintosh documentation for details on using the color wheel to specify a color.

Chapter 4
Formatting a Document

Formatting Lines of Text

Now that you know how to format individual characters to suit your taste and the requirements of the document, the next step in formatting a document is adjusting the line format. The main line formatting features are tab stops, line spacing (and related commands), and alignment. The topics of line numbering, hyphenation, and subtitles also are covered in the following sections.

Applying Formatting Changes

Before you look at the different line-formatting capabilities, you must decide how you want WordPerfect to treat the options you choose. When you change any line or paragraph formatting option, WordPerfect can apply the change in one of two ways. The setting in the Format menu of the Environment dialog box determines the method used (see fig. 4.20). Open this dialog box by choosing Preferences from the File menu and then choosing Environment from the submenu.

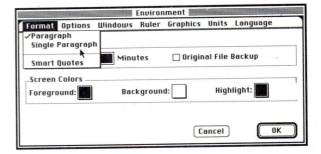

Fig. 4.20
The Format menu in the Environment dialog box.

If you choose Paragraph, WordPerfect inserts the new formatting codes at the beginning of the paragraph that contains the insertion point and applies the changes to the current paragraph and any following paragraphs until another change is encountered. If you change margins, for example, the new margins affect the current paragraph and any following paragraphs until the program encounters another margin change. The Paragraph option is likely to produce the fewest surprises for a new user of the program.

The other Format option, Single Paragraph, applies formatting changes to only the paragraph containing the insertion point. If the insertion point is in the last paragraph of a document, however, the program continues the formatting in new paragraphs that you add to the end of the document.

Using Tabs

Tab settings—called tab stops on a typewriter for their mechanical effect on carriage motion—enable you to achieve precise horizontal alignment of words or numbers typed on different lines in your document.

On a typewriter or in a monospaced font such as Monaco or Courier, you can achieve alignment by inserting spaces until the text lines up. With proportional fonts (nearly all fonts available for the Mac), inserting spaces doesn't work because the space character is a different width than other characters. The spaces on-screen also are not exactly the same width as spaces on a printed page; what looks perfect on-screen frequently is slightly misaligned on a printed page if you use spaces for horizontal alignment.

WordPerfect offers nine kinds of tabs. The main tab types—Left, Center, Right, and Decimal—can appear alone or with leader dots (for a total of eight tab types). The Bar tab enables you to draw a vertical line down the page as you enter tabular text.

In the following sections, you learn how to set tabs, using the ruler. Additional options available through the Layout menu are covered later in the section.

Understanding Tab Types

To see how each tab type works, try the following exercise:

1. Open a new document and display the ruler by pressing ⌘-R or choosing Show Ruler from the Layout menu.

2. Clear all the tabs by clicking the Tab Type pop-up menu in the ruler and choosing Clear Tabs (see fig. 4.21). Notice that the default tab type shown in the ruler Tab Type pop-up menu is the left-aligned tab.

Fig. 4.21
Clearing all tabs from the ruler.

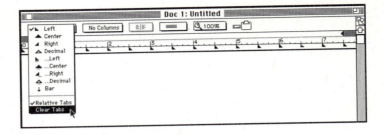

3. Place the mouse pointer just below the 2-inch mark on the ruler. Press and hold the mouse button.

   A dotted vertical line drops from the tab location of the pointer. This line helps when you set tabs in an existing document and want to align the tab relative to text elsewhere on the page. The exact position of the tab—from the edge of the page and from the left margin—is reported in the status bar (see fig. 4.22).

Fig. 4.22
Setting a tab in the ruler.

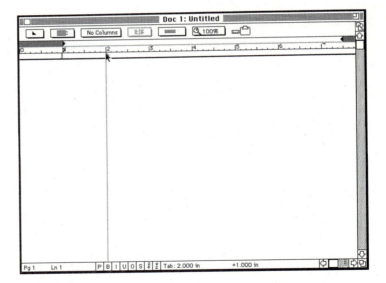

4. When you get the tab on or near the 2-inch position, release the mouse button.

5. Use the Tab Type pop-up menu to choose Center; then place a center tab at the 3-inch ruler mark.

Part I
Getting Started

6. Choose Right in the Tab Type pop-up menu; then place a right tab at the 4-inch ruler mark.

7. Choose Decimal tab from the Tab Type pop-up menu; then place a decimal tab at the 5-inch ruler mark.

8. Type the following, pressing the Tab key once before each word:

   Left
   Center
   Right
   123.654

Your screen should resemble the screen shown in figure 4.23. Notice that each tab type on the ruler has its own shape to help you recognize the types easily when the ruler is displayed. After you choose a tab type in the Tab Type pop-up menu, the type remains the active type; and you can add any number of tabs of that type to the ruler by clicking in the tab segment of the ruler (under the numbered section and above the bottom of the ruler). You use the Tab Type pop-up menu only to change tab types.

> **Tip**
> You can use any type of tab stop temporarily as a Decimal tab by pressing ⌘-Tab instead of pressing the Tab key alone.

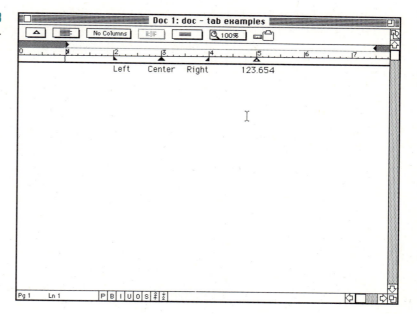

Fig. 4.23
Four types of tab.

Chapter 4
Formatting a Document

Each tab type can have an associated leader. The leader tabs are signified by three dots in front of the names in the Tab Type pop-up menu (refer to fig. 4.21) and by three dots appearing by the tab symbol that shows on the ruler. The most common use of leader tabs is to create a row of dots from text on the left of a page to associated text at the right margin. Price lists and tables of contents frequently use leader tabs.

To see the effect of the leader tabs, perform the following steps:

1. Go to the beginning of a blank line and clear the tabs by choosing Clear Tabs from the Tab Type pop-up menu.

2. Choose the Right Leader tab from the Tab Type pop-up menu.

3. Move the mouse pointer to the 7-inch mark and click.

4. Type *first item*, press Tab, and type *$9.95*. Your document should resemble the document shown in figure 4.24.

Fig. 4.24
Using a Right Leader tab.

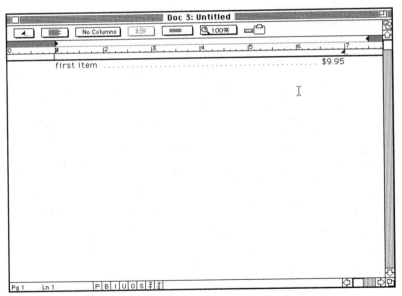

The last type of tab is the Bar tab. Its ruler symbol is a downward-pointing arrow (refer to fig. 4.21). When you press Tab to move the insertion point to the position of the Bar tab, WordPerfect places a vertical bar in front of text typed after the tab character. To practice using the Bar tab, follow these steps:

1. Clear the tabs on the ruler.
2. Set a Bar tab at the 3-inch mark.
3. Type several lines of two words each, pressing Tab between words. Your document should resemble the document in figure 4.25.

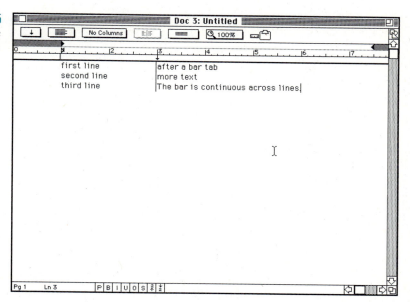

Fig. 4.25
Using the Bar tab to create a vertical line.

Using columns and column borders provides a more flexible method to accomplish many tasks for which you can use a Bar tab, but a Bar tab is a quick way to place a vertical line in a document.

Specifying Relative and Absolute Tabs

Another option, Relative Tabs, appears on the ruler's Tab Type pop-up menu. A relative tab retains its position with respect to the left margin. If you set multiple tabs (refer to fig. 4.23) and then drag the left margin of a ruler to the right, all the tabs move to the right the same distance the margin moves (see fig. 4.26).

Chapter 4
Formatting a Document

Fig. 4.26
Relative tabs moving with the left margin.

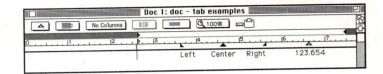

If you choose Relative Tabs in the Tab Type pop-up menu, the check mark disappears, and the tab stops become absolute tabs. Absolute tabs do not move when you change the left margin.

For most general writing tasks, relative tabs are more convenient. Moving the left margin does not require resetting tabs to retain a particular indent distance. Absolute tabs are a better choice, however, when you fill out a form and need to align tabbed text at a specific point, regardless of the left margin setting.

Setting Tabs with the Tabs Dialog Box

Although using the Ruler to set a few tabs is convenient, using the Tabs dialog box is faster and more accurate when you must set a series of regularly spaced tabs—for columns or tables, for example.

To set a tab stop every one inch, follow these steps:

1. Position the insertion point at the appropriate location.

2. Choose Line from the Layout menu; then choose Tabs from the submenu. Alternatively, you can double-click any tab mark in the ruler. The Tabs dialog box appears (see fig. 4.27).

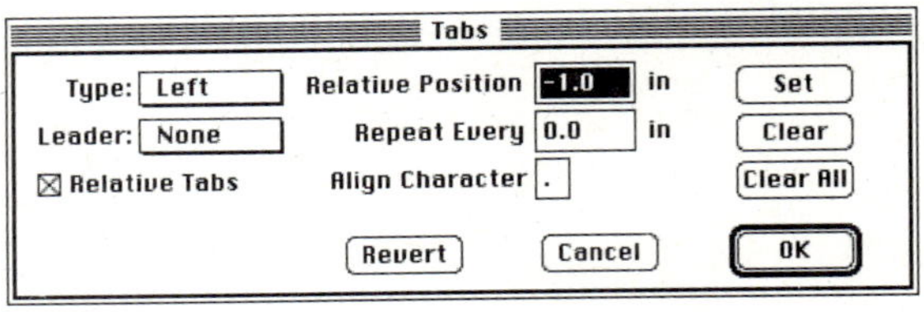

Fig. 4.27
The Tabs dialog box.

3. Choose the type of tab from the Type pop-up menu in the dialog box.

Part I
Getting Started

4. Type the location of the tab in the Relative Position text box. For this example, type *-1.0*.

   The relative position is the distance from the left margin of the first tab in a series. The value -1.0 in the Relative Position text box means that you can place a tab to the left of the left margin if you use the Margin Release function. The Margin Release function moves the insertion point one tab setting to the left of the current location. (Margin release is described more completely later in this chapter.)

   If you turn off the Relative Tabs check box, Relative Position changes to Absolute Position. The value in the Absolute Position text box is the distance from the left edge of the paper.

5. Type the repeat value in the Repeat Every text box. For this example, type *1.0*.

   The repeat value is the distance between adjacent tabs in the series being created. If the Repeat Every value is 0.0, the Tabs dialog box inserts a single tab at the relative or absolute position value when you click Set.

6. Click the Clear All button or press ⌘-A.

   If you don't click Clear All, WordPerfect adds the tab series to tabs currently set. For placing single tabs, you may want to add to current settings; otherwise, you should replace settings when you define a series.

7. Click the Set button or press ⌘-S.

8. Click OK or press Return to return to the document.

If something goes wrong and you must recover the preceding tab settings, click Revert or Cancel. Revert resets the tabs to their locations before you entered the dialog box and leaves the dialog box active so that you can try other changes. Cancel resets the tabs and closes the dialog box, taking you back to the document.

You also can use the Tabs dialog box to set and clear individual tabs. Make sure that the Repeat Every text box contains the value 0.0. Use the Tabs dialog box to set an individual tab if you have trouble setting a precise location by dragging a tab icon along the ruler.

If you want a tab to have a leader, choose one of the four leader styles from the Leader pop-up menu in the Tabs dialog box. You can choose from a series of hyphens, a solid line, or two styles of dotted leaders.

Chapter 4
Formatting a Document

The Align Character text box in the Tabs dialog box controls the character on which the Decimal tab aligns. To align text with an asterisk, for example, select the period (.) in the Alignment Character text box (refer to fig. 4.27), type *, and click OK. You can enter any character.

Clearing Tabs

You can clear all tabs by choosing Clear Tabs from the Tab Type pop-up menu in the ruler or by clicking Clear All in the Tabs dialog box. The easiest way to clear a single tab, however, is to drag it off the bottom of the ruler. As mentioned in the preceding section, you also can use the Tabs dialog box to clear a single tab setting.

Aligning Text

WordPerfect alignment functions frequently are referred to as *justification*. In the menus and in the documentation, however, only text that is flush with both margins is referred to as *justified*.

The commands you use to apply any of the main alignment attributes are available from the Alignment pop-up menu in the ruler, from the Style menu, and as keyboard shortcuts. Two other alignment commands, Center Line and Flush Right, are available only if you have an extended keyboard or if you redefine the keyboard command layout. (See Chapter 15, "Customizing WordPerfect," for information on redefining keyboards.)

The Alignment pop-up menu also has the Justify All option, which is available only in the pop-up menu. Justify All is a special setting that you may never use. This setting provides a quick way to space out a word or phrase to fill a whole line.

Alignment Settings

The default setting for alignment is Left. All lines fill from the left margin. When the text meets the right margin, the line wraps, and the text fills the next line from the left to the right margin. The left margin is flush, and the right margin is jagged. To see how each alignment command affects text, follow these steps:

1. Open a new document (press ⌘-N); then, if you have not done so already, turn on the ruler by pressing ⌘-R. The default alignment setting is Left.

2. Type a few short lines; end each line by pressing Return. WordPerfect aligns the text with the left margin, and the right edge of the text is jagged.

   (You press Return in this step to save the time of entering enough text to fill the entire line or two. As with most text you enter in a word processor, however, pressing Return when you reach the end of a line is not necessary. WordPerfect wraps the text to the next line according to the alignment setting you choose.)

3. Choose Right from the ruler's Alignment pop-up menu (see fig. 4.28). Notice that the Alignment pop-up menu displays the currently active alignment setting after the menu closes.

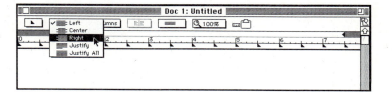

Fig. 4.28
The Alignment pop-up menu on the ruler.

4. Type a few more lines, pressing Return after each line. WordPerfect aligns the text flush right, and the left edge is jagged.

5. Choose Center from the Style menu and type a few more lines. The alignment icon in the ruler switches again, and WordPerfect centers the new lines between the margins.

6. Press ⌘-Shift-J or choose Justify from the Alignment pop-up menu; then enter a paragraph of text. Again the pop-up menu changes to reflect the current alignment setting. WordPerfect adds space between words to make the lines end flush with left and right margins.

7. Choose Justify All from the Alignment pop-up menu and then type a few words. Press Return and type a single word.

When you finish, your screen—despite the fact that the text is different—should resemble the screen shown in figure 4.29.

Chapter 4
Formatting a Document

Fig. 4.29
Text alignment examples.

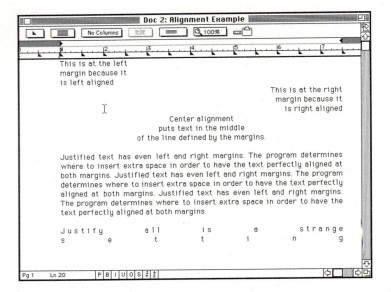

Center Line and Flush Right

The Center Line and Flush Right commands are useful if you mix alignments on a single line. Although you can accomplish multiple alignments on a single line by using tabs, the Center Line and Flush Right commands are much more convenient if you use an extended keyboard. The commands are most useful for setting up headers and footers where only one or two lines contain multiple alignment.

To see an example of left-, center-, and right-aligned text on a single line, follow these steps:

1. Type *July, 1991*.

2. Press Option-F5.

3. Type *-1-* and press Shift-F5.

4. Type *topic* and press Return. Your screen should resemble the screen shown in figure 4.30.

Part I
Getting Started

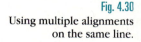

Fig. 4.30
Using multiple alignments on the same line.

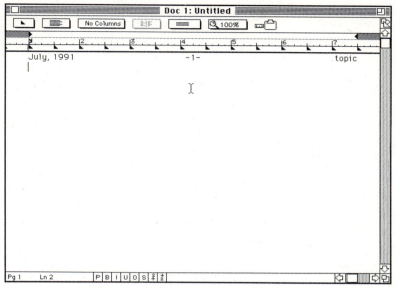

Setting Line Spacing, Line Height, and Leading

By setting line spacing, line height, and leading, you can control the vertical distance between adjacent lines of text. The options are explained in the following list:

- ■ *Line spacing.* This option is an extension of the way a typewriter spaces lines in increments of half a typewritten line.

- ■ *Line height.* This option enables you to assign a specific amount of space for each line, regardless of the size of the characters.

- ■ *Leading.* This option refers to the amount of space between lines, measured from the bottom of the lowest descender on one line to the top of the highest ascender on the next line. The practice of adjusting leading independent of type size comes to microcomputers from the typesetting world, where such spacing was accomplished by inserting lead strips between rows of type.

You can set these three options in the Line Format dialog box, as described in the following sections.

Chapter 4
Formatting a Document

Line Spacing

Most typewriters, which have a fixed line spacing of six lines per inch, can space in only half-line increments. WordPerfect enables you to set any value for line spacing. To choose between single, double, and 1 1/2-inch line spacing, choose the value from the Line Spacing pop-up menu on the ruler (see fig. 4.31).

Fig. 4.31
The Line Spacing pop-up menu.

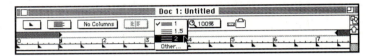

To change the line spacing, follow these steps:

1. Choose Other from the Line Spacing pop-up menu on the ruler, or press Shift-F8 on an extended keyboard. Alternatively, you can choose Line from the Layout menu and Format from the submenu.

   The Line Format dialog box appears (see fig. 4.32).

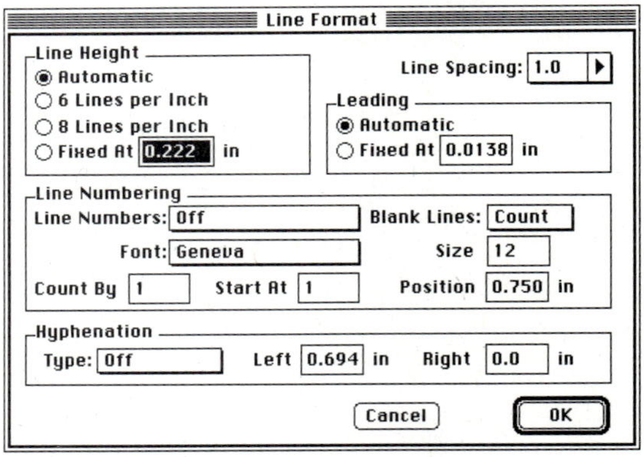

Fig. 4.32
The Line Format dialog box.

2. Type any number between 0.5 and 160.0 in the Line Spacing text box. You also can choose an option from an expanded pop-up list that appears when you click the triangle beside the Line Spacing text box.

3. Click OK or press Return.

Entering 160.0 in the Line Spacing text box results in one line of 5-point text per page of standard letter paper. Entering 0.5 spacing usually results in unreadable text because the letters overlap so much that the printed characters are illegible. On-screen, WordPerfect crops each line of characters, showing only as much of each character as can fit in the specified space.

Line Height and Leading

Line height and leading are mutually exclusive adjustments. If you choose anything other than Automatic for either option in the Line Format dialog box, the other option is disabled.

Use the Line Height options to print a form with fixed line spacing. Choose the 6 Lines per Inch option to print on a form designed for a typewriter. The 8 Lines per Inch option matches another, less common, fixed-line spacing choice from pre-computer days. The last option, Fixed At, enables you to set any line height between 0.014 inch (1 point) and 11.111 inches.

The Line Height and Line Spacing options work together. If you set a fixed line height of 0.2 inch and choose double-spacing, the lines print at 0.4-inch intervals.

The Leading option is convenient if you must insert a space between lines. To set a leading, click Fixed At in the Leading area of the Line Format dialog box. Type a number between -0.222 and 11.111 inches (-16 to 800 points). Press Return. If you enter a positive number for the leading value, WordPerfect adds space between each line. Negative leading values enable you to close up the space between lines when too much space separates lines (usually a problem with large fonts).

Numbering Lines

The Line Numbering feature in the Line Format dialog box enables you to show line numbers next to text on all or part of a document. To number lines on a page, follow these steps:

1. Open a document that is already typed or type several lines, including one or more blank lines.

2. Move the insertion point to the beginning of the text you want numbered.

3. Choose Line from the Layout menu; then choose Format from the submenu. The Line Format dialog box appears.

4. In the Line Numbering section, choose Restart Each Page from the Line Numbers pop-up menu.

Chapter 4
Formatting a Document

> **Tip**
>
> By entering a new value in the Count By text box, you can change the number by which the program counts. So that the program counts in units of ten, for example (10, 20, 30, and so on rather than 1, 2, 3, and so on), change the Count By value to 10 rather than 1.

5. Choose a font from the Font pop-up menu.

6. Leave the Count By value set to 1. Set the Start At value to 1 by double-clicking the Start At text box and typing 1.

   When you open the Line Format dialog box, the Start At value is set to the line number of the line containing the insertion point, as counted from the beginning of your document.

7. Choose Count in the Blank Lines pop-up menu so that WordPerfect counts blank lines.

   If you choose the Skip Blank Lines option, WordPerfect counts the blank lines but doesn't print the number next to a blank line. To leave blank lines out of the counting sequence, you must choose Ignore in the Blank Lines pop-up menu.

8. Leave the Position value set to 0.75 inch. This value is the distance from the left edge of the page to where the line numbers appear. So that the numbers appear in the right margin rather than the left, set a number between 7.5 and 8.5.

9. Click OK or press Return.

When you finish choosing line numbering options, your screen should resemble, for the most part, the screen shown in figure 4.33, which shows the result of other line numbering options.

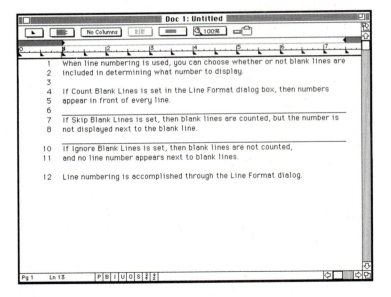

Fig. 4.33
An example of numbered lines.

Part I
Getting Started

Don't plan on using the Line Numbers feature in parts of your document that are set up in columns unless the first column is full and longer than other columns. The line counter counts lines only in the first column and starts over at every column break unless you choose the Continuous numbering option.

Using Hyphenation

Using hyphenation makes the right margin less ragged in left-aligned text or reduces the amount of space added between words in justified text. The result of hyphenating text is a document that is visually more appealing.

WordPerfect's hyphenation utility can hyphenate text automatically while you type. The location of the hyphens is determined by information contained in the Speller dictionary or by linguistic rules that, although not appearing in the dictionary, are included in the program. A manual mode of hyphenation is included, however, if you want more control over the hyphenation process.

Turning Hyphenation On and Off

As with any other formatting setting in WordPerfect, hyphenation can apply to an entire document or a section of a document. When you turn hyphenation on, WordPerfect hyphenates words from the current paragraph to the end of the document or until you turn hyphenation off. If you select text and then activate hyphenation, WordPerfect hyphenates only the appropriate words in the selected paragraphs.

Hyphenation applies only to whole paragraphs. If you select part of a paragraph and turn hyphenation on, all lines in the paragraph are subject to hyphenation.

Depending on your personal working style, you can choose to have hyphenation on while you create a document, or you can wait until the document is complete before you hyphenate.

To turn on hyphenation, follow these steps:

1. Choose Line from the Layout menu and Format from the submenu. The Line Format dialog box appears.

Chapter 4
Formatting a Document

2. From the Type pop-up menu in the Hyphenation section, choose Automatic or Auto Aided.

   Choose Automatic if you want WordPerfect to hyphenate the appropriate words according to the spelling dictionary; choose Auto Aided if you want WordPerfect to ask for confirmation before hyphenating a word. These options are explained in more detail following these steps.

3. Click OK or press Return.

Automatic hyphenation uses information in the spelling dictionary to determine where to hyphenate a word. If a word is not in the dictionary, WordPerfect uses general rules about hyphenation to set a suitable breaking point in a word. If WordPerfect fails to find a rule that fits the word, the program wraps the word to the next line.

Auto Aided hyphenation asks you to confirm the choice of hyphenation location. The Position Hyphen dialog box shows a dotted line where the margin lies, the location that the program has picked for the hyphen, arrow controls to enable the user to pick a new hyphen location, and a Wrap button to make the program move the whole word to the next line (see fig. 4.34). Clicking the Hyphenate button tells WordPerfect to hyphenate the word as hyphenated in the dialog box.

Fig. 4.34
The Position Hyphen dialog box.

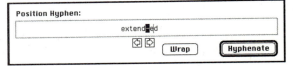

Auto Aided hyphenation offers complete control over hyphenation but is intrusive while you create or edit a document. Having the Position Hyphen dialog box appear as you enter text is probably more distracting than most people want. If you want the control this option offers, hyphenate after you complete the document. Place the insertion point at the top of the finished document, turn on Auto Aided hyphenation, and respond to the dialog boxes and prompts as the program works its way through the document.

Inserting Soft Hyphens

To provide suggestions for hyphenation locations while you type, press ⌘-hyphen at the location where you think the hyphen should be. WordPerfect inserts a hidden code into the word at that location. If editing the document moves that word to the end of the line so that the word requires hyphenation, the hyphenation occurs at the soft hyphen.

Understanding the Hyphenation Zone

In determining what words are long enough to hyphenate, WordPerfect uses a hyphenation zone to determine how long a word must be before WordPerfect hyphenates it. You set the hyphenation zone in the Line Format dialog box (refer to fig. 4.32). Entering a number smaller than the default (0.694 inch) in the Left text box in the Hyphenation section of the Line Format dialog box results in more words hyphenated and, consequently, a more even margin.

The hyphenation zone (or H-zone, as the WordPerfect manual sometimes calls it) has no concise definition. If you have used a typewriter, you can think of the Left value in the Hyphenation section of the Line Format dialog box as the distance from the right margin where the line-end warning bell rings. If you are in the middle of a word when the bell rings—that is, when you enter the H-zone—you must finish the word or hyphenate it before reaching the right margin. If you finish the word after the bell rings, continue to the next line (that is, wrap the text) rather than start a new word at the end of a line. When you use WordPerfect, all these "decisions" are made automatically, and the program automatically wraps text as necessary.

Leave the value of the Right text box set at 0.000. Although setting a slightly larger number in this box enables you to squeeze an extra letter or two onto a line (rather than hyphenating or wrapping a word), the resulting text often appears crowded.

Using the Hard Space and Nonbreaking Hyphen

Although hard spaces and nonbreaking hyphens are not specifically related to hyphenation, they do affect how WordPerfect wraps lines. Suppose that you enter the following sentence in a document:

> The book by A.B. Smith was an important text book in the field.

You probably don't want WordPerfect to wrap the line in the middle of the author's name. Rather than use the space bar to insert spaces in the name, press ⌘-space bar; WordPerfect keeps the name together. Similarly, you may not want the hyphen in hyphenated surnames or telephone numbers to cause a line break. If you press ⌘-Shift-hyphen rather than just a hyphen, WordPerfect treats the hyphen like an alphabetic character.

Chapter 4
Formatting a Document

Using Subtitles

The Subtitle option, accessed through the Language submenu of the Tools menu, is designed to enable linguists to insert translations or phonetic pronunciations above or below selected text. You can use subtitles to insert any text between two lines.

To practice using subtitles, follow these steps:

1. Type *Deadly nightshade is a poisonous plant with black fruit. The plant also has small white flowers.*

2. Select *Deadly nightshade*. Choose Language from the Tools menu; then choose Subtitle from the submenu (see fig. 4.35). The Subtitles dialog box appears.

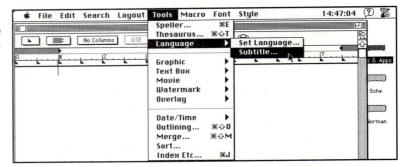

Fig. 4.35
Choosing Subtitle from the Language submenu.

3. Choose Italics from the Style menu on the Subtitles dialog box.

4. Choose Small from the dialog box's Size menu (see fig. 4.36).

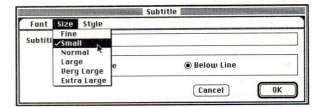

Fig. 4.36
Choosing a size in the Subtitle dialog box.

The choices on the Size menu are the same relative font sizes discussed earlier in this chapter. WordPerfect always scales a subtitle relative to its associated text; you cannot choose a fixed font size for a subtitle.

Part I
Getting Started

5. By default, the font of the subtitle is the same as the font of the text you are annotating. To use another font for the subtitle, choose a font from the Font menu in the Subtitle dialog box.

6. In the Position area of the dialog box, the selected radio button (Above Line or Below Line) indicates where WordPerfect places the subtitle. You can change the position by clicking the other radio button. For the example, make sure the Below Line button is selected.

7. Type *Solanum nigrum* in the Subtitle text box and click OK or press Return. Your subtitle should resemble the subtitle shown in figure 4.37.

Fig. 4.37
An example of a subtitle below a line of text.

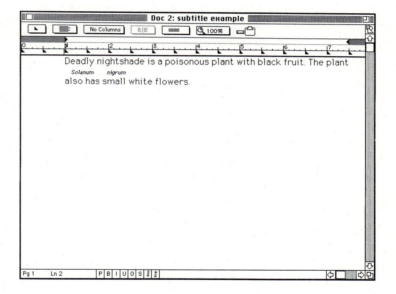

To delete a subtitle, follow these steps:

1. Click anywhere in the subtitled text.

2. Choose Language from the Tools menu; then choose Subtitle from the submenu. The Subtitle dialog box, with the entire subtitle selected, appears.

3. Press Delete; then click OK.

Chapter 4
Formatting a Document

You can edit the subtitled text by selecting and changing the text instead of pressing the Delete key in step 3. You can edit subtitle text only in the Subtitle dialog box; you cannot change the subtitle in the document window.

Formatting Paragraphs

The paragraph formatting commands control left and right margins, first-line indents, and any extra space between paragraphs. As usual, WordPerfect provides several ways to accomplish each setting. Some choices determine whether a paragraph setting affects all subsequent paragraphs or only the paragraph for which you enter the command. This section assumes that you have not changed the default Format mode (Paragraph) in the Environment dialog box.

Setting Left and Right Margins

Setting margins is the most fundamental aspect of paragraph formatting. Some people set their margins once and never change them; other people change margins several times per page. (See Chapter 15, "Customizing WordPerfect," for instructions on changing the margins WordPerfect uses by default for a new document.)

Again, WordPerfect provides more than one way to accomplish a formatting task. You can use the ruler, which is the easier way to set left and right margins, or a dialog box. To set margins by using the ruler, follow these steps:

1. If you have not done so already, display the ruler by pressing ⌘-R.

2. Drag the margin markers to the desired location.

Because the exact location of the margin marker is reported in the status bar when you press the mouse button, you easily can position the margin accurately with the mouse and ruler.

If you need more precise control over the margin settings, or if you have trouble with the mouse moving slightly when you release the button, open the Page Format dialog box (press ⌘-M, press Option-F5, or choose Format from the Page submenu in the Layout menu). You can enter the values for the margins directly in the Left and Right text boxes in the dialog box (see fig. 4.38).

Part I
Getting Started

Fig. 4.38
Setting margins from the Page Format dialog box.

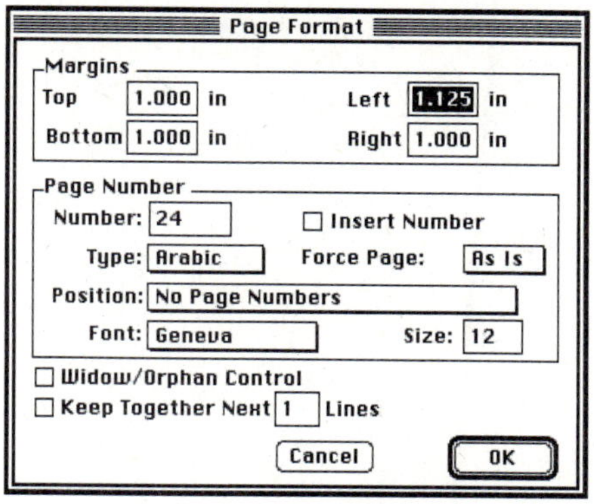

> **Tip**
> In WordPerfect, you can set a 0.000 left or right margin even if the printer selected in the Chooser cannot print to the edge of the page. Laser and inkjet printers, for example, use narrow areas at both sides of the paper to feed the paper through the printer and, therefore, cannot print all the way to the edges. If your text is getting chopped off at the edges of the page, check your printer manual for minimum margin settings and adjust the margins in WordPerfect accordingly.

WordPerfect doesn't enable you to set margins so large that the left and right margins cross. Remember, however, that the ruler displays the distance from the left edge of the page, but the Page Format value for Right is a distance from the right edge of the paper.

Indenting Text

Indenting can affect the first line or every line of a paragraph. You can indent an entire paragraph on the left or left and right margins. Indenting an entire paragraph frequently is used to set off long quotations. Hanging indents, in which the first line of a paragraph starts to the left of the rest of the lines, are often used for bulleted or numbered lists.

First-Line Indent

First-line indents frequently are used to indicate that a new paragraph has started. Block style (no indent—like this paragraph) is more common in most correspondence today; however, you must leave a blank line between paragraphs, or the text is hard to read.

To set a first-line indent, follow these steps:

1. Display the ruler by pressing ⌘-R.

2. Drag the indent marker (the open triangle just below the left margin marker) to the desired location. Notice that the status bar reports the absolute position from the left edge of the page and the relative offset from the left margin.

Chapter 4
Formatting a Document

You also can set a first-line indent by choosing Paragraph from the Layout menu or by pressing ⌘-F8. When the Paragraph Format dialog box appears, as shown in figure 4.39, enter the offset from the left margin in the First Line Indent text box.

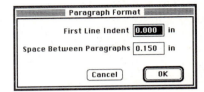

Fig. 4.39
Setting first-line indent in the Paragraph Format dialog box.

Paragraph Indent

For a whole paragraph indent, you must have at least one tab set to the right of the left margin. Only the tab settings determine the distance of indentation in the text. If no tabs are set, WordPerfect places an indent code in the document but does not indent the paragraph. If you set tabs later in that paragraph, WordPerfect indents the text to the first tab.

To indent an entire paragraph, follow these steps:

1. Place the insertion point at the beginning of the paragraph.
2. Choose Indent from the Layout menu, press ⌘-Shift-I, or press F5.
3. To indent the left and right sides of the paragraph, choose Left/Right Indent from the Layout menu or press ⌘-F5.

Either indent affects only the paragraph in which the command is entered. To indent several consecutive paragraphs, select the paragraphs before choosing the command. To indent paragraphs as you create them, issue an indent command at the beginning of each paragraph.

Hanging Indent

A paragraph with a first line that begins closer to the left edge of the page than the rest of the paragraph has a hanging indent. You can create a hanging indent in any of the following ways:

- Drag the first-line indent marker of the ruler to a position left of the left margin.

- Type a negative number in the First Line Offset text box of the Paragraph Format dialog box.

- Issue an Indent command followed immediately by a Margin Release command. (Press Shift-Tab or choose Margin Release in the Layout menu.)

- Enter the Indent command after typing a bullet or number.

Bulleted lists, like the preceding, are examples of hanging indents. To create a bulleted list with a hanging indent, follow these steps:

1. Set a tab at about 0.25 inch from the left margin.

2. Enter the bullet character by pressing Option-8.

3. Press F5 or choose Indent from the Layout menu.

4. Type the text of the paragraph. End the paragraph with two carriage returns.

Repeat the steps to add paragraphs to the list. When you finish, your list, although different in content, should resemble the list shown in figure 4.40.

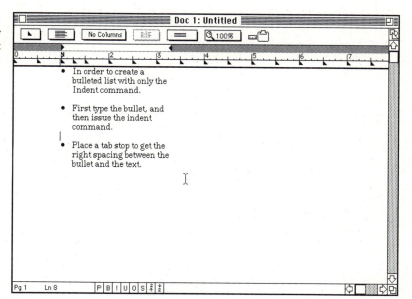

Fig. 4.40
A bulleted list created by using the Indent command.

Chapter 4
Formatting a Document

Adding Space between Paragraphs

In the last example, you ended each paragraph with two carriage returns to set off each bulleted item with a blank line. You can insert extra space after every paragraph without entering an extra carriage return, however. Choose Paragraph from the Layout menu (or press ⌘-F8) and enter a number in the Space between Paragraphs text box of the Paragraph Format dialog box.

You can enter any number in the Space Between Paragraphs text box. Entering negative numbers, however, doesn't make much sense because negative numbers cause adjacent paragraphs to overlap. Values greater than the length of your paper also are frivolous, but you can enter such values without an error message appearing.

For practical purposes, when you use Space Between Paragraphs only to provide a little extra space between paragraphs, a value between 0.05 and 0.20 inches probably is a good choice. The exact value depends on the font size in use and your personal taste.

The advantage of using the Paragraph Format dialog box to set space between paragraphs is that you aren't limited to using full line spaces. The Paragraph Format method also enables you to set a fixed amount of space, regardless of font size.

Formatting Pages

Page formatting options control the features that appear only once per page. Page numbers, headers, and footers are items that actually appear on the page. Other page formatting options—such as top and bottom margins, widow and orphan control, vertical centering, and format suppression—are examples of options that control other aspects of page formatting.

Setting Top and Bottom Margins

To set top and bottom margins, you must access the Page Format dialog box. Press ⌘-M, press Option-F5, or choose Page from the Layout menu and Format from the submenu (see fig. 4.41). The Page Format dialog box appears. Type the values of the margins in the Top and Bottom text boxes in the Margins section of the dialog box, shown in figure 4.42.

Fig. 4.41
Choosing Page Format from the Layout menu.

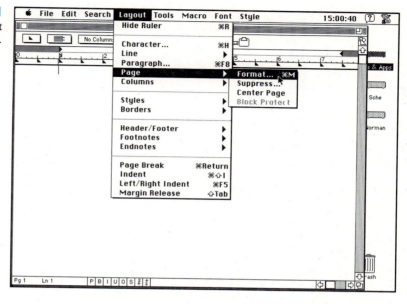

Fig. 4.42
The Page Format dialog box.

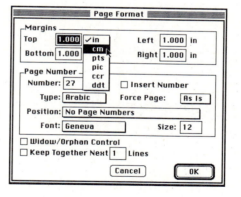

Tip

This measurement conversion trick (accessing a hidden pop-up menu of measurement options) works in any dialog box for any measurement abbreviation, such as `in`, next to a value text box.

To change the measurement system you use for a particular margin, click the abbreviation for inch (`in`) next to the Top text box and choose one of the options from the previously hidden pop-up menu (refer to fig. 4.42). Notice that when you pick a new measurement system, WordPerfect converts the value of the margin in the box to the new measurement system.

Chapter 4
Formatting a Document

If you leave the dialog box by clicking OK and then reopen the dialog box, you may notice that WordPerfect converts your measurement to inches and displays all values in inches. To use a unit other than inches as the default measurement, use the Units menu in the Environment dialog box (see Chapter 15, "Customizing WordPerfect," for details).

WordPerfect is one of the few word processors that enables you to change your top and bottom margins on each page, independent of the margins of the other pages. If you are in the middle of a document when you enter new numbers in the Top or Bottom text box, an alert box appears to ask whether you want the change to affect the current page. If you click Yes, WordPerfect inserts a hard page break at the top of the current page and applies the new margins. If you click No, WordPerfect applies the margin change to the whole document by inserting the margin set code at the beginning of the document before any text. If you click Cancel, WordPerfect ignores your margin changes and uses the existing margins.

Inserting a Hard Page Break

While you enter text into a document, you don't need to know how much space is left on a page. WordPerfect automatically starts a new page when you fill a page. To force something to appear at the top of a new page, however, you can insert a hard page break by pressing ⌘-Return or choosing Page Break from the Layout menu.

You can see the locations of the page breaks inserted by WordPerfect (soft page breaks) and the breaks you insert (hard page breaks). A soft break appears as a thin gray line across the page; a hard page break appears as a thicker gray line across the page (see fig. 4.43).

Adding Page Numbers

To add page numbers to your printed output, you can include the numbers in headers or footers, as described in the next section, or you can set page numbers separately in the Page Format dialog box. Page numbers can appear in one of six locations listed in the Location pop-up menu (see fig. 4.44). WordPerfect places the page numbers at the margins in effect at the page number location.

Fig. 4.43
Soft and hard page breaks in the document and codes windows.

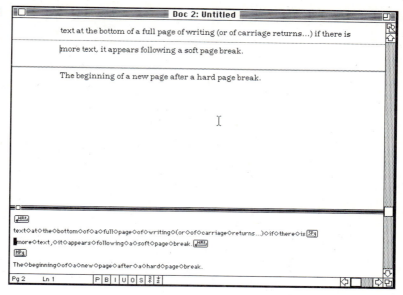

Fig. 4.44
Setting the page number position.

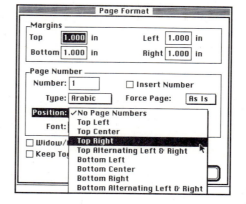

Tip
If you add page numbers after you type a document, page through the document in Print Preview to make sure that the extra space taken up by the new page numbers hasn't disrupted your page breaks.

Although the page numbers are not visible in the document window, you can see the numbers in Print Preview. WordPerfect adds a blank line between the page number and the text on the page.

Page numbers can be in Arabic or Roman numerals. (Choose Arabic or Roman Numerals from the Type pop-up menu in the Page Number section of the Page Format dialog box.) You also can assign to page numbers any font or size in the Page Format dialog box by choosing a

Chapter 4
Formatting a Document

font from the Font pop-up menu and typing the size in the Size text box. (Both items are in the Page Numbering section of the Page Format dialog box.)

The Insert Number check box in the Page Format dialog box enables you to insert the current page number in the text at the insertion point location. Using this check box puts a page number code (`Page#`) in your document, text box, column, and so forth. If you use one of the normal page number locations, including headers or footers, the Insert Number option has little use. You can use this option, however, to indicate to the reader that she is on page four, for example, of a ten page document.

The Force Page pop-up menu in the Page Format dialog box enables you to ensure that a given page appears on an odd or even page. To make the first page of a chapter appear on the right-hand page, for example, set Force Page to Odd while the insertion point is on the first page of the chapter. If Force Page is set to Even, the page holding the insertion point appears on the left side of a two page spread. If whether the page appears on the odd or even side is unimportant, choose As Is from the Force Page pop-up menu.

Adding Headers and Footers

You use headers and footers to print recurring information at the top (*header*) or bottom (*footer*) of each page. One common use of headers and footers is putting a chapter or section title and a page number on each page of a book. Lengthy office memos often include a topic, date, and page number in a header or footer.

To insert a header consisting of a topic and page number at the top of each page in a multipage document, follow these steps:

1. Place the insertion point on the page where you want the header to begin.

2. Choose Header/Footer from the Layout menu; then choose New from the submenu. Alternatively, press ⌘-Shift-H. The New Header/Footer dialog box appears (see fig. 4.45).

3. Click Header A in the Type section.

4. Click OK or press Return.

    A header window appears with the insertion point inside (see fig. 4.46).

Fig. 4.45
The New Header/Footer dialog box.

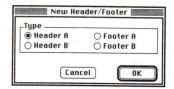

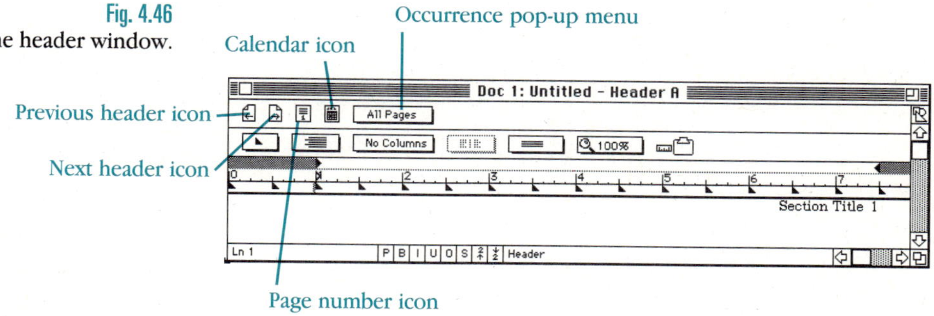

Fig. 4.46
The header window.

5. Choose Odd Pages from the Occurrence pop-up menu.

6. Display the ruler in the Header window (if the ruler isn't showing already) by pressing ⌘-R. Choose Right from the ruler Alignment pop-up menu.

7. Type *Section Title* followed by two spaces.

8. Click the Page Number icon in the Header window to insert the page number at the right margin (refer to fig. 4.46).

9. Close the Header window by clicking the close box or pressing ⌘-W.

10. Repeat the process, specifying Header B in the Header/Footer dialog box, choosing Even Pages from the Occurrence pop-up menu, choosing Left in the Alignment menu of the Header window, and inserting the page number code before typing *Section Title*. Your header and footer should resemble figure 4.47 in Print Preview.

If you want the same header to appear on all pages, choose All Pages in the Occurrence pop-up menu.

Chapter 4
Formatting a Document

Fig. 4.47
Odd and even page headers.

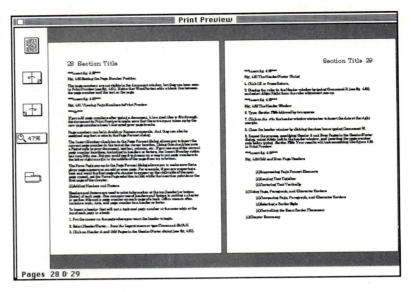

The same status bar appears in the header window as in the document window. You can do any formatting in the header window (independent of the formatting in the main document). If you use many different headers in a document, clicking the Next or Previous Header icon displays the following or preceding Header window for editing. You can have as many A and B headers in a document as the document has pages.

By default, the headers and footers have the same font as Normal Style. If you change the main font in your document by inserting a font choice in the document instead of editing the Normal Style, you also must set the font in headers and footers. In fact, because all subdocument types are based on the Normal Style font, updating your Normal Style to include your main font choice is a good idea.

The Calendar icon in the Header window inserts a date function code into your header (refer to fig. 4.46). See Chapter 15, "Customizing WordPerfect," for information about how to customize the information inserted at a date code.

Part I

Getting Started

After you define a header or footer, you may want to edit the item to correct mistakes or include new information. You can edit a header or footer by choosing Header/Footer from the Layout menu and Edit from the submenu. The Edit Header/Footer dialog box appears. With the exception of the title, this dialog box is identical to the New Header/Footer dialog box (refer to fig. 4.45).

Choose the header or footer you want to edit (A or B) by clicking the radio button next to the name, and then click OK. WordPerfect searches the document to find the header or footer definition and opens the window of the header or footer. You then can edit the window contents and close the window just as though you are defining the header or footer for the first time.

To stop a header or footer from appearing on any page after the page holding the insertion point, you can use the Discontinue Header/Footer command. Most documents that have headers and footers use the header or footers throughout the document; however, you may use two headers for a while and then return to using a single one. To discontinue a header or footer, follow these steps:

1. Choose Header/Footer from the Layout menu and Discontinue from the submenu.

   Another Header/Footer dialog box appears (see fig. 4.48). This dialog box is slightly different from the other Header/Footer dialog boxes in that the options in the Discontinue box have check boxes rather than radio buttons. The check boxes enable you to discontinue more than one header or footer at a time.

Fig. 4.48
The Discontinue Header/Footer dialog box.

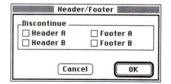

2. Click the check boxes for items you want to discontinue.

3. Click OK or press Return.

WordPerfect discontinues the items you checked, starting with the page containing the insertion point. The discontinue function affects only the active items. If you define another header or footer of the same type (that is, A or B) later in the document, WordPerfect does not discontinue those items.

Chapter 4
Formatting a Document

Using Watermarks

On a piece of paper a watermark is, literally, a water mark. Paper manufacturers use water to put a logo or identification mark that is visible when you hold the paper in front of a light. Corporations frequently have bond paper watermarked with their company logo—as a status symbol and as a means of authenticating correspondence and reports.

Naturally, WordPerfect's watermark feature doesn't add a nearly invisible item to your paper, but one that is very similar to a paper watermark. A WordPerfect watermark is an object, usually a graphic object, that appears on every page and that does not affect the formatting of any text on the page.

You can use watermarks to put your company logo on every page of a document, place a notice—such as *draft* or *confidential*, for example—in large type across the page to inform readers of the document status, or insert a copyright notice outside the normal margins on each page of overhead transparency slides.

WordPerfect watermarks also have much in common with headers and footers. You can define up to two watermarks (Watermark A and Watermark B) to appear on any page. You can place a different watermark on every page, a technique accomplished more logically by using the graphic overlay feature. You can create and edit watermarks at any time. You also can discontinue the display of watermarks at any point in your document.

Although you may recognize many similarities in the handling of headers, footers, and watermarks, several differences exist. WordPerfect watermarks are graphics objects. Because Mac graphics objects can contain text, you can create a watermark that contains only text. You must enter that text, however, in WordPerfect's Graphics Editor, which is discussed in detail in Chapter 11, "Using the Drawing Window." This section deals solely with watermark management.

To create a watermark, follow these steps:

1. Place the insertion point on the first page on which you want the watermark to appear.

2. Choose Watermark from the Tools menu and New from the submenu. The New Watermark dialog box appears, asking you to choose which kind of watermark to create (Watermark A or Watermark B).

Part I

Getting Started

3. Click the radio button of Watermark A or B in the New Watermark dialog box.

4. Click OK or press Return.

   A new graphic window appears in which you create and edit the watermark graphic. (See Chapter 11, "Using the Drawing Window," for details on graphic editing.)

5. After you finish your watermark, close the graphic window by pressing ⌘-W, clicking the close box of the graphic window, or clicking the document icon at the top of the vertical scroll bar.

The graphic window closes, and you return to your document. The watermark does not appear in your document window while you are editing (just as headers and footers are not displayed). To see how your watermark looks on the page, you must use Print Preview.

After you define a watermark, you can edit it by following these steps:

1. Choose Watermark from the Tools menu and Edit from the submenu.

2. Click the radio button of Watermark A or Watermark B in the Edit Watermark dialog box to select the watermark to edit.

3. Click OK or press Return.

The graphic editing window of the watermark you have chosen opens. After you finish editing, close the graphic window to return to your main document window.

The rest of the watermark management functions are accomplished from the Watermark Options dialog box. To change the occurrence setting or to discontinue a watermark, follow these steps:

1. Choose Watermark from the Tools menu and Options from the submenu. The Watermark Options dialog box appears (see fig. 4.49).

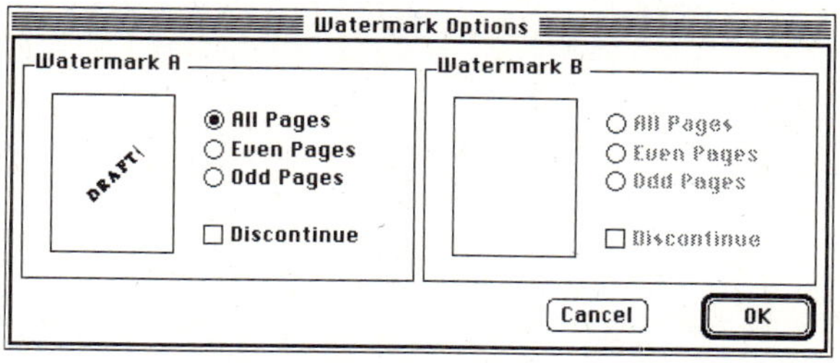

Fig. 4.49
The Watermark Options dialog box.

Chapter 4
Formatting a Document

Notice that the dialog box shows a small image of the page containing the watermark. If you haven't defined an A or a B watermark, one side of the dialog box dims.

2. To change the occurrence frequency of your watermark, click the radio button beside Odd Pages, Even Pages, or All Pages. The watermark appears on the pages specified by the active radio button.

   To discontinue a watermark, click the Discontinue check box. If this box is checked and you want the watermark to appear on subsequent pages, click the check box again to turn the option off.

3. After you finish setting the watermark options, click OK or press Return.

The option settings you make take effect on the page containing the insertion point. Again, you must use Print Preview or print the document to see the changes.

Suppressing Page Format Elements

You may want to specify a single header for a whole document but don't want the header to print on a particular page, or you may want to leave a watermark off a page that contains an extensive table. You may want to suppress all headers, footers, watermarks, and page numbers on the first page of a chapter in a book. You can accomplish each of these tasks by using the Suppress Format dialog box.

To stop a header from printing on a page, follow these steps:

1. Make sure that the insertion point is on the page for which you are suppressing the header.

2. Choose Page from the Layout menu and Suppress from the submenu. The Suppress Format dialog box appears (see fig. 4.50).

Fig. 4.50
The Suppress Format dialog box.

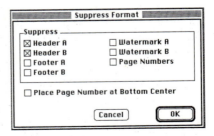

Part I
Getting Started

3. Click Header A, Header B, or both in the Suppress Format dialog box.

4. Click OK or press Return.

By checking the appropriate boxes in the Suppress Format dialog box (and then clicking OK), you can suppress one or more of the page formatting elements.

If you are using page numbers (not headers) from the Page Format dialog box, you can use the Suppress Format dialog box to move the page number to the bottom center of a single page. The typical use for this feature is to move the page number to the bottom center and suppress all other page formatting elements on the first page of a book chapter.

To move the page number and suppress other elements, follow these steps:

1. Open the Suppress Format dialog box.

2. Activate all the options in the Suppress section of the dialog box. All the boxes in the Suppress section should be checked.

   (*Note:* The Place Page Number at Bottom Center option is independent of the Page Number option. Even though you suppress the page number here, you can display a page number at the bottom of the page by clicking the Place Page Number at Bottom Center option.)

3. Click Place Page Number at Bottom Center.

4. Click OK or press Return.

When you print the page, WordPerfect does not print headers, footers, or watermarks on that page, and the page number appears at the bottom center of the page.

Suppress Format acts on only one page at a time. To suppress items on other pages, you must move the insertion point to each page in turn and use Suppress Format again. To stop using a header, footer, or watermark for the rest of the document, use the Discontinue function for each element individually (as discussed earlier in the chapter).

Keeping Text Together

In some circumstances, you may not want two or more lines separated across a soft page break. WordPerfect provides three different control options for preventing unwanted text separation across page boundaries.

Chapter 4
Formatting a Document

By convention, leaving a single line of a paragraph alone at the top or the bottom of a page is considered a poor practice. These single lines are referred to as *widows* and *orphans*, respectively. If you choose Widow/Orphan control in the Page Format dialog box, WordPerfect prevents widows and orphans from occurring.

To ensure that a particular section of text remains together on a page, you can use the Keep Together Next option from the Page Format dialog box or the Block Protect command from the Page submenu under the Layout menu. The commands are slightly different, but they accomplish much the same thing.

To use the Keep Together Next option, follow these steps:

1. Put the insertion point in the first line of the group you want to keep together.

2. Open the Page Format dialog box by pressing ⌘-M, pressing Option-F8, or choosing Format from the Page submenu under the Layout menu.

3. Set the number of lines you want to protect in the text box in the Keep Together Next option.

4. Click OK or press Return.

You also can use the Block Protect command. The difference between these two methods is that the size of a block increases as you insert text inside the block. Theoretically, you can make a block grow larger than an entire page. The Keep Together Next option keeps together only the same number of lines, no matter how much text you insert or where you insert it.

To use Block Protect, follow these steps:

1. Select the text you want to keep together.

2. Choose Page from the Layout menu and Block Protect from the submenu.

The protected text block always appears as a block, no matter where page breaks normally fall.

Using Block Protect for a large block can leave you with an almost empty page if WordPerfect moves the protected block to a new page.

Part I
Getting Started

Centering Text Vertically

If you are preparing promotional fliers or overhead transparencies for a business presentation, you may have only a few lines of text on the page. You also may have several pages, each with a different number of lines. To make these pages attractive when printed, use the Center Page command. To practice the Center Page command, follow these steps:

1. Open a new document and set the font and size to 24-point Times.
2. Choose Page from the Layout menu and Center Page from the submenu. Alternatively, press Option-F9.
3. Choose Center from the ruler Alignment pop-up menu or the Style menu. Alternatively, press ⌘-Shift-C.
4. Type the following, pressing Return at the end of each line:

   Announcing
   a
   New Standard
   in
   Word Processing

5. Press ⌘-Return to enter a hard page break.

Notice that the editing screen shows only the text. In Print Preview, however, you can see the effects of the Center Page function (see fig. 4.51).

To turn off Center Page, place the insertion point on the page to be modified and choose Center Page from the Page submenu in the Layout menu. If the page uses the Center Page option, you can see a check mark beside the menu choice. You activate and turn off the Center Page option one page at a time.

> **Tip**
> To center text slightly above center on a page, you use the Center Page function and reset the bottom margin to an inch or two more than the top margin.

Adding Page, Paragraph, and Character Borders

One of the major additions to Version 2.x of WordPerfect is the capability to put a border around characters, paragraphs, columns, or pages. Column borders are covered in Chapter 9, "Using Columns and Text Boxes," but many of the features available to all the borders are the same.

Chapter 4
Formatting a Document

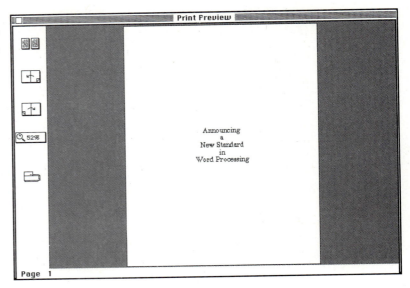

Fig. 4.51
Results of using the Center Page function.

Any border can use one of 64 patterns (see fig. 4.52), one of 36 border types (see fig. 4.53), and any one of the colors available to the Mac. Similarly, you also can fill the area bounded by the border with one of the 64 patterns, any one of the colors, or both. One of the few limitations of borders in WordPerfect is that the minimum line thickness is 1 point (0.014 inch). That restriction may not sound like much of a limitation, but a 1-point line looks like a boldface line in some borders.

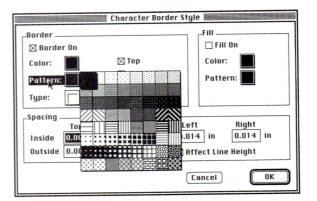

Fig. 4.52
The border patterns.

Part I
Getting Started

Fig. 4.53
The border types.

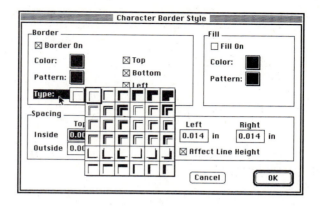

Although these figures show the pattern and border type pop-up palettes of the Character Border Style dialog box, the same selection of borders and patterns is available for each kind of object—character, page, and paragraph—that you can surround with the border. In each case, you apply the borders to selected text or to all text following the insertion of the border code. In most cases, selecting some text before applying a border makes sense.

Page Borders

To apply a border to a single page, follow these steps:

1. Select at least one character on the page.

2. Choose Borders from the Layout menu and Page from the submenu. Alternatively, press Option-F7. The Page Border Style dialog box appears (see fig. 4.54).

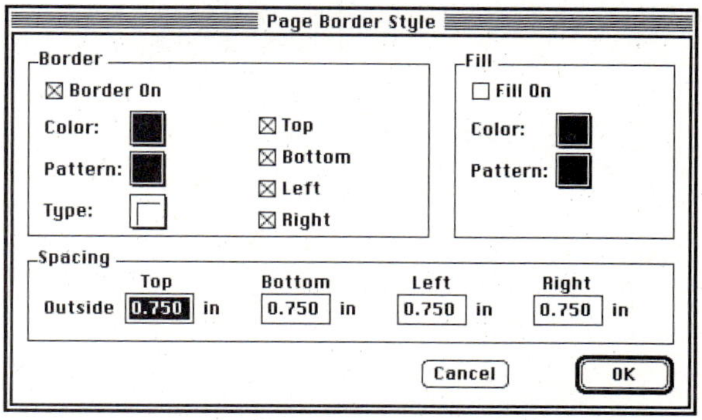

Fig. 4.54
The Page Border Style dialog box.

Chapter 4
Formatting a Document

The Page Border Style dialog box is almost identical to the Character Border Style dialog box shown in figures 4.52 and 4.53. The only differences are in the Spacing options, which are covered in the last section of this chapter.

3. On the Page Border Style dialog box, choose a border type and pattern from the pop-up palettes.

4. Leave the Top, Bottom, Left, and Right check boxes selected to create a border on all four sides.

5. Leave the Spacing settings at their default values.

6. Click OK or press Return.

7. Click Yes or press Return in response to the alert box, which asks whether you want the change applied only to the selected pages.

You do not get the alert box if you are applying a border to the first page in a document. Even if you select just the first page, the border spills over to the subsequent pages. You must move the insertion point to the second page, open the Page Border Style dialog box, click the Border On check box (to turn off the border), and then click OK.

In the document window, you can tell that a page border is active because the border shows in the right and left margins (see fig. 4.55). If you go to Print Preview, you see the entire border (see fig. 4.56).

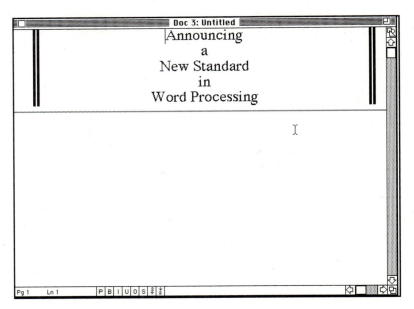

Fig. 4.55
An active page border in the document window.

Part I
Getting Started

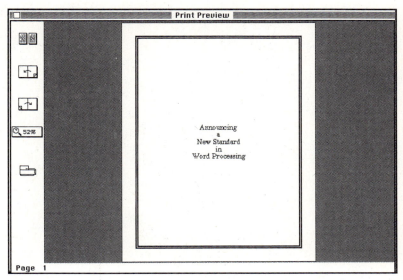

Fig. 4.56
A bordered page in Print Preview.

Paragraph and Character Borders

The only difference between a paragraph and character border is that a paragraph border is guaranteed to be rectangular in shape, but a character border, while still having square corners, may not be a rectangle. If you apply a character border to selected text, WordPerfect outlines the selection with a border.

To put a border around a single paragraph, follow the instructions given for a page border, but use the Paragraph Border Style dialog box, which you open by choosing Border from the Layout menu and Paragraph from the submenu, or pressing ⌘-F7. To put a border around more than one paragraph, you must select at least a piece of every paragraph to be enclosed in the border.

To put a border around some characters but not a whole paragraph, follow these steps:

1. Select the characters to be enclosed in the border.

2. Choose Borders from the Layout menu and Character from the submenu. Alternatively, press F7. The Character Border Style dialog box appears.

Chapter 4
Formatting a Document

3. Choose the border type and pattern.

4. Click OK or press Return.

WordPerfect places a border around the selected text (see fig. 4.57).

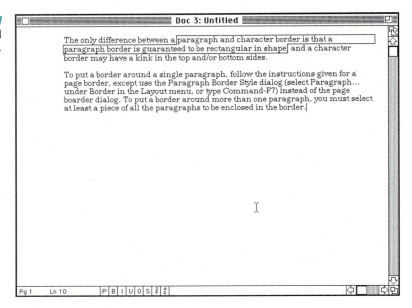

Fig. 4.57
A character border around part of a paragraph.

You can substitute a character border for the Redline text style, which is described in Chapter 3, "Editing a Document." You also may use a character border to emphasize a group of words (in the same manner that boldface, italics, underlining, outline, or shadow styles are used).

Filled Regions

In addition to enclosing text in a border, you can additionally emphasize text by filling the bordered region with a color or a pattern. To fill the bordered region in figure 4.57 with gray, follow these steps:

1. Select the text again.

2. Press F7 to display the Character Border Style dialog box.

3. Choose a light gray from the bottom row of the Color pop-up menu in the Fill section. Note that when you choose a color, the Fill On check box is checked.

Part I
Getting Started

4. Leave the Pattern option in the Fill section set to black.

5. Click OK or press Return. WordPerfect fills the selected text (see fig. 4.58).

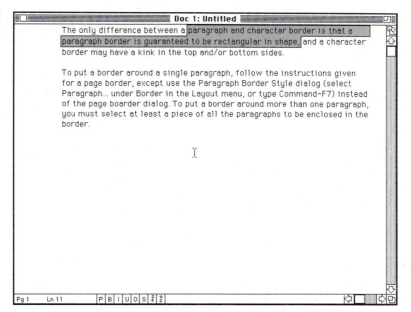

Fig. 4.58
A character border filled with gray.

Border Location

Until now, the Spacing area of the Border Style dialog boxes, shown in figure 4.59 has not been explained. The default values are usually a good choice for general purpose borders. The Affect Line Height check box is on so that you don't print a border over text on lines above and below the border. The Inside Right and Inside Left boxes have the value 0.014 inch (1 point) so that the text inside the border doesn't run into the border. The Inside and Outside boxes for Top and Bottom have 0.000 inch because the normal font leading prevents the border from overwriting text.

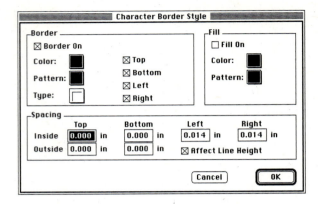

Fig. 4.59
The Spacing area of the Character Border Style dialog box.

The Page Border Style dialog box does not have the Spacing options for Outside or Affect Line Height because only blank paper appears outside a page border; therefore, nothing needs to be protected from overprinting by a border.

To provide more or less space between the text adjacent to a border and the border itself, adjust the values in the spacing boxes.

Chapter Summary

This chapter covered formatting text and documents—from the spacing between characters (kerning) to borders around complete pages. Along the way, the chapter covered a progression of character, line, paragraph, and page formatting commands. Not only did you use commands from the Layout, Font, and Style menus, but you also used shortcut key commands and dialog boxes to enhance documents. As you create and format documents in the future, remember that the on-line help system provides a guide to where the commands are located.

CHAPTER 5

Using the WordPerfect Speller and Thesaurus

WordPerfect includes two features useful in writing and reviewing your documents: a 116,000-word expandable spelling checker and a thesaurus feature that contains more than 111,000 reference words.

With the Speller, you can check an entire document or parts of a document for misspelled words. The Speller also enables you to check the spelling of words not contained in a document.

If you work in a field that requires the use of special terms, the Speller enables you to create a user dictionary that includes frequently used terms not found in the WordPerfect dictionary. You even can create more than one English user dictionary; however, you may find the multiple files inconvenient to manage. (You can use only one user dictionary at a time for any specific language.)

You can use the Thesaurus to enliven your writing by replacing repetitious words within a document with suggested synonyms and antonyms. You also can use the Thesaurus to look up words not included in a document.

The following list includes some of the features discussed in this chapter:

- Locating and replacing misspelled words within a document
- Adding words to the user dictionary
- Checking the spelling of words—including parts of words—not included in a document
- Looking up words in the Thesaurus and inserting them into the text

Using the Speller

WordPerfect comes with a dictionary, the WordPerfect dictionary, that you can use to check for misspellings within your document. Although the this dictionary is extensive, it may not contain all the words that appear in your document. If you routinely use technical words or proper names not found in the WordPerfect dictionary, you can put them into a *user dictionary*.

When you check a document for spelling, the WordPerfect Speller compares each word in the document first to the list of words in the WordPerfect dictionary and then in the user dictionary. If the Speller fails to find the word in either location, the Speller flags the word as misspelled. You can replace the flagged word by choosing a word from the list provided, typing your own replacement, adding the word to the user dictionary, or leaving the word as it is.

The following sections fully explain each option. A practice session also is provided so that you can develop your skills using the Speller.

Selecting Text To Spell-Check

With the WordPerfect Speller, you can spell-check an entire document (the default setting), a selected section within a document, or text from the insertion point to the end of the document.

To spell-check a part of the document, you select the text you intend to spell-check. Choosing another option from a menu is not necessary. To spell-check the document from the insertion point to the end, choose To End from the Check menu of the Speller dialog box.

Spell-Checking an Entire Document

The Speller checks the entire document unless you highlighted a section of text. The Speller also checks the entire document regardless of the location of the insertion point within the document.

Follow these steps to spell-check an entire document:

1. Open the Speller dialog box, shown in figure 5.1, by choosing Speller from the Tools menu.

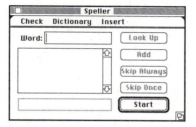

Fig. 5.1 The Speller dialog box.

You can view the default settings by clicking the Check menu (see fig. 5.2). A check mark appears beside the active settings. By default, the Speller checks the entire document, checks for words with numbers, checks for duplicate words, and suggests spelling corrections based on an analysis of the phonetics of misspelled words.

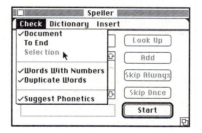

Fig. 5.2 The Speller's default settings.

2. Click Start.

WordPerfect checks the entire document for misspelled words, for words combined with numbers, and duplicate words.

Chapter 5
Using the WordPerfect Speller and Thesaurus

Spell-Checking a Part of a Document

At times, you may want to check the spelling of only a part of a document. The Speller enables you to check the spelling of a single word, a paragraph, or several pages. You may find this feature useful if you are unsure of the spelling of a particular word, for example, or if you added several paragraphs to a document after spell-checking the rest of the document.

Follow these steps to spell-check a section of a document:

1. Select the text to be spell-checked.
2. Choose Speller from the Tools menu. Because you selected text, the check mark has moved from Document (the default setting) to Selection on the Check menu (see fig. 5.3).

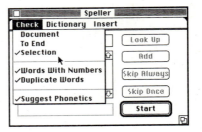

Fig. 5.3
Changing the default setting to Selection.

3. Click Start.

The Speller checks the selected text for misspelled words.

Spell-Checking from the Insertion Point to the End

Suppose that you type and spell-check a 10-page document. The next day, you add 5 pages. Because the first 10 pages include several proper names not listed in the WordPerfect dictionary or the user dictionary, spell-checking those pages is more time-consuming than usual. To avoid rechecking the first 10 pages, you can check the spelling of the last 5 pages by using another Speller feature—spell-checking from the insertion point to the end of the document.

To spell-check a document from the insertion point location to the end of the document, follow these steps:

1. Place the insertion point at the beginning of the text to be checked.

Tip
You can select as much of the document to spell-check as you want—up to several pages. Consider, however, the time needed to select the text compared with the time needed to use another spell-checking method.

Part I
Getting Started

2. Choose Speller from the Tools menu.
3. Pull down the Check menu and choose To End. The check mark appears beside To End.
4. Click Start.

The Speller checks the document from the location of the insertion point to the end.

Using Other Check Menu Options

The Check menu has three other options. The first two—Words With Numbers and Duplicate Words—affect how the Speller checks your document. The third option, Suggest Phonetics, affects the list of suggested alternate spellings offered for a misspelled word.

Checking Words with Numbers

The Speller recognizes some number-letter combinations—for example, the ordinal numbers *1st* through *20th*. The Speller stops, however, at any combination not in the dictionary and flags the combination as a misspelled word. If you frequently use certain number-letter combinations—for example, you live on 25th Street and often write a friend who lives in Apt. 2A— you can add these combinations to your user dictionary. (The next section covers adding words to the user dictionary.)

If you have several one-time uses of number-letter combinations, however, you may prefer to deactivate the Words With Numbers option. Turn off the Words With Numbers option by following these steps:

1. Choose Speller from the Tools menu.
2. Pull down the Check menu in the Speller dialog box. You see a check mark in front of the Words With Numbers option.
3. Drag the pointer to the Words With Numbers option and release the mouse button. The check mark indicator disappears, indicating that the Words With Numbers option is turned off.

The Speller now ignores any words with numbers, an action that is useful when you use formulas or equations, such as H_2O or $E=mc^2$. The Speller also ignores legitimate misspellings, however, such as *y4ar* for *year*.

If you do another spell-check of this document, the Speller returns to the default setting of Words With Numbers and checks the document for number-letter combinations.

Checking for Duplicate Words

If your document contains two identical consecutive words, the Speller flags the words and displays an alert box asking whether you want to delete one of the words (see fig. 5.4). Choose Yes to delete the duplicate; choose No to skip the duplicate. To return to the Speller dialog box, choose Cancel.

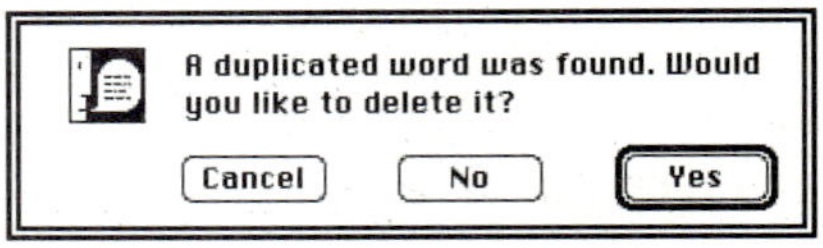

Fig. 5.4
The alert box for duplicate words.

To turn off this feature, click Duplicate Words in the Speller's Check menu so that the check mark disappears (refer to fig. 5.3).

> **Tip**
> WordPerfect provides an alternative to turning off Words With Numbers for the entire document. If you have several formulas in one section of your document, mark that text as Generic Language (covered later in this chapter). The Speller skips that section.

Controlling the Search for Phonetic Suggestions

When the Speller finds a word that is not in the WordPerfect or user dictionary, the feature applies two sets of rules to make suggestions for alternate spellings. The first set of rules is alphabetic—which checks for what is usually thought of as a typo—and the second set of rules is phonetic.

The suggested alternate spellings are grouped together. WordPerfect lists the alphabetic suggestions first and the phonetic suggestions next. A line separates the two groups (see fig. 5.5).

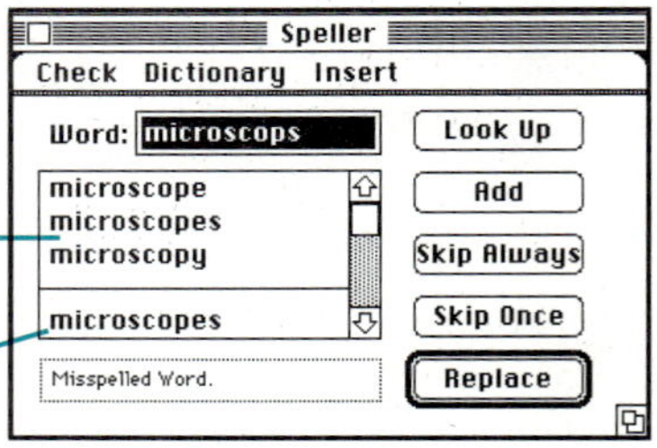

Fig. 5.5
Alphabetic and phonetic spelling suggestions.

Typographic suggestions

Phonetic suggestions

Part I
Getting Started

Disabling Suggest Phonetics reduces the length of time required to check spelling. If you are a good speller or if you are spell-checking a long document, you may want to turn Suggest Phonetics off. (With the Suggest Phonetics option off, however, you may have to type the correct spelling into the Word text box for a flagged word.)

If your spelling abilities are a little rusty, however, you may want to rely on a more extensive word list from which you can select the correctly spelled word. The next section covers replacing misspelled words.

Running the Speller

After you set the options on the Check menu in the Speller dialog box, you can spell-check your document.

When the Speller flags a misspelled word, you have several options. You can replace the word with one of the suggestions from the dictionaries, add the word to your user dictionary so that the Speller doesn't stop at the word in the future, skip the word once or throughout the document, or type the correction in the Word text box.

Replacing Misspelled Words

When the Speller cannot find a word in either dictionary, the Speller flags the word as misspelled and displays the word in the Word text box. Similarly spelled words included in the WordPerfect dictionary appear in a list box as alternative spelling choices. If the appropriate spelling appears in the list, click the word and then click Replace. WordPerfect replaces the misspelled word in the document with the alternative spelling you selected.

Adding Words to the User Dictionary

You should add to the user dictionary frequently used technical words and proper names not included in the WordPerfect dictionary. You can add as many words to the user dictionary as you want (as long as you have disk space), but the more words you add, the longer spell-checking a document takes.

To add a word to the user dictionary, follow these steps:

1. When the program flags a word that you want to add to your user dictionary during a routine spell-check, make sure that the word is spelled correctly. If necessary, check a technical manual, a map, or the phone book for the correct spelling.

2. Click Add in the Speller dialog box. The computer beeps, indicating that the program added the word to the user dictionary.

If you misspell a word spelled correctly in your user dictionary, the Speller does not display an alternative spelling. You must type the correct spelling in the Word text box and click Replace. Suppose, for example, that you correspond with a business in Roseville, MI. You add Roseville to your user dictionary. If you misspell the word as *Rooseville*, the word *Roseville* does not appear among the choices in the word list. All alternate spellings come from the WordPerfect dictionary, not the user dictionary.

You can incorporate your user dictionary words into the WordPerfect dictionary by using the ST Utility application, which is included on the WordPerfect 2.1 distribution disks. The application also is installed on your hard disk if you used the Easy Install method of installing the program (see Appendix A). See the "Using ST Utility" section at the end of this chapter for more information.

Skipping Words

Sometimes words in a document are spelled correctly but do not appear in the dictionary and are not likely to be used again. Rather than add these words to the user dictionary, you can skip the word and move on to the next word. You can skip words by choosing Skip Once or Skip Always.

If you click Skip Once, the Speller ignores that occurrence of the word but flags later occurrences of the word. If you click Skip Always, the Speller ignores all occurrences of the word during that session with the Speller. (WordPerfect flags the word the next time you spell-check the document, however.)

Practicing with the Speller

To practice checking spelling, do the following exercise. Type the following list of words and phrases in a new document window. Type the words exactly as they appear (the numbers are for your reference):

1. serch
2. Their is the book.
3. amygdala
4. corpora quadrigemina

Part I
Getting Started

5. Peter
6. Schnecksville
7. 22nd Street
8. I had had a terrible day.
9. eariest
10. paradocks
11. quadrigemina
12. Schnecksville

As you spell-check the words in this list, you can see a demonstration of the different features of the Speller. First, choose Speller from the Tools menu and press ⌘-E to check the entire document. Click Start to begin the spell-check, and then follow along with the list as the Speller checks each word:

1. The first word to be flagged is *serch*. The most likely correction appears at the top of the word list box. Other possible words, including the closest match again, appear below in the word list box (see fig. 5.6).

Fig. 5.6
Possible alternatives for a misspelled word.

In this case, click *search*; then click Replace to replace *serch* with *search* in your document. The Speller moves to the next word.

2. Although *Their* is used incorrectly in this sentence, the program doesn't flag the word because it is spelled correctly. The Speller checks spelling only, not grammar.

3. *Amygdala*, a region in the brain, is not a household word but is in the WordPerfect dictionary and, therefore, is not flagged.

4. The word *quadrigemina* in *corpora quadrigemina* (another region in the brain) is neither a household word nor found the WordPerfect dictionary. You can choose to Skip Once, Skip Always, or Add (to add the word to the user dictionary). In this case, click Skip Always.

5. *Peter* is a proper name listed in the WordPerfect dictionary. The program doesn't flag this name.

6. *Schnecksville*, another proper name that is spelled correctly, is not in the dictionary and is flagged. Again, you can Skip Once, Skip Always, or Add. In this case, click Skip Once.

7. The Speller flags *22nd* next and asks whether you meant *2nd*. Choose Skip (Once or Always).

8. The program flags the double occurrence of *had* in this sentence. The program asks whether you want to delete one of the words. Whether you click Yes or No depends on what meaning you are trying to convey in that sentence.

    You also can click Cancel to return to the Speller dialog box. If you choose Cancel, the To End option in the Check pull-down menu automatically is active so that you can continue with the Speller from where you left off.

9. The next word flagged is *eariest*. Unlike *serch*, *eariest* does not have a closest match because this spelling is equally similar to more than one word. Select the appropriate word from the list and replace the misspelled word.

10. The word *paradocks* shows a limitation to the Speller. The word *paradox* is the correct spelling, but because the misspelled word ends with an *s*, the Speller searches for an alternative word that also ends with *s* and gives as the only choice the word *paradoxes*. You must type the word *paradox* in the Word text box and click Replace.

11. The program doesn't flag the second occurrence of *quadrigemina* because you pressed Skip Always for this entry earlier.

12. The program flags the second occurrence of *Schnecksville* because you clicked Skip Once at the first occurrence. Skip the word again and click the close box.

In this exercise, you have seen several features of the Speller. You experienced how easy the Speller is to use and saw that some limitations exist, especially with grammatical errors.

Part I
Getting Started

> **Tip**
>
> To return to your document without exiting the Speller, drag the Speller dialog box part of the way out of your document window. By doing this, you easily can click the visible part of the dialog box to return to the Speller.

You can exit the Speller at any time by clicking the close box. You also can interrupt the spell-checking process at any time to return to your document without exiting the Speller, and then return to the Speller to resume spell-checking. After you return to the Speller, the To End option in the Check pull-down menu is selected. After you click the Start button, the Speller begins from the location of the insertion point and continues to the end.

Looking Up a Word Not in the Document

You also can use the Speller to look up words not included in your document. Type the word directly into the Word text box in the Speller dialog box, and click Look Up.

You're not likely to use this feature often, but if you are in the Speller, you may decide to look up a word that you expect to use later in your document.

Entering the Word

Type the word you want to look up or as close an approximation as possible. When you enter just one letter in the Word text box, the Look Up button changes from gray to black, indicating that this option is enabled. Click the Look Up button so that the Speller checks the word and provides alternative spellings if the word is misspelled.

Using Wild Cards

If you are unsure of one or more letters in a word, you can type the letters you know and insert special characters, called *wild cards*, for the letters of which you are unsure. The Speller uses a question mark to replace one unknown character and an ellipsis to replace multiple adjacent unknown letters.

You choose Speller from the Tools menu or press ⌘-E. When the mouse pointer appears in the Word text box, type the portion of the word you know. Insert wild cards where necessary by pulling down the Insert menu and choosing the appropriate option (see fig. 5.7).

Fig. 5.7
Pulling down the Insert menu to choose a wild card.

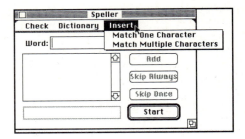

Suppose that you are not sure whether a word ends in *able* or *ible*. Follow these steps to choose a wild card:

1. Type *cap* in the Word text box of the Speller dialog box.
2. Pull down the Insert menu and choose Match One Character. The program inserts a question mark after the *p*.
3. Type the remainder of the word, *ble*, and click Look Up.

The Speller compares the word you typed with words in its dictionary and finds a match. The word *capable* appears in the Word text box (see fig. 5.8).

Fig. 5.8
Looking up a word with one unknown letter.

> **Tip**
> When inserting a single-character wild card, you can save time by typing a question mark from the keyboard instead of pulling down the Insert menu.

You can use more than one single-character wild card in a word, but each entry represents a single letter. If you are not sure whether *height* or *hieght* is correct, for example, you can type *h??ght* in the Word text box and click Look Up. The Speller displays the word *height*.

Suppose that you want a list of words (of any length) that end in *cate*. You can use a multiple-character wild card to represent the beginning of the word, and then type *cate* at the end.

Part I
Getting Started

Follow these steps to insert a multiple-character wild card:

1. Choose Speller from the Tools menu or press ⌘-E. The insertion point appears at the beginning of the Word text box.

2. Pull down the dialog box's Insert menu and choose Match Multiple Characters (or press Option-;). WordPerfect inserts an ellipsis into the Word text box. You also can use the asterisk (*) to match multiple characters.

3. Type *cate* after the dots and click Look Up.

Five words appear in the Word List box, and at the bottom of the dialog box, the Speller notes that it found 106 words (see fig. 5.9). You can scroll down the list to see the other 101 words.

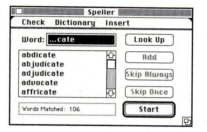

Fig. 5.9
Using a multiple-character wild card.

The multiple-character wild card cannot be produced by typing three periods from the keyboard.

Using Set Language To Limit Spell-Checking

If you have a section of a document that you do not want spell-checked, you can put a generic language marker around that section. Using this option is ideal if you included a foreign language passage, for example, or a mathematical equation into your document. You can set generic language as you enter the text or mark this setting after the text has been entered.

To set generic language as you type, follow these steps:

1. Choose Language from the Tools menu; then choose Set Language.

Chapter 5
Using the WordPerfect Speller and Thesaurus

2. Scroll down the list until you come to Generic (No Spell). Click the option (see fig. 5.10).

Fig. 5.10
Choosing Generic (No Spell) in the Set Language dialog box.

3. Click OK or double-click Generic (No Spell).
4. Type the text that should not be spell-checked.
5. After you finish entering the text, return to Set Language and choose US-English. The program checks the text you type after that point for spelling errors.

To set generic language after you enter the text, follow these steps:

1. Select the text.
2. Choose Language from the Tools menu; then choose Set Language.
3. Scroll down the list until you come to Generic (No Spell). Click the option. The program marks the highlighted text as generic.

> **Tip**
> Selecting the text after it has been entered is easier and saves a few keystrokes.

Selecting Alternate-Language Dictionaries

In the United States, WordPerfect normally is shipped with a US-English language dictionary. If you write documents in another language and have installed a WordPerfect dictionary for that language, you can choose that language's dictionary from Language in the Tools menu before you begin entering text in your document. When the language is marked in your document, WordPerfect uses the selected dictionary as it does a spell-check.

If no other language codes are in the document, you can use another method to get WordPerfect to use a dictionary other than the one determined by the installed language module (your default language).

Part I
Getting Started

The only time this method is useful is when the Speller is open, and you realize that the document is not in your default language and doesn't have a language code in the document to indicate the correct language.

Using the Dictionary menu in the Speller dialog box is easier than returning to the document and inserting a language code. To change dictionaries after you are in the Speller, pull down the Dictionary menu and choose the new dictionary (see fig. 5.11). Then proceed with the normal spell-checking operations.

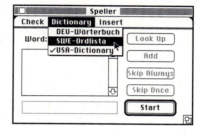

Fig. 5.11
Choosing a different dictionary in the Speller dialog box.

If any language codes are in the document (see the preceding section for more on Set Language), the Speller switches dictionaries when it reaches the language code and doesn't return to the choice you made in the Dictionary menu.

Using the Thesaurus

Suppose that you used the same word several times throughout your document, and you know that another word—which you cannot remember—can convey the same meaning. Instead of racking your brain for a synonym, reach for a thesaurus.

WordPerfect comes with a thesaurus, which you use to look up synonyms and antonyms for many words. You even can look up words that are not in your document.

Looking Up a Word

Looking up a word in the WordPerfect Thesaurus is easy, simple, a snap. The feature even can provide some entertainment on a slow afternoon.

Chapter 5
Using the WordPerfect Speller and Thesaurus

To look up a word in your document, follow these steps:

1. Place the insertion point at the word you want to look up—*document*, for example. You can place the insertion point before, after, or within the word. You also can select the word.

2. Choose Thesaurus from the Tools menu or press ⌘-Shift-T. The Thesaurus dialog box appears with the word *document* in the Word text box (see fig. 5.12).

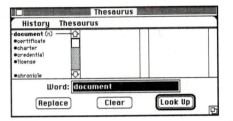

Fig. 5.12
Looking up a word in the Thesaurus.

The word *document* also appears as the *headword*, the word at the top of the first column. Below the headword is a list of synonyms and antonyms called *reference* words. WordPerfect groups reference words by similarities in connotation or by parts of speech, such as noun or verb. These groupings are *subgroups*.

Scroll down the list. Near the end, after the synonyms, you again see document (ant), which indicates that the following words are antonyms.

3. To replace the word in your document with a word from the list, click the new word; then click the Replace button. The new word replaces the selected word in your document.

To look up a word that is not in your document, follow these steps:

1. Open the Thesaurus.

2. Type the word into the Word text box.

3. Click Look Up.

If the computer beeps when you open the Thesaurus, the word you selected is not among the headwords. You must try another word.

Extending a Document Word Search

If you do not find an appropriate word from the list, you can extend your search by looking up synonyms and antonyms of the words included in the list. A bullet in front of a word indicates a word with other entries in the Thesaurus. Click one of these words—for example, *certificate*—then click Look Up. *Certificate* becomes the headword in the second column, and synonyms and antonyms appear below (see fig. 5.13).

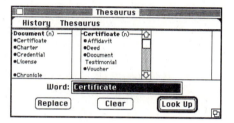

Fig. 5.13
Headwords in two columns in the thesaurus.

To extend the search further, click another word in either list and click Look Up. Another list appears in the third column. Each time you select a new word from either list, the new list of synonyms and antonyms appears in the third column.

Displaying a Search History

Suppose that you start your search by looking for synonyms for the word *pretty*. You extend the search until you arrive at the word *nonpartisan*. If you wonder how you got from *pretty* to *nonpartisan*, click History in the Thesaurus dialog box to see the list of headwords you looked up during your search. The words appear in reverse order, with the most recent headword at the top of the list and the original headword at the bottom (see fig. 5.14).

As you look at the list of words on the History menu, you may decide to look up additional synonyms for one of those words listed in the history. Click the word on the History list; that word replaces the word in the active column. You now can continue your search along a new branch.

Chapter 5
Using the WordPerfect Speller and Thesaurus

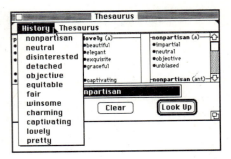

Fig. 5.14
Displaying the history of a Thesaurus search.

If you look up the same word more than once, only the last search with that word shows up in the history. WordPerfect removes from the list previous searches using that word. For example, if you look up *sad*, *melancholy*, *gloom*, *melancholy*, in that order, the History menu lists (from bottom to top) *sad*, *gloom*, *melancholy*.

Clearing a Column

With the Thesaurus, when all three columns are full and you look up another word, WordPerfect replaces the third column. To retain the third column, you must clear the first or second column. The next word list then appears in the cleared column.

To clear a column, follow these steps:

1. Click the column you want to clear.

2. Click Clear. After all three columns are full again, WordPerfect replaces the third column—not the column that you cleared—if you continue your word search.

> **Tip**
> Clicking the Clear button clears only a column. The History remains intact.

Looking Up a Nondocument Word

In the preceding section, you learned how to replace a word in your document with a word from the Thesaurus. This section explains how to insert a new word from the Thesaurus into your document. If you do not want to use the word *document* again, for example, you can go directly to the Thesaurus for a new word by following these steps:

1. Place the insertion point where you want the new word to appear. Make sure that the insertion point is not touching another word in the document; otherwise, that word is selected and replaced when you choose a word in the Thesaurus.

Part I
Getting Started

2. Choose Thesaurus from the Tools menu.

3. Type *document* in the Word text box and click Look Up. Select a word in the list—for example, *chronicle*—and click Replace. WordPerfect inserts *chronicle* into your document.

If you are at the end of your document, WordPerfect inserts the new word at the insertion point. If you are within the document, the word appears one space beyond the insertion point.

Using ST Utility

WordPerfect 2.1 is shipped with a second application, ST Utility, which, among other things, enables you to make changes to your existing dictionaries. All previous versions of WordPerfect for the Macintosh enable you to view and edit your user dictionary as a text file. With ST Utility, you can make changes to the WordPerfect dictionary.

ST Utility is so new that the original Version 2.1 documentation doesn't mention the feature at all. Undoubtedly, many changes will be made to the details of how ST Utility works, but for now you can make changes to dictionaries, find out how many words are in the dictionary and thesaurus, and make a list of the headwords in the thesaurus.

The installer places ST Utility in the WordPerfect 2.1 folder when you install the rest of the WordPerfect application and associated files. If you did a custom installation and did not include ST Utility, you can copy the feature directly from the WordPerfect 3 floppy disk. See Appendix A, "Installing WordPerfect," for more information on installation and the distribution disks.

Modifying Existing Dictionaries

The most useful aspect of ST Utility is the capability of adding words to the WordPerfect dictionary. You even can incorporate your entire user dictionary in the WordPerfect dictionary.

If you merge the dictionaries, the Speller includes your added words in the suggested alternative spellings for flagged words. The Speller also may be slightly faster when checking a document because the Speller doesn't have to check a second file for the words added to the main dictionary.

Follow these steps to open the WordPerfect dictionary for editing:

1. In the Finder, double-click the WordPerfect 2.1 folder to open the folder.

2. Double-click the ST Utility icon. You may have to use the window scroll bars to find the application because the installer isn't particularly neat when arranging the icons of files it installs.

   A standard Macintosh file list appears (see fig. 5.15). This list shows only the dictionaries, thesaurus files, and other folders in the folder containing ST Utility. You can switch folders using the standard file list navigation techniques for the Mac.

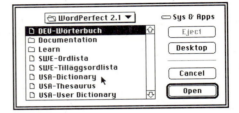

Fig. 5.15
The Open Dictionary/Thesaurus dialog box.

   Your list may show only USA-Dictionary and USA-Thesaurus unless you used the Speller to add words to your user dictionary, USA-user dictionary. You also probably don't see the Swedish and German dictionaries shown in fig. 5.15.

3. Open the file by double-clicking the USA-Dictionary file name. Alternatively, clicking the file once; then click the Open button or press Return.

The ST Utility window for the USA-Dictionary opens (see fig. 5.16). Most of the window is blank. You use the text box near the bottom to enter words for searching the dictionary. Because this text box is the only one in the window, anything you type appears there; you don't have to select the text box first.

This dialog box also includes buttons you use to add, delete, and look up words in the dictionary. Another button in the dialog box, Add From Dictionary File, enables you to combine whole dictionaries—for example, adding all the words in your user dictionary to the main WordPerfect dictionary. You also can use this button to import a PC WordPerfect dictionary to the Mac, provided that you can get the dictionary onto a Mac disk or file server accessible to your Mac.

Fig. 5.16
The ST Utility window.

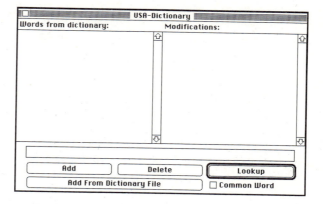

The single check box option in the ST Utility speller window, Common Word, affects words added to the open dictionary. WordPerfect maintains a short list of the most common words used in any particular language so that spelling searches can be faster. If you add to the dictionary a word that you want to be on the Common Word list, click the Common Word check box before you add the word to the dictionary. To see the list of common words in your dictionary, press ⌘-R or choose Show Common from the Speller menu after you open a dictionary.

> **Tip**
> Searching the dictionary before adding a word is a good idea so that you don't duplicate a word that already exists in the dictionary.

As an example of adding words to the dictionary, follow these steps:

1. In the ST Utility (opened in the preceding steps), type *electroch**. (You also can press Option-; for the ellipsis rather than use the asterisk for the Match Many Characters function.)

2. Press Return or click the Lookup button. ST Utility searches the dictionary and displays the words that match the search criteria (see fig. 5.17).

   Notice that ST Utility displays the possible hyphenation locations for each word it finds in the dictionary. You cannot edit the hyphenation information. You also cannot supply any hyphenation information for the words you are adding to the dictionary.

3. Type *electrochemist*; then click the Add button or press ⌘-=.

4. Type *electrochemists*; then click Add or press ⌘-=. The Modifications section of the ST Utility window lists the words you add (see fig. 5.18).

Chapter 5
Using the WordPerfect Speller and Thesaurus

Fig. 5.17
The results of a word search in ST Utility.

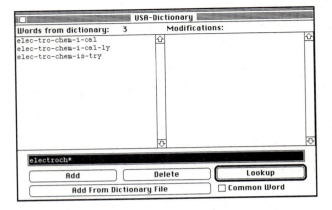

Fig. 5.18
Words to be added to the dictionary.

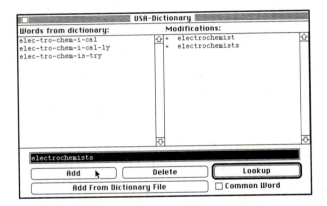

5. Choose Save from the File menu or press ⌘-S to save the changes in the dictionary.

If you perform the same search as described in steps 1 and 2, you can see the words you added in the Words from Dictionary section of the ST Utility window. The added words don't have any hyphenation information, which is one way to determine which words originally came with the dictionary. (Of course, if you are adding words to your user dictionary, because no words should be hyphenated in the Words from Dictionary list, you cannot tell what words have been added.)

After you save the changes, you can close the dictionary window by clicking the close box or choosing Close from the File menu. After you finish using ST Utility, you can choose Quit from the File menu or press ⌘-Q to close the dictionary window and quit ST Utility.

Deleting Words from a Dictionary

You can delete words from a dictionary file. Deleting words should be necessary only if you make a mistake adding words to one of your dictionaries or if you want to delete some temporary words (such as unusual proper names) in your user dictionary.

To delete a word from a dictionary, follow these steps:

1. Launch ST Utility and open the dictionary, as described earlier.
2. Type the word you want to delete in the ST Utility text box.
3. Click Lookup or press Return.
4. Select the word you are deleting from the Words from Dictionary list.
5. Click the Delete button or press ⌘- –. The word you are deleting appears in the Modifications list with a – next to it.
6. Choose Save from the File menu or press ⌘-S. WordPerfect removes the word from the dictionary and the Modifications list box. Changes you make to the dictionary are not permanent until you save the changes.

If you make a mistake and accidentally add something to the Modifications list that doesn't belong there, click the word in the Modifications list box and click the Delete button. WordPerfect removes the word from the Modifications list, and no change is made to the word when you save the dictionary.

Creating New Dictionaries

You can use ST Utility to create new dictionaries, but the task is likely to cause you more trouble than it is worth. WordPerfect expects dictionaries to have specific names, and unusual names make the dictionary more difficult to use.

The only way to use a specially created dictionary is to choose it from the Dictionaries menu in the Speller dialog box, as described earlier in the "Selecting Alternate-Language Dictionaries" section. Any language codes inserted in your document deselects the special dictionary. Also, while using your special dictionary in the Speller, if you click the Add button to add a word to your user dictionary, WordPerfect renames your existing user dictionary to something like Bak_USA-User Dictionary and creates a new USA-User Dictionary file to hold the word you were trying to add.

User dictionaries created in ST Utility *must* have the same name that WordPerfect would give a user dictionary created by the Speller (USA-User Dictionary for most people in the United States). If you create a user dictionary with a different name, WordPerfect will never use that dictionary from the Speller.

If you can live with the limitations listed in the preceding paragraphs and want to create your own dictionary, follow these steps:

1. If ST Utility is not running, launch ST Utility and click Cancel after the Mac file list appears.

2. If ST Utility is running, close any open dictionary or thesaurus files.

3. Choose New from the File menu or press ⌘-N. The New File dialog box appears (see fig. 5.19).

Fig. 5.19
The New File dialog box in ST Utility.

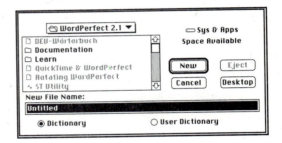

4. Type the name of your new dictionary in the New File name text box.

5. Click the Dictionary or user dictionary radio button at the bottom of the dialog box to set the type of dictionary you are creating.

6. If you are creating a user dictionary and a user dictionary already exists in the same folder containing ST Utility, change folders by using the standard Mac file navigation methods.

7. Click the New button or press Return.

ST Utility creates the new, empty dictionary file and displays the editing window (refer to fig. 5.17). You can add as many words as you want. Save the dictionary before you quit ST Utility, however, or the dictionary—although present—will be empty.

Using ST Utility with Thesaurus Files

ST Utility performs only two functions on thesaurus files that you cannot perform with the WordPerfect Thesaurus function: creating a list of headwords and counting the number of headwords and cross-references in the thesaurus file. Although you can look up words in the thesaurus by using ST Utility, you get only a single word list with no history information. The WordPerfect Thesaurus provides more flexibility for looking up words.

To count headwords and cross-references or to create a headword list, you first must open a thesaurus file. If you have a dictionary open, you must close it before you open a thesaurus.

If ST Utility is open, and you have closed any other files opened by ST Utility, follow these steps:

1. Choose Open from the File menu or press ⌘-O.

2. Use the file list to find the thesaurus file (USA-Thesaurus for most users in the United States).

3. Double-click the thesaurus file name to open the file. The ST Utility thesaurus window, USA-Thesaurus, opens (see fig. 5.20).

Fig. 5.20
The ST Utility thesaurus window.

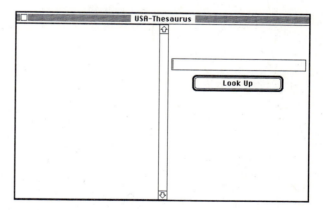

4. Choose Word Count from the Thesaurus menu or press ⌘-N. After a minute or so, an alert box appears (see fig. 5.21).

Chapter 5
Using the WordPerfect Speller and Thesaurus

Fig. 5.21
The word count alert box.

5. Click OK or press Return to remove the alert box.
6. Choose List Headwords from the Thesaurus menu or press ⌘-H.
7. A standard Mac save file dialog box appears. Type the appropriate file name and click Save (or press Return).

ST Utility creates a text file containing all the headwords from the thesaurus file. To look at the list, launch WordPerfect and open the file in the usual fashion.

After you finish with the thesaurus file, you can close the Thesaurus by clicking the close box of the ST Utility thesaurus window, choosing Close from the File menu, or pressing ⌘-W. Because you cannot make any changes to a thesaurus file in ST Utility, you also can quit ST Utility (press ⌘-Q or choose Quit from the File menu); the thesaurus file closes before the application quits.

Counting Words in a Dictionary

Not many compelling reasons exist for counting words in a dictionary, but the task is possible in the ST Utility. Although ST Utility has no specific command to tell you how many words are in a dictionary, you can find out the number by using the Lookup function. Type an asterisk (*) or create an ellipsis (...) by pressing Option-; as the only character in the ST Utility window text box, and then click Lookup.

After several seconds (or more, depending on the size of your dictionary and the speed of your Mac), ST Utility displays an alert box to tell you that only 2,844 out of however many words are in the dictionary can be displayed at one time.

Part I
Getting Started

Chapter Summary

This chapter explained how to check all or part of a document for misspelled words, how to check the spelling of a particular word, and how to replace misspelled words in a document. You also learned how to create your own user dictionary for frequently used technical words and other unusual words.

This chapter also reviewed how to use the Thesaurus to replace repetitious words in a document and to enhance the text with a well-placed adverb or adjective. Finally, several features of the speller/thesaurus utility (called ST Utility) were discussed, the most important being the capability to add and delete words from any WordPerfect dictionary file.

Chapter 5
Using the WordPerfect Speller and Thesaurus

CHAPTER 6

Printing a Document

In Chapter 1, "Quick Start: Creating a Business Letter," you learned how to print a basic document without using any of the special features WordPerfect makes available. In this chapter, you learn how to print a larger document, print selected portions of a document, and make multiple copies. You also learn ways to make a printed document look more professional.

When you complete this chapter, you will be able to do the following:

- Choose a printer
- Set up a page for printing
- Preview documents before printing
- Choose print features
- Print documents and envelopes

Choosing a Printer

The first time you print from your Macintosh, you must choose your printer. (If you have not yet installed your printer, see the printer manual for instructions.) You choose a printer through the Chooser option in the Apple menu. Even though you may have only one printer driver installed, you must perform this step. If you have previously printed documents from your Macintosh, however, you perform this step only to change printers.

The type of printer determines which port is used. Serial printers connect to the printer port or communications port. Networked printers connect to the printer port using the AppleTalk network system, or to an EtherNet port if a high-speed network is available. SCSI (Small Computer System Interface) printers connect to the SCSI port—the same port used by external hard disk drives.

To make things more confusing, you can connect simultaneously to the same Macintosh printers using different cabling and communications methods. Although you must choose one printer to use at any given time, you may have other printers connected. The method of choosing a printer is similar, regardless of how the printer is connected to the computer; however, the few differences may lead to confusion.

To choose a printer, follow these steps:

1. Select Chooser from the Apple menu. The Chooser dialog box appears (see fig. 6.1).

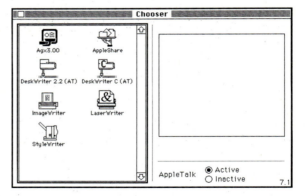

Fig. 6.1
The Chooser dialog box.

2. Click the icon of the printer you want to use.

   If you click the icon of a LaserWriter or other networked printer, a list of the available printers appears in the right box of the Chooser dialog box (see fig. 6.2). If you have previously used the selected printer, the name of that printer is highlighted in the printer name list.

Fig. 6.2
Choosing a networked printer.

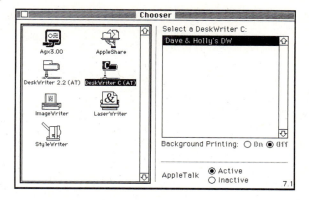

3. From the printer list in the right box, click the name of the appropriate printer.
4. Click the close box of the Chooser dialog box.

Although these steps are fairly straightforward, several things may happen as you choose a printer. AppleTalk, a communications protocol built into the Macintosh system, must be active to print to a networked printer. If you choose a networked printer and leave the AppleTalk radio button in the lower right of the Chooser dialog box set to Inactive, your Macintosh presents a warning box that reminds you to make sure that the printer is connected properly to the Mac and offers to activate AppleTalk. Make sure you are not connected to a serial printer before the system activates AppleTalk.

Don't connect printers or other devices to your Macintosh while the Macintosh or the printer is turned on. Shut down the Mac and turn off the printer before connecting or disconnecting cables on the Mac.

If your Mac is connected to a large network with many zones, you must choose a *zone*, which is a smaller section of a larger network, before you choose a printer in the Chooser dialog box. The list of zones appears at the lower left of the Chooser dialog box. Because zones normally are named by work group (for example, Engineering) or by location (Bldg B, 3rd fl), figuring out the zone for your computer and nearby printers is usually easy.

Chapter 6
Printing a Document

If you choose a serial printer rather than a networked printer in the Chooser dialog box, a list of ports appears in the right scroll box (see fig. 6.3). Click the icon of the port to which you have attached the printer. The Printer port is the top icon; the Modem port is the bottom icon. These icons match the icons that are embossed in the case of the Macintosh next to the connector ports on the back of the computer. After you choose the appropriate port, click the close box of the Chooser.

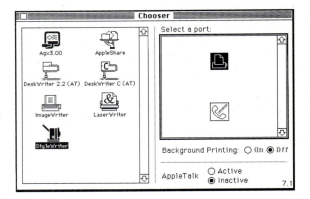

Fig. 6.3
Choosing a serial printer.

If, while the AppleTalk option is active, you choose a serial printer that is connected to the Printer port, a dialog box warning you that AppleTalk must be off appears. Clicking the Cancel button in the warning box enables you to choose a different printer from the Chooser dialog box. If you deactivate AppleTalk, you lose access to all the network services (file sharing with other Macs and communication with file servers), not just the networked printers.

If you use the Chooser to change printers (even when you change from no printer to your only printer the first time you use your Mac), a dialog box indicating that you changed printers and must use Page Setup in each open application appears. Because the dialog box is only a reminder, you can proceed by clicking OK.

The system also reminds you to use Page Setup because applications such as WordPerfect check which printer is used only when you first open the application, just before you print, or when you click OK in the Page Setup dialog box. In addition, if you change printers without telling WordPerfect, the line and page breaks of your printed document may be different than the line and page breaks of the document displayed onscreen because different printers may space fonts differently. The next section discusses using the Page Setup dialog box.

Part I
Getting Started

Another setting in the Chooser dialog box is the Background Printing option (refer to fig. 6.2). *Background printing* (or *print spooling*) is a wonderful idea. Most computers can send a document to a printer faster than the printer can print the pages. With background printing, the computer sends the document being printed to an intermediate file and from the intermediate file to the printer. If you use background printing, waiting for the printing to finish before you can continue working at the computer is unnecessary.

> **Tip**
>
> If you frequently send several documents to the printer one after the other, you may find that the Macintosh freezes up. When this happens, you must restart the computer, turn off Background Printing, and send each file to the printer individually.

If you have the background printing controller installed—it normally is installed with the rest of the Macintosh system files—and are printing to a printer that uses the Apple LaserWriter driver, you can turn on Background Printing by clicking the On radio button in the Chooser dialog box after you select the printer.

Although background printing on the Macintosh is not perfect, the feature can save you much time. Few computer delays are more aggravating than waiting for your colleague's 100-page report to print on your networked printer so that you can print your document or continue your work on the computer.

Using Page Setup

ordPerfect and other applications use several settings that vary from printer to printer. These settings are controlled in the Page Setup dialog box.

Previously, describing every page setup option available on the Mac was easy—only two printers existed, the ImageWriter and the LaserWriter. Now dozens of Mac-compatible printers are available. Some third-party printers use the Apple printer drivers, and some manufacturers have written their own drivers. Consequently, each driver and printer have slightly different capabilities and settings. Despite the variety, many similarities exist between the Page Setup dialog boxes for Macintosh printers.

Although the preceding section emphasizes using Page Setup after you choose a printer, you also can use Page Setup to change the options for the current document any time in WordPerfect. In addition, the program saves the Page Setup settings with each document; therefore, returning settings to "normal" if you change settings in other documents is unnecessary. To access the Page Setup dialog box, choose Page Setup from the File menu (see fig. 6.4).

Chapter 6
Printing a Document

Fig. 6.4
Choosing Page Setup from the File menu.

The Page Setup dialog box enables you to choose a paper size and specify the orientation of the paper (tall or wide) for any printer. In addition, many printers offer the capability to scale the print on a page and to choose other options, some of which are provided by an application (see fig. 6.5).

Fig. 6.5
The LaserWriter Page Setup dialog box.

Paper sizes
Print scaling
Paper orientation
Options added by WordPerfect

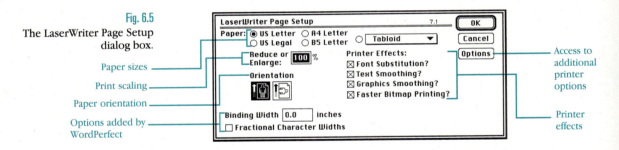

Access to additional printer options

Printer effects

Tip
Remember that Page Setup options apply to an entire document, not just a single page.

The following sections detail the Page Setup options for an Apple LaserWriter printer. The options for other printers depend on the printer's specific capabilities, such as paper bin size, color capabilities, and other hardware-related items. Consult your printer manual for a list of the options specifically available for your printer.

Part I
Getting Started

Paper Size

You can choose among several paper sizes on most printers. The most common paper sizes in the United States are US Letter and US Legal, which are the standard sizes for business and legal correspondence. Table 6.1 lists the paper sizes available in the Apple LaserWriter driver.

Table 6.1
Available Apple LaserWriter Paper Sizes

Paper size	Dimensions	Typical use
US Letter	8 1/2-by-11 inches	Standard business correspondence in U.S.
US Legal	8 1/2-by-14 inches	Standard legal paper in U.S.
A4 Letter	210mm-by-297mm	Metric standard letter size (commonly used in Europe)
B5 Letter	180mm-by-250mm	Another standard European size
Tabloid	11-by-17 inches	Twice the width of US Letter, used for pamphlets and larger artwork
A3 Tabloid	420mm-by-594mm	Twice the size of A4 Letter
Envelope	4 1/8-by-9 1/2 inches	Standard US letter envelope (No. 10)
LaserWriter II B5	A couple of millimeters wider than B5 letter	

Rather than cluttering the dialog box with an ever-expanding set of paper size choices, Apple added a pop-up menu that contains the last four sizes listed in table 6.1 (see fig. 6.6).

Fig. 6.6
Additional paper sizes in the Apple LaserWriter Page Setup dialog box.

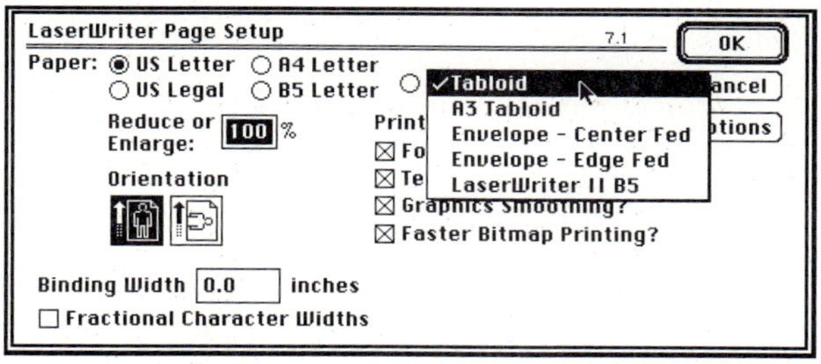

Chapter 6
Printing a Document

Although several paper sizes are listed, your printer must be able to accept the selected size. When you can print on smaller paper sizes, make sure the printer prints on the paper and not on some internal part of the printer.

You use the envelope options in the pop-up menu to indicate how the printer handles an envelope. The original LaserWriter printers (and several current third-party printers) use the edge of the manual feed paper tray to guide an envelope through the printer. To use this method of envelope handling, choose Envelope–Edge Fed in the Page Setup dialog box.

The newer LaserWriter II family of printers has a paper guide that closes down near the middle of the manual feed tray to guide envelopes down the center of the printer's paper path. To use this method, choose Envelope–Center Fed. (*Note:* WordPerfect does not yet recognize the Envelope–Center Fed and Envelope–Edge Fed settings in the LaserWriter Page Setup dialog box. See "Printing Envelopes" at the end of this chapter for instructions on printing envelopes.)

Reduce or Enlarge

With the Reduce or Enlarge setting, you can scale the printing and margins to smaller or larger sizes. Suppose, for example, that a typical document has 10-point text and 1-inch margins. If you type 50 in the Reduce or Enlarge text box of the Page Setup dialog box, the document prints in 5-point text with 1/2-inch margins (50 percent of the text and margin sizes used in the document). Similarly, if you enter 200 in the Reduce or Enlarge text box, the document prints in 20-point text with 2-inch margins (200 percent of your normal settings).

> **Tip**
> Before you print in landscape orientation a document you created in portrait orientation, check your document by using Print Preview. The margins and alignment change with the orientation, but tab settings remain the same.

Because WordPerfect scales the margins and the text size with the Reduce or Enlarge setting, the best use of this option is limited to small adjustments around the 100 percent normal size (90 through 120 percent). To squeeze more of a document onto each page, enter a number between 90 and 98 percent in the Reduce or Enlarge text box in Page Setup. If you want a short note to fill more of a page, set the Reduce or Enlarge option to 105 to 120 percent. Use Print Preview to check the effects of your setting before you print the scaled document.

Part I
Getting Started

Orientation

You can orient your text in one of two ways on the printed page: portrait and landscape orientation. The text in this book, with the print aligned across the width (shortest measure) of the paper, is an example of *portrait orientation* (see fig. 6.7). In *landscape orientation*, the text prints across the length (longest measure) of the paper (see fig. 6.8). Wide tables and trifold brochures frequently are printed in landscape orientation.

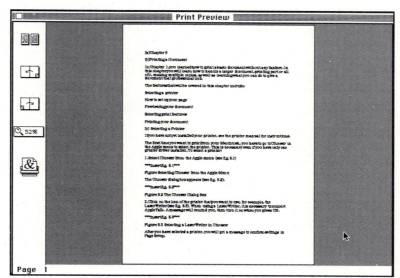

Fig. 6.7
A document in portrait orientation.

Options Added by WordPerfect

If you regularly use other Macintosh applications, you may notice that the Page Setup dialog box is not the same as it appears in other applications (refer to fig. 6.5). Apple enables software developers to add options to the Page Setup dialog box. The added options generally appear at the bottom of the dialog box.

WordPerfect has added the Binding Width and Fractional Character Widths options to the Page Setup dialog box. You can use these options with any printer you choose in the Chooser.

Chapter 6
Printing a Document

Fig. 6.8
A document in landscape orientation.

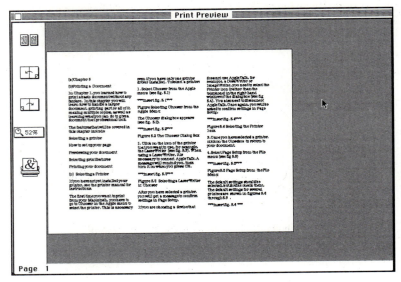

Binding Width

When printing documents, you often use even margins on all sides of your document. If you plan to bind your document, side-staple it, or put it into a notebook, however, you must allow margin space for the binding or holes. If you are printing on one side of the paper, adjust one margin—probably the left margin—and print.

If you intend to bind two-sided printing, however, you must adjust the right margin for even-numbered pages and the left margin for odd-numbered pages. To avoid the difficulties of doing this job by hand, add an automatic adjustment for binding width to your document by following these steps:

1. Choose Page Setup from the File menu. The Page Setup dialog box appears.

2. Click the Binding Width text box and type an appropriate width. If you enter 0.5 inch, for example, WordPerfect adds a half-inch to the right margin on even pages and to the left margin on odd pages of your document (see fig. 6.9).

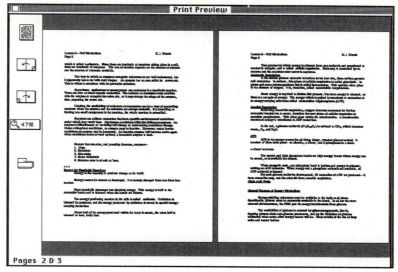

Fig. 6.9
Pages with margins adjusted for binding.

You can change the binding width unit to something other than inches by clicking the word inches next to the Binding Width text box. On the pop-up menu, drag the pointer to the appropriate unit of measure—centimeters, points, and picas, for example—and release the mouse button. The new unit is selected.

Fractional Character Widths

The smallest dot displayed on your monitor is called a *pixel*. The monitor displays 72 pixels per inch. Because a laser printer prints 300 pixels per inch, this printer can print character widths more accurately than the monitor can display them.

Choosing Fractional Character Widths enables a LaserWriter or other high-resolution printer to create more accurate proportional spacing. Leave Fractional Character Widths off until you are ready to print, however. Because the monitor cannot display fractions of a pixel, the screen display is more difficult to read with this feature turned on.

Printer Effects

You use the Printer Effects options in the Page Setup dialog box to enhance the speed or quality of printing. Whether you use these options is largely a matter of personal preference and experimentation. Try printing a few documents with the options on, turn the options off, and then print the documents again to see which options work best for you.

To turn a Printer Effect option on or off, follow these steps:

1. Choose Page Setup from the File menu.

2. Click the option title or the check box next to the option. An X appears in the check box if the option is on. When you click the option again, the X disappears, indicating that the option is off.

3. Click OK to close the Page Setup dialog box.

The following sections describe the functions of each option.

Font Substitution

When you activate the Font Substitution option, which was originated to enable early Macintosh users to print existing documents on a LaserWriter that didn't have high-quality fonts, the printer substitutes an available printer font for a font not offered by the printer. Helvetica, for example, is substituted for Geneva, Times for New York, and Courier for Monaco.

Font substitution worsens alignment problems if you use the space bar to align text. Do not use the space bar to align text in columns. Because proportional spacing is different for different fonts, using the space bar to line up text results in irregular alignment. You can avoid this problem by using tabs or the Columns feature to line up text.

If you deactivate the Font Substitution option, the printer tries to create a bit map for the unavailable font. (A *bit map* is the representation of a video image stored in a computer's memory. Each pixel is represented by bits stored in memory.) The results may be less than desirable because the fonts may appear jagged. With TrueType fonts installed in System 7, however, your Macintosh can create attractive print in Geneva, New York, Monaco, and Chicago fonts.

Part I

Getting Started

Text Smoothing

Text Smoothing smooths some of the jagged edges on a bit-mapped font but slows printing. Because the smoothing algorithm may be more successful on some fonts than others, try text smoothing on each font to see which works best. With the advent of TrueType fonts and the expanding use of Adobe Type Manager with PostScript fonts, however, you may never need to use the Text Smoothing option on bit-mapped screen fonts.

Graphics Smoothing

Although the Graphics Smoothing option smooths bit-mapped graphics, the usefulness of this option depends on what you print.

In the early days of the Macintosh, nearly all graphics were bit maps at 72 dots per inch (the resolution of the screen). Printing these images without smoothing produced printed graphics that had slightly rough edges. Now, because most graphics programs create their own smooth curves, the Graphics Smoothing option is not generally necessary. In fact, when you are trying to create a specific effect with a bit-mapped graphic image, the option can get in the way.

Faster Bitmap Printing

This option enables bit-mapped text to be printed faster. If you get an error message while the document prints, turn off this option and print the document again.

The Faster Bitmap Printing option also survives from the original LaserWriter. Computers and printers are significantly faster now. Given the possibility of errors in printing, you are probably better off deactivating this option.

Additional Options

The Options button on the Page Setup dialog box for the LaserWriter appears below the OK button. Clicking this button gives you access to other options that enable you to rearrange further your text or graphics for printing (see fig. 6.10).

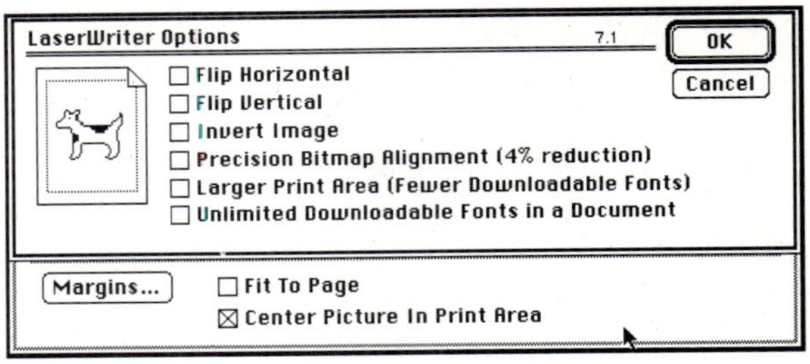

Fig. 6.10
Choosing Options.

Flip Horizontal and Flip Vertical

The Flip Horizontal option flips your document around an imaginary vertical line at the middle of the page. The graphic to the left of the check boxes changes to show the result of the chosen option. If you horizontally flip the image from figure 6.10, for example, the dog flips to face right instead of left.

Choosing Flip Vertical flips your document around an imaginary horizontal line through the center of the page. In this case, the dog of figure 6.10 flips to an upside-down position.

Individually, the Flip Horizontal and Flip Vertical options aren't too useful for any documents containing text (unless you are creating an iron-on transfer master). Using both options, however, has the effect of "turning the paper around." If your printer normally feeds the top of the page first, using both options feeds the bottom of the page.

The only time this reversal helps you is if you are manually feeding smaller than full-size sheets and need to print closer to one edge of the sheet than the printer normally permits (even if Larger Print Area is selected). Trying to print near the edge of a small sheet is a hassle; the flip options can help.

Invert Image

This option reverses the white and black in an image. Black becomes white and white becomes black, much like a negative of a photograph.

Precision Bitmap Alignment

The Precision Bitmap Alignment (4% reduction) option corrects for the slight discrepancy that may occur between the monitor and the printed page if you use bit-mapped graphics. LaserWriters, for example, print 300 pixels per inch, but the monitor displays only 72 pixels per inch. Because 300 is not a multiple of 72, you may see some distortion when the screen image is printed. By reducing the printer pixels per inch to 96 percent of the original 300, this option makes the printer output a multiple of the screen display and reduces distortion.

Choosing this option is not necessary if you created your graphics in WordPerfect.

Larger Print Area

Normally, the LaserWriter's print area is bounded on top and bottom by a half-inch margin and on each side by a three-eighths-inch margin. If you choose the Larger Print Area (Fewer Downloadable Fonts) option, you can expand that print area to within a quarter inch of the edge of the paper.

In the early days of the LaserWriter, the Larger Print Area option required most of the free memory in the printer; as a result, multiple-font use was severely limited. Now most printers have enough memory to handle the larger print area and a reasonable number of fonts easily.

Unlimited Downloadable Fonts

If you use in one document several fonts that are not built-in to the printer, you can choose the Unlimited Downloadable Fonts in a Document option. The program downloads extra fonts to the printer from a file on your hard disk and clears unused fonts from memory if the printer requires more space for a new downloaded font.

You use Unlimited Downloadable Fonts only if your document uses many different fonts that aren't built-in to your printer (see your printer manual for a list of built-in fonts). Because a font must be downloaded to available memory in the printer as needed, using this option may increase the amount of time needed to print your document.

Help

Apple describes all the Page Setup options in the Help files that are included in the printer driver. For the System 7 driver, however, you must activate Balloon Help. (Choose Show Balloons from the Balloon Help menu; then choose Page Setup from the File menu.) With Balloon Help, a description of the option appears when you place the mouse pointer on an option.

Earlier versions of the printer driver have a Help button in the Page Setup dialog box. Clicking the Help button displays a list of the options and their descriptions.

Previewing Your Document

Before printing your document, you can preview it. The Print Preview option enables you to see a full-page view of your document, including headers, page numbers, footnotes, and other special features that do not appear in your document as you enter text.

By using Print Preview, you can check the document's formatting without wasting paper. Does the page break leave the last word in a paragraph by itself on the next page? Did you accidentally set a three-inch margin at the top of the page and a half-inch margin at the bottom? Are the headers incorrect? Print Preview exposes these problems before they appear on paper.

One important point to remember, however, is that you cannot edit the document in Print Preview. Make a note of any changes you want to make; then return to your document to edit it.

To preview your document, choose Print Preview from the File menu or press ⌘-Shift-P. You see the page that currently is being edited or viewed (see fig. 6.11). The Print Preview screen has several important features. At the bottom left, you see the page number of the page being previewed. On the left side of the screen are five icons that represent preview options.

The first icon enables you to choose a one-page display or to view two pages side by side. When you first enter Print Preview, you see only one page at a time. Click the Two-Page icon at the top of the left column to see two pages side by side (see fig. 6.12). When you click the Two-Page icon, the icon becomes a single page.

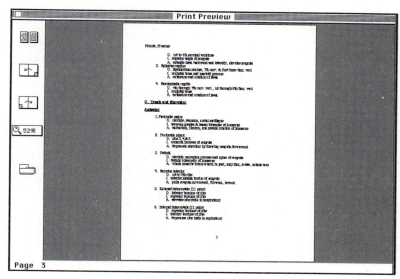

Fig. 6.11
Using Print Preview.

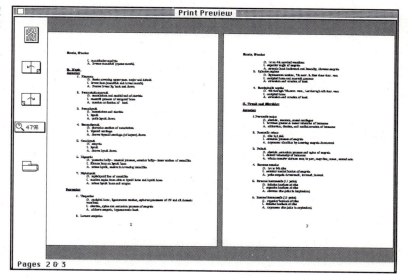

Fig. 6.12
Viewing two pages in Print Preview.

Chapter 6
Printing a Document

The next two book-shaped icons enable you to move through your document by "turning" pages. By clicking the icon with the arrow pointing from right to left, you "turn" to the next page. To turn to the preceding page, click the icon containing the arrow pointing from left to right.

The fourth option is a pop-up menu with a magnifying glass and a percentage (52% in this example). This icon indicates the size of the page you are viewing relative to an 8 1/2-by-11-inch sheet of paper. The default magnification size is 52 percent for a U.S. letter page displayed on a 13-inch monitor. WordPerfect automatically chooses a magnification that displays the largest magnification (up to 100 percent) that shows a complete page on your monitor.

You can change the magnification of your document by choosing one of the preselected sizes (75%, 100%, 200%, or 400%) or entering your own magnification. To set a custom magnification in Print Preview, follow these steps:

1. Choose Other from the magnification pop-up menu. A dialog box appears.

2. In the text box, type the percent value of the appropriate magnification.

3. Click OK or press Return.

Figure 6.13 shows a document enlarged to 200 percent, which enables you to examine the page in detail.

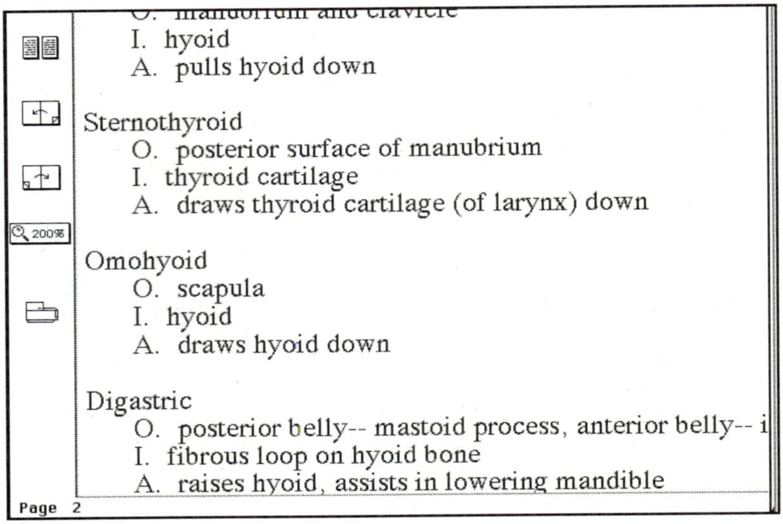

Fig. 6.13
A Print Preview document magnified to 200 percent.

```
O. mandibium and clavicle
I. hyoid
A. pulls hyoid down

Sternothyroid
    O. posterior surface of manubrium
    I. thyroid cartilage
    A. draws thyroid cartilage (of larynx) down

Omohyoid
    O. scapula
    I. hyoid
    A. draws hyoid down

Digastric
    O. posterior belly-- mastoid process, anterior belly-- i
    I. fibrous loop on hyoid bone
    A. raises hyoid, assists in lowering mandible
Page 2
```

Part I

Getting Started

You can return the document to its original preview size by choosing 52% or Full Page from the magnification pop-up menu.

In full page view, the type is too small to read. When you move the pointer over text, however, the pointer becomes a magnifying glass, enabling you to enlarge a particular area of your document. To select an area for closer examination, move the magnifying glass to the desired location and click.

When you magnify an area of your document in this way, the document size changes to 100 percent and the magnifying glass changes to a hand (see fig. 6.14). You can use the hand to drag the document page around the screen. To return the document to its original preview size, use the magnification pop-up menu on the left side of the page.

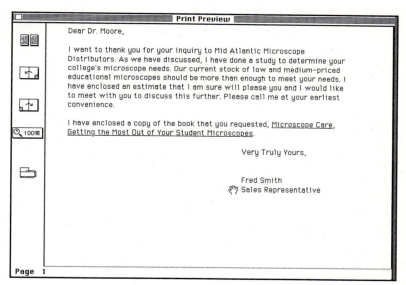

Fig. 6.14
Enlarging the document to examine an area.

You can print a document directly from the Print Preview screen. This feature saves time and keystrokes if the preview indicates that no changes are necessary before printing. Click the printer icon at the bottom of the left column. The Print dialog box, which is the same dialog box that appears when you choose Print from the File menu, appears.

Chapter 6
Printing a Document

Using the Print Dialog Box

hen you choose Print from the File menu, you see a dialog box in which you indicate what to print and how it should be printed (see fig. 6.15).

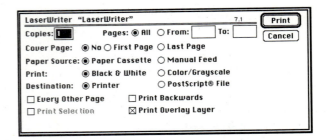

Fig. 6.15
The LaserWriter Print dialog box.

The print dialog boxes for other printers are usually very similar to the LaserWriter Print dialog box. The most common difference is that most inkjet and dot-matrix printers offer a choice between *best* print quality and *draft* quality, which is faster but not as attractive. The LaserWriter has only one print quality—300 dpi (dots per inch).

Printing Part of the Document

Although you frequently may print an entire document by clicking the All button in the Print dialog box, times may occur when you only need two or three pages from the document. WordPerfect provides two ways to print a portion of a document: you can enter a page range, or you can select text from your document.

To print one or more consecutive pages of a document, you must enter the page range in the Page Range entry area of the Print dialog box (refer to fig. 6.15). Click the From text box and type the number of the first page that should print; then click the To text box (or press Tab) and type the number of the last page that should print. To print one page, type that page number in both text boxes. If you are making no other changes, click OK. Only the specified pages print.

You also can select a specific portion of your document for printing—for example, one or more sentences, a paragraph, or a table. In your document, select the text by dragging the I-beam pointer while you press the mouse button. Open the Print dialog box and click the Print

Part I
Getting Started

Selection check box. If Print Selection is unavailable (dimmed), you have not selected text in your document. After you choose Print Selection, click OK to start printing.

Specifying the Number of Copies

Although the default number of copies is 1, you can print as many as 99 copies of a document in a single run. To create more than one copy of your document, type the appropriate number in the Copies text box.

The specified number of copies are generated page by page—first all copies of page 1, then all copies of page 2, and so on. You must collate the pages manually into complete documents after the print job is finished. (WordPerfect includes a macro that prints collated copies. See Chapter 14, "Using Macros," for more information.)

Using Other Print Options

Although you may use the other options in the Print dialog box less frequently than the options discussed previously, each option provides additional control of the printing process that can be useful in some situations.

Cover Page

You can choose to print a cover page, which can be the first or the last page printed. A cover page contains information about the document, including the user (as listed in the File Sharing Control Panel in System 7), the application, the document name, the date and time, and the printer. Cover pages are particularly useful if you print to a network printer used by many other people.

Paper Source

Paper sources vary from printer to printer. On the LaserWriter, the default source is the paper cassette; however, you can choose to manually feed the paper through the printer. To print one letter on letterhead, for example, you can specify Manual Feed; then feed one or two pages of letterhead through the printer. By indicating an alternate paper source, you don't have to switch the paper in the paper cassette.

Chapter 6
Printing a Document

Print Color

Some of the newest LaserWriters can print in gray scales (shades ranging from white to black) and convert colors in a document to shades of gray when printed. Unless you have a "gray capable" printer, leave the Print option set to Black & White. Even if you use a grayscale or color printer, choosing the Black & White option speeds up printing when producing a grayscale or color image is not necessary.

Destination

Normally you send your document to a printer to print. To create a PostScript file that you can print on a PostScript device (such as a high-resolution image setter) that is not connected to a Macintosh, set the Destination option to PostScript File. You still must find a way to transfer the file, but this method is easier than running WordPerfect Mac on a DOS computer.

Every Other Page

To print on both sides of the paper, you print on one side, turn the paper over, and print on the other side. Doing this task page by page is cumbersome. With the Every Other Page option, however, you can save time and effort.

If you don't specify a page number, the printer starts on page 1 and prints the odd-numbered pages on the front of the paper. After you turn the stack of paper over, type *2* in the From text box. The printer then starts with page 2 and prints the even-numbered pages on the back of the paper.

Print Overlay Layer

Any draw overlays that you create in your document are printed unless you turn off the Print Overlay Layer option, which is active by default. To turn the option off, click the check box so that the X disappears. (See Chapter 11, "Using the Drawing Window," for more information on graphic overlays.)

Part I
Getting Started

Print Backwards

When you print a document in normal order, the first printed page ends up at the bottom of the stack, and the last page ends up at the top. You must reverse the order of the pages manually. To avoid this effort, choose Print Backwards so that the last page of the document prints first and, consequently, ends up at the bottom of the pile. This option does not slow the printing process.

Some printers turn the pages over before depositing them in the exit paper tray. For these printers, using the Print Backwards option is unnecessary.

Printing a Document

ow that you have learned about the various options available when printing your document, the actual printing is easy. To print a document, follow these steps:

1. Make sure that your printer is on-line (connected to the computer and ready to accept the computer's output).

2. Choose Print from the File menu or press ⌘-P.

3. Choose the appropriate options in the Print dialog box.

4. Click OK or press Return. Your document starts printing.

Printing Envelopes

One subject that seems to raise quite an emotional response among computer users is how to get a computer and printer to produce a printed envelope without making the user tie him- or herself in knots to accomplish the task. In some offices, envelopes and multipart forms are the only things standing in the way of junking the typewriter and reclaiming the precious desk space it occupies. Although this section doesn't help you with the multipart forms, it can guide you in creating an easy-to-use envelope document.

WordPerfect has helped and hindered the envelope printing process. As mentioned earlier in this chapter, WordPerfect 2.1 does not accept the Envelope–Center Fed or Envelope–Edge Fed options in the paper size section of the Page Setup dialog box for the LaserWriter. You can set these sizes, but WordPerfect doesn't set the page margins automatically.

If, on the other hand, you use a printer that feeds envelopes down the center of the paper path (the Apple LaserWriter II family, for example), you can use the Envelopes macro that WordPerfect installs with the application. The following sections tell you how to handle three different envelope printing situations.

Center-Fed Envelopes with No Return Address

If you don't need to print a return address on an envelope, you are in luck. The Envelopes macro that WordPerfect ships with Version 2.1 (and even some of the later 2.0.x versions) makes printing envelopes easy. To print an envelope that doesn't require a return address, follow these steps:

1. Select the recipient's name and address from the document containing the letter you are sending. If the document is not open, you can type the name and address in any open document and then select the address.

2. Choose Envelopes from the Macros menu. If your Macros menu doesn't list the Envelopes macro, see Chapter 14, "Using Macros," for information on moving macros from the WordPerfect distribution disks to your WordPerfect Private Library.

3. WordPerfect opens a new document, sets the margins, inserts the name and address, and presents an alert box stating that the program is ready to print the envelope.

4. Click OK in the alert box or press Return. WordPerfect opens the Print dialog box.

5. Set Paper Source to Manual Feed if you feed envelopes through the printer by hand; otherwise, choose the correct paper tray for envelopes in the Print dialog box.

6. Click OK or press Return. WordPerfect sends the envelope document to the printer, closes and discards the document it created to print the envelope, and returns you to the document that contained the selected name and address.

You must know which end of the envelope to put into the printer first and whether the envelope should face up or down in the feed tray. You can find this information in your printer manual. Aside from these two minor details, printing envelopes cannot get much easier.

Center-Fed Envelopes with a Return Address

To print a return address on your envelopes, the WordPerfect Envelopes macro doesn't do you much good. Modifying the macro is possible but beyond the scope of discussion in this chapter. See Chapter 14, "Using Macros," to modify the macro.

An envelope is just another piece of paper to the printer; the only trick is getting the text on the envelope instead of on some internal part of the printer. To create a template document that includes a return address for printing center-fed envelopes on a laser printer, do the following:

1. Open a new document by typing ⌘-N or choosing New from the File menu.
2. Choose Page Setup from the File menu. The Page Setup dialog box appears.
3. Click the Landscape orientation icon.
4. If the return address should start less than 1/2 inch from the left edge of the envelope, click the Options button in the Page Setup dialog box.
5. In the Options dialog box, click the check box for the Larger Print Area option; then click OK to return to the Page Setup dialog box.
6. Click OK or press Return to return to your blank document.
7. Set the page top margin to 2.3 inches and the left margin to approximately 0.25 inch. (See Chapter 4, "Formatting a Document," for information on setting page margins.)
8. Type the return address in any font and type size.
9. Press Return a few times to create the space between the return address and the address. The number of returns depends on font and font size. For 12-point New Century Schoolbook text, 8 blank lines are reasonable.

    You can use a single blank line with a large, fixed line height to set a precise distance between the return address and address. See Chapter 4, "Formatting a Document," for more information on setting line height.
10. Reset the left margin to 4.5 inches.
11. Type the address.
12. Choose Save As from the File menu.

Chapter 6
Printing a Document

13. Give your envelope template document a name, such as *Envelope Template*.

14. Set the Format pop-up menu in the Save As dialog box to WordPerfect 2.1 Stationery. By making your envelope template a stationary document, you prevent changes you make later to individual envelopes from affecting the template document. (See Chapter 7, "Managing Files," for more information on stationary documents.)

15. Click OK or press Return to save your envelope template.

Experimenting with full sheets of paper is a good idea to make sure the alignment is correct before you feed envelopes through the printer.

Some laser printers print a page image as much as 1/8 inch off center. Adjust the page top margin of your envelope template to compensate for your printer's precise page alignment.

Check your envelope alignment by printing the template on a full sheet of paper; then line up the center of the left edge of the full sheet with the center of the left edge of an envelope to see where the printing falls. Hold the overlapping paper up to a light if you have trouble seeing the envelope edges through the paper.

To print an envelope, using your template document, do the following:

1. Copy the address to the Clipboard (select the address and press ⌘-C or choose Copy from the Edit menu).

2. Open the envelope template document.

3. Select the address in your template document.

4. Paste the address from the Clipboard into the envelope template (press ⌘-V or choose Paste from the Edit menu). The address copied from your letter source document replaces the selected template address.

5. Choose Print from the File menu or press ⌘-P.

6. Set the proper paper feed option in the Print dialog box and click OK or press Return to print the envelope.

This scheme isn't quite as convenient as the Envelopes macro, but it does enable you to print a return address on an envelope without requiring that you realign the information for each envelope.

> **Tip**
> You don't have to measure to find the center of the paper or envelope. Pinch a small crease in both pieces after lining up opposite edges of each piece; then line up the creases to check your layout.

Part I
Getting Started

Edge-Fed Envelopes with a Return Address

The original LaserWriters and at least some of the current NEC and QMS (among others) laser printers feed envelopes along one edge of the paper feed trays. To create an envelope template document for this type of printer, follow all the directions given in the preceding section, except set the top margin to 4.5 inches instead of 2.3 inches (step 7).

Again, printing the envelope template on a full sheet of paper to check your alignment is a good idea. Line up the lower left corner of an envelope with the lower left corner of the full sheet sample and see if all your printing falls within the bounds of the envelope edges. Adjust the top and left margins to move the printing to the proper place.

Chapter Summary

In this chapter, you learned how to preview your document before printing. You also learned how to view the document at different magnifications, how to print from within Print Preview, and how to print envelopes on a LaserWriter. This chapter showed you how to set important printing options, such as page orientation (landscape or portrait), the size and type of paper to be used, and the number of copies to print. In addition, this chapter explained how to print envelopes—a previously time-consuming and often frustrating task—with little effort. With this information, you can confidently print documents from a single-page letter to a two-sided bound "book."

PART III

Refining Documents

Includes

Managing Files and Documents
Formatting with Styles
Using Columns and Text Boxes
Creating Outlines and Lists
Using the Drawing Window

CHAPTER 7

Managing Files and Documents

Until now, you have learned primarily about handling a single document. In the real world, however, you are likely to have many documents on your hard disk. You must be able to keep track of the location of those documents. After you create several files, for instance, you may want to locate documents containing a certain phrase, or you may want to create new documents with parts of one or more old documents. You can consider all these tasks aspects of "managing" files.

With the Macintosh Finder, you can arrange and manage files on disk. WordPerfect, in addition, provides many of the same capabilities within the program and adds to those capabilities by providing a search function that you can use to find phrases in unopened files. This chapter shows you how to use the WordPerfect File Manager to manage files and folders, how to work with multiple documents simultaneously, and how to convert file formats.

Understanding the File Manager Dialog Box

After you choose File Manager from the File menu, the File Manager dialog box appears (see fig. 7.1). Although this dialog box at first glance looks very much like the Open dialog box, upon closer inspection you can see the File, Folder, and Search menus across the top of the dialog box.

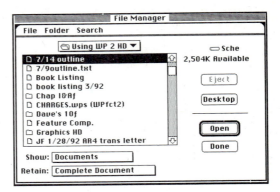

Fig. 7.1
The File Manager dialog box.

These menus provide the extra file management power that enables you to change names of files or folders, create new folders, delete files or folders, and search closed files for text phrases. You also can print files, copy files, and get information about file or folder size and modification dates while you have the File Manager dialog box open.

Finding a File in the File List

The file list in the File Manager dialog box is based on the standard file list that you get in all Mac programs when you use an Open dialog box. (See Chapter 3, "Editing a Document," for more information on the Open dialog box.) Some extra capabilities added to the standard list manager make choosing the desired file easier. The most significant added capability is being able to search through all files in a folder to find files that contain a specified phrase.

Most long-time Macintosh users are likely to find using the Macintosh Finder more convenient for all functions except the text search. Because System 7 requires that Finder be active in the background at all times, you can switch to the Finder without losing time. If you are using System 6.0.5 or 6.0.7 (WordPerfect requires 6.0.5 or newer), however, and don't have the Finder running in the background, using WordPerfect's File Manager dialog box instead of quitting WordPerfect to access the Finder can save time.

Part II

Refining Documents

Navigating the File List

To use the File Manager dialog box, you must be able to select the appropriate files, commands, and folder levels. You use the same techniques and commands to navigate this dialog box that you use to navigate other dialog boxes. These standard techniques are discussed in the following list:

- To open a file or folder, you can choose a file or folder name and click the Open button; you can double-click the file or folder name; or you can use the up- and down-arrow keys to highlight a file or folder and then press Return.

- To select a folder that is higher in the file hierarchy, you click the pop-up menu containing the folder name at the top of the list and choose a new folder from the list that appears (see fig. 7.2). The disk name (Sys & Apps in figure 7.2) appears above the Desktop option at the bottom of the folder pop-up list.

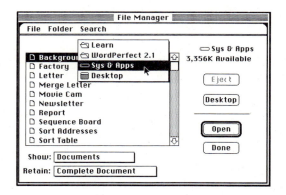

Fig. 7.2
Changing folders in the file list.

Choosing Desktop from the folder title pop-up menu has the same effect as clicking the Desktop button. In System 6, the Desktop button was the Drive button, and the disk name appeared at the bottom of the file list folder name pop-up menu. Clicking the Drive button cycled through any disk drives and partitions attached to your Mac.

A Macintosh *file hierarchy* is the collection of folders within folders, within folders, and so on. That the top of the hierarchy appears at the bottom of the pop-up list probably is due to screen size limitations on the early Mac.

- To move up one folder level on a disk, press ⌘-↑ or click the disk name in the upper right of the dialog box.

- To advance through a long list of files and folders, use the scroll bar and arrows.

- To choose among hard disk partition, floppy drive, and network server file lists, click the Desktop button. (A *drive partition* is a part of a hard disk that acts like a separate disk drive. Partitions make file "housekeeping" easier on large-capacity hard disks.)

- To eject a floppy disk, click the Eject button when the name of the disk appears in the upper right corner of the dialog box. Although you usually use the Eject button to insert a different floppy disk in the drive, using Eject in the File Manager is the only way to eject a disk without closing the File Manager first.

- Click the Done button to close the File Manager.

Using the Show Menu

If your folder contains many files or if you want to see files other than WordPerfect files, use the Show pop-up menu at the bottom of the dialog box (see fig. 7.3). Of the options available in the Show pop-up menu, the WordPerfect 2.x and Documents options generally are the most useful. The active option in the Show pop-up menu (the option that's visible when the pop-up menu is closed) describes the type of files shown in the file list.

> **Tip**
> WordPerfect displays keyboard shortcuts for buttons when you hold down the Command (⌘) key while the dialog box is open.

Fig. 7.3
The Show pop-up menu in the File Manager dialog box.

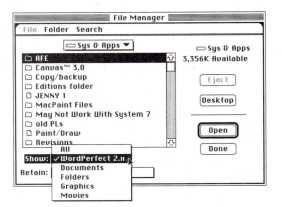

> **Tip**
>
> To open a document that is not a WordPerfect file, you need a file conversion resource in the Conversions folder in the WordPerfect Preferences folder. (See "Converting File Formats" later in this chapter for more details.)

The default option, WordPerfect 2.x, results in only folders and WordPerfect 2.x files appearing in the file list. The Documents option adds all types of documents to the list of folders and WordPerfect files. The files that appear as Documents but not as WordPerfect files include files from DOS versions and earlier Mac versions of WordPerfect, as well as files from other word processors and graphics packages.

To see the names of system files, system extensions, and control panels in the file list, choose All from the Show pop-up menu. Because you shouldn't do anything with or to system files from inside WordPerfect, the All option is not particularly useful.

The other Show menu options offer some special-purpose file selections for navigating in the disk file lists. The All option, for example, shows all file types—even applications—at a particular folder level. (You cannot open an application from the File Manager, but you can copy, rename, delete, and get information about an application.)

The Movies option limits the file list to show folders and QuickTime movies. Unless you have your own video digitizing equipment, you must get QuickTime movies from software suppliers or on-line services. WordPerfect includes one sample movie with Version 2.1.

If you have many *nested folders*—that is, folders in folders in folders—and many files at each folder level and want to open a file at a low folder level, you can use the Folders option. This option hides all documents from the file list, resulting in a short list of folders. With the Folders option, you can open many folder levels in succession (double-click the folder name) without scrolling through the file list that contains both folders and documents. To open a file in a folder, however, you must locate the folder that contains the file and then use the Show pop-up menu again to display the appropriate files.

The Graphics option is useful when you create, in another application, graphics that you want to include in a WordPerfect file. In the Finder, you easily can distinguish graphics files from other types of files by the graphics file icon, but that information is not available in a file dialog box. By choosing the Graphics option, you at least can make sure that you are inserting a graphic into your document.

Using the Retain Menu

Retain, the other pop-up menu at the bottom of the File Manager dialog box, also appears in the Open, Save As, and File Manager dialog boxes (see fig. 7.4). The Retain menu's options give you considerable flexibility in dealing with WordPerfect files and files from other word processors.

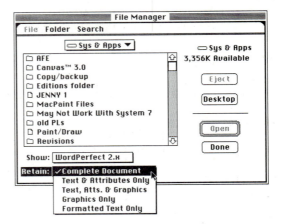

Fig. 7.4
The Retain pop-up menu in the File Manager.

The Retain options enable you to control how much of a document remains when you use the File Manager to open or insert a file. You can keep a whole document, just the graphics, or just the text (with or without text styles and ruler settings).

On the Retain menu, the default option is Complete Document. WordPerfect inserts everything—text, formatting, styles, and graphics—in the document into the editing window. The Complete Document option is the same as the standard Macintosh Open or Save As function in WordPerfect. The other available options are explained in the following list:

■ *Text & Attributes Only.* This option retains the words and the associated character styles. WordPerfect retains attributes—such as boldface, italic, underline, font choice, and type size—when you open or save a file with this option. Page margins, tab settings, and other line-formatting details are not retained. Graphics also are excluded in file operations using the Text & Attributes Only option.

Text & Attributes Only is a useful option if you must change substantially the structure of a file. If you created a file before learning how to use styles, as explained in Chapter 8, "Formatting with Styles," for example, and decide to use styles later to clean up the document formatting, open the file by using the Text & Attributes Only option to make selecting text and applying a style easier. Reformatting without the graphics in the file speeds up the operation, especially for a long document.

Part II

Refining Documents

- *Text, Atts. & Graphics.* This option retains graphics in addition to the text and attributes opened or saved with a document. The option works with everything but page and line formatting.

    You may find the Text, Atts. & Graphics option useful in some file importing situations. When you open a file from another word processor, you may end up with tab set codes or line format codes inserted with every paragraph. So many codes can make reformatting your document difficult. Because you must change many imported files anyway, you can choose Text, Atts. & Graphics when you open the file and then insert line-formatting codes later to save time and effort.

- *Graphics Only.* If you open a file with this option, only graphics elements appear in the opened document window. Use this option to save all your graphic elements to a separate file. Many publishers, for example, handle text and graphics separately; therefore, if you have a complete compound document (text and graphics) to be typeset, you may have to separate the graphics from the rest of the document. You can use the Graphics Only option to separate the graphics from the text.

- *Formatted Text Only.* This option excludes graphics but includes text attributes and page, paragraph, and line formatting. You can use this option with the Graphics Only option to divide documents into text and graphics files. To separate text from graphics, for example, you can use the formatted Text Only option.

Using the File Manager Menus

The preceding section shows you how to navigate through the file list, change the files shown, and specify what attributes to retain. The File Manager, however, does not limit you to these options. Unlike other dialog boxes, the File Manager dialog box contains three menus—File, Folder, and Search—that enable you to perform additional file management tasks.

The File and Folder menus enable you to do several tasks that you can do from the main File menu at the top of the screen or in the Macintosh Finder. If you are using MultiFinder, you can do most of the system-level tasks of the File Manager without quitting WordPerfect.

The Search menu provides a convenient way to identify files containing a particular phrase. If, from a file list of all the documents you wrote in one year, you must find the memo that mentions third-quarter results, the Search menu makes the task easy.

The File Menu

The File menu in the File Manager dialog box is dimmed until you select (click) a file from the file list. The first two options on the File menu, Open and Insert, produce the same result that choosing these options from the main File menu produces (see fig. 7.5).

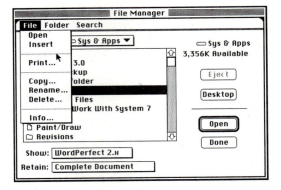

Fig. 7.5
The File Manager's File menu.

If you select a file, you also can click the Open button or press Return to open the file. The Open option is probably on the dialog box pull-down menu to satisfy an Apple guideline that all File menus should contain an Open command.

The Print option closes the File Manager dialog box, opens the selected document, and opens the Print dialog box. You can set any option in the Print dialog box (see Chapter 6, "Printing a Document," for more details) and then click Print in the Print dialog box or press Return to print the document. After WordPerfect finishes printing, the file closes.

The Copy, Rename, and Delete commands enable you to do just what their names imply. Each option accesses a corresponding dialog box, from which you can save a copy of the file to a different location (Copy), rename and leave the file in its present folder (Rename), or delete the file (Delete). Of course, the Delete option gives you one last chance to cancel before deleting a file (see fig. 7.6).

If you answer Yes to the Delete File Confirmation alert box, the file is *gone*. Although special file recovery software may retrieve the file, you should consider the delete confirmation alert box as your last chance to keep the file.

Part II

Refining Documents

Fig. 7.6
The Delete Confirmation alert box.

The last option on the File Manager's File menu, Info, offers a feature not available in the Macintosh Finder. When you choose Info, the File Info dialog box appears (see fig. 7.7). The Dates and Sizes section reports file directory information: when the file was created, when the file was last saved (modified), and how big the file is. Documents don't have a version number—n/a appears next to Version instead—but applications have an entry in the Version space. In the Attributes section of the dialog box are two four-character attributes called Creator and Type. You ordinarily don't need to change these values.

Fig. 7.7
The File Info dialog box.

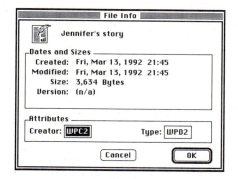

Do not change the values of the Creator and Type attributes unless you know what you are doing. These values determine how the system and applications recognize files. WordPerfect technical support can talk you through using this feature to recover WordPerfect backup files that don't open when you launch WordPerfect after a system crash. As of this time, the support number is 800-336-3614. You also can find the number under Customer Support in your WordPerfect manual.

Related to the idea of file information is that of document information. Although document information is not part of the File Manager dialog box, considering the complementary aspects of the two types of information is useful.

Chapter 7
Managing Files and Documents

The Document Info option on the main File menu details the number of characters, words, sentences, and paragraphs in the active document (see fig. 7.8). The Document Information dialog box provides more internal writing information than the file system type information presented in the File Manager's File Info dialog box.

Fig. 7.8
The Document Information dialog box.

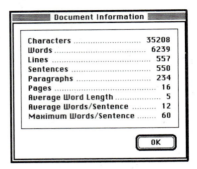

If the File Manager dialog box is open, you must close it (click Done) before you can access the Document Info command.

The Folder Menu

When you select a folder in the file list box, all options in the Folder menu become active (see fig. 7.9). The first option, New, is always available in the File Manager, but the other three options are available only if you select a folder from the file list.

Fig. 7.9
The File Manager's Folder menu.

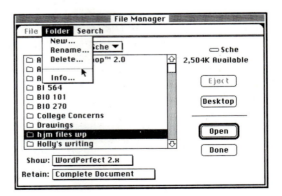

Part II

Refining Documents

The New option enables you to create a new folder on your hard or floppy disk. If you are using System 7— or MultiFinder in System 6—this method of creating a new folder is slower than switching to the Finder and creating a new folder there. If you are using System 6 without MultiFinder, however, using the File Manager's Folder menu saves you the hassle of quitting WordPerfect, creating the new folder, and re-launching WordPerfect.

Create a new folder on your hard disk by following these steps:

1. In the File Manager dialog box, make sure you are in the folder where the new folder should appear. Use the file list navigating steps discussed earlier in the chapter to switch folders.

2. Choose New from the Folder menu. The New Folder dialog box appears (see fig. 7.10).

Fig. 7.10
The New Folder dialog box.

3. Type the folder name in the New Folder Name text box and click OK. The program creates the new folder.

With the Rename and Delete options, you can change a folder's name or delete a folder without going to the Finder. If you choose a folder in the file list and choose Rename from the Folder menu, the Rename dialog box, which is identical (except for the name) to the New Folder dialog box, appears. Type a new name in the text box and click OK or press Return to finish renaming the folder.

If you choose a folder in the file list and then choose Delete from the Folder menu, the Delete Confirmation alert box appears (refer to fig. 7.6). After you click Yes in the alert box, you cannot undo the deletion.

Always check a folder's contents before deleting the folder. Because a folder can contain other files and folders, you easily may delete files or folders unintentionally.

Chapter 7

Managing Files and Documents

The Info option on the Folder menu is similar to the Info option in the File menu, except no creator or type attributes are associated with folders. The Folder Info dialog box shows the name of the folder, the dates and times that the folder was created and changed, and the number of items in the folder (see fig. 7.11).

Fig. 7.11
A Folder Info dialog box.

The Search Menu

The Search menu, shown in figure 7.12, is the most useful part of the File Manager dialog box. You can use the File Manager's Search menu to search for a word or phrase in all documents at one folder level without opening each file and using the Find/Change command from WordPerfect's main Search menu.

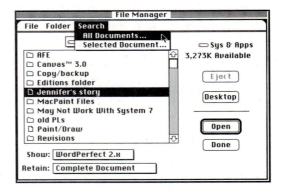

Fig. 7.12
The File Manager's Search menu.

If, for example, you know you mentioned *continental drift* in a document you stored in a folder named Geology but cannot remember which of the 50 files in the folder the phrase was in, the Search All Documents option can help you. Similarly, if you want to know whether you mentioned a certain phrase in a 100-page document, you can use the Search Selected Document option.

The Search All Documents option weeds out files in the file list that don't contain your search phrase. After this kind of search, the file list shows only the names of any folder and its files that contain your search phrase.

To limit the file list in a particular folder to show only files containing a certain word or phrase, follow these steps:

1. In the File Manager, open the folder that you want to search. The files and folders in the folder you are going to search appear in the file list.

   If the folder being searched contains WordPerfect documents and files from other applications (such as spreadsheets), you can use the Show pop-up menu to define which files should be searched.

2. Choose Documents from the Show pop-up menu to search all documents; choose WordPerfect to search only WordPerfect files. The file list changes accordingly.

3. Choose All Documents from the File Manager's Search menu to search all the documents that appear in the file list.

   The Word Search dialog box appears (see fig. 7.13).

Fig. 7.13
The Word Search dialog box.

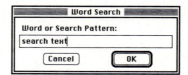

4. Type the word or phrase you want to find and click OK.

   WordPerfect searches the specified files for occurrences of the text. (The search is not case specific.) After WordPerfect completes the search, an information box appears, telling you how many files contain the search phrase (see fig. 7.14) or that no files contain the phrase (see fig. 7.15).

Fig. 7.14
A successful search information box.

Fig. 7.15
A search information box indicating that no match was found.

5. Click OK.

   The file list shows only files that contain the search phrase, plus any folders on the list.

The search process does not look in folders that appear in the file list. To search inside these folders, you must open the folder in the file list and redo the search.

You cannot do nested All Documents searches. In other words, you cannot search for files containing *third quarter* and then search the files containing *third quarter* for the word *deficit*. If you choose All Documents a second time, the search routine returns to all the files in the folder, not just the ones found by the first search.

To do a partial nested search, follow these steps:

1. Choose one of the files from a previously successful search.
2. Choose Selected Document from the Search menu.
3. Enter a word or phrase in the dialog box and click OK. An information box tells you whether WordPerfect found the new phrase.

To reset the file list to show all the documents listed prior to the search, choose one of the Show options or click Show.

Don't confuse the File Manager Search option with the Find/Change command for an open document. The File Manager search tells you only that a file contains a phrase. To see where the phrase is, you must open the document and use the Find dialog box to search for the phrase and show its location.

After you finish with the File Manager dialog box, click Done. The dialog box closes, and you return to the document (if any) from which you started the File Manager. The dialog box also closes when you open a file from the File Manager dialog box.

> **Tip**
> Some third-party programs, such as On Location by ON Technology, give you more flexibility in searching a disk full of files. If you must search frequently through a large number of files, consider buying a third-party program.

Part II

Refining Documents

Working with Multiple Documents

As you gain confidence with the program, chances are that you will work with more than one open document at a time. One reason for working with more than one document, for instance, is to copy parts of one or more documents into a new summary document. Switching back and forth between documents is much easier than retyping material.

When you open more than one document in WordPerfect, you must decide how to arrange the document windows so that you can make the best use of screen space and accomplish editing tasks efficiently. Screen size, the amount of editing you must do in each document, and personal preference determine the best way to handle several open documents.

Arranging Windows On-Screen

You can arrange multiple windows by *stacking* full-size windows, *tiling* windows (see fig. 7.16), or *overlapping* windows (see fig. 7.17). Handling windows in WordPerfect is exactly the same as in any Macintosh application. See your Macintosh reference manual for more information on sizing and positioning windows.

Fig. 7.16
Tiling multiple windows.

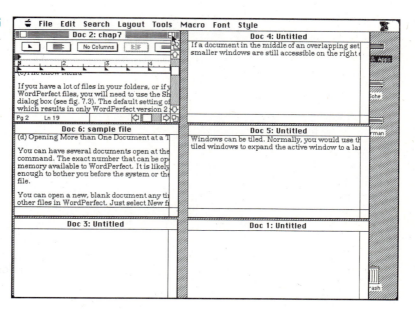

Chapter 7
Managing Files and Documents

Fig. 7.17
Overlapping windows.

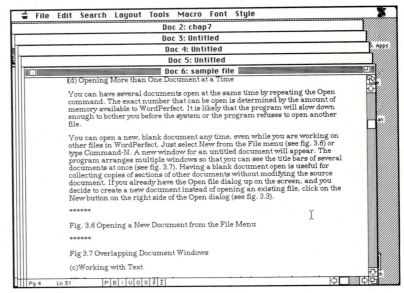

If you like to work in document windows that fill the screen, you should stack your windows. Stacked windows fill the screen; to stack windows, click the Zoom box of each document window when it opens.

Tiled windows are arranged like a section of ceramic tile—small, regularly spaced panels that don't overlap. Use the size box to shrink your windows for tiling.

When you open a series of documents, WordPerfect overlaps the windows. WordPerfect also overlaps existing documents if you turn off the Remember Window Location attribute in the Options menu of the Environment dialog box. (See Chapter 15, "Customizing WordPerfect," for a complete discussion of the environment options).

The overlapping window approach provides several advantages. If you're working on the most recently opened file, you can see all the document titles. If you click the largest window (the first document opened), that window comes to the front of the pile so that you can edit the document. (Because the windows don't resize automatically, the largest window obscures most of the other windows.)

Even though larger windows may obscure other open windows, as shown in figure 7.18, a little bit of each window is exposed so that you can click an opened window to bring it to the front for editing. Use the

Tip

If you use the Show Style Buttons or Show Position options in the Environment dialog box, you cannot make the windows as small as shown in figure 7.16. With both options enabled, the minimum window width is almost the entire width of a Macintosh Classic screen.

Part II

Refining Documents

list of open windows at the bottom of the Edit menu to choose a new front window if you cannot remember the contents of each window. (See the section "Changing the Active Window" later in this chapter for more information on switching windows.)

Fig. 7.18
Clicking an exposed corner to activate a window.

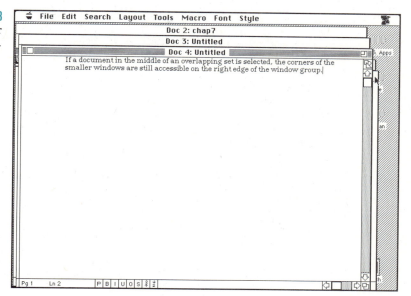

Using Two Windows with a Single Document

WordPerfect enables you to open a second copy of a currently open file. If you are writing an executive summary of a long report, for example, having a second window open enables you to refer to other parts of the report while you write the summary. If you tell WordPerfect to open a currently open file, an information box appears to remind you that the file is open (see fig. 7.19).

Fig. 7.19
The information box indicating that the file is open.

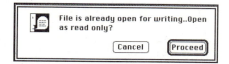

Chapter 7
Managing Files and Documents

> **Tip**
>
> WordPerfect enables you to make changes in the window that displays the read-only file, but you cannot save the changes unless you rename the file. Save yourself some confusion and don't make changes in a window that has a padlock icon in the title bar.

You cannot save changes to a read-only document. If you change a document that is read-only, you can save these changes only by using the Save As command to create a new document with a different name. A window open for writing means that you can use the Save command to write changes to the disk copy of the file.

To open a second copy of the current document, follow these steps:

1. Choose Open from the File menu.
2. Choose the appropriate file from the file list; then click OK or press Return. The information box appears.
3. Click Proceed in the information box.
4. Use the size box in the lower right corner of the windows to resize the original document and its copy; then drag the windows by the title bars so that you can see both versions of the file (see fig. 7.20).

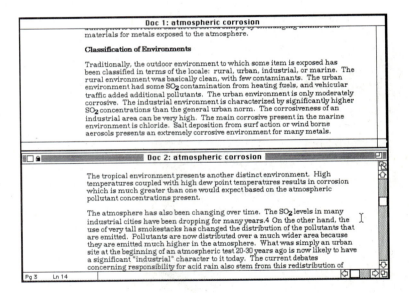

Fig. 7.20
Viewing two copies of the same document.

Notice in figure 7.20 that the second copy of the file (the read-only copy) has a padlock symbol next to the window close box. This padlock reminds you that the file in that window is "locked" and can be read only. (Remember, you cannot save any changes you make to a locked document unless you rename it.) When you try to save a read-only file, WordPerfect displays the Save As dialog box so that you can give the read-only file a new name.

Part II

Refining Documents

> **Tip**
>
> Using two copies of a file on-screen is not the same as split-screen editing of a single copy. (Split-screen editing is available in some word processors, but not in WordPerfect for the Mac.) To avoid confusion, make all your changes to the first copy of the file you opened.

The second copy you open is a copy of the file as it exists on disk when you issue the second Open command. If you open a file, make changes that you don't save, and then open a second copy of the file, the second open document is a copy of the version of the file without the changes (and the second copy is still read-only). Similarly, none of the changes you make in one window appear in the other window.

Changing the Active Window

If you have several files open at the same time, you can switch between the files to view and edit them. Changing the active window is very important because the commands you issue and the changes you make affect the active window only.

WordPerfect enables you to switch the active window in several ways. In a stack of overlapping windows, the active window is always the front window. As in all other Mac applications, the title bar of the active window has horizontal lines and visible scroll bars. In a group of tiled windows, the title and scroll bars indicate which window is active.

Perhaps the easiest way to make a window active is to click the window. If you can see any portion of a window, no matter how small, you can click that portion to activate the window. The second method available for activating a window is to choose the window from the list at the bottom of the main Edit menu (see fig. 7.21). The current window, with a check mark next to the window name, appears below the Cycle Windows option.

A padlock icon appears next to read-only files (Doc 2: Atmospheric Corrosion in figure 7.21, for example). Be sure to pay attention to the padlock symbol for read-only windows. The read-only version doesn't necessarily have a higher document number (DOC2 versus DOC1) than the regular version.

The last method for activating a window is to use the Cycle Windows command. Choosing this command activates the window that is at the bottom of the Edit menu and moves the window's name to the top of the list. If only two files, each of which use the entire screen, are open and you want to switch between the two documents, you should use the Cycle Windows command. To cycle through the open windows, press ⌘-Shift-W. You also can choose Cycle Windows from the Edit menu; however, if you access the Edit menu, you may as well pick the window you want directly.

Chapter 7
Managing Files and Documents

Fig. 7.21
Using the Edit menu to change windows.

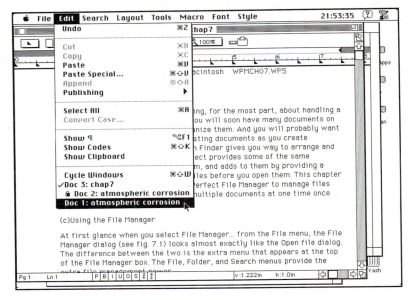

Combining Two Files

Large projects often are split up into several pieces to make working on the various sections easier. Smaller files are handled faster by WordPerfect, and multiple authors usually find working with separate files easier for early drafts. When the work is finished, you may want to combine all the sections into a single document.

Combining the contents of two files in WordPerfect is easy. Follow these steps:

1. Open one of the files to be combined.

2. Place the insertion point in the open file where the other file should be inserted.

3. Choose Insert from the File menu. The Open File dialog box appears.

4. Choose the file to be inserted from the file list.

5. Click Insert in the Open File dialog box. WordPerfect inserts the specified file at the location of the insertion point.

Part II

Refining Documents

To insert parts of several files into another file, open all the files you need and alternately copy the text from the source files, switch to the destination document window, and paste the material into the destination document. See Chapter 3, "Editing a Document," for information about moving text by using the Copy and Paste commands.

Converting File Formats

If you share files with someone outside your work group or get files from outside your company, you may have to convert a source file to WordPerfect Mac Version 2.1 format. Different word processing applications use different ways (file formats) of storing the commands that control the formatting of text and graphics on a page.

You must convert files from other word processors before you can edit the foreign file in WordPerfect for the Mac. (To WordPerfect, all other file formats are "foreign.") If you send files to someone else, you also may have to convert your document to the appropriate format before sending the document because the WordPerfect Mac format is new enough that many other programs may not recognize it. (Converting a file from another format to WordPerfect for the Mac is called *importing*. Converting from WordPerfect Mac to another format is called *exporting*.)

Reviewing File Conversion Filters

Besides the native 2.1 format, WordPerfect provides 14 word processing file import conversion filters, 7 graphics file import filters, and 6 export filters. The WordPerfect 2.1 installer places conversion filters inside the Conversions folder that is in the WordPerfect folder inside the Preferences folder in the System Folder of your hard disk. The conversion filters supplied with Version 2.1 are shown in figure 7.22.

Fig. 7.22
File conversion filters in the Conversions folder.

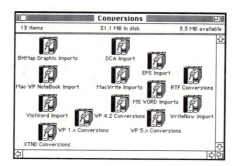

Chapter 7
Managing Files and Documents

WordPerfect Corporation is adding to the list of available conversion filters. New filters can be completed and distributed independently of a new version of the program. You should check with WordPerfect Customer Support to see whether a filter you want has been completed since the release of your version of the program.

RTF Documents

Microsoft Corporation developed a file format known as *RTF* (Rich Text Format) to ease document transfers between different computers and programs. The RTF specification is a set of commands for describing the format (font, size, style, margins, and so forth) and content (text and graphics) of the material that resides in a computer file.

Nearly all Macintosh word processors can read an RTF file. Although you lose some formatting when you convert RTF between systems, using RTF is better than the alternative—plain, unformatted text. WordPerfect now recommends RTF as the way to send Version 2.1 files to Microsoft Word and Aldus PageMaker.

The XTND Conversion Utility

Claris Corporation developed the XTND conversion scheme for many of the same reasons that Microsoft developed RTF. With the XTND utility, you gain greater compatibility between many different systems; however, each file type must have its own filter. Claris provides several filters with many of its applications. XTND conversion filters also are available from DataViz Inc. in its MacLink Plus Translators package.

If you already have XTND filters installed with a Claris application, the filters should be available for importing and exporting files with WordPerfect. If you get the filters from another source, such as the Claris forum on CompuServe, carefully follow the instructions in the Read Me file on the WordPerfect Installer disk to make the filters available.

Importing Files

To edit a file in WordPerfect that you or someone else created in another word processor, you must *import* the file into WordPerfect. WordPerfect uses an import file conversion filter to translate the other word processor's formatting commands into equivalent WordPerfect formatting.

WordPerfect recognizes the format of most files for which WordPerfect has an import filter. To open a Microsoft Word document, for example, follow these steps:

1. Choose Open from the File menu or press ⌘-O.

2. From the Show pop-up menu in the Open dialog box, choose All or Documents.

3. From the Retain pop-up menu, choose the appropriate option for the amount of formatting you want to retain. (See "Using the Retain Menu" earlier in this chapter.)

4. Double-click the file name to open the document.

   Alternatively, you can choose the file from the file list and then click Open.

If WordPerfect recognizes the file type you are opening, a progress information box appears to indicate which filter is in use and how much of the conversion is complete (see fig. 7.23). After WordPerfect completes the conversion, the file opens in a new window with the same name as the source file.

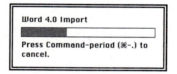

Fig. 7.23
A File Import Progress information box.

To keep the original file, be sure to use Save As to rename the new document or save the document to a different folder. If you use just the Save command, the WordPerfect version of the file overwrites the original version.

If, using the steps given earlier, you try to open a text file or a file that WordPerfect doesn't recognize, the Input Conversion Format dialog box appears (see fig. 7.24). If you are opening a text file, choose Text Import. Choose WP4.2 Import if you are opening a DOS WordPerfect Version 4.2 file. Choose XTND Import for any other type of file. (Remember that WordPerfect already has compared the format of the file being opened to the know conversion filter formats—XTND Import is your last chance.) Then click OK or press Return.

Chapter 7
Managing Files and Documents

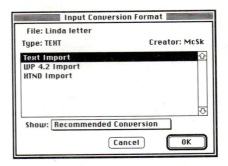

Fig. 7.24
The Input Conversion Format dialog box.

WordPerfect searches the XTND files in your WordPerfect folder and the System Folder for an XTND filter that matches the file. If WordPerfect finds one, the file opens in a new window.

You can change from the Recommended Conversion option to All Conversions with the Show pop-up menu in the Input Conversion Format dialog box. All Conversions lists all the conversion filters WordPerfect can find. Recommended Conversion lists the filters that are most likely to succeed at converting the file being opened. Chances are fairly good that if WordPerfect didn't put a conversion filter on the Recommended list, that filter cannot convert the file being opened.

That a text file created in WordPerfect causes the Input Conversion Format dialog box to appear may seem strange, but consistent handling of text files is the result. The dialog box appears for text files because some files that have a file type of TEXT are really a different format. The dialog box thus gives you a chance to compensate for the strange assignment of file type.

Exporting Files

If you share a WordPerfect file with someone who doesn't have WordPerfect for the Macintosh Version 2 or who has a different type of computer altogether, you must export the file before the other person can use it on her system. WordPerfect has several exporting options.

Exporting in Other Word Processing Formats

As you may guess from the similarities between importing (described earlier) and opening a WordPerfect file, exporting a file has much in common with saving a file. You use the Save As dialog box to export all files.

Part II
Refining Documents

To convert your WordPerfect 2.1 document to another file format, follow these steps:

1. Choose Save As from the File menu or press ⌘-Shift-S.

2. In the Save As dialog box, choose the export conversion filter from the Format pop-up menu (see fig. 7.25).

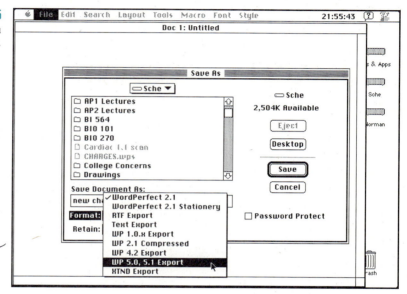

Fig. 7.25
The Format pop-up menu in the Save As dialog box.

The formats that begin with WP and end with Export are for WordPerfect products (DOS systems or older Mac WordPerfect versions). RTF, Text, and STND Exports are discussed later.

3. From the Retain pop-up menu, choose a value according to the amount of formatting the exported document must contain. (See "Using the Retain Menu" earlier in this chapter.)

4. Rename the document by typing a new name in the Save Document As text box in the Save As dialog box if you are saving the file to the same folder as the source file and want to keep your WordPerfect 2.1 copy of the file.

5. Click Save or press Return to start the export process.

Chapter 7

Managing Files and Documents

The XTND Export filter may provide additional file conversion formats, but those formats don't handle as many of the special features of WordPerfect 2.1 as specific filters provided by WordPerfect. If you have XTND filters installed on your hard disk and choose XTND Export in the Format pop-up menu, a list of available formats appears when you click Save (see fig 7.26). Choose a format by clicking the name or typing the letter next to the format name.

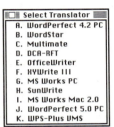

Fig. 7.26
An XTND Export filter list.

Notice that some of the listed XTND conversions match conversions available in the Format pop-up menu. If the file type is available in the Format pop-up menu, use that conversion filter instead of an XTND filter because more formatting information translates with the WordPerfect export filter.

Because Microsoft holds the leading market position in Mac word processing, at least for the moment, you may need to send a file to someone who wants a Word format file. WordPerfect, however, does not supply a direct Microsoft Word export conversion. Instead, send RTF and WP 5.0, 5.1 versions of the file. The other user can pick the file retaining the most important formatting features.

The current recommendation of WordPerfect is to use the RTF Export. Although some formatting is lost, the resulting file may be as close as you can get to a complete conversion. Alternatively, if you save your WordPerfect Mac file as a DOS WordPerfect file with the WP 5.0, 5.1 Export option, the recipient of your files can use import filters that enable Mac Microsoft Word users to open DOS WordPerfect files.

You also should use RTF to create a file that you can import into page layout programs, such as PageMaker. You can choose WP 1.0.x Export (the earlier version of WordPerfect for the Mac) from the Format pop-up menu. A PageMaker filter exists for the Version 1 series Mac program. Because a PageMaker filter has been requested frequently by customers, one probably will appear sometime soon. Check with WordPerfect Corporation and Aldus to see whether a PageMaker filter is ready.

Part II

Refining Documents

Exporting Text Files

To save only the words and none of the formatting information in a file, choose Text Export from the Save As dialog box's Format pop-up menu. The Text Type dialog box appears, enabling you to specify how WordPerfect should handle line breaks (soft returns) during an export operation (see fig. 7.27).

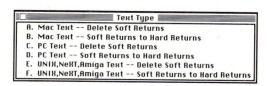

Fig. 7.27
The Text Type dialog box.

Choose Mac Text—Delete Soft Returns, PC Text—Delete Soft Returns, or UNIX, NeXT, Amiga Text—Delete Soft Returns, depending on the type of computer that will use the text file next. You should use the options that convert soft returns to hard returns only in special cases in which each line must end in a carriage return. A VAX computer, for example, expects to see a carriage return before 255 characters are entered in a file.

If you must send text on-line to a VAX computer, you probably must choose option D (PC Text—Soft Returns to Hard Returns) in the Text Type dialog box to get a file you can upload directly into a VAX text editor. Better ways exist to move a file to a mainframe or minicomputer these days, but occasionally sending raw text directly into a text editor on the minicomputer gets the job done.

Using WordPerfect Special Format Files

The Format pop-up menu on the Save As dialog box includes two special-format WordPerfect file types: WordPerfect 2.1 Stationery and WP 2.1 Compressed. You use these formats to create special types of files. Stationary documents enable you to set up documents as templates for frequently used reports, letters, or memos. Compressed files save space on your hard disk.

Chapter 7
Managing Files and Documents

Stationary Files

A *stationary document* can contain any text and formatting information you can put in an ordinary WordPerfect file. The difference between an ordinary file and a stationary file, however, is that a stationary file opens into an untitled document window. You keep the original stationary file on disk but create a copy to edit when you "open" the stationary file.

A stationary document is useful if you must create repetitive documents with minor changes. Save a copy of the file as a WordPerfect 2.1 Stationery format file. After you open the stationary file, you can make the necessary changes and save the new document with its own name.

Compressed Files

Not all the disk space taken up by a WordPerfect file is necessary to describe the formatting and contents of your documents. This inefficient storage helps speed up the process of opening a file. A compressed file stores document information more efficiently on disk but slows down your work.

A WordPerfect 2.1 file containing only text and no graphics takes up approximately twice as many bytes of disk space as the number of characters in the file. Graphics tend to be stored even less efficiently in files. Saving a 2.1 document in compressed form reclaims extra disk space at the expense of a significant decrease in speed when you open the file. After the file is open, you have little, if any, speed penalty while editing.

Although you may not want to compress files you use frequently, compressing old files for storage is a good idea. Save your current documents as normal files, for example, but after you edit them, save them as compressed files; then store them on disk.

Chapter Summary

This chapter covered several aspects of managing files in WordPerfect, including a File Manager option that goes beyond the system's capabilities: searching through several files for a text phrase without opening the files in WordPerfect.

Part II
Refining Documents

You learned how to save various portions of files (text and/or graphics) with or without page- and line-formatting detail. You also learned several techniques for arranging multiple document windows on-screen at the same time.

This chapter discussed importing and exporting, as well as the two special WordPerfect file formats. With these special formats, you can create repetitive documents easily and save disk space by compressing WordPerfect files.

Chapter 7
Managing Files and Documents

CHAPTER 8

Formatting with Styles

WordPerfect *styles* are collections of character, line, paragraph, and page formatting attributes that you define. You can apply these styles to text by issuing a single command. By defining a group of styles that are linked to each other, you also can format an entire document with few trips to the menu bar, and you can eliminate these trips by assigning a keystroke command to your base style.

Using styles to format text instead of formatting text manually enables you to accomplish complex formatting tasks more easily. If you define a Headline style of 14 point Helvetica bold, for instance, you can apply this style to selected text, and WordPerfect formats the text for you. Without using the style, you must manually choose the font, font size, and attribute for each headline in your document. Another way that using WordPerfect makes formatting easier is that, if you change a style description for a style used in your document, WordPerfect reformats the text linked to the style according to the changes. Scrolling through many pages of text to modify a series of formatting commands is unnecessary.

WordPerfect provides several ways that you can define a style: you can use sample text; you can modify an existing style; or you can start from scratch and define every formatting feature to be included in the style. WordPerfect also makes changing an existing style easy by enabling you to use the style editor or to update a style assigned to selected text.

In this chapter, you learn how to create, modify, apply, remove, and delete styles. With a few exceptions, using styles can simplify the process of creating a complex document. You must be careful, however, when you edit style definitions after you complete a document and when you exchange documents with a user who uses styles that, although named the same as yours, are defined differently.

Understanding Styles

Each document created with WordPerfect begins in the *Normal* style. WordPerfect comes with a built-in Normal style, which you can edit to suit your needs. In many cases, the definition of the Normal style determines the formatting of special features such as headers, footers, footnotes, endnotes, and box captions.

Do not confuse styles with the character attributes that you assign through the Style menu. (WordPerfect Corporation decided not to rename the Style menu because the menu appears under that name in virtually every Macintosh application.) The styles covered in this chapter are paragraph- rather than character-based—that is, when you apply a paragraph-based style to any part of a paragraph, WordPerfect applies the style elements to the whole paragraph.

Default Styles

All formatting in WordPerfect begins with the Normal style. WordPerfect stores the Normal style settings in the Defaults file, which is created when you install the program. You can edit the Normal style to change its format settings, but WordPerfect retains the original settings in the Defaults file so that you can retrieve them if needed. See the "Editing a Style" section for information on editing any style, including the Normal style.

Besides the Normal style, the WordPerfect installer creates the following additional default styles:

    Endnote

    Endnote # in Document

    Figure Box Caption

    Footer

    Footnote

Footnote # in Document

Header

Normal

Table Box Caption

Text Box

Text Box Caption

User Box Caption

Some default style names may look familiar because these style names also are the names of WordPerfect features or commands. WordPerfect uses these styles to generate the formatting for the respective features.

You can edit any of these styles to reflect your formatting choices. If you delete the Normal style, however, WordPerfect re-creates the style from the settings in the Defaults file the next time you start the application. If you change the other predefined styles, on the other hand, you must re-create the standard style definitions manually or use the Librarian to copy the original styles from the Installation disk. See Chapter 15, "Customizing WordPerfect," for information about using the Librarian.

Style Definitions

If you use style definitions instead of manually formatting documents, you ensure consistency of formats and eliminate the need for extensive searches to make formatting changes. If you collaborate with other users, style definitions enable you to maintain a uniform format for all documents. In addition, if the group leader decides that the standard format should change, only the style definition must be edited to accomplish the formatting changes.

Suppose, for example, that you have section headings formatted as 14-point boldface Geneva. Rather than apply the formatting to each section heading, you can define and apply a Heading style. By using a Heading style, you can format all headings correctly and consistently. Suppose you later decide to change the Heading style from boldface to italics, for example. If you formatted manually, you must find and change each head. With styles, you make the change once.

Problems may sometimes arise, however, if you edit styles after you complete a document. See "Avoiding Common Problems" at the end of this chapter for more information.

Chapter 8
Formatting with Styles

Style Precedence

To provide flexibility and control, WordPerfect provides three levels of style definitions. When you apply a particular style to one or more paragraphs in your document, WordPerfect first tries to use the style definition that is stored in the current document. If the style is not defined in the current document, the program searches the Private Library; if the style is not found in the Private Library, the program searches the Common Library, if available.

This arrangement ensures that style alterations made for a particular document are consistent throughout that document. This arrangement also enables you to make single document style changes without altering the library styles; the two libraries then provide document-to-document consistency in formatting.

Document Styles

After you create a style, WordPerfect installs the new style definition in the current document. When you choose the style name, the program uses this document style even if a style with the same name exists in the libraries.

Document styles enable you to share documents with other people without their style definitions interfering with the formatting of your document. Document styles also enable you to make minor formatting changes for one document without affecting other documents.

As you learn to use styles, saving the style definition in the document rather than one of the libraries is a good idea. After you define a style, you can use the Librarian to transfer a copy of the style to the Private Library (see Chapter 15, "Customizing WordPerfect").

Private and Common Library Styles

The *Private Library* is a permanent file that contains styles and other resources that the program uses with documents you create. WordPerfect created the Private Library in the System Folder's Preferences folder when you installed the program. The Private Library is dedicated to your work only. After you install a style in the Private Library, you can use that style in any document.

The *Common Library*, which is the same type of file as the Private Library, is installed on a network server, enabling an entire work group to access a single set of style definitions. By using a common set of definitions, a group can create documents that are consistent in format. Remember, however, that the Common Library is the last place WordPerfect looks for a style definition. If you are working in a network environment, see Chapter 15, "Customizing WordPerfect," for instructions on setting the path to pick up Common Library style definitions first.

Creating Styles

Frequently, when people begin using a word processor, they format all text manually. As they become more familiar with the software and tire of repeating formatting commands, they begin to format with styles.

WordPerfect provides an easy way to define a style according to the formatting of existing text. This style-by-example feature enables you to choose whether to include in the style definition the character attributes and ruler formatting of the existing text. You also can create, at any time, a new style not related to existing text. When you define a style, you can save the style definition in the current document or in one of the libraries.

Defining a Style

To define a style, you can use existing text that contains the desired formatting. Suppose, for example, that you are using boldfaced characters to emphasize section headings in your reports, as shown in figure 8.1. You can define a boldfaced Section Heading style that you use each time you enter a heading.

You can choose how much of the sample text formatting to preserve in your style definition. You can choose to preserve the attributes, formatting (ruler settings), both, or neither. If you preserve neither the attributes nor the formatting, you are, in effect, creating a style from scratch, with no connection to existing text.

Chapter 8

Formatting with Styles

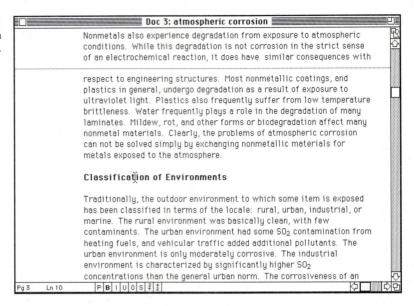

Fig. 8.1
A typical document with boldface section headings.

Preserving Attributes

For the purpose of defining a style, *attributes* determine the appearance of a single character. Font, size, and text style (boldface, italic, and so on) are the attributes a style can include. To create a style that formats only the attributes—14 point boldface text, for example—you should define the style-preserving attributes only.

Follow these steps to define a style that preserves attributes:

1. Click anywhere in the text that contains the desired character attributes (or use the arrow keys to place the insertion point within the appropriate text). For the example in figure 8.1, the chosen text is the boldface section heading.

2. Choose New from the Styles submenu in the Layout menu, as shown in figure 8.2, or press ⌘-F10 on an extended keyboard. WordPerfect displays the New Style dialog box (see fig. 8.3).

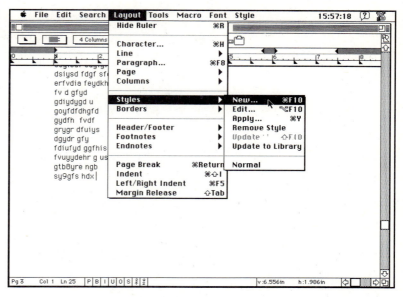

Fig. 8.2
Choosing New from the Styles submenu.

Fig. 8.3
The New Style dialog box.

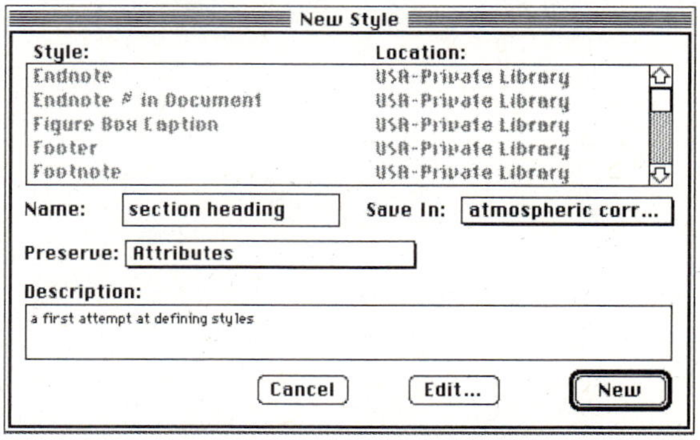

3. Type the style name—*section heading*, for the example—in the Name text box.

4. Check to see that the Preserve pop-up menu indicates Attributes and the Save In pop-up menu displays the document name.

5. Place the insertion point in the Description text box (click the text box or press Tab) and type a description of the new style. When you edit the style in the future, this information can help you remember why you defined the style.

Chapter 8
Formatting with Styles

6. Click the New button or press Return.

These steps define a style that formats any paragraph with the same character attributes (font, font size, color, and other special attributes) as the selected text.

Preserving Attributes and Formatting

Character attributes are only a small part of the formatting information that you can include in a style. Styles also can preserve a paragraph's margin settings and text alignment.

Any formatting setting that you can make on the ruler are transferred to the style definition if you choose to preserve formatting. (See Chapter 4, "Formatting a Document," for more information on formatting with the ruler.) If your document title is centered, boldfaced, and entered in a font size larger than the rest of the text, as shown in fig. 8.4, you can include all that information in your Title style definition by preserving attributes and formatting.

Fig. 8.4
A sample report title.

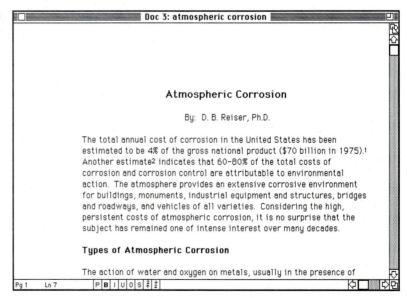

To define a style that retains character attributes and formatting, follow these steps:

1. Place the insertion point in the chosen sample text—for the example, in the title.

2. Choose New from the Styles submenu in the Layout menu or press ⌘-F10 to access the New Style dialog box.

3. Type the style name—for example, *Title*—in the Name text box; then type a short description of the style in the Description text box.

4. Choose Attributes and Formatting from the Preserve pop-up menu (see fig. 8.5).

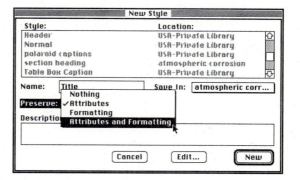

Fig. 8.5
Choosing Attributes and Formatting from the Preserve pop-up menu.

5. Choose USA-Private Library from the Save In pop-up menu (see fig. 8.6).

   Because the title appears only once in a document, defining a Title style for a single document is unnecessary. If you were to define a Title style for the document, however, you would choose the document name from the Save In pop-up menu—in this case, Atmospheric Corrosion. (Notice that the default for the Save In pop-up menu is the document, not the library.)

6. Click the New button or press Return to define the style and save it in the Private Library. You now can apply the defined style to the sample text.

Chapter 8
Formatting with Styles

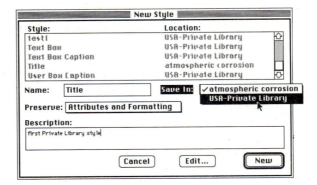

Fig. 8.6
Setting the Save In pop-up menu to Private Library.

Preserving Formatting

If you choose Formatting from the Preserve pop-up menu, only ruler formatting information (margins, alignment, column definitions, tab settings, and so forth) are transferred to a style definition. You may use this option, for example, when your documents require consistent margins, but you frequently change the font or size of text within those margins.

Preserving Nothing

Creating a new style with the Nothing option set in the Preserve pop-up menu creates a blank style. To create a style from scratch, you should choose the Preserve Nothing option from the pop-up menu. See "Editing a Style" later to see how to add formatting and attribute information to blank styles created with the Preserve Nothing setting.

Applying a Style

Even though you use existing text to define a new style, that text remains manually formatted. To gain the advantage of being able to update all occurrences of a particular style by editing a single style definition, you now must *apply* the style to the sample text. To do so, follow these steps:

1. Select text in the heading that you used to define the new style.

   If you don't select any text, WordPerfect applies the style to all paragraphs from the current paragraph to the end of the

Part II
Refining Documents

document (unless you are using the Environment Format Single Paragraph option described in Chapter 15, "Customizing WordPerfect").

2. Choose Apply from the Styles submenu in the Layout menu, press ⌘-Y, or press F10. The Apply Styles dialog box appears, with the style you just defined highlighted in the Style list (see fig. 8.7). To apply a different style to the paragraph, click the name of the appropriate style.

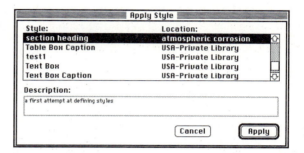

Fig. 8.7
Choosing a style to apply.

3. Click the Apply button or press Return to apply the style to the highlighted text.

In the Apply Style dialog box, you can find a style name by typing the first few letters of the name. As you type, the style selection highlight bar scrolls to the proper place in the list and selects the first style name beginning with the characters you enter. You then can use the arrow keys to move through the list. When you enter more than a character or two, type quickly; if you hesitate, the program may complete one search and initiate a second search for the last few characters that you type.

After you apply the style, notice that the name of the applied style appears in the status bar at the bottom of the document window. The status bar always indicates the style in effect at the current insertion point location (see fig. 8.8).

Although you can use regular formatting techniques to apply the boldface attribute to your section heading, using a style makes applying attributes easier, particularly if you want to change the appearance of your document in the future. If you decide later that all the section headings should be boldface italic type in a larger font size, for example, you can edit the Section Heading style definition. By editing style definitions, you do not need to scroll through the document to find and change the headings; WordPerfect changes all the section headings for you.

Chapter 8
Formatting with Styles

Fig. 8.8
Indication of current style on the status bar.

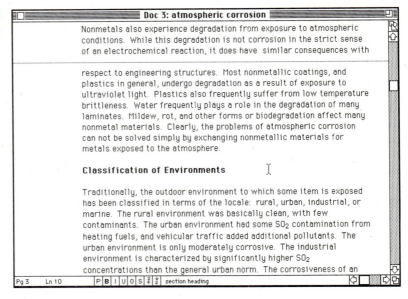

Editing a Style

Styles that you define by using sample text often fall short of the style idea with which you began. The formatting information that is included by the Preserve Formatting option is limited to the formatting you can accomplish from the ruler. You can add many more formatting commands, however, by editing your style definition. Editing also enables you to eliminate some information from the style definition created by the New Style Preserve options.

Suppose, for example, that you don't want a specific font defined in the Title style and that you want the titles centered between the existing margins. You can apply the Title style to existing titles in such a way that size and other attribute information is changed, but the font remains the same.

To edit the Title style defined in the preceding section, follow these steps:

1. Choose Edit from the Styles submenu in the Layout menu or press Option-F10. WordPerfect displays the Edit Style dialog box (see fig. 8.9).

Part II

Refining Documents

Fig. 8.9
The Edit Style dialog box.

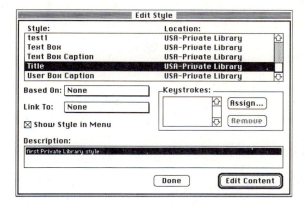

2. Select the Title style from the Style list.

3. Click the Edit Content button or press Return to open the style definition window (see fig. 8.10).

Fig. 8.10
Examining the Title style in the style definition window.

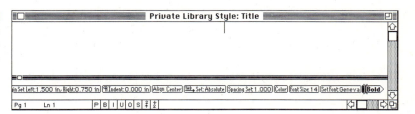

When you first open a style definition window, the codes window appears at the bottom. When you edit a style, the codes window provides a quick way to see what formatting commands are included in the style. (Chapter 3, "Editing a Document," provides more details about using codes.)

Notice that the title bar of the style definition window indicates the name and location of the style. `Private Library Style: Title`, for this example, indicates that the style name is *Title* and that this style is saved in the Private Library.

4. Click the right side of the font code (`Set Font Geneva` in figure 8.9), or use the arrow keys to move the wide, black codes cursor to the right of the font code and press Delete. WordPerfect removes the font code.

Chapter 8
Formatting with Styles

5. Move the codes cursor to the right of the margin definition (at the beginning of the line) and press Delete. WordPerfect removes the margin definition.

6. Close the style definition window by clicking the close box or pressing ⌘-W.

After you close the style definition window, the changes you made take effect. In the example, no noticeable change occurs because the codes removed from the style definition also exist in the document as a whole. Because the Title style is now more generic, however, you can apply it to documents that use different margins or different fonts without changing the formatting.

Adding a Style to the Styles Submenu

When you define a new style, WordPerfect adds the name of the new style to the bottom section of the Styles submenu (see fig. 8.11). Any styles in the Private Library or in the current document appear in this menu if you activate the Show Style in Menu option in the Edit Style dialog box.

Fig. 8.11
Defined styles shown in the Styles submenu.

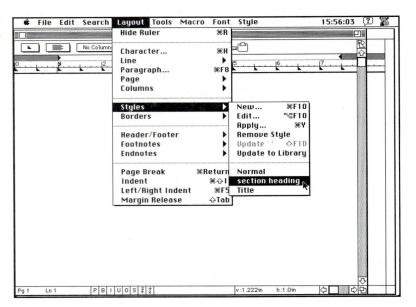

Part II
Refining Documents

To include or exclude a particular style on the Styles menu, follow these steps:

1. Choose Edit from the Styles menu or press Option-F10. WordPerfect displays the Edit Style dialog box (refer to fig. 8.9).

2. Select the style from the list.

3. To display a style on the Styles submenu, click the Show Style in Menu check box or press ⌘-S so that an X appears in the box. By clicking the check box again, the X disappears, indicating that the style is not displayed on the submenu.

4. Click the Done button or press ⌘-period (.) to leave the Edit Style dialog box.

To apply a style from the Styles submenu, place the insertion point in the paragraph where you want the style to start (or select a few characters to limit the style to the specified paragraph); then choose the style name from the Styles submenu in the Layout menu.

Assigning a Keystroke Command

The Edit Style dialog box also enables you to define a keystroke command for applying a style. Keystroke commands save you the effort of going to a submenu every time you intend to change styles in a document.

To assign a keystroke command to the Title style, for example, follow these steps:

1. Choose Edit from the Styles submenu in the Layout menu or press Option-F10. The Edit Style dialog box appears.

2. Select the Title style from the Style list.

3. Click the Assign button in the Keystrokes section (refer to fig. 8.9). WordPerfect displays the Assign Keystroke dialog box (see fig. 8.12).

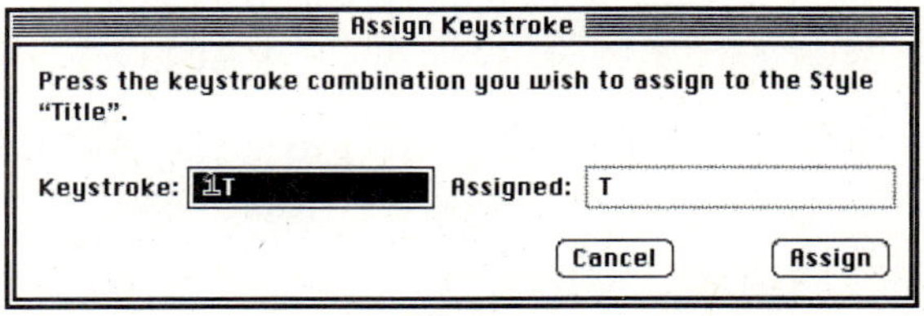

Fig. 8.12
The Assign Keystroke dialog box.

Chapter 8
Formatting with Styles

4. Enter the keystroke combination you want to assign to the style. For the example, press the Gold key (the Keypad-7 key); then type the letter *T*.

   The *Gold key* is represented by an outlined *1* when pressed once before a keystroke (refer to fig. 8.12). By using the Gold key, you can avoid conflicts with other keyboard commands. See Chapter 15, "Customizing WordPerfect," for more information about assigning keystroke commands.

   If anything appears in the Assigned text box when you type a keystroke sequence in the Assign Keystroke dialog box, you have a conflict with a keystroke defined by WordPerfect (or you). A *T* appears in the Assigned text box in figure 8.12, indicating that, as defined by WordPerfect, this keystroke combination—Gold-T—is currently assigned.

   For this example, replacing the current Gold-T assignment (inserting a *T* in your document) with a new assignment (applying the Title style) shouldn't cause any problems.

5. Click the Assign button to save the new assignment. WordPerfect replaces the old assignment with the new.

   Your new definition—that is, applying the style—overrides the old keystroke assignment. If you don't want to override a prior definition, return to step 4 and enter a different keystroke.

   The assigned keystroke appears in the Edit Style dialog box and next to Title in the Styles submenu.

6. Click the Done button in the Edit Style dialog box. You now can apply the Title style by pressing Gold-T.

You can assign a keystroke to any style when the Edit Style dialog box is open. To assign a keystroke to a style being created, click the Edit button in the New Style dialog box (refer to fig. 8.6) to access the Edit Style dialog box. You then can assign a keystroke to your new style. The Keyboards command under Preferences in the File menu also enables you to assign keystrokes to styles. See Chapter 15, "Customizing WordPerfect," for more information on this method of defining keystrokes.

The Assign Keystroke dialog box is the only dialog box that does not have Command-key equivalents for the buttons; you must use the mouse to assign or cancel keystrokes. You can use the Command (⌘), Option, or Shift keys in your keystroke definitions, but you cannot use the Control key.

Part II

Refining Documents

Updating a Style

To make a small change in your style definition, using the Update command is frequently easier than using the Edit Style dialog box. To make a quick change to the Title style, for example, follow these steps:

1. Select text—the title—entered in the style you want to change.

2. Change the font, font size, character attributes, or formatting alignment.

3. Leave the title selected (or make sure that the insertion point is somewhere in the modified title) and choose Update from the Styles submenu in the Layout menu or press Shift-F10.

   The Update Style dialog box appears (see fig. 8.13). Notice the warning that tells you that you cannot use the Edit menu's Undo command to reverse an update operation.

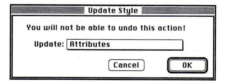

Fig. 8.13
The Update Style dialog box.

4. Use the Update pop-up menu to specify the update as Attributes only, Formatting only, or both.

5. Click OK or press Return. WordPerfect updates the style according to the specifications and changes you made.

Using Text in a Style Definition

While you edit the content of the Title style, you may notice that the style definition window looks similar to a document window. You can enter text in a style definition window. The capability to include text in a style can be quite useful.

When, in addition to the formatting specifications, you include regular text in a style definition, the text appears in your document at the beginning of the paragraph to which you apply the style. If you have standard section headings for frequently issued reports, for example, you can add the headings to the style definition and save yourself the trouble of typing the headings. Consider, for example, one of the simplest paragraph headings frequently added—a bullet.

You can create a Bullet List style, for example, by following these steps:

1. Choose New from the Styles submenu in the Layout menu or press ⌘-F10. WordPerfect displays the New Style dialog box.

2. Type *Bullet List* (or any name that helps you remember the style being defined) in the Name text box; then type a description in the Description text box.

3. Choose Nothing from the Preserve pop-up menu and Private Library from the Save In pop-up menu so that the New Style dialog box resembles the dialog box shown in figure 8.14.

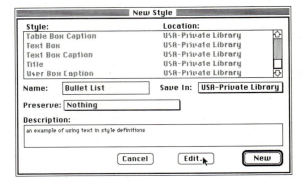

Fig. 8.14
Entering a Bullet List style in the New Style dialog box.

Remember that Preserve Nothing creates a blank style (no formatting or text). To keep attributes, formatting, or attributes and formatting of the text surrounding the insertion point, you can choose another Preserve option.

4. Click the Edit button or press ⌘-E. The Edit Style dialog box appears.

5. Click the Assign button in the Edit Style dialog box or press ⌘-A to access the Assign Keystroke dialog box. Assign a keystroke command (such as Gold-B) to the style.

6. When you return to the Edit Style dialog box, click the Edit Content button or press Return.

   A new style definition window appears, bearing the title that you gave the style. Now you can enter any text and formatting that the style should contain.

7. Press ⌘-R to display the ruler in the style definition window and set a tab stop 1/4 inch from the left margin.

8. Press Option-8 (the 8 from the main keyboard) to insert the round bullet character.

   The bullet (or any text you enter) appears in the style definition window above the line that marks the beginning of the codes window.

9. Press F5, press ⌘-Shift-I, or choose Indent from the Layout menu.

   Your style definition window should resemble figure 8.15. The style definition now includes text (the bullet character) and the indent formatting that sets off the bullet from other text you enter in the document.

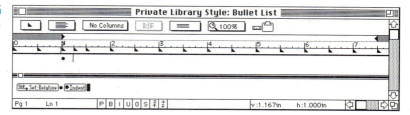

Fig. 8.15
Entering text in the style definition window.

10. Close the style definition window by clicking the close box or pressing ⌘-W.

To use the new style to create a bulleted list in your document, follow these steps:

1. Press Return or move the insertion point to a new line.

2. Press Gold-B (or the keystroke combination you assigned); then type the text of the first item on your list.

3. Repeat step 2 for each item on your list, pressing the appropriate keystroke combination each time you want the bullet to appear.

4. When the list is complete, press Return to start a new paragraph and choose a new style—Normal, for example—from the Styles submenu in the Layout menu.

You also can define a macro, as explained in Chapter 14, "Using Macros," to insert a bullet followed by an Indent command. If you are inclined to work with macros, you may think using a macro is an easier way to create a bulleted list. Such an opinion may be correct concerning the style definition shown in this section. Later in this chapter, however, you modify the style definition created here to make it even easier to use—easier even than extending a simple bullet list macro.

Chapter 8
Formatting with Styles

Removing a Style from Text

If you apply a style by mistake or decide that you don't like the way your document looks with a particular style, you can remove that style from the text.

Removing a style does not delete the style definition from your file or from the Private Library. You remove the application of a style's attribute and formatting commands from selected text. To remove a style from some text, follow these steps:

1. Select the paragraphs you want to change.

2. Choose Remove from the Styles submenu in the Layout menu.

WordPerfect removes the formatting controlled by the style from the text. If you applied no other formatting manually, the text reverts to the Normal style. Removing a style does not affect manually applied formatting changes.

Using Advanced Style Features

By reading the preceding sections, you know how to create single styles and apply these styles one at a time; however, WordPerfect also enables you to link one style to another and to base new styles on previously defined styles. Using these style features, you can create a collection of styles that enables you to apply complex formatting to documents with much less effort.

Linking Styles

Linking styles enables you to switch from one style to another while you edit. You initiate the link by pressing the Enter key on the numeric keypad. Pressing Enter inserts a hard carriage return in the document (much like pressing Return) and switches from one style to another, according to the link designated in the first style definition. You can enter as many paragraphs as you want in the first style before pressing Enter to force the link to the second style.

To create a linked list of styles, you first must make sure that you have defined all the styles to be linked, and then do the following:

1. Access the Edit Style dialog box by choosing Edit from the Styles submenu in the Layout menu.

2. Choose a style from the list at the top of the Edit Style dialog box.

3. Use the Link To pop-up menu to pick the name of the style that should follow in the chain of styles.

   Repeat these steps for each link in the chain.

Although you can define the links in any order, you can keep track of the styles more easily if you form the links in order.

The following example demonstrates the special case of linking a style to itself. Earlier in the chapter you defined a Bullet List style for creating lists of paragraphs. With the Bullet List style linked to itself, you can start a new bullet paragraph by pressing the Enter key instead of the keyboard command you assigned to the style.

To link the Bullet List style to itself, follow these steps:

1. Choose Edit from the Styles submenu in the Layout menu or press Option-F10. The Edit Style dialog box appears.

2. Select Bullet List from the styles list.

3. Click the Link To pop-up menu and choose Bullet List (see fig. 8.16).

Fig. 8.16
Linking the Bullet List style to itself.

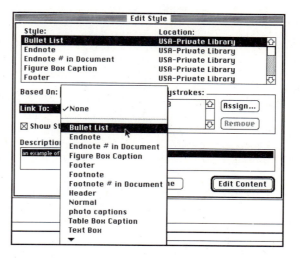

The real advantage of linking styles is being able to define an extended series of linked styles to format a large report. Instead of remembering and using several style command keys, link the styles in the appropriate order and use the Enter key to switch styles for each section.

Chapter 8
Formatting with Styles

Basing One Style on Another

Another convenience feature provided by WordPerfect is the capability of basing one style on a previously defined style. If your section headings are only slightly different from your titles, for example, you can use this feature to base your Section Heading style on the Title style definition. After the connection is made, most changes made to the Title style definition also are reflected in text formatted by the Section Heading style.

You can create a new Section Heading style based on the Title style defined earlier by following these steps:

1. Choose New from the Styles submenu in the Layout menu or press ⌘-F10. The New Style dialog box appears.

2. Type *Section Header* in the Name text box and give the style a description.

3. Choose Nothing from the Preserve pop-up menu; then choose Private Library from the Save In pop-up menu.

4. Click the Edit button or press ⌘-E to open the Edit Style dialog box.

5. Select Title, which you defined earlier in this chapter, from the Based On pop-up menu.

6. Click Edit Content or press Return to open the style definition window.

7. Choose Left from the Style menu (do not confuse this menu with the Styles submenu in the Layout menu), or press ⌘-Shift-L to set left alignment for the Section Heading style. You also can enter any other formatting information specific to the new style.

8. Close the style definition window by clicking the close box or pressing ⌘-W.

This style contains one code—the left alignment code—and a reference to the Title style. If you change anything except the alignment in the Title style definition, the Section Heading style also changes. Any formatting defined in a style (alignment, in this case) takes precedence over the formatting of the style on which the applied style is based (the Title style in this example).

These convenience features are most helpful if you work with clear rules governing the formatting of documents. Many corporations, for instance, have well-defined formatting rules for their internal documents. After these rules have been translated into style descriptions, you can create documents that conform to the rules by applying the correct styles. If you work on a network, the styles can be made available and controlled through the Common Library.

Deleting a Style

Sooner or later, you may want to delete a style. You may define styles you don't use, for example, or your formatting needs may change. You use the Librarian to delete styles. Chapter 15, "Customizing WordPerfect," deals with the Librarian in more detail, but the basic steps are explained here.

To delete a style from a document or from the Private Library, follow these steps:

1. Choose Librarian from the File menu. The Librarian dialog box appears.

2. Choose Styles from the Resource pop-up menu in the Librarian dialog box (see fig. 8.17).

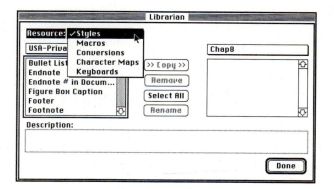

Fig. 8.17
Setting the Resource pop-up menu to Styles.

3. Select the style to be deleted from the Private Library style list (left side of the dialog box) or the current document style list (right side).

4. Click the Remove button or press ⌘-R to delete the style definition.

Chapter 8
Formatting with Styles

5. Click the Done button or press Return to close the Librarian dialog box. WordPerfect deletes the selected style.

As described earlier, the Remove Style command does not delete the style description from your document or Private Library. Similarly, deleting a style definition by removing it with the Librarian does not perform an automatic Remove Style command on your text. Text formatted by a style before you delete the style retains the formatting and attributes of the style definition.

Although WordPerfect deletes the style from the Private Library, the text retains not only its formatting, but a reference to the name of the deleted style, as well. If you later define a new style with the same name or give the file to someone who has a style with the same name, the new style definition reformats the text assigned to the old style. Be careful about deleting style definitions from documents.

Avoiding Common Problems

lthough styles are easy to create and use, some common problems do occur. The goal of this section is to describe problems that you may encounter and to explain how to avoid or correct these problems.

Retaining Style Formatting

When you create a document, the document contains a Normal style code that you cannot remove. If you give a copy of that document to an associate who uses a different version of WordPerfect, WordPerfect formats the file according to the Normal style on the your associate's machine.

By choosing Update to Library from the Layout Styles submenu, you can install in the document all default style definitions so that your formatting is retained. This command writes a copy of all default styles from your Private Library to your document. These definitions increase the size of your document by about 4,000 bytes—a small price to pay for formatting sanity if you share files with other workers.

Part II

Refining Documents

You also can use the Librarian to move a subset of the default styles to the document. You must use the Librarian to move style definitions of styles you create yourself. See Chapter 15, "Customizing WordPerfect," for instructions on using the Librarian.

After copying the default styles to the document, the document copy controls formatting. To change the Normal style, be sure to choose the document version in the Librarian dialog box.

Retaining Manual Formatting

Because WordPerfect's styles are paragraph based, applied styles affect entire paragraphs. Applying a style to a paragraph that contains manual formatting may change the existing format. If you enter a paragraph with one word in boldface and then apply a style to that paragraph, for example, the boldface attribute disappears from the word you emphasized. To avoid this problem, apply styles to text before you make manual formatting additions.

If you edit a style definition that affects text containing manual font or formatting changes, WordPerfect does not apply the style definition changes to the text that follows the point from which the manual change should switch back to the style definition. To see an example of this effect, follow these steps:

1. Type a sentence in a new document.

2. Move the insertion point to the middle of the sentence.

3. Choose Symbol or Zapf Dingbats from the Font menu and enter a few characters.

4. Choose Edit Style from the Styles submenu in the Layout menu or press Option-F10. The Edit Style dialog box appears.

5. Choose Normal from the styles list (Normal in the active document if you copied Normal into the document) and click the Edit Content button. The Normal style definition window appears.

6. Choose a different font from the Font menu.

7. Close the style definition window by clicking the close box or by pressing ⌘-W.

Your sentence should resemble figure 8.18. Notice that the font change in the edited style definition affects only text before the Symbol characters. To avoid this problem, do not edit styles after you enter text, apply a style, and add additional manual formatting commands.

Chapter 8
Formatting with Styles

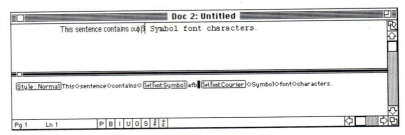

Fig. 8.18
Side effects of editing a style definition.

> **Tip**
> Edit the Normal style in your Private Library so that Normal style contains the font and margins you use most often. Use the Librarian to copy the Normal style into each document you create, and modify the document copy of the Normal style to change your major font and formatting information.

All default styles are based on the Normal style, despite the fact that the Based On pop-up menu in the Edit Style dialog box reports that they are based on None. The biggest consequence of this hidden connection is that when you enter a note, a header, or one of the other predefined style features, the font and formatting are those of the Normal style rather than the formatting you manually assign to the text containing the feature.

Suppose that the font defined in your Normal style is Times, and that for one document you decide to use the New Century Schoolbook font. If you select the new font when you open a new document rather than edit the Normal style, you must change the font manually in your headers, footers, notes, and so forth because the font of each of these elements is your default font, Times.

Chapter Summary

This chapter, in addition to covering the basics of using styles to automate document formatting, introduced you to such advanced features as basing one style on another and linking styles in a series. You learned how to create styles by formatting text first and then assigning that formatting information to a style. You also learned how to apply, edit, remove, and delete styles.

Styles offer a powerful and convenient way to achieve consistent, complex formatting of the documents you create. As long as you are aware of the limitations mentioned in the last section, using styles in WordPerfect makes the task of formatting documents much easier.

Part II
Refining Documents

CHAPTER 9

Using Columns and Text Boxes

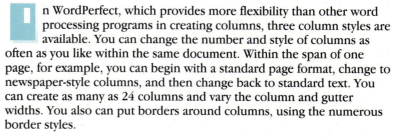

In WordPerfect, which provides more flexibility than other word processing programs in creating columns, three column styles are available. You can change the number and style of columns as often as you like within the same document. Within the span of one page, for example, you can begin with a standard page format, change to newspaper-style columns, and then change back to standard text. You can create as many as 24 columns and vary the column and gutter widths. You also can put borders around columns, using the numerous border styles.

Using WordPerfect, you also can create text boxes, which enable you to isolate text within a document. By setting text apart from the rest of the document, you essentially create a document within a document—a perfect way to highlight important information. You can use most WordPerfect features within a text box; for example, you can enter text, change the fonts, or create columns. You also can move a text box—anchored to or independent of text—around your document. To make the text box more distinctive, you can frame it (put a border around it) and add a background pattern.

After you finish this chapter, you will be able to do the following:

- Define the types of columns
- Set column margins
- Add borders to columns

- Create text boxes
- Edit and move text boxes
- Add frames and captions to text boxes

Defining Types of Columns

You can create three types of column formats with WordPerfect: newspaper, parallel, and extended parallel. Text in newspaper column format, shown in figure 9.1, flows from the bottom of one column to the top of the next column. Newsletters, brochures, and newspapers frequently use this column style. You use parallel columns, also shown in figure 9.1, to arrange text side by side. The parallel column style frequently is used to make tables or lists of related materials.

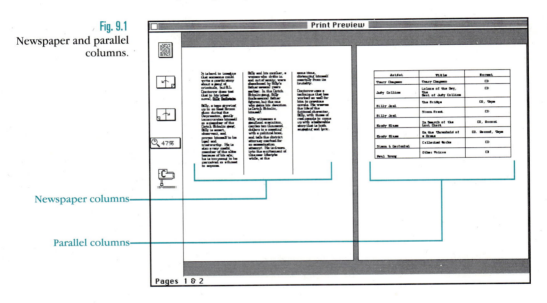

Fig. 9.1
Newspaper and parallel columns.

Newspaper columns

Parallel columns

The extended column style is a variation of parallel columns. The text in an extended column can continue across a page break, as shown in figure 9.2. WordPerfect does not move the entire row to the next page.

Part II

Refining Documents

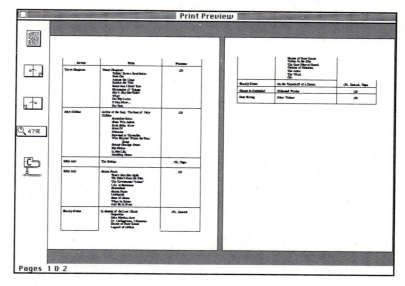

Fig. 9.2
Extended columns.

Adding and Adjusting Columns

A *column* is a vertical unit into which you can enter text. By creating more than one column, you change the placement of text on the page. The most common style for standard documents is a single newspaper style column; in fact, most of the text in this book uses the one-column newspaper style. As you create columns, you should be familiar with the components of a column.

The *gutter* is the space between adjacent columns. A *row* is a unit of adjacent columns that begins at the left margin of the page and ends at the column break. A *column break* moves the insertion point to the beginning of the next column. You insert a column break by pressing ⌘-Shift-Return or by choosing Column Break from the Columns submenu in the Layout menu.

A *set* of columns begins when you define one column style and ends when you define another column style. When you start with newspaper style and switch to parallel style after a few pages, for example, you have two sets of columns. Similarly, if you switch from three columns to four columns, even though the column style remains the same, you have two sets of columns.

To create columns, place the insertion point at the location where the column should begin. If you place the insertion point within an existing paragraph, the column starts at the beginning of that paragraph.

WordPerfect provides two methods of specifying the number of columns: you can use the Columns pop-up menu on the ruler or the Columns option from the Layout menu. Although you can use either method to specify the number of columns, one method may be easier than the other in certain situations. To create two to five columns, for example, clicking the ruler's Columns pop-up menu is easier because you simply choose the appropriate column number from the menu. When you choose two to five columns, the Columns pop-up menu reflects your choice. To create more than five columns, you must access the Column Format dialog box. You can access this dialog box by clicking the Other option on the Columns pop-up menu or by choosing Format from the Columns submenu in the Layout menu.

When you create columns, WordPerfect calculates the spacing of the columns; you can use the ruler or the Columns Format dialog box to adjust column width, however. Which method you use depends on personal preference. If you prefer to adjust the column width visually, you can drag the margin markers (the black triangles on the ruler) to the appropriate location. If precise column spacing is important, however, you should use the Column Formats dialog box to specify the column width.

To create columns and the adjust column width from the ruler, do the following:

1. Choose Show Ruler from the Layout menu or press ⌘-R.

2. Click the Columns pop-up menu on the ruler to show the available options (see fig. 9.3). For more information on the ruler, refer to Chapter 4, "Formatting a Document."

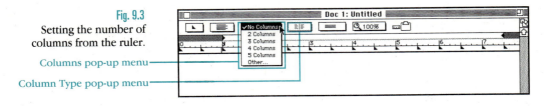

Fig. 9.3
Setting the number of columns from the ruler.

Columns pop-up menu
Column Type pop-up menu

3. Choose the appropriate number of columns. Although you can specify as many as 24 columns, only 2 through 5 columns are available directly on the menu; to choose more than 5 columns, you must choose Other.

When you choose Other, the Column Format dialog box appears (see fig. 9.4). The defaults—one column and newspaper style—appear in the dialog box.

Part II
Refining Documents

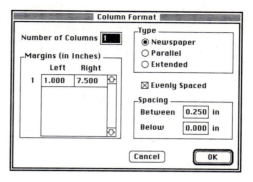

Fig. 9.4
The Column Format dialog box.

4. Type the appropriate number in the Number of Columns text box. For the example, type *10*.

    WordPerfect calculates and displays the spacing of the first five columns in the Margins section of the dialog box (see fig. 9.5). To see the spacing for the remaining columns, use the scroll arrows.

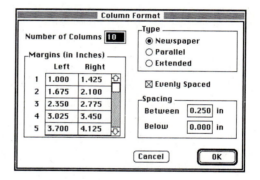

Fig. 9.5
Margin spacing for 10 columns.

5. To accept these settings and return to your document, click OK.

    Observe the margin markers above the numbers on the ruler. The markers face left and right and have gray shading between them (see fig 9.6). The black triangles of the markers represent column margins, and the gray areas represent the gutters.

6. To change a column or a gutter width, click and drag a margin marker to the appropriate location on the ruler.

Chapter 9
Using Columns and Text Boxes

Fig. 9.6
Viewing column and gutter widths on the ruler.

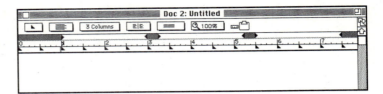

As you drag the marker, a dotted vertical line appears. This line makes aligning the column margins easier. Also notice that as you move the column margins, the location of the margin appears in the status bar.

To create columns and adjust column widths by using the Layout menu, follow these steps:

1. Choose Columns from the Layout menu; then choose Format from the Columns submenu. The Column Format dialog box appears (refer to fig. 9.4).

    The choices displayed in the dialog box reflect the last column definition choices that you made within your document. If you did not change the column defaults, one column and newspaper style are specified in the dialog box.

2. In the Number of Columns text box, type the number of columns being created. For the example, type *3*. (Because the box already is highlighted, clicking the box is not necessary.) WordPerfect calculates and enters column and gutter widths into the Margins list box.

3. To adjust column margin widths, click the first margin you want to change (see fig. 9.7). Then type a value (in inches) from the left side of the page where the column margin should appear. Use the same technique to change other margins; you also can press Tab to advance through the boxes.

Fig. 9.7
Adjusting columns from the Column Format dialog box.

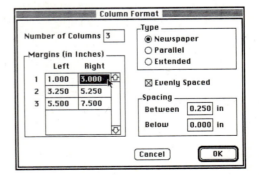

Part II
Refining Documents

When you change the column margins, notice that the Evenly Spaced check box on the right side of the dialog box is no longer selected.

4. Click OK to accept the new settings and return to your document.

5. If you have not done so already, choose Show Ruler from the Layout menu so that you can see the new column margins on the ruler.

Choosing the Column Type

The ruler's Column Type pop-up menu, which is dimmed unless you chose two or more columns from the Columns pop-up menu, displays the column style. Three column styles from which to choose—Newspaper, Parallel, and Extended—are discussed in the following sections.

Newspaper

Newspaper is the default column style. You find this column style in newspapers, brochures, pamphlets, and many textbooks. When you enter text into a newspaper column, the text wraps from the bottom of one column to the top of the next. After you fill the page, the insertion point moves to the beginning of the first column of the next page. If you don't want to fill one column before you move to the next column, you can insert a column break by pressing ⌘-Shift-Return or choosing Column Break from the Columns submenu in the Layout menu. Figure 9.8 shows a typical document using newspaper-style columns.

Parallel

Parallel columns, frequently used in tables, catalogs, and inventory lists, provide a convenient format for arranging text or information side by side (refer to fig. 9.1). To choose the parallel columns style, choose Parallel from the Column Type pop-up menu on the ruler.

In parallel columns, you enter text in the first column; as you enter column breaks across the row, the insertion points line up with the first line of text in the first column. When you enter a column break in the last column of a row, WordPerfect places the insertion point in the first column, one line below the longest text entry in the preceding row. This feature enables you to align text across a row regardless of whether one column has one line of text and another column has 10 lines. In the

Chapter 9
Using Columns and Text Boxes

table shown in figure 9.9, notice that the Judy Collins entry appears one line below the last Tracy Chapman title. This table has been enhanced with borders to help you discern the various entries.

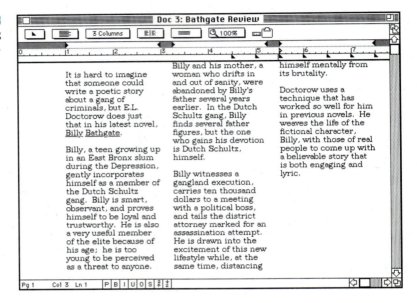

Fig. 9.8
A typical document using newspaper-style columns.

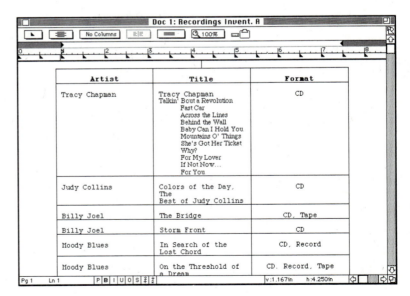

Fig. 9.9
Lining up related text across parallel columns.

Part II

Refining Documents

> **Tip**
>
> If you have superscripts or subscripts in a parallel column, the text may appear misaligned. Setting a fixed line height larger than normal for that font can improve the appearance of the text. Start with a 25 percent increase and experiment from there. For details on how to set line height, see Chapter 4, "Formatting a Document."

A single column of text in parallel columns does not extend past a page break. Like a newspaper column, the parallel column text wraps from the bottom of one column to the top of the next, thus defeating the intent of parallel columns. If a parallel column should extend past a page break, you must use the extended column style.

Extended

Although similar to parallel columns, extended columns provide one additional feature: these columns can extend over page breaks (refer to fig. 9.2). The reference manual that comes with your software is set up in extended columns. Section headings appear in one column, the text appears in another, and the columns continue over page breaks. You may use extended columns for a script from a play, for example, in which one character is speaking at great length, yet you want to keep the dialog in a single column.

Adding Column Borders

You can enhance columns by adding borders. With borders, you can set columns apart or create a table. WordPerfect provides 36 border styles and 68 border and shading patterns. Not only can you add and fill borders, but you also can change the spacing between the border and the column and document text.

You add and enhance borders by using the Column Border Style dialog box (see fig. 9.10). This dialog box contains sections in which you set the color and style of borders, color and fill patterns of the area enclosed by the border, and the spacing between the border and the text.

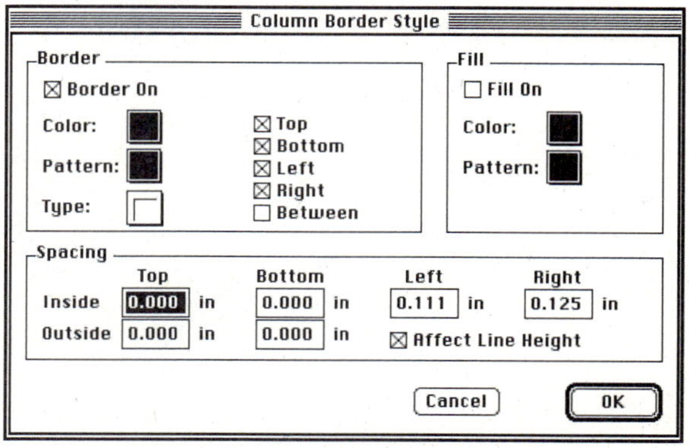

Fig. 9.10
The Column Border Style dialog box.

You can add borders to all column types. If you use newspaper columns, WordPerfect places a border around each column. With parallel and extended columns, WordPerfect places a border around each *cell*—all text between two column breaks. (WordPerfect refers to columns as cells.) Column borders do have some limits, however. You cannot place a single border around a set of columns, for example. To create a single border surrounding more than one column, you must put the columns in a text box, which is explained in the section "Creating a Text Box" later in this chapter.

You can add a border to your columns as you type the column text or after you enter text. To create borders as you type the text, place the insertion point at the beginning of the area where you intend to enter the column. WordPerfect creates the border as you type.

To create borders after you enter text in the columns, you first must indicate the column or text to be surrounded. If you place the insertion point within a column of text, WordPerfect creates a border around that column and all columns that follow it. By selecting the appropriate text, you can create a border around one of several columns, or you can create a border around a part of a column. To place a border around a specific row, for example, you must select text in that row before you open the Column Border Style dialog box and choose a border style. You don't have to select all the text in the row; selecting any portion of text is sufficient.

After you select the column or place the insertion point, you access the Column Border Style dialog box by choosing Column from the Borders submenu in the Layout menu. Alternatively, you can press Shift-F7. When the Column Border Style dialog box appears, the Border On option is selected by default. If you do nothing more than click OK, WordPerfect places the default style border around your columns; however, you can change the default border style by choosing other options in the dialog box. By changing these options, you change the appearance and color of your border, its fill, and spacing. The following sections detail these options.

> **Tip**
> If the screen redraw is slow or distracting while WordPerfect creates a border as you type, add the borders after you enter text.

Designing the Border

Within the Border area of the Column Border Style dialog box, you make several choices regarding the appearance and placement of the border. The first choice is Border On, which is checked by default. With this option checked, you can change border color, pattern, and so on. To turn borders off, click the box; the X disappears. If you close the Column Border Style dialog box with the Border On box unchecked and then open the dialog box again, the dialog box reverts to the default choice.

If you use a color monitor, you can choose from several screen colors for your border. If you have 4-bit color, you can choose from 16 colors on the palette; with 8-bit or greater color capability, you can choose from 256 colors on the palette. By double-clicking the Color pop-up palette, the color wheel appears. You can choose from 16 million shades and hues from this color wheel. If your Macintosh is not equipped with a color video display card, you can choose from eight colors (you see only the names) or Other, which opens the color wheel. The colors appear black on-screen.

You also can add a pattern to your border. To see the available patterns, click the Pattern pop-up palette and drag the pointer to one of the 64 patterns available (see fig. 9.11). The chosen pattern appears on the Pattern pop-up palette.

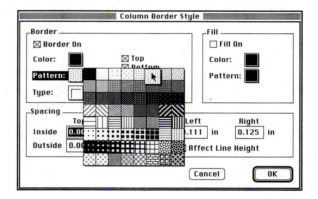

Fig. 9.11
Choosing from the 64 border patterns.

Because the borders are narrow, most border patterns have minimal impact. You can create some interesting effects, however, with a little experimentation. WordPerfect offers 36 types of borders, including a range of single narrow lines, thick double lines, and shadowed borders. Click the Type pop-up palette and drag the arrow to the style of your choice (see fig. 9.12).

Chapter 9
Using Columns and Text Boxes

Fig. 9.12
Choosing one of the 36 borders types.

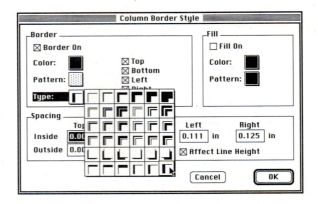

You can place borders on any or all sides of a column by clicking the appropriate button—Top, Bottom, Left, and so on—in the Border section of the dialog box. If you click the Top, Bottom, Left, and Right check boxes, the specified border style surrounds each column (see fig. 9.13). To separate columns without adding a border on all sides, as shown in figure 9.14, you can click the Between check box and leave the Left and Right boxes unchecked.

Fig. 9.13
Surrounding columns with borders.

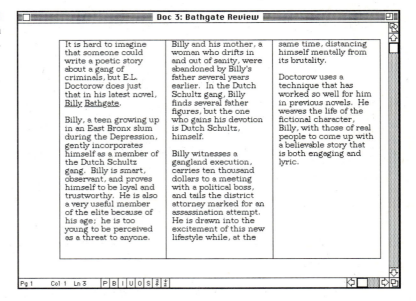

Part II

Refining Documents

Fig. 9.14
Separating unbordered columns.

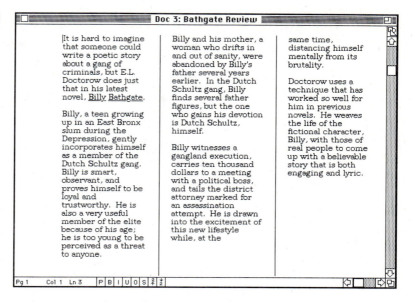

The default spacing between columns is 0.25 inch. If you choose Right and Left borders (but not Between) and don't change the spacing, the right border of one column overlaps the left border of the next column so that only one border appears between the columns. As you increase the gutter width, two borders appear.

If you choose Right, Left, and Between, however, the Between border option overrides the Right and Left options between the columns so that a single, evenly spaced border appears between the columns, regardless of the width of the gutter.

Adding Fill Styles

In the Fill area of the Column Border Style dialog box, you can add a pattern and color to the text area in your column. You choose fill color the same way you choose border color. Click the Color pop-up palette in the Fill area and drag the pointer to a color. To choose a fill pattern, click the Pattern pop-up palette and drag the arrow to one of the 64 available patterns.

Although you can choose fill styles before or after you enter text, adding these features after you enter the text may be less distracting. You can fill the entire set of columns with a pattern, or you can selectively fill rows to make the text in the columns easier to read, as shown in figure 9.15.

Chapter 9
Using Columns and Text Boxes

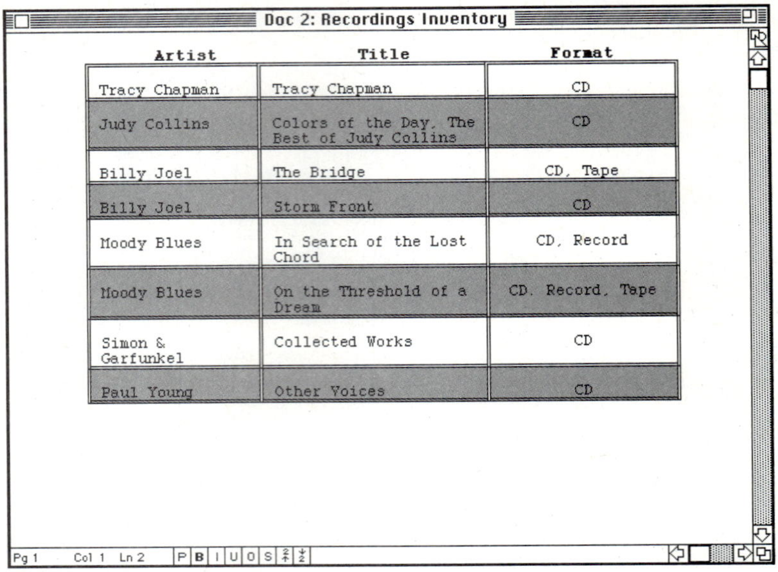

Fig. 9.15
Filling selected text in a column.

> **Tip**
> Keep in mind that not all fill patterns are suitable as background filler for text. Make sure that you can read the text through the pattern by printing a sample.

> **Tip**
> Check the document for overlapping border and text by going into Print Preview and increasing the magnification to 200 percent, which provides a good view of the text and border.

When you fill columns after you enter text, you must indicate the location where WordPerfect should add the fill. If you place the insertion point anywhere in the first row, WordPerfect fills the entire set of columns. If you place the insertion point in any row but the first, WordPerfect fills the columns from that row on. To fill a selected row, select any text within that row before opening the Column Border Style dialog box.

Changing the Spacing

You can adjust the spacing between the text and the border in the Spacing area of the Column Border Style dialog box. The default values leave no space between text and border at the top or bottom of columns. At the left side of the column, the border is 0.111 inch from the text. The right border is 0.125 inch from the text. To reset the spacing, click the appropriate box and type the new number.

To change the units of measurement for spacing, click in (inches). The Units pop-up menu appears. Click one of the following units: cm (centimeters), pts (points), pic (picas), ccr (cicéros), or ddt (didots).

If you use something other than a narrow, single-line border, you must increase the spacing to keep the border from running into your text. Add

Part II
Refining Documents

space between the text and border, as necessary. Begin by adding 0.020 inch. Continue to add space until the text is out of the border.

Creating a Text Box

Text boxes are regions of text that, although appearing next to or within the main document, are entered and edited independently of the rest of the document. You can move text boxes from one location to another, or you can anchor text boxes to a specific location or text.

By using text boxes and graphic boxes you can add almost anything to your document, including figures, tables, pictures, and sidebars. You can use text boxes to highlight text, tables, or columns, and add material that supplements your main document. (See Chapter 11, "Using the Drawing Window," for information on graphics boxes.)

To create a text box, follow these steps:

1. Place the insertion point where the box should appear.

2. Choose Text Box from the Tools menu; then choose New from the Text Box submenu (see fig. 9.16). Alternatively, press ⌘-F2.

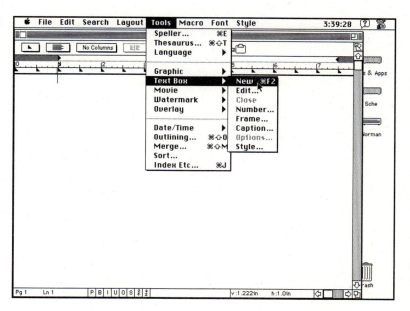

Fig. 9.16
Creating a new text box.

Chapter 9
Using Columns and Text Boxes

A rectangle with dotted lines appears at the insertion point (see fig. 9.17). A newly created text box is 2 1/2 inches wide.

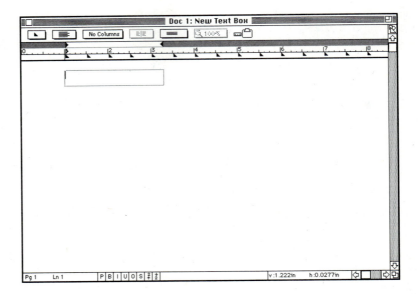

Fig. 9.17
A new text box.

Entering Text

When you create a new text box, the insertion point appears in the upper left corner of the text box. You can make the same formatting adjustments to text within a text box that you can make to other text. You can change the font or the type size, for example; the changes affect the text in the box only. Enter the necessary formatting changes and then type the text.

As you enter text, WordPerfect wraps the text automatically, pushing the bottom margin of the text box down. You cannot adjust the right margin (making the box wider or narrower), however, until you exit the box and then go back to edit it. (See "Resizing a Text Box" later in this chapter for more information.) Although the bottom of the text box drops to accommodate the text you add, text boxes cannot continue across a page break. After the box reaches the bottom of the page, no more text appears on-screen or on a printed page. After you finish entering your text, leave the text box by clicking outside the box.

Editing a Text Box

To edit a text box after you unselect it (click outside the box), you must enter edit mode by double-clicking within the text box or by using the Tools menu. Double-clicking the text box, which is perhaps the easiest way to enter edit mode, accesses the text box, which you can edit as necessary.

When you use the Tools menu, you specify the text box to be edited by single-clicking the appropriate box and then accessing the Edit Text Box dialog box. Alternatively, you can access the dialog box first and then specify the text box to be edited. Both of these methods are discussed in the following paragraphs.

To specify the text box before you access the Edit Text Box dialog box, click the appropriate text box so that a frame appears; then choose Edit from the Text Box submenu in the Tools menu to open the Edit Text Box dialog box (see fig. 9.18).

Fig. 9.18
The Edit Text Box dialog box.

The Content option already is chosen. If you are adding, deleting, or rearranging text, the Content option is the setting you want; click OK to edit the text in the selected box. (The other options, Caption and Options, are explained later in the chapter.)

To specify the text box to be edited after you access the Edit Text Box dialog box, choose Edit from the Text Box submenu in the Tools menu. When the Edit Text Box dialog box appears, type the number of the text box to be edited in the Find Text Box Number box and click OK. (WordPerfect numbers text boxes in the order in which the boxes appear in the document; remembering the contents of each text box is up to you.)

This method is particularly useful if you're not sure on which page of the document your text box is located; you also may want to use this method if you create a text box on a blank page, exit the text box before entering any text, and, as a result, cannot find the text box on the blank page. (Unless you add text or a border, text boxes are invisible.)

Resizing a Text Box

New text boxes are 2 1/2 inches wide. If this size does not suit your needs, you must resize the box. To resize a new text box, you must exit the text box and then select it.

Follow these steps to resize a text box:

1. Click the text box. If the insertion point is in the text box, click outside the box; then click the text box. A frame with handles (three small squares) appears around the text box.

2. To resize the text box, drag one of the handles (see fig. 9.19).

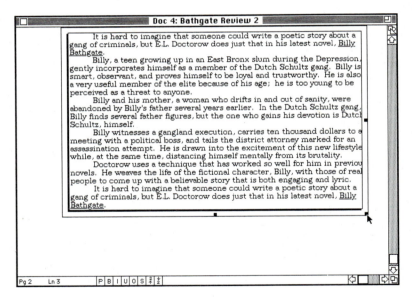

Fig. 9.19
Resizing a selected text box.

To change the box's width, drag the handle on the right border; to change the box's length, drag the bottom handle. You can change width and length simultaneously by dragging the handle in the lower right corner.

If you resize the box to be larger than the area used by text, blank space appears in your text box. If you make your text box smaller than the area taken up by text, your text disappears under the edges of the box. Although the text is still present, you cannot see it on-screen unless you readjust the size of the box to accommodate the area of text.

Resizing a text box by dragging a handle is the easiest—but not the most precise—way to change the dimensions of the text. You must do precise resizing—explained in "Setting Text Box Options" later in this chapter—from the Graphic Options dialog box.

> **Tip**
> To resize a text box before you enter text, type something—a single letter, for example—in the box before exiting it so that you have something to click when you want to access the text box.

Changing Margins

You change margins within a text box the same way that you change margins within the document: you use the ruler. To display the ruler, choose Show Ruler from the Layout menu or press ⌘-R. When the insertion point is in a text box, the ruler reflects the spacing within the box only (refer to fig. 9.17).

The default width of the text box and the margin is approximately 2.25 inches. You change the margins by dragging the margin markers above the numbers on the ruler. Although you may change the text box margins, the text box remains at its default width. If you enlarge the margins but do not change the default size of the text box, you still can enter text; however, the text disappears under the right side of the box (see fig. 9.20). When you enlarge the size of the box, the text reappears.

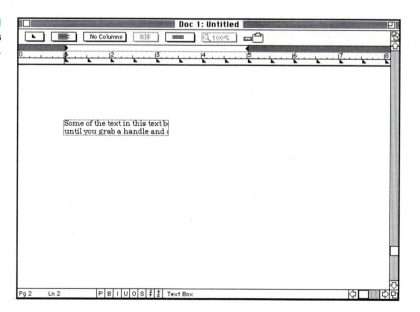

Fig. 9.20
Changing only the margins of a text box.

Chapter 9
Using Columns and Text Boxes

Using Columns in Text Boxes

To create columns in a text box, you can use the pop-up menus on the ruler, or you can choose Columns from the Layout menu. The column spacing fits within the margins of the text box (see fig. 9.21).

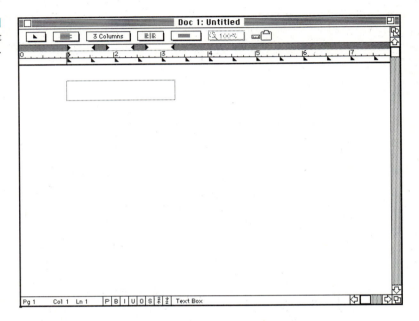

Fig. 9.21
Columns fit within the text box.

You can change column width by dragging the right or left column margin marker to a new margin setting. All the columns adjust to even widths within the new margin setting; however, the text box margins still appear in the window at the default setting (see fig. 9.22).

Setting Text Box Options

After you create a text box, you can choose options that change the text box's function. You can anchor a box as a character, or you can anchor the box to a specific page or paragraph. You can label text boxes as figures, tables, text, or user boxes. (By labeling a box, you can number certain types of boxes consecutively and create separate lists for each type of box.) You set up these options through the Options command on the Text Box submenu.

Fig. 9.22
The same text box size with new margin settings.

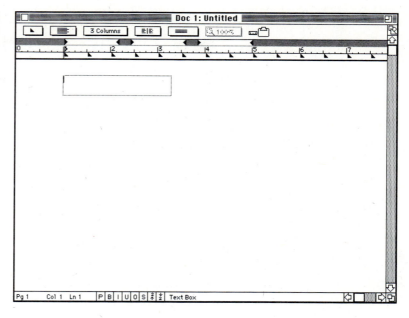

The Options command on the Text Box submenu is not available while you enter text in a text box. To choose Options, you first must create a text box, click outside the box (exit the text box), and then click the box. The sizing handles appear. Now you can choose text box options by choosing Options from the Text Box submenu in the Tools menu. The Graphic Options dialog box appears (see fig. 9.23).

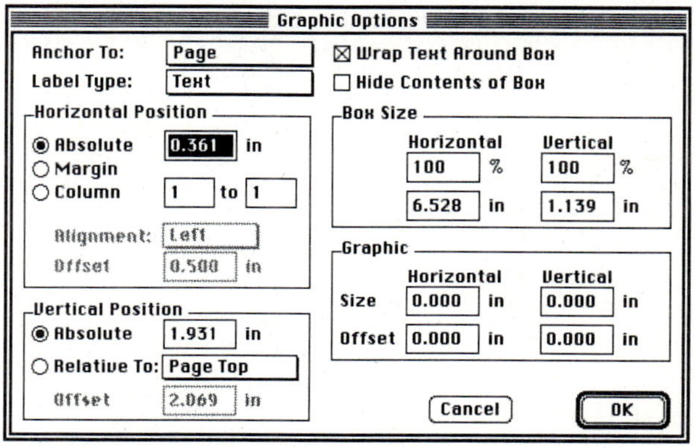

Fig. 9.23
The Graphic Options dialog box.

Chapter 9
Using Columns and Text Boxes

Because of its many options, the Graphic Options dialog box appears confusing at first glance. By studying each area individually, however, you soon can make sense of the dialog box. The following sections explain the available options. *Note:* Text boxes and graphic boxes use this dialog box. You use the Graphic section in the Graphic Options dialog box for graphics only; the Graphic settings do not affect text boxes.

Anchoring a Text Box

WordPerfect anchors a new text box as a character. Regardless of the box's size, you treat the text box as you would any other character when you edit the document. When you insert text above the text box, WordPerfect pushes the box farther down the page; when you delete text that precedes the text box, WordPerfect moves the text box up.

You may not want to anchor a text box as a character, however. You may want the text box to remain in a specific location on a page or within a paragraph, regardless of how you edit the text around it. The Anchor To pop-up menu on the Graphic Options dialog box enables you to anchor the text box to a page or paragraph. To change anchoring, open the Anchor To pop-up menu and choose the appropriate option: Page, Character, or Paragraph.

Anchoring As a Character

The default choice is to anchor a text box as a character so that the entire box functions as though it were a character. The line height at the location where the box is anchored changes to accommodate the height of the box. If a text box that takes up several lines is anchored as a character, a very large flashing insertion point appears next to the box when you return to your document.

Text does not wrap around the side of a text box that is anchored as a character. Instead, text above the box remains above, and text below the box remains below. If you add text in front of (above) the text box, the box is pushed down the page.

Anchoring to a Page

Anchoring a text box to a page keeps the box in the same position, regardless of how much text you add or delete. You may find this type of placement useful if you are adding a sidebar to an article and the appearance of the page is more important than linking the text box to specific text. Text in the document wraps around the box on the side that has more space (see fig. 9.24). Even though you may place the text box in the middle of the page, text wraps only around one side of the box (see fig. 9.25).

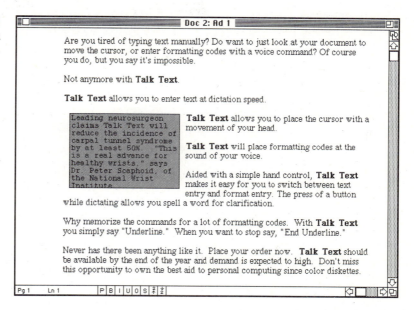

Fig. 9.24
A text box anchored to a page.

You can anchor a text box to a page in two ways: by choosing Page from the Anchor To pop-up menu or by moving the text box within the document. After you move a box, the anchor switches from character (or paragraph) to page.

Anchoring to a Paragraph

Anchoring a text box to a paragraph keeps the box in the same position, relative to the top left of the paragraph. Use this type of placement to link the text box to specific text in your document. Document text flows around the text box. Text wraps around a paragraph-anchored text box in the same way it wraps around a page-anchored box.

> **Tip**
> If you move a text box, regardless of how you previously anchored it, the box becomes anchored to a page. To anchor the text box as a character or to a paragraph, you must reanchor the moved text box.

Chapter 9
Using Columns and Text Boxes

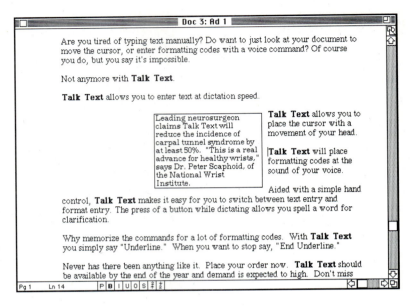

Fig. 9.25
A text box anchored to the middle of a page.

Changing the Label Type

The next option in the Graphic Options dialog box is Label Type, which enables you to create four types of boxes. You use labels to generate lists in the Index, Etc. feature, for example. When you create a text box, WordPerfect labels the box as text and assigns a number. WordPerfect numbers consecutively the text boxes that you create. You may label a text box as a table, a figure, or something specific to your document, such as Graph.

The Label Type pop-up menu on the Graphics Options dialog box enables you to change the label of the text box to Figure, Table, or User. You can customize the User label for a particular document (such as Graph, for example). The label assigned to a text box can be important for the following reasons:

- WordPerfect numbers each text box consecutively, according to its label type. (Boxes labeled as text are numbered consecutively and separately from boxes labeled as figures, for example.)

- You can generate a list of all text boxes in your document by using the Index, Etc. command. For example, you can generate a list of all figures or graphs used in your document.

- You can define a frame for each type of box so that if you change the label for that box, the frame style changes to match.

When you add a caption to the text box, the box's label determines the caption style, as explained in the following list:

- If the box is labeled as text, the number of the box appears in front of the caption.
- The word *Figure* followed by the box number precedes the caption of a figure box.
- The word *Table* appears in front of the box number in boxes designated as tables.
- User boxes display the box number only. You can edit the user box caption style, however, to include whatever you want. All user box captions can include words such as *Graph* or *Quote*, for example.

> **Tip**
> You can edit all caption styles by using the Edit Style dialog box, explained in Chapter 8, "Formatting with Styles."

Changing the Horizontal Position

The next options available in the Graphic Options dialog box appear in Horizontal Position section. These options, like the Vertical Position options, are available only if the text box is anchored to a page.

Although you can position text boxes in two ways—by using the mouse or by using Horizontal Position options—the Horizontal Position options enable you to place your text box precisely between the left and right sides of your page. The following sections describe the available options.

Absolute

The Absolute setting places a text box a specified distance (in inches) from the left edge of the paper. The box remains in the specified position regardless of margin changes.

To set an absolute position, click the Absolute radio button and then type the distance in the box. To specify distances in a unit of measurement other than inches, click in to the right of the box. From the pop-up menu that appears, you can choose centimeters (cm), points (pts), picas (pic), cicéros (ccr), or didots (ddt).

Margin

If you choose Margin, WordPerfect anchors the box to the page relative to a margin so that the text box remains aligned with other text in your document even though you change the margin settings. When you choose Margin, the Alignment and Offset options become enabled.

The default alignment is Left; the text box lines up with the left margin. When you click the Alignment box, a list of available alignments appears (see fig. 9.26). You can align the box with the right margin, center the box between margins, or justify the box—that is, have the width of the box increase to match the width of the margins.

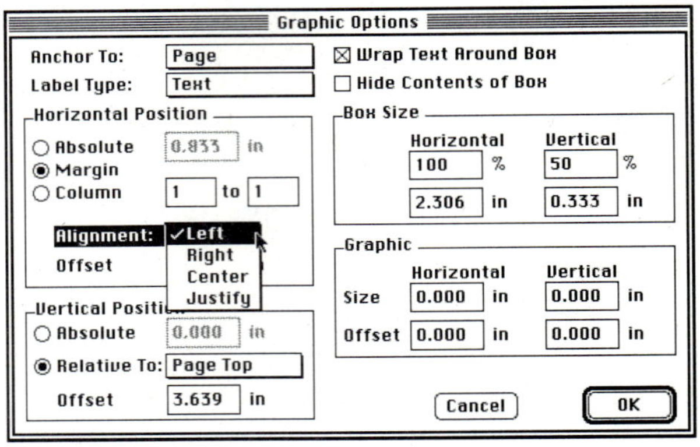

Fig. 9.26
The list of available alignments.

By using the Offset option, you can offset a text box from the margin to which it is anchored. If you want the text box anchored relative to the left margin but indented 1.5 inches from the margin, for example, type *1.5* in the Offset text box. WordPerfect moves the text box the specified distance to the right.

To move the text box to the left of the right margin, you must enter a negative number in the Offset text box. If you choose right alignment and type a positive number in the Offset box, the text box moves to the right. Suppose that you choose right alignment and 2.0 inches for your offset. The right edge of the text box moves 2 inches to the right of the right margin and partially off the page. Similarly, typing a negative number with a Left alignment enables you to move the box only to the left edge of the page.

When you enter an offset distance with Center alignment, the text box moves to the right of the center position (or to the left, if you enter a negative number). When you justify a text box, the Offset option is dimmed.

Part II

Refining Documents

Column

When you place a text box in a column, you can anchor the box to any location within the column. When you choose Column, the Alignment and Offset options become available.

To the right of the Column option are two number boxes (refer to fig. 9.26). When you choose Left, the text box aligns with the left margin of the column designated in the first number box. If you type *2* in this Column number box, for example, your text box lines up with the left margin of the second column.

When you choose right alignment, your text box lines up with the right margin of the column designated in the second Column number box. By choosing center alignment, the text box lines up between the outside margins of the columns specified in the Column number boxes. If you type *1* into the first box and *3* into the second box, for example, WordPerfect centers the text box between the left margin of the first column and the right margin of the third column.

When you choose Justify, the margins of the text box align to match the outside margins of the columns specified in the column number boxes. As with the Margin option, Offset is available for all column alignments except Justify.

Changing the Vertical Position

The next options available on the Graphic Options dialog box are in the Vertical Position section. These options enable you to set the vertical position of a page-anchored text box. If you anchor the text box as a character, you can change the position of text outside the text box.

Absolute

If you choose the Absolute option, the text box is set relative to the top margin that you set in Page Format (from the Layout menu). The number box next to Absolute enables you to place the text box a specified distance from the top margin (a relative absolute setting). If you set a 1-inch margin in Page Format and type *0* into the position box, for example, WordPerfect places the text box 1 inch from the top of the page. If you set a 3-inch top of page margin in Page Format and type *2* in the Absolute box, WordPerfect places the text box 5 inches from the top of the page.

Chapter 9
Using Columns and Text Boxes

Relative To

By choosing Relative To on the Graphic Options dialog box, you can position the text box relative to the whole page or the top, bottom, or middle of the page. When a text box is placed relative to the top margin, for example, the box remains the specified distance from the top margin even though you may change the margin setting. The Relative To options are explained in the following list:

- *Whole Page.* This option resizes the text box to fit the top, bottom, left, and right margins. (In other words, the text box takes up the entire page.) Offset is not available when you choose Whole Page.

- *Page Top.* This option, which is the default, places the text box in a position relative to the top of page margin. Although you can place the box at some point below the margin with Offset, you cannot enter a negative number into the Offset box to move the text box above the margin.

- *Page Middle.* This option aligns the text box with the vertical center of the page. Typing a number in the Offset box moves the text box down the specified number of inches.

- *Page Bottom.* This option places the text box at the bottom of the page margin. Typing a number into the Offset box has no effect on this option.

When anchoring a box as a character, you can use the Relative To pop-up menu to adjust the position of the text outside the text box. The default setting, Box Bottom, aligns the bottom of the text with the bottom of the box. The Baseline option aligns the baseline of the text (the bottom of a letter without a descender) with the bottom of the box. If you choose Box Top, the top of the text aligns with the top of the box. Box Middle positions the text next to the text box at the vertical center (see fig. 9.27). (Offset is not available when you anchor a text box as a character.)

Wrapping Text around a Box

The next option on the Graphic Options dialog box is the default Wrap Text Around Box check box. When this option is checked, text outside the text box flows around the box.

If you *unselect* (or turn off) this feature, WordPerfect writes the document text over the text box. The text box remains but does not appear on-screen. If you look in Print Preview or print the document, the text box and the document text appear and are printed in the same location. You should leave this option checked unless you also choose Hide Contents of Box (see the next section, "Hiding the Contents of a Text Box").

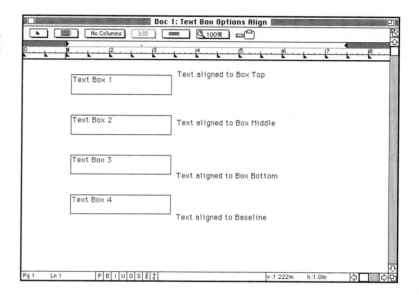

Fig. 9.27
Aligning text next to a character-anchored text box.

> **Tip**
> Rearranging text around a text box you cannot see can be tricky. Line codes behave differently than they would if the text box weren't in the way. Experiment with and check the spacing in Print Preview as often as necessary.

If you turn off the wrap feature, you must use an alternate method to access the text box so that you can edit or change options or create a caption. To access a text box when the wrap feature is turned off, do the following:

1. Choose Edit from the Text Box submenu in the Tools menu. The Edit Text Box dialog box containing the Edit, Caption, or Options commands appears.

2. Type the number of the text box you want to edit in the Find Text Box Number box.

3. Choose the appropriate function: Edit, Caption, or Options.

You now can edit the box, add a caption, or change features with the Graphic Options dialog box.

Chapter 9
Using Columns and Text Boxes

Hiding the Contents of a Text Box

Hide Contents of Box is the next option on the Graphic Options dialog box. If you hide the contents of a box by choosing this option, the document text wraps around a blank space on the page. The text box does not print or appear in Print Preview.

If you choose the Hide Contents of Box option and unselect Wrap Text Around Box, the box is hidden and overwritten. The space and text do not appear in Print Preview or on the printed document. You can use this technique to make comments or suggestions for changes to a document without changing the document's layout. To read the comments, you can run a macro to find hidden boxes. For information on creating macros, see Chapter 14, "Using Macros."

Changing Box Size

With the Box Size option on the Graphic Options dialog box, you can change the size of a text box. You already know that you can drag sizing handles to resize the text box. With the Box Size option, however, you can change the box size by setting specific dimensions.

You can choose horizontal and vertical dimensions as a percentage of the original box size or in absolute numbers. Below the percentage boxes are absolute size boxes. You can type in a box width (Horizontal) and length (Vertical). To change the units of measurement, click in (inches) and choose a measurement.

Moving a Box

ou can move text boxes a short distance within the same page or cut and paste them onto another page. To reposition a text box on the same page, follow these steps:

1. Click the text box once. If the insertion point is in the text box, click outside the box and then click the box.

2. Place the pointer anywhere inside the box and drag the box to its new location.

3. When the text box is in the appropriate location, click outside the text box to unselect it and fix the box location.

Because you moved the box, it now is anchored to the page. To anchor the text box as a character or to a paragraph, click the box and then

Part II

Refining Documents

choose Options from the Text Box submenu in the Tools menu (see the explanation in the preceding section for complete instructions on using the Graphic Options dialog box).

Adding a Caption

You can add captions to text boxes. If you frame a text box, you can place a caption inside or outside the frame. You also can place a caption above or below the text.

Labels have specific caption text associated with them; for example, if you label a text box as a figure, the word *figure* appears in the caption. You can edit the caption style by choosing Edit Style from the Layout menu (see Chapter 4, "Formatting a Document").

Creating a Caption

To create a caption, as shown in figure 9.28, follow these steps:

1. Click the text box.

2. Choose Text Box from the Tools menu; then choose Caption from the Text Box submenu. The insertion point appears at the bottom of the text box next to the box number or, if you added a frame, within the frame. You can change the font or text size or make other text style changes. You also can delete the box number.

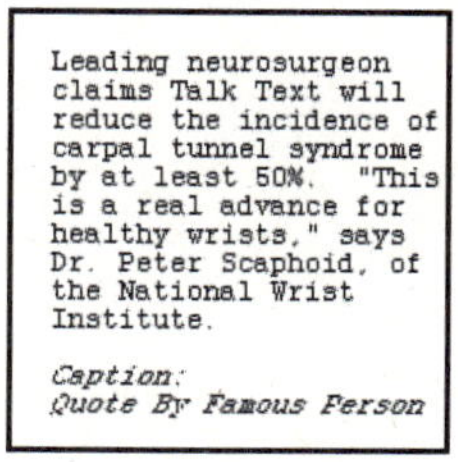

Fig. 9.28
Adding a caption to a text box.

3. Type the caption. The only limits to caption length are the same limits that govern the length of the text box: the text box and caption cannot cross a page break.

4. Click outside the text box after you finish the caption to set the caption.

Using the Text Box Frame dialog box, which is discussed in the section "Creating Frames," you can change the location of the caption.

Editing a Caption

Like any other text in WordPerfect, you can edit your caption. You can enter edit mode to change a caption in one of the following ways:

- Double-click the caption to go directly into edit mode.

- Click the text box; a frame appears around the text box and the caption. Choose Text Box from the Tools menu; then choose Caption from the Text Box submenu.

- Choose Edit from the Text Box submenu, type the number of the box you want to edit, and choose Caption from the Edit Text Box dialog box. (If you click the text box first, WordPerfect enters the correct box number for you.)

When you use the double-click method, be sure to click the caption. If you double-click the text, you go to text box edit mode, not caption edit mode.

In edit mode, you can add or delete text and change text styles, fonts, or font sizes of your captions. To remove the caption, delete all the caption text, including the box number. The caption disappears when you exit the text box. Click outside the text box after you complete your changes.

Creating Frames

You can add frames to text boxes much the same way that you add borders to columns. Several frame styles are available, and you can fill the frame with color or a pattern. You also can change the location of a caption.

To create a frame around your text box, follow these steps:

1. Select the text box.

2. Choose Text Box from the Tools menu; then choose Frame from the Text Box submenu. The Text Box Frame dialog box appears (see fig. 9.29).

Part II

Refining Documents

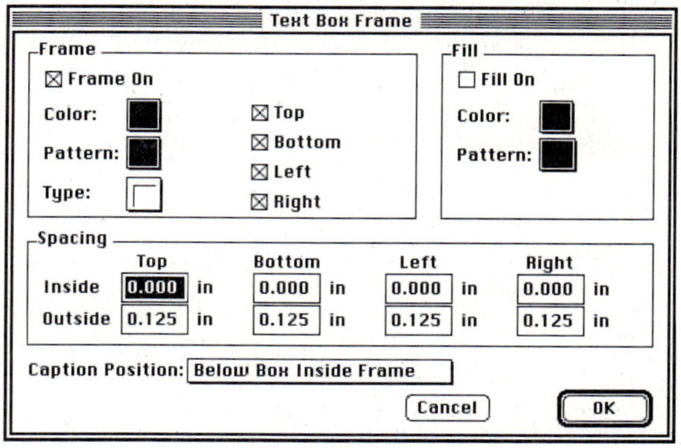

Fig. 9.29
The Text Box Frame dialog box.

You have essentially the same choices for framing a text box as you have for creating a column border. The specific components of the Frame dialog box are discussed in the following sections.

Adding a Frame

An X in the Frame On check box means that the Frame On option is activated. You can unselect the option by clicking the check box so that the X disappears.

You can create a frame around any or all sides of the text box. If you have a text box in the lower left corner of a page and want only the top and the right side framed, for example, click Bottom and Left to unselect those options.

You can choose a screen color for the frame by clicking the Color pop-up palette and dragging the pointer to the color of your choice. The Pattern pop-up palette contains 64 choices for frame patterns. Click the Pattern box and choose a pattern for your frame from the 36 frame styles that appear when you click the Type pop-up palette.

Adding a Fill

The Fill box enables you to fill the text box with color or a pattern. To choose Fill On, click the check box so that an X appears; then choose a color and pattern from the pop-up palettes. Be careful when you choose patterns, however, because some patterns may obscure your text.

Chapter 9
Using Columns and Text Boxes

If you choose a pattern and no pattern appears, the background color and the pattern color may be the same; therefore, be sure to choose a color other than white.

Changing the Spacing

Spacing, the next option on the Text Box Frame dialog box, enables you to change the spacing between the text within the box and the frame and the spacing between the frame and the document text. To change the spacing, type the distance (in inches) in the appropriate box (refer to fig. 9.29). To change the units of measurement, click in; then choose a different unit from the pop-up menu.

Compare figures 9.30 and 9.31. In figure 9.30, the spacing parameters for inside and outside the text box are 0.000. In figure 9.31, the inside positions for top, bottom, and left are 0.100 inch, and the outside right spacing is 0.125 inch.

Fig. 9.30
No space between text and frame.

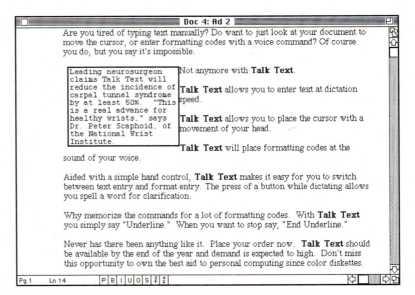

Changing the Caption Position

To change the position of the caption, choose Caption Position from the Text Box Frame dialog box. The default option, Below Box Inside

Frame, places a caption below the text within the text box (see fig. 9.32). You can change the position to one of the following options: Below Box Outside Frame, Above Box Inside Frame, and Above Box Outside Frame.

Fig. 9.31
Adjusted spacing inside and outside the frame.

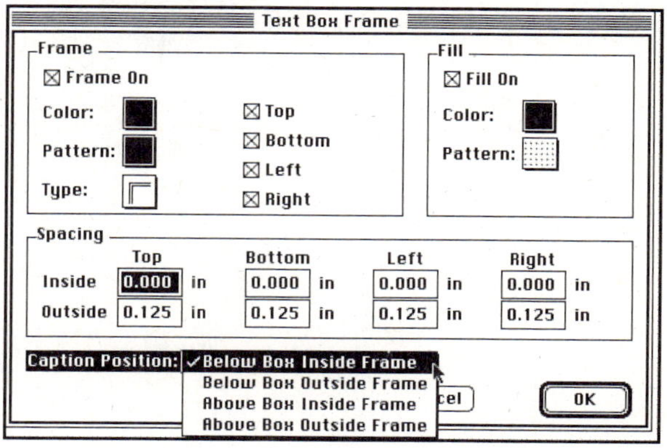

Fig. 9.32
Changing the caption position.

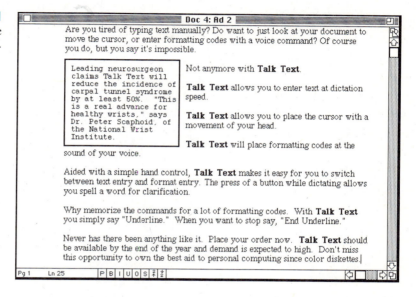

Chapter 9
Using Columns and Text Boxes

Chapter Summary

With a little practice, you can become proficient in the use of columns and text boxes to enhance your documents. You can choose from three column styles and create up to 24 columns. You can place sidebars, graphs, figures, and quotes within text boxes in a document, and then move or edit these boxes separately from the main text.

In this chapter, you learned how to create and manipulate text boxes. You also learned how to change the label type of text boxes, how to add and edit captions, and how to enhance boxes with frames. As you learned in this chapter, the flexibility of text boxes in WordPerfect exceeds any other word processing software.

CHAPTER 10

Creating Outlines and Lists

Although the main component of professional-quality documents is the body of text, care also must be given to support materials such as lists, indexes, and tables of contents. WordPerfect enables you to create these and other types of support material to make your reports and research papers more informative.

Using WordPerfect, you can create simple outlines, footnotes and endnotes, as well as several types of lists. You can generate lists of figures, tables, graphs, tables of contents, indexes, and tables of authorities. (WordPerfect, in fact, is the only word processing program for the Macintosh that is capable of creating tables of authorities.) This chapter explains how to create these supplemental materials. When you complete this chapter, you will be able to do the following:

- Create, customize, and edit an outline
- Create endnotes or footnotes for research papers
- Assemble an index
- Create a table of contents
- Create a table of authorities
- Create cross-reference items within a document
- Create a custom list

Creating an Outline

Creating outlines as part of a document or an entire document is an easy procedure in WordPerfect. You can create an outline in a new or existing document. These outlines, which can consist of up to eight levels, use standard outline formatting. WordPerfect aligns level 1 topics, for example, vertically down the page; level 2 subtopics are indented below level 1 topics, level 3 subtopics are indented below level 2 subtopics, and so on. Figure 10.1 shows the paragraph and tab insertions at each level of the outline.

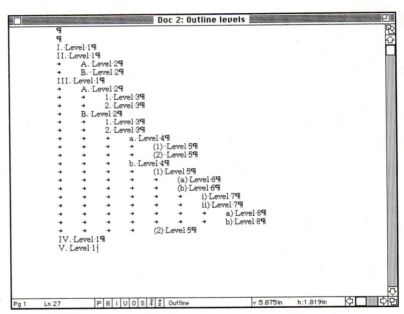

Fig. 10.1
Paragraph and tab insertions of a standard outline.

Selecting levels is easy. After you select Outlining, press Return. The first level 1 entry appears. Pressing Return again inserts the second level 1 entry. (When Outlining is activated, pressing Return always results in a new level 1.) To insert a level 2 entry, press Tab; the most recent level 1 entry changes to level 2. By pressing Tab, the insertion point moves through the levels. If you tab too far, you can go back a level by pressing Shift-Tab.

To create an outline, follow these steps:

1. In a new or existing document, place the insertion point in the location where the outline should begin; then choose Outlining from the Tools menu or press ⌘-Shift-O. The Outlining dialog box appears (see fig. 10.2).

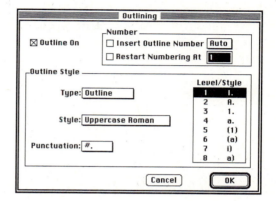

Fig. 10.2
The Outlining dialog box.

2. Choose an appropriate option in the Number section of the dialog box (see the section "Selecting Number Options" for information on this step).

3. Select an outline style (see the section "Selecting an Outline Style" for help with this step).

4. Click OK or press Return. WordPerfect returns you to the document.

When you press Return in your document, the first level 1 heading appears; you can begin entering the text of your outline. When you enter outline text, remember that you create a new level 1 when you press Return. Press Tab to move to subordinate levels; press Shift-Tab to move back up a level. When the insertion point is next to the level number, you can delete the outline number by pressing Delete.

Selecting Number Options

Two options are available in the Number box. The first, Insert Outline Number, enables you to insert a single outline number where you choose. By checking Insert Outline Number when you turn on Outlining, pressing Return to get a new level heading is not necessary ; however, this option is used primarily to number text sections after you enter the text.

Chapter 10
Creating Outlines and Lists

To number sections in a report or research paper, for example, you can select Insert Outline Number at the beginning of each section; each time you select Insert Outline Number and click OK, WordPerfect inserts the next number (see fig. 10.3). When you rearrange sections, WordPerfect automatically renumbers the sections.

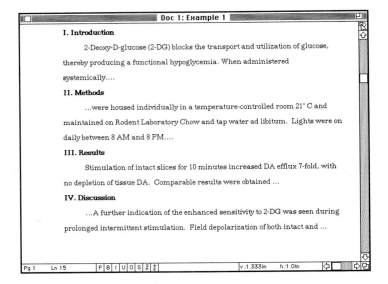

Fig. 10.3
Inserting individual outline numbers in a document.

To insert outline numbers, follow these steps:

1. In your document, place the insertion point where the outline number should appear; then open the Outlining dialog box by choosing Outlining from the Tools menu or pressing ⌘-Shift-O.

2. When you enter the Outlining dialog box, Outline On is always checked. To enter an outline number only, click the check box so that the X disappears.

3. Click Insert Outline Number so that an X appears. The selected outline type determines the numbering style that WordPerfect inserts into your document.

   The Insert Outline Number pop-up menu, shown in figure 10.4, determines what level number to insert when you close the Outlining dialog box. If you leave the pop-up menu set to Auto, which is the default, WordPerfect determines the number of tabs or indents from the left margin and enters the number for the appropriate level. To enter a level 8 number in front of a paragraph that isn't tabbed, for example, you must choose 8 from this pop-up menu.

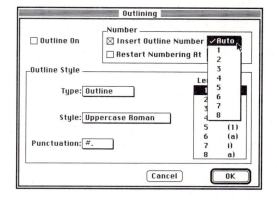

Fig. 10.4
The Insert Outline Number pop-up menu.

4. Click OK to return to your document. WordPerfect inserts the specified outline number at the insertion point.

The second feature in the Number box of the Outlining dialog box is the Restart Numbering At option. This feature enables you to make more than one outline in a document and start each new outline with a I (or another level 1 numbering style that you specify). When you check the Restart Numbering check box and click OK, one line ends and a new one begins.

> **Tip**
> To insert several outline numbers throughout a document, enter the Insert Outline Number keystrokes into a Macro so that the operation becomes one keystroke instead of several. See Chapter 14, "Using Macros," for instructions on creating a macro.

Selecting an Outline Style

The Level/Style box shows the lettering or numbering style and the punctuation at each level of the specified outline style. When you open the Outlining dialog box, for example, you see that the outline type is Outline. You also see that level 1 is highlighted, the style is Uppercase Roman, and punctuation is #. (refer to fig. 10.2). These settings indicate that the level 1 style of the Outline type is an uppercase Roman numeral followed by a period. If you select level 6 in the Level/Style box, you can see that the style for level 6 subtopics is Lowercase Letters, and the punctuation is (#), as shown in figure 10.5.

To establish an outline style, the first thing you must decide is the type of outline you plan to create. Choose the appropriate type of outline from the Type pop-up menu in the Outlining dialog box (see fig. 10.6).

Chapter 10
Creating Outlines and Lists

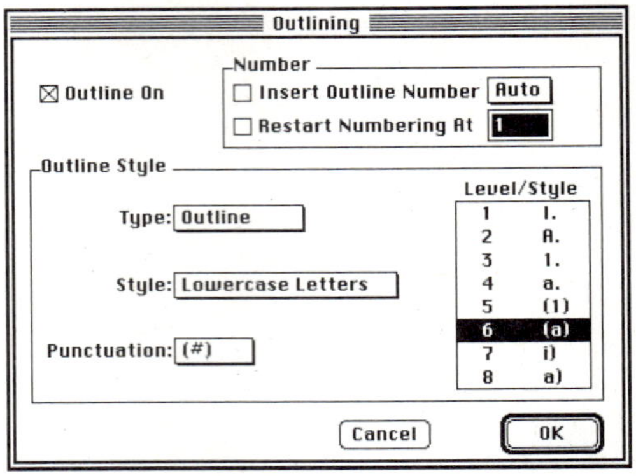

Fig. 10.5
The level 6 outline style.

Fig. 10.6
Choosing an outline type.

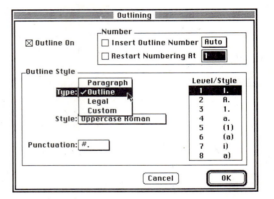

You can choose one of three predefined styles for your outline: Outline, Paragraph, and Legal. These outline styles use predetermined numbering styles and punctuation. The default outlining style is Outline (see fig. 10.7). In the Paragraph outlining style, shown in figure 10.8, level 1 consists of numbers (1, 2, 3, and so on), and level 2 consists of letters. The Legal style overwhelms you with numbers and decimal points (see fig. 10.9). The Custom Number option, which is discussed in the next section, enables you to use any numbering style variation that is most useful.

When you specify an outline type, the Level/Style box displays the predefined numbering styles for that outline type. If you change the features in the Style pop-up menu or the Punctuation pop-up menu, the outline type changes automatically to Custom, which is covered in the following section.

Part II

Refining Documents

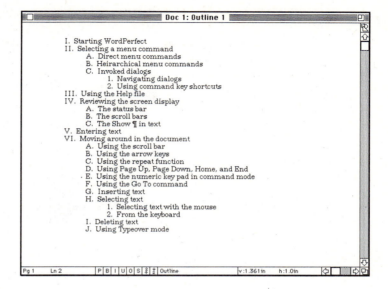

Fig. 10.7
The Outline style.

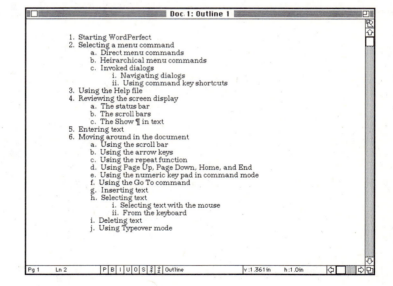

Fig. 10.8
The Paragraph style.

Chapter 10
Creating Outlines and Lists

Fig. 10.9
The Legal style.

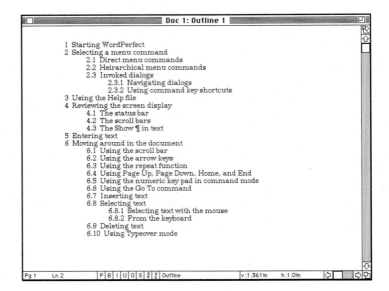

Customizing a Style

To use an outline scheme other than the Paragraph, Outline, or Legal outline type, you can create a custom outline type. WordPerfect provides two methods of customizing a numbering style: you can choose options from the Type, Style, and Punctuation pop-up menus, or you can change an item in the Level/Style list box. You must access the Outlining dialog box to use either method.

To use the first method, you must choose Custom from the Type pop-up menu; then select a level in the Level/Style list box. To change the style for the selected level, use the Style or Punctuation boxes. The faster way of customizing a style, however, is to select and change any level in the Level/Style box. The Outline Type automatically changes to Custom.

The limitation of customizing an outline style is that you must choose from the selections available in the Style and Punctuation pop-up menus. Suppose, for example, that the customized outline type should use the same level numbering as the Paragraph outline type, with the exception that level 2 style should use uppercase letters. To change the level 2 outline style, do the following:

1. Place the insertion point in the location where the outline type should take effect; then choose Outlining from the Tools menu or press ⌘-Shift-O. The Outlining dialog box appears.

2. To modify the style and punctuation of level 2, click the 2 at the left side of the Level/Style area of the dialog box.

3. Choose Uppercase Letters from the Style pop-up menu (see fig. 10.10). WordPerfect applies the specified style to the level 2 headings.

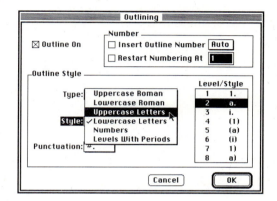

Fig. 10.10
Choosing Uppercase Letters from the Outline style pop-up menu.

4. Click OK. You now can enter your outline text, using the custom outline type.

To change the punctuation of an outline style, you use the Punctuation pop-up menu in the Outlining dialog box. To enclose level 2 headings in parentheses, for example, choose (#) from the punctuation pop-up menu. In addition, you can follow a heading with a period (#.), a single right parenthesis (#)), or no punctuation (None).

Editing an Outline

You can edit the text of your outline the same way you edit other text in WordPerfect. To automatically renumber outline text that you rearrange, however, you must activate Outlining On. With Outlining On checked, you can add or delete outline levels. When you change levels, the other entries automatically renumber. You also can change outlining style. Place the insertion point at the location where the change should begin and choose a new style from the Outlining dialog box. WordPerfect renumbers the outline to fit the new style.

When Outlining is activated, remember that you create a new level 1 heading each time you press Return. To change the level of the new entry, press Tab. To move outline text, use Cut, Copy, or Paste—just as you would in any other WordPerfect document.

Chapter 10
Creating Outlines and Lists

Creating Endnotes

Endnotes, which are similar to footnotes, are explanations or reference citations that you find at the end of a document, such as a book chapter or research paper, for example. In this section, you learn how to create, edit, and delete endnotes. You also learn how to move quickly from one endnote to the next.

When you create an endnote, WordPerfect automatically adds the endnote number to your document and stores the endnote itself in a hidden location. If you add an endnote to precede an existing endnote, the endnote numbers change automatically to accommodate the addition. Because the endnotes are not visible in the normal document editing window, you must look in Print Preview or print the document to see the endnotes list. Of course, you can look at each endnote separately to enter and edit text.

To create an endnote, follow these steps:

1. In any document window, place the insertion point where the endnote number should appear.

2. Choose Endnotes from the Layout menu; then choose New from the Endnotes submenu (see fig. 10.11). WordPerfect enters the proper endnote number in your document, using the Endnote # in Document style.

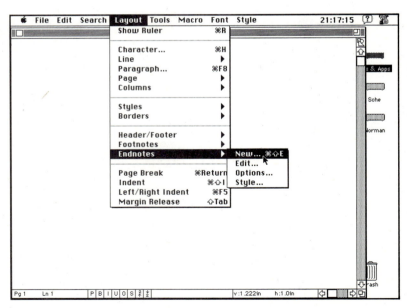

Fig. 10.11
Creating an endnote.

Part II
Refining Documents

An endnote window, containing the endnote number, appears (see fig. 10.12).

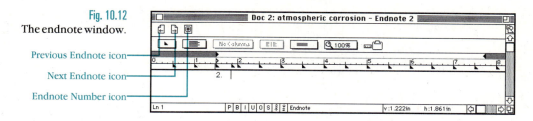

Fig. 10.12
The endnote window.

Previous Endnote icon
Next Endnote icon
Endnote Number icon

3. Type the text of the endnote (see fig. 10.13). You can use most WordPerfect formatting features, such as the ruler, Speller, and Thesaurus, in the endnote window.

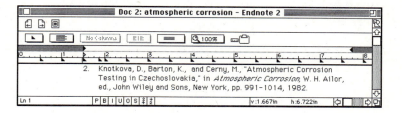

Fig. 10.13
Adding endnote text.

4. When you complete the endnote, click the close box in the endnote window to return to your document. In your document, only the endnote number appears.

To scroll through the existing endnotes one endnote at a time, you click the Previous and Next Endnote icons in the endnote window (refer to fig. 10.12). When you click these icons, the current endnote window closes and the previous or next endnote window, as specified, opens.

By clicking the Endnote Number icon, you insert the current note number in the endnote window at the location of the insertion point. Because the Endnote style places the note number at the beginning of the endnote, clicking the Endnote Number icon may be unnecessary.

Editing an Endnote

Because WordPerfect doesn't display endnotes in the document window, you must edit endnotes in the endnote window. The simplest way to open the endnote window is to use the I-beam pointer to double-click the endnote number in your document. The endnote window for the specified endnote number opens. When you work with a long document that contains numerous endnote references, you can avoid scrolling through the document to find the references by following these steps:

1. Choose Endnotes from the Layout menu; then choose Edit from the submenu. An Edit Note dialog box appears (see fig. 10.14).

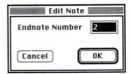

Fig. 10.14
The Edit Note dialog box.

2. Type the number of the appropriate endnote in the Endnote Number text box. The specified endnote appears in an endnote window.

3. Make the necessary changes; then click the close box when you are done. You can edit endnotes just as you edit other text.

When you open the endnote window, the endnote number appears automatically at the top left of the box. Be careful not to delete the endnote number when you edit; otherwise, the note appears without the number in the endnote list.

If you move a section of text containing an endnote number as you edit your document, WordPerfect automatically renumbers the notes. Similarly, if you insert a new endnote in a document, WordPerfect renumbers all the following endnotes.

Viewing Endnotes

When your document is complete and all endnotes have been entered, you may want to view your endnotes. Move the insertion point to the end of the document and choose Print Preview from the File menu. WordPerfect displays the document (see fig. 10.15).

To create a title—*References*, for example—for the endnote list, you must place the title and any blank space that appears between the title and the list at the end of your document. If the endnote list should begin on a new page, you must insert a Page Break before you type the title of the endnote list.

Part II
Refining Documents

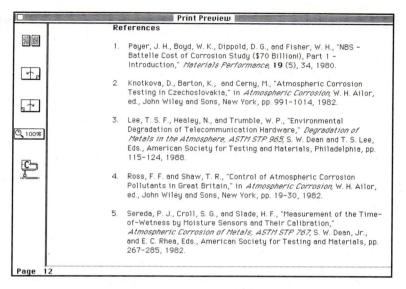

Fig. 10.15
Looking at the completed endnotes in Print Preview.

Deleting an Endnote

To delete an endnote, you must delete the endnote number in the document. Follow these steps:

1. Place the insertion point to the right of the endnote number in your document, or select the number so that it is highlighted.

2. Press Delete to delete the endnote.

When you delete the endnote number in your document, WordPerfect deletes the endnote from the endnote list and renumbers the subsequent endnotes.

Changing Endnote Options

You use the Endnote Options dialog box to restart the endnote numbering sequence or change the citation marker from a number to a character. Restarting an endnote numbering sequence has few, if any, applications. If you create a document that contains only a few notes, for example, you may want the endnote "number" to be a character, such as an asterisk (*).

To change endnote options, follow these steps:

Chapter 10
Creating Outlines and Lists

1. Place the insertion point in front of the appropriate endnote number.

2. Choose Endnotes from the Layout menu; then choose Options from the submenu. The Endnote Options dialog box appears (see fig. 10.16).

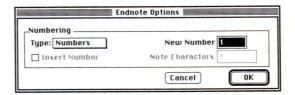

Fig. 10.16
The Endnote Options dialog box.

3. Make the appropriate changes; for example, you can change the citation markers and the numbers assigned to endnotes. You also can insert numbers. (These options are explained in the following section.)

4. Click OK to exit the dialog box and save the changes. The specified endnote number and all subsequent endnotes numbers appear in the document and in the printed list, using the type and characters you choose in the Endnote Options dialog box.

In the Endnote Options dialog box, you can change the citation marker from numbers to letters or characters. If you choose Letters from the Type pop-up menu, endnotes are lettered consecutively beginning with *a*. If you have more than 26 endnotes, the letters double, for example, aa, bb, cc, and so on, after the 26th letter.

If you choose Characters from the Type pop-up menu, the Note Characters box is enabled. The default character is an asterisk (*). One asterisk labels the first endnote, two asterisks (**) label the second endnote, and so on. You can choose up to 5 characters to represent endnote labels by entering the appropriate characters in the Note Characters text box (see fig. 10.17). Do not put spaces between the characters, or WordPerfect uses the space as an endnote label. You can specify any printable characters, including numbers and letters, as the endnote character. Remember, however, that if you specify the note as I, WordPerfect marks the first note as I, the second note as II, the third as III, and so on.

You use the New Number box to change the numbers assigned to endnotes. Normally, endnotes are numbered consecutively (beginning with 1) within a single document. If, for some reason, you must restart endnote numbering, place the insertion point in front of the appropriate endnote *before* you open the Endnote Options dialog box. After you access the dialog box, type the new number in the New Number box and click OK. The endnote number changes, and WordPerfect adjusts all subsequent endnote numbers.

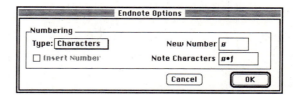

Fig. 10.17
Changing endnote characters.

> **Tip**
> Even though you can use letters and characters for endnotes, using numbers is easier for the person reading your document, unless your document contains very few endnotes; otherwise, your reader may have to remember whether she is looking up the citation for **** or *****.

Insert Number, which is disabled unless you are in a Style editing window, inserts endnote numbers on the endnotes page at the end of a document. If you removed numbers—which you may do when you edit styles, for example—you can reinsert the numbers by selecting Insert Number. This option is particularly helpful if you accidentally delete the endnote number code from your endnote style definition. For more information on style definitions, see Chapter 8, "Formatting with Styles."

To insert a number, follow these steps:

1. Choose Style from the Endnotes submenu in the Layout menu. The Endnote style definition window appears.

2. Place the insertion point in the Endnote Style Definition window where the note number should appear. Remember that changes in a style definition affect all text containing that style—in this example, every endnote.

3. Open the Endnote Options window and click Insert Number.

4. Click OK. WordPerfect inserts the endnote number code in your endnote style definition. This code enables WordPerfect to display the sequence number of your endnotes in the printed list when you print your document.

Creating Footnotes

Creating footnotes is similar to creating endnotes. When you create a footnote, WordPerfect adds a footnote number to your document at the location of the insertion point. WordPerfect numbers footnotes consecutively throughout the document and adjusts the numbers if you add or delete a footnote.

Chapter 10
Creating Outlines and Lists

> **Tip**
> Because of the placement of footnotes, WordPerfect must adjust the text to accommodate the number of footnotes on a page; consequently, your document text may move to a new page sooner than you expect.

Like endnotes, footnotes do not show up in your document, but you can see them in Print Preview. The main difference between endnotes and footnotes is that, because footnotes appear on the same page as the footnote numbers, WordPerfect must adjust the spacing at the bottom of the document page to accommodate the addition of the footnotes in printing.

To create a footnote, follow these steps:

1. Place the insertion point in your document where the footnote number should appear.

2. Choose Footnotes from the Layout menu; then choose New from the Footnotes submenu. The footnote window, which is very similar to the endnote window, appears (see fig. 10.18). As a result of WordPerfect's default Footnote style definition, the footnote number appears automatically in the editing window.

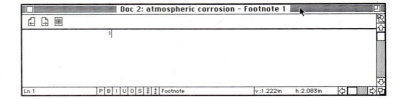

Fig. 10.18
The footnote window.

3. Enter the text for your footnote. As with endnotes, you can use most Wordperfect editing and formatting commands in footnotes.

4. When you finish the footnote, click the footnote window close box. WordPerfect adds the footnote number to the document and stores the footnote until you print your document or use Print Preview to view your document.

To see the footnotes as they appear on a page, select Print Preview from the File menu. Figure 10.19 shows a typical document containing footnotes displayed in Print Preview mode.

Editing a Footnote

You easily can edit footnotes from anywhere within the document. To edit a footnote, follow these steps:

1. Choose Footnotes from the Layout menu; then choose Edit from the Footnotes submenu. The Edit Note dialog box appears. This dialog box is similar to the dialog box shown in figure 10.14.

Fig. 10.19
Viewing footnotes in Print Preview.

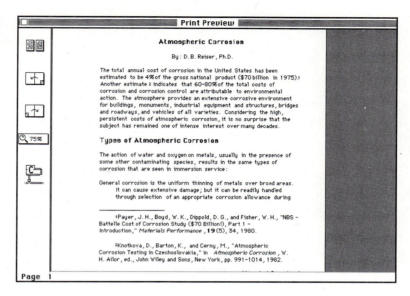

2. In the Footnote Number text box, type the number of the footnote to be edited; then click OK. The footnote window containing the selected footnote appears.

3. Make any additions or corrections to the footnote content and formatting.

4. Click the close box to accept the changes. WordPerfect returns you to the main document window with the insertion point following the footnote number.

Tip
Double-clicking a footnote number in your document window opens the footnote editing window for the specified footnote.

Be careful not to delete the footnote number in the footnote window as you edit. Although the text of the footnote remains, no identifying number is attached to it.

Deleting a Footnote

You use the same technique to delete a footnote that you use to delete an endnote. Follow these steps:

1. Place the insertion point to the right of the footnote number in the document.

Chapter 10
Creating Outlines and Lists

2. Press Delete to delete the footnote number. WordPerfect deletes the footnote code and, therefore, the footnote itself. All subsequent footnote numbers are adjusted accordingly.

Changing Footnote Options

You can change footnote formatting in the Footnote Options dialog box. In addition to the numbering options explained in the Endnote Options dialog box, the Footnote Options dialog box enables you to set the spacing between adjacent notes on a page and to indicate how WordPerfect separates footnotes from the main text on the page.

To change footnote options, follow these steps:

1. Place the insertion point where formatting changes should begin.

    If you place the insertion point within a paragraph, all footnotes in that paragraph and subsequent paragraphs are affected. To apply the footnote options to all notes within your document, place the insertion point at the beginning of the document.

2. Choose Footnotes from the Layout menu; then choose Options from the Footnotes submenu. The Footnote Options dialog box appears (see fig. 10.20).

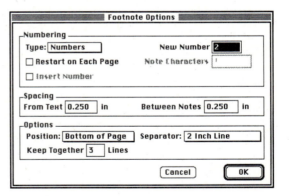

Fig. 10.20
The Footnote Options dialog box.

3. Make the appropriate changes; you can change the numbering, spacing, and position of footnotes. These options are discussed in the following sections.

4. Click OK to save the changes and return to your document.

Changing the Footnote Label

The features in the Numbering box change the footnote label. You can use numbers (the default), letters, or characters as your footnote labels. To change the label type, click the Type pop-up menu and choose another label type.

Numbers start with 1 and continue consecutively. Letters start with *a* and continue through the alphabet. If you choose Character, the default character is an asterisk (*). Each subsequent footnote label adds another asterisk.

When you choose Character as the label type, the Note Characters box is enabled. As with endnotes, you can choose up to 5 characters for labelling footnotes. Enter the appropriate characters in the Note Characters box. Do not put spaces between the characters; if you do, WordPerfect uses the space as a footnote label.

To restart the labelling format from the beginning of each page, choose Restart on Each Page. You should use this option when you use character labels; otherwise, the string of characters may become too long or complex. If you use this option with number labels, the first footnote on each page is 1.

The Insert Number option is disabled unless you are editing the style of the footnote or the footnote number. For more information on this option, see the appropriate section in the discussion of endnotes earlier.

As with endnotes, you can change the number label on footnotes. To change the number of a footnote, place the insertion point to the left of the footnote number in your document; then access the Footnote Options dialog box. Type the new number in the New Number box and click OK. WordPerfect renumbers all footnotes following the insertion point with the number you specified in the Options dialog box.

Changing Spacing

In the Footnote Options dialog box, you can change the spacing between the end of the text and the first footnote, as well as the spacing between footnotes. The default spacing for both options is 0.25 inch.

To change the spacing between the text and footnotes, select the From Text box and type in the new measurement. Similarly, to change the spacing between footnotes, select the Between Notes box and enter the new measurement.

Chapter 10
Creating Outlines and Lists

You can change the units of measure for both options from inches to centimeters, points, picas, ciceros, or didots. Click in to display the pop-up menu containing the available units of measurement and select another unit.

Changing Footnote Position

The Position pop-up menu controls where WordPerfect places the footnotes on the page. Although footnotes usually are placed at the bottom of the page, you may want the footnotes to follow the text directly, particularly if the combination of text and footnotes does not fill the page. To change the footnote location, click the Position box to display the pop-up menu, and choose Bottom of Page or After Text. The Bottom of Page option places footnotes at the bottom of the page. The After Text option places footnotes at the end of the text, according to the value of the Spacing From Text option.

The Keep Together option indicates how many lines of a footnote must be kept together if the footnote is split between two pages. The default number is 3, but you can type another number in the Keep Together text box.

Normally, a two-inch line separates the text from the footnotes. You can choose no line or a line across the page instead. Click the Separator pop-up menu and choose None, Two-Inch Line, or Line Across Page, as appropriate.

Creating Generated Lists

In contrast to endnotes and footnotes, which are created one at a time and automatically placed in the printed document, you must specifically generate other lists before they appear in your document. Among these lists are indexes, tables of contents, tables of authorities, lists of figures and text boxes, custom lists, and cross-references. You set up and control each of these generated lists through the Index, Etc. command in the Tools menu (see fig. 10.21).

You prepare all lists in essentially the same way, as explained in the following steps:

1. Select the items or mark the locations to be included in the list.

2. Define the format of the list. Each list has several options that determine the appearance of the list on a printed page.

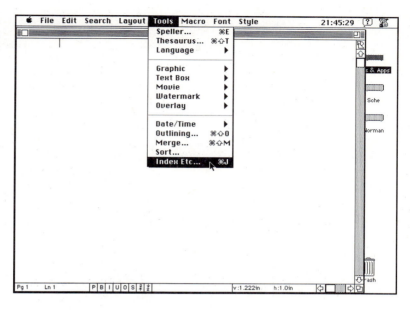

Fig. 10.21
Choosing Index Etc. from the Tools Menu.

3. Generate the lists.

The following sections explain in detail how to create, define, and generate the various lists.

Creating Indexes

WordPerfect enables you to create indexes containing entries and subentries that you can cross-index. Rather than marking individual entries for the index, you can use a concordance, which is a separate document containing a list of words and terms to be indexed. When you create a concordance, WordPerfect searches for occurrences of the listed words and includes these words in the index. In addition, WordPerfect alphabetizes the entries during list generation.

Your index can use any of the five numbering styles for the page number references that WordPerfect includes. These styles determine how a page number is formatted in a printed index—next to the indexed item or right-aligned to a column margin, for example.

> **Tip**
> WordPerfect provides only one Generate command, which generates *all* defined lists any time you issue the command. Because generating some lists requires a great deal of time, you should postpone the generation step until you complete the document.

Chapter 10
Creating Outlines and Lists

Marking Index Entries

To mark a single item for inclusion in the index, follow these steps:

1. In any document containing text to be indexed, select the word or words to be included in the index.

2. Choose Index Etc. from the Tools menu or press ⌘-J. The Index, Table of Contents, Etc. dialog box appears.

3. Choose Mark for Index from the Type pop-up menu (see fig. 10.22).

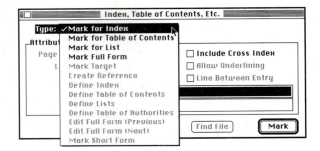

Fig. 10.22
Choosing Mark for Index.

WordPerfect inserts the selected text in the Entry box (see fig. 10.23).

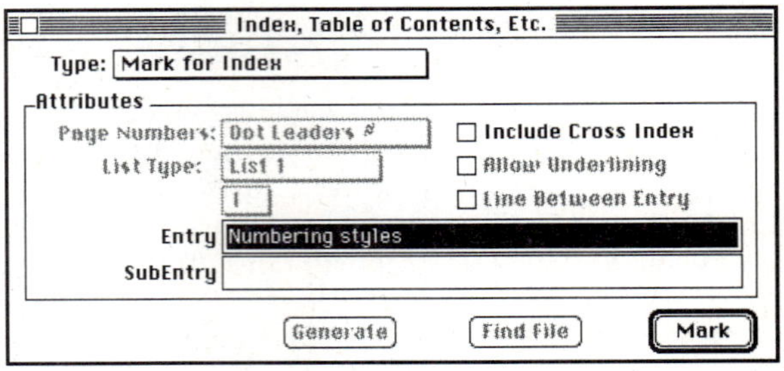

Fig. 10.23
Selected text in the Entry box.

4. To include a subentry for this term, press the Tab key and type a subentry in the SubEntry text box. Make sure the capitalization and punctuation of the entry and subentry are exactly as you want them in the generated index.

5. If you entered a subentry and want the two entries cross-indexed, click the Include Cross Index box so that an X appears. A

cross-indexed entry appears twice in the index—as a primary entry in the Entry box and as a secondary entry in the SubEntry box.

6. To mark the index entry, click Mark or press Return.

To see the marked text, choose Show ¶ from the Edit menu. You also can choose Show Codes to display the codes window (see fig. 10.24). In this figure, the words *numbering styles* are marked for indexing. The Marked Text symbol appears in the document window at the beginning of the marked text. In the codes window, the marked text appears twice—inside an index code and in the general text of the codes window. The marked text is easier to see in the codes window than the small triangle at the beginning of the marked text in the document window itself, but the triangle can help you locate the markings if Show ¶ is active.

Fig. 10.24
The marked text appearing in the codes window.

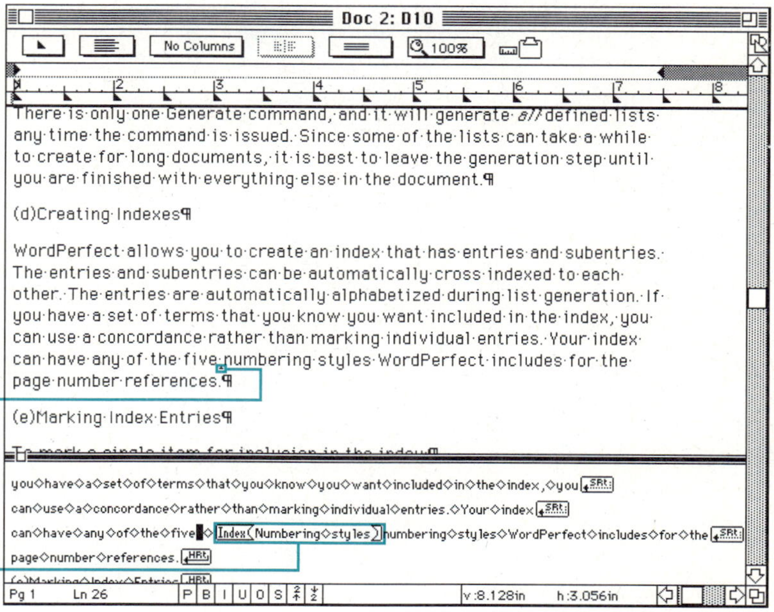

To mark several entries in sequence, follow these steps:

1. Arrange the main document window and the Index, Table of Contents, Etc. dialog box so that you can see the window and dialog box at the same time. Arranging the window and dialog box in this way enables you to switch quickly between the document and the dialog box as you index terms.

Chapter 10
Creating Outlines and Lists

2. In the document window, select text to be indexed.

3. Click anywhere in the Index, Table of Contents, Etc. dialog box; WordPerfect transfers the selected text, and Mark for Index appears in the Type box (see fig. 10.25).

Fig. 10.25
Marking an entry.

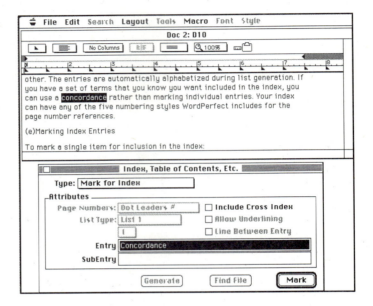

4. Click the Mark button. To enter a subentry, type the subentry into the SubEntry text box.

5. Return to the document window and select another term for the index.

6. Repeat steps 2 through 5 until you have marked all the terms to be indexed.

   You are ready now to define the index format and generate the index.

> **Tip**
> If you don't need to enter subentry information for a particular index entry, select the text for the entry and press Shift-F11 to add the entry to the index list.

You can leave the document window full size and simply click the Index, Table of Contents, Etc. dialog box (or press ⌘-J) to mark a term; however, when you must mark many terms in sequence, the resized window approach saves time because WordPerfect doesn't have to redraw the screen each time you switch windows.

Another way to mark text is to create a concordance, which is a list of terms to be indexed. WordPerfect includes in the index the terms listed

Part II
Refining Documents

in the concordance and any terms you mark in the document. Using a concordance can save you a tremendous amount of time if you have a long document that contains several references to index entries. Rather than searching through your document to find and mark each item for the index, you can include the term in a concordance so that WordPerfect automatically indexes each occurrence.

To create a concordance, follow these steps:

1. Open a new document.
2. Type the terms to be indexed, pressing Return after each term.
3. Save the file in which all appropriate terms have been listed.

When you define the index, as explained in the next section, you specify the concordance file that WordPerfect should use to generate the index.

> **Tip**
> Although you don't have to alphabetize the concordance file, an alphabetical concordance can speed up the indexing process. Don't try to alphabetize your list as you enter it—use Sort after you enter terms. See Chapter 13, "Sorting Data," for information on the Sorting utility.

Defining the Index Format

Although you can define an index at any time, you must remember that WordPerfect places the index format definition code at the location of the insertion point when you finish defining the index format. If you define an index before you generate the index, be sure to keep track of the ``«« Index Generated Here »»`` text, which indicates where the generated index appears.

> **CAUTION**
> If you position the index definition anywhere but at the end of a document, entries following the index are likely to be numbered incorrectly because the index itself changes the subsequent page numbering.

To define an index format, follow these steps:

1. Place the insertion point at the location where the index should begin. Be sure to enter any page breaks and titles before defining the index.
2. Choose Index Etc. from the Tools menu or press ⌘-J. The Index, Table of Contents, Etc. dialog box appears.
3. Choose Define Index from the Type pop-up menu.
4. Choose a page numbering style from the Page Numbers pop-up menu. Five styles of page numbers are available (see fig. 10.26).

Chapter 10
Creating Outlines and Lists

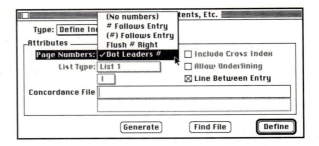

Fig. 10.26
The Page Numbers pop-up menu.

5. If you use a concordance, click the Find File button or press ⌘-F; then select your concordance file from the standard Mac file selector.

6. Click the Set button or press Return to transfer the concordance file name to the Define Index box.

7. If you don't want WordPerfect to add a blank line at the top of the generated index, click the Line Between Entry box to remove the check mark.

8. Click the Define button or press return to insert the index format definition in the document. WordPerfect inserts ««`Index Generated Here`»» in your document to remind you that an index is defined at that location.

9. Unless you are ready to generate the index immediately, as explained in the next section, close the Index, Table of Contents, Etc. dialog box by clicking its close box or typing ⌘-W.

    WordPerfect returns you to your document. You can edit, mark text, format, and so on, as necessary.

Generating an Index

When you complete your list definitions, or if you plan to generate only an index, you can generate the index immediately after defining it. When you generate an index, WordPerfect finds all occurrences of the specified terms, assembles the index, and inserts the index in your document at the location of the index definition code.

To generate the index, follow these steps:

1. Choose Index Etc. from the Tools menu, press ⌘-J, or click the Index, Table of Contents, Etc. dialog box if it is still present on your desktop.

Part II
Refining Documents

2. Click the Generate button or press ⌘-G to start the generation process. WordPerfect displays a message reminding you that all other defined lists will be regenerated in addition to the index (see fig. 10.27).

Fig. 10.27
The replace existing lists message box.

3. Click the OK button or press Return to continue generation of the lists. Click the Cancel button or press ⌘-period (.) to prevent all the lists from being generated.

   If you suddenly remember that you must edit another list definition and don't want to sit through a possibly long generation operation twice, you should click Cancel.

WordPerfect updates all lists and places them in the document at their defined positions.

Tip
If you have an extended keyboard, you can generate a list by pressing Option-F11 instead of opening the Index, Table of Contents, Etc. dialog box.

Creating a Table of Contents

A table of contents in WordPerfect can be as many as five levels deep. The generated table of contents list contains all marked items at the appropriate level and the appropriate page numbers. Creating a table of contents is much like creating an index; however, some additional formatting options are available in the list definition step.

Marking Table of Contents Entries

To mark entries for the table of contents, follow these steps:

1. Select the text for one entry.
2. Choose Index Etc. from the Tools menu or press ⌘-J. The Index, Table of Contents, Etc. dialog box appears.
3. Choose Mark for Table of Contents from the Type pop-up menu.
4. Choose the appropriate level of the selected text from the Level pop-up menu (see fig. 10.28).
5. Click the Mark button or press Return to mark the entry.

Chapter 10
Creating Outlines and Lists

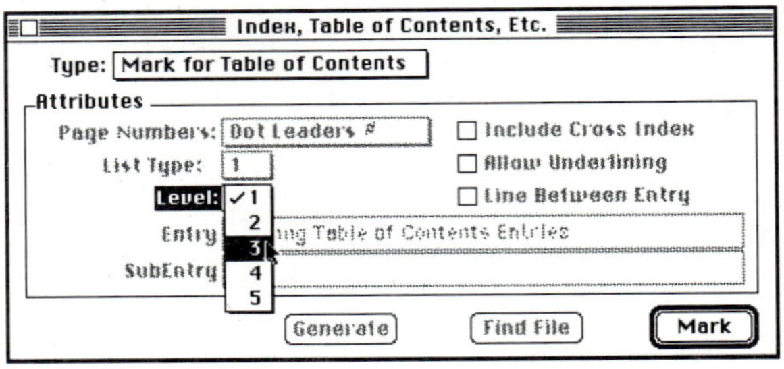

Fig. 10.28
Setting the table of contents level for selected text.

6. To select and mark additional entries, switch between the document window and the Index, Table of Contents, Etc. dialog box.

Defining the Table of Contents Format

You can define the format of the table of contents at any time. Like the index definition described earlier, WordPerfect inserts the definition of the table of contents as a code in the document at the location of the insertion point.

To define the table of contents format, follow these steps:

1. Move the insertion point in the document to the location you want the generated table of contents to appear.

2. Choose Index Etc. from the Tools menu or press ⌘-J. The Index, Table of Contents, Etc. dialog box appears.

3. Choose Define Table of Contents from the Type pop-up menu.

4. Set the maximum number of levels you want in the table by choosing a number in the Max Level pop-up menu.

   This setting is useful if you mark text for many levels and later decide to limit the entries in the table. By setting Max Levels, WordPerfect can generate only the specified number of levels.

5. Choose a page number format for each table of contents level from the Page Numbers pop-up menu.

   You can choose several formats. The page numbers can follow entries, for example, with only a space between the last character and the page number. You can align page numbers flush with the right margin, with or without a dot leader between the entry and number. You also can generate a table of contents without displaying page numbers.

> **Tip**
>
> If you are marking first or second level table of contents entries, you can select the text for the entry and press F11 (to mark a level 1 entry) or ⌘-F11 (to mark a level 2 entry) on an extended keyboard. If you don't have an extended keyboard, you can redefine these commands, using the Keyboard Management dialog box described in Chapter 15, "Customizing WordPerfect."

Part II
Refining Documents

6. The Line Between Entry option is only active for level 1 entries. If WordPerfect should insert a blank line before each level 1 entry, click this box so that an X appears.

7. Click the Define button or press Return to insert the table of contents definition into the document. WordPerfect inserts `«« Table of Contents Generated Here »»` in your document to indicate where the generated table appears.

Figure 10.29 shows a table of contents defined so that the page numbers for all levels use a dot leader followed by the page number and blank lines separate level 1 entries.

Fig. 10.29
A sample table of contents.

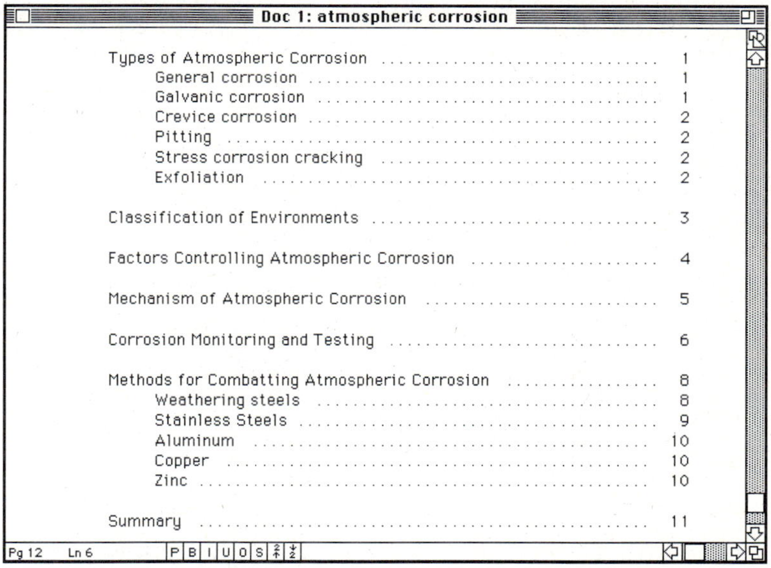

```
Doc 1: atmospheric corrosion

Types of Atmospheric Corrosion ..................... 1
     General corrosion ............................. 1
     Galvanic corrosion ............................ 1
     Crevice corrosion ............................. 2
     Pitting ....................................... 2
     Stress corrosion cracking ..................... 2
     Exfoliation ................................... 2

Classification of Environments ..................... 3

Factors Controlling Atmospheric Corrosion .......... 4

Mechanism of Atmospheric Corrosion ................. 5

Corrosion Monitoring and Testing ................... 6

Methods for Combatting Atmospheric Corrosion ....... 8
     Weathering steels ............................. 8
     Stainless Steels .............................. 9
     Aluminum ...................................... 10
     Copper ........................................ 10
     Zinc .......................................... 10

Summary ............................................ 11
```

Figure 10.30 shows the same table of contents without a blank line separating level 1 entries (the Line Between Entry option is unchecked) and the level 2 page numbers set to # Follows Entry so that the page numbers appear immediately after the number.

The Wrap Last Level option in the Index, Table of Contents, Etc. dialog box enables you to condense the last level of a table of contents. Instead of each entry appearing on its own line, WordPerfect wraps the entries like a regular paragraph (see fig. 10.31). The wrapped level is defined by the Max Levels setting. If you choose the Wrap Last Level option, you also must choose the (#) Follows Entry setting.

Chapter 10
Creating Outlines and Lists

Fig. 10.30
The same table of contents using a different format.

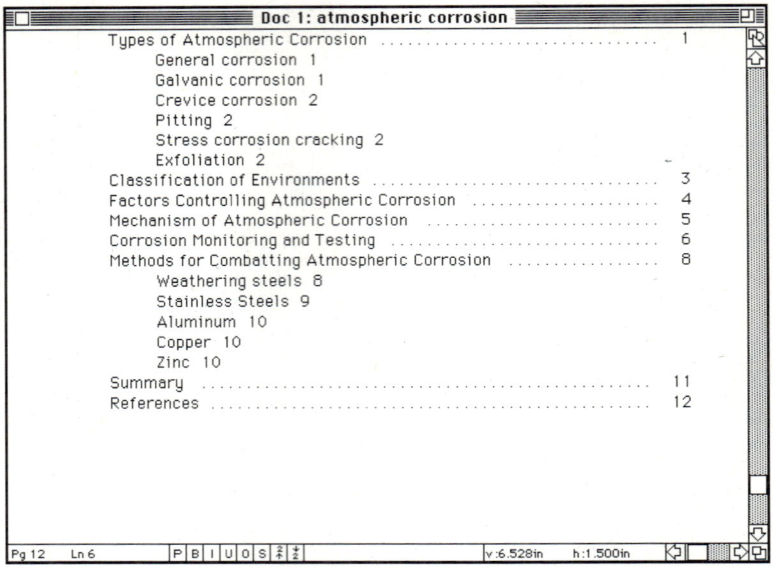

```
Doc 1: atmospheric corrosion
        Types of Atmospheric Corrosion ..................... 1
                General corrosion  1
                Galvanic corrosion  1
                Crevice corrosion  2
                Pitting  2
                Stress corrosion cracking  2
                Exfoliation  2
        Classification of Environments ..................... 3
        Factors Controlling Atmospheric Corrosion .......... 4
        Mechanism of Atmospheric Corrosion ................. 5
        Corrosion Monitoring and Testing ................... 6
        Methods for Combatting Atmospheric Corrosion ....... 8
                Weathering steels  8
                Stainless Steels  9
                Aluminum  10
                Copper  10
                Zinc  10
        Summary ............................................ 11
        References ......................................... 12
```

Fig. 10.31
A table of contents using the Wrap Last Level option.

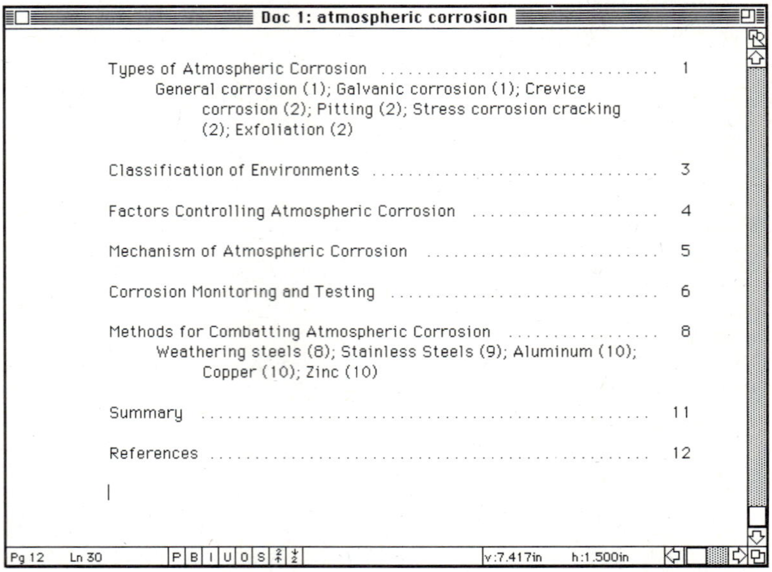

```
Doc 1: atmospheric corrosion
        Types of Atmospheric Corrosion ..................... 1
                General corrosion (1); Galvanic corrosion (1); Crevice
                        corrosion (2); Pitting (2); Stress corrosion cracking
                        (2); Exfoliation (2)

        Classification of Environments ..................... 3

        Factors Controlling Atmospheric Corrosion .......... 4

        Mechanism of Atmospheric Corrosion ................. 5

        Corrosion Monitoring and Testing ................... 6

        Methods for Combatting Atmospheric Corrosion ....... 8
                Weathering steels (8); Stainless Steels (9); Aluminum (10);
                        Copper (10); Zinc (10)

        Summary ............................................ 11

        References ......................................... 12
```

Part II

Refining Documents

Generating a Table of Contents

Remember that the Generate command regenerates any lists you defined (a possibly time consuming task). To generate the table of contents, do the following:

1. Choose Index Etc. from the Tools menu, press ⌘-J, or click the Index, Table of Contents, Etc. dialog box if it is accessible.//
2. Click the Generate button or press ⌘-G. The message box indicating that other lists will be replaced appears (refer to fig. 10.27).
3. Click the OK button or press Return.

WordPerfect replaces any existing lists, including tables of contents, with the new version. New lists are placed at the location of the appropriate definition code.

Tip
If you have an extended keyboard, press Option-F11 to initiate a list generation operation.

Creating a Table of Authorities

Tables of authorities are used in legal documents to list all the citations of other legal documents cited. Using WordPerfect, you can create a table of authorities containing as many as 16 sections, each with its own formatting. A *section* divides the table of authorities citations in some structured way. For example, you may have one section for citations on tax court decisions, another for criminal cases, and so on.

Like other generated lists, you create a table of authorities by marking text, defining the list format, and generating the table. The table of authorities is more involved, however, because you define both a short (easy to use) form and a long form (complete reference) of the citation. You also must format each section of the table of authorities separately.

Marking Citations

Marking a table of authorities entry involves marking a location in the document and defining the format of the citation (long and short forms). After you define both forms, you can mark another citation of the same reference, using only the short form.

To mark a table of authorities entry, follow these steps:

1. Place the insertion point at the location of the citation or select the citation in the text.

Chapter 10
Creating Outlines and Lists

2. Choose Index Etc. from the Tools menu or press ⌘-J. The Index, Table of Contents, Etc. dialog box appears.

3. Choose Mark Full Form from the Type pop-up menu.

4. In the Section pop-up menu, choose the number of the section that should contain the citation.

   Because the dialog box enables you to set the section by number only, you must remember which section number goes with which type of citation.

5. Type the short form of the citation in the Short Form text box (see fig. 10.32). If you selected text in the document, that text appears in the Short Form box already.

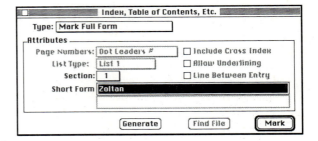

Fig. 10.32
Using the Mark Full Form option.

6. Click the Mark button or press Return to mark the citation.

   At the bottom of your screen, a window appears in which you enter the full form of the citation.

7. Enter the full form citation. Be sure to enter the text and punctuation of the citation exactly as you want it to appear in the table of authorities (see fig. 10.33).

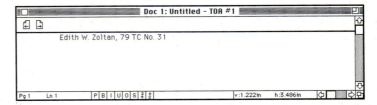

Fig. 10.33
Entering the full form of a table of authorities citation

8. To complete the full form definition, close the window by clicking its close box or pressing ⌘-W.

Part II
Refining Documents

To make another citation to the same source later, do the following:

1. Place the insertion point where the second (short form) citation should appear in the document.
2. Choose Index Etc. from the Tools menu or press ⌘-J. The Index, Table of Contents, Etc. dialog box appears.
3. Choose Mark Short Form in the Type pop-up menu.
4. Enter the short form of your citation in the Short Form text box.
5. Click the Mark button or press Return to mark the citation.

   WordPerfect inserts the short form citation into your document.

Defining Table of Authorities Section Formats

You define the sections of the table of authorities separately. You must type the section headings in your document for each section of the table. To define a section format for a table of authorities, follow these steps:

1. Type the section heading in the document where the table section should appear. Make sure the insertion point is on the line where you want the generated section to begin.
2. Choose Index Etc. from the Tools menu or press ⌘-J. The Index, Table of Contents, Etc. dialog box appears.
3. Choose Define Table of Authorities from the Type pop-up menu.
4. Choose the section number from the Section pop-up menu.
5. Choose the page numbering style from the Page Numbers pop-up menu.
6. If you don't want blank lines between table entries, click Line Between Entry so that the X disappears. Similarly, if the full form definition should not be underlined in the table, deselect Allow Underlining (the X disappears).
7. Click the Define button or press Return to put the table definition code in your document. The phrase «« Table of Authority Generated Here »» appears in your document where the section format is defined.
8. Repeat steps 1 through 7 for each section of the table of authorities. You can define the sections to appear sequentially or individually within your document.

Chapter 10
Creating Outlines and Lists

Editing a Full Form of a Citation

You can edit the text in your full form citation definition by using the Edit Full Form (Previous) and Edit Full Form (Next) options in the Type pop-up menu of the Index, Table of Contents, Etc. dialog box (see fig. 10.34). As with endnotes and footnotes, you can switch between the current full form definition and the next or previous definitions by clicking the respective icons at the top of the definition window. Next and previous refer to the order in which the definitions appear in the document.

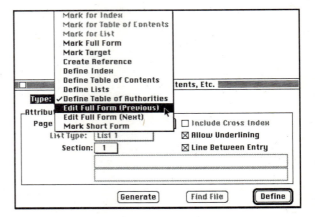

Fig. 10.34
Choosing Edit Full Form.

To edit the full form definition of a citation, follow these steps:

1. Place the insertion point next to the full form definition. Use the Show ¶ command or the Codes window to find the marked text.

2. Choose Index Etc. from the Tools menu or press ⌘-J. The Index, Table of Contents, Etc. dialog box appears.

3. Depending on whether you placed the insertion point in front of or behind the text marked in the document, choose Edit Full Form (Next) or Edit Full Form (Previous) from the Type pop-up menu. The short form definition of the respective full form appears in the Short Form box in the Index, Table of Contents, Etc. dialog box.

4. Click the Edit button, which appears in place of Define after you choose Edit Full Form in step 3, or press Return to open the full form definition window.

5. Edit the citation, using any of the usual editing and formatting commands.

6. Click the close box or press ⌘-W to close the full form window.

Part II

Refining Documents

Generating a Table of Authorities

Remember that generating a table of authorities also generates other lists that you defined. To generate a table of authorities, follow these steps:

1. Choose Index Etc. from the Tools menu or press ⌘-J. The Index, Table of Contents, Etc. dialog box appears.

2. Click the Generate button or press ⌘-G.

3. Click the OK button or press Return when the message box appears that indicates existing lists will be replaced also.

You can avoid steps 1 and 2 if you have an extended keyboard; from the document window, press Option-F11.

Creating Custom Lists

In addition to the standard lists covered, WordPerfect enables you to create up to nine additional lists (see fig. 10.35). Four of these lists—figure, table, text box, and user defined—are especially easy to create because WordPerfect keeps track of these boxes; you don't have to mark the boxes prior to defining and generating a list.

Fig. 10.35
Custom lists that you can define in WordPerfect.

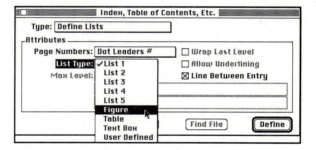

You use the process outlined earlier to create custom lists (List 1 through List 5): mark the text to be included, define the list format, and generate the list. List 1 through List 5 can include any text to be collected in list form.

Creating Lists of Boxes

You may recognize the four special kinds of lists (figure, table, text box, and user defined) as having the same names as the types of boxes discussed in Chapters 9 and 11, which include information on setting text and graphics box options. If you assigned a caption to the boxes of a specific type, marking text to create a list of that box type is unnecessary; simply define the list format and generate the list. WordPerfect creates the list, using the captions assigned to each box of the specified type for the list text.

If you add captions to your graphics boxes (figures), for example, you can create a list of figures by following these steps:

1. In any document for which you want to create a list of figures, move the insertion point to the location where the list should appear.
2. Choose Index Etc. from the Tools menu or press ⌘-J. The Index, Table of Contents, Etc. dialog box appears.
3. Choose Define Lists from the Type pop-up menu.
4. Choose Figure from the List Type pop-up menu.
5. Choose the type of numbering for the list from the Page Numbers pop-up menu.
6. Click the Define button or press Return to insert the list definition into the document.
7. Generate the list by clicking the Generate button or pressing ⌘-G. Alternatively, if you have an extended keyboard, you can press Option-F11 when the document window is active.
8. Click the OK button or press Return when the message box appears that indicates existing lists will be replaced.

Creating Other Lists

You can use the other available options under Define Lists—List 1 through List 5—to create lists of any text in your document. You can use these lists, for example, as selective tables of contents or to replace one of the existing lists. If you type your tables in columnar text instead of table boxes, you can select and mark the title of each table for inclusion in one of these lists. Again, you use the same process to create lists: you mark the entries, define the format, and generate the list.

To create a custom list not included in any of the other types of lists, follow these steps:

1. Select the text to be included in the list.

2. Choose Index Etc. from the Tools menu or press ⌘-J. The Index, Table of Contents, Etc. dialog box appears.

3. Choose Mark for List from the Type pop-up menu.

4. Choose a list type—List 1, List 2, and so on—from the List Type pop-up menu.

5. Click the Mark button or press Return to mark the selected text.

6. Return to the document and select another entry for the list.

7. Press ⌘-J; the Mark for Lists and List type should be set to the list you are defining.

8. Click the Mark button or press Return.

9. Repeat steps 6 through 8 until all entries for the list are marked.

10. Press ⌘-J and choose Define Lists from the Type pop-up menu.

11. In the List Type pop-up menu, choose the list you used to mark the entries.

12. Choose a numbering format from the Page Numbers pop-up menu.

13. If you don't want a blank line between each entry in the list, click the Line Between Entry box so that the check mark disappears.

14. Click the Define button or press Return to insert the list definition in your document.

15. When you finish defining your lists, generate the custom list by clicking the Generate button or pressing ⌘-G while the Index, Table of Contents, Etc. dialog box is active. You also can generate your lists from the document by pressing Option-F11 on an extended keyboard.

The generated custom list appears in your document at the location of the definition code—the location of the insertion point when you entered the Define Lists options.

Creating Cross-References

You use cross-references to refer to some item or location remote from the reference. In a long report, for example, you may want to refer to a figure shown earlier in the document. As you enter and modify text in your document, the location and numbers of figures may change. Although you can enter a specific reference to a figure, such as "see figure 10, page 15," you cannot be sure that figure 10 doesn't become figure 13 or end up on page 20.

WordPerfect cross-references enable you to set up links between locations so that references can be updated by the Generate command; consequently, the time-consuming task of searching your document to check the references is unnecessary.

You create a reference by using many of the same steps you use to mark text in the list creation process. The items that you cite in a cross-reference are *targets*.

To create a reference between the location of the insertion point and a figure elsewhere in your document, follow these steps:

1. Type the part of the reference text that isn't the number of the page or figure being cited. For example, type *see figure , page* . Be sure to include any spaces which should appear in the final phrase.

   If you forget to include the spaces, you can add them in the usual way: click the I-beam pointer to move the insertion point to the appropriate location and press the space bar.

2. Place the insertion point in front of the comma (where the figure number should appear).

3. Choose Index Etc. from the Tools menu or press ⌘-J. The Index, Table of Contents, Etc. dialog box appears.

4. Choose Create Reference from the Type pop-up menu.

5. Choose Figure from the Target Type pop-up menu.

6. Enter a descriptive name of the target in the Target ID text box (see fig. 10.36). Use a distinctive name for the target so that you can recognize the ID. Avoid using current figure numbers as ID's because the figure number may change later.

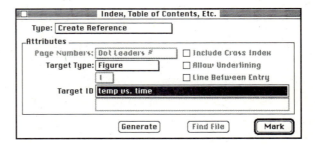

Fig. 10.36
Entering the target ID.

7. Click the Mark button or press Return to create the reference. Your current document becomes the front window, and a ? appears in the text where WordPerfect creates the reference. Do not delete the question mark; otherwise, you lose your reference.

8. Place the insertion point after the space following page in your text.

9. Press ⌘-J or click the Index, Table of Contents, Etc. window to bring it to the front.

10. Choose Page from the Target Type pop-up menu. Your previous Target ID is still in ID box; because both the figure and page citations refer to the same target, leave the target ID in place.

11. Click the Mark button or press Return to create the reference to the page containing the figure. Your text should now read see figure ?, page ?.

> **Tip**
> Use Show Codes from the Edit menu to check whether a question mark is an incomplete cross-reference or a normal question mark.

You are now ready to mark the target so that WordPerfect can complete the link between reference and target when you generate the cross-reference. Creating references and marking targets at the same time is a good idea because your last target ID remains available in the Index, Table of Contents, Etc. dialog box; therefore, you don't have to remember the exact wording of the ID. Also, if you create and mark at the same time, you are less likely to forget to finish the link preparation.

Marking Targets

You can use any of the following items as targets: pages, paragraphs, endnotes, footnotes, and the four types of text and graphics boxes. To identify a target to the list generator, you must place the insertion point immediately following the item to be cross-referenced. If you select the item, the Mark Target option in the Index, Table of Contents, Etc. dialog box is not available in the Type pop-up menu. To mark a target, follow these steps:

1. Click the figure you are citing. If you are citing something other than a box, place the insertion point next to the item to be cited.

Marking text, figure, table, and user-defined boxes as cross-reference targets requires special care. A page or paragraph anchored box does not necessarily appear on the page near the text that is adjacent to the figure code. Because you want the target code adjacent to the box code, click the box (the bounding rectangle with size handles appears around the box) before marking the target.

Chapter 10
Creating Outlines and Lists

2. Choose Index Etc. from the Tools menu or press ⌘-J. The Index, Table of Contents, Etc. dialog box appears.

3. Choose Mark Target from the Type pop-up menu.

   If you have just created the reference, your target ID is still in the Target ID box. If you created an intervening reference, you may have to reenter the target ID. Be sure to use exactly the same text when you create and mark references and targets. (The target ID's are not case sensitive, however.)

4. Click the Mark button or press Return to mark the target. If Show ¶ is active, a small triangle appears in the baseline of the text at the location of the target mark. This is the same mark that appears for other list item marks.

Unlike deleting the reference question mark, which deletes a reference, deleting a figure or note does not necessarily remove the target code from the document. When you cut and paste marked figures, open the codes window and make sure both the figure (or box) code and the target code are selected before you cut the figure.

You have now prepared both ends of the cross-reference link. When you generate your lists, WordPerfect inserts numbers appropriate to the type and location of your targets in the cross-references.

Generating Cross-References

You should wait to generate your cross-references until you finish modifying your document. Although seeing the question marks where the references go may be annoying, the references may be wrong if you generate your lists before you finish adding and removing figures.

To generate your lists and cross-references, follow these steps:

1. Choose Index Etc. from the Tools menu or press ⌘-J. The Index, Table of Contents, Etc. dialog box appears.

2. Click the Generate button or press ⌘-G.

3. Click the OK button or press Return when the message box indicating that existing lists will be replaced appears.

(Remember, if you have an extended keyboard, you can generate the reference by pressing Option-F11 when the document window is active.)

After WordPerfect generates the cross-reference, all question marks inserted when you created the reference are replaced with the numbers defined by the target type.

Chapter Summary

In this chapter, you learned how to create outlines using one of three predefined styles and how to create a custom outline numbering style. In addition, you learned that the outlining features can be used for numbering paragraphs, that outlines can be easily edited, and levels are automatically renumbered.

You found that endnotes and footnotes are simple to create and edit. You also learned that you can designate numbers for endnotes and footnotes to accommodate your particular needs when you divide a large document into multiple chapters or combine more than one document into a single chapter. Finally, you learned that several types of lists—including lists of figures or tables, indexes, and tables of contents—can be created and generated, using the same techniques.

CHAPTER 11

Using the Drawing Window

With WordPerfect's graphics features, you can create graphics within your document or import graphics created in other software programs. You can stretch or rotate your graphics, add captions, or layer a graphic as a watermark or an overlay. You can edit, move, and save graphics in separate files or your document.

Because many graphics features are similar to text box features, which are explained in Chapter 9, "Using Columns and Text Boxes," you have a head start on graphics if you understand text boxes. WordPerfect graphics are created in a separate area from the main document. After you finish editing a drawing, you return to your document, and the graphic exists as an element of your page—just like a text box. You can position graphics on a page, apply a caption or a frame, and resize graphics the same way you resize a text box.

By reading this chapter and doing the exercises, you can understand and use WordPerfect's graphics features. After you have a solid understanding of these features, you can experiment and create more advanced graphics as you need them. When you complete this chapter, you will be able to define figure boxes, overlays, and watermarks; understand and use WordPerfect's graphics tools; create and edit objects; and import graphics from other programs.

Defining WordPerfect Graphics

Software applications use one of two basic types of graphics: paint or draw. A *paint graphic* is created and stored as a series of pixels (dots). A *draw graphic* is stored as a collection of mathematically defined objects. When you enlarge a paint image, the individual dots are enlarged, and the image may appear jagged. When you enlarge a draw image, however, the resolution is maintained, and the object remains smooth.

Figure 11.1 shows four circles—two original and two enlarged. The top circles are draw objects; the others are paint objects. The quality of the original circles (the small circles on the left) appears similar. When enlarged, however, the paint object appears much more jagged than the draw object.

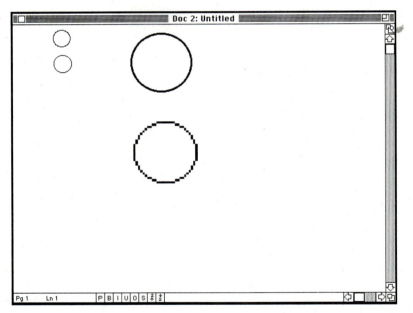

Fig. 11.1
Draw and paint objects.

WordPerfect creates only draw objects. You can import paint objects from other applications by using the Clipboard or the Insert command in the File menu. You cannot edit imported paint objects (also called *bit maps*) in WordPerfect. With draw images, you must edit the entire object. You can change the object's dimensions, rotate the object, or delete it altogether, but you cannot edit just part of the draw image.

Figure Boxes

WordPerfect usually stores and displays graphic images in *figure boxes*. These boxes are just big enough to display the entire image; they do not obscure the document text. You create or import a graphic, which appears within a box in your document. You can move the graphic, add a caption or frame, wrap text around the graphic, and so on. If you change the size of the graphic box, the document text rearranges to accommodate the box's new size.

WordPerfect also creates and manages two other kinds of graphics: overlays and watermarks. The following sections cover these two types of graphics.

Graphic Overlays

An *overlay* is a graphic placed on top of your text as a separate layer. You can use overlays to place a drawing over the text or to add comments or editing remarks without disturbing the main document, for example. You can edit the overlay separately or remove it altogether so that the document is not altered.

To insert a graphic overlay on a page in your document, follow these steps:

1. Place the insertion point at the location where the overlay should appear.

2. From the Tools menu, choose Overlay and then Draw. A graphic editing window appears (see fig. 11.2).

    You now can create your overlay by using all the graphic editing tools and techniques that this chapter presents.

An overlay is different than a figure box in that you can see your document text while you edit the overlay. Being able to see the text and overlay simultaneously enables you to see where the objects in your overlay appear in relation to the text. Also, objects in the overlay block out text in the document under them, just as the white rectangle in figure 11.2 blocks the text beneath it. Usually, you place solid objects in the overlay in areas of the page that don't contain text. You also can choose to include or exclude graphic overlays from printed documents by using the Print Overlay Layer check box in the Print dialog box. (See Chapter 6, "Printing a Document," for more information.)

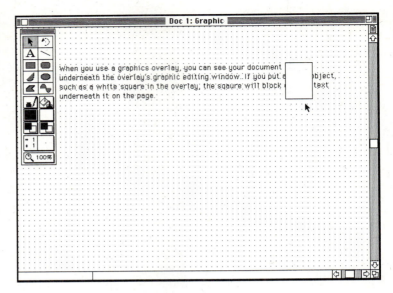

Fig. 11.2
The overlay graphic editing window.

> **Tip**
> By turning on the Display Overlay option on the Graphics menu of the Environment dialog box, you can display the overlay while you work on the document. (See Chapter 15, "Customizing WordPerfect," for a complete discussion of the Environment dialog box.)

After you finish editing your overlay, you can return to the document window by clicking the graphic window close box or the document icon above the vertical scroll bar. You also can choose Close Graphic from the File menu or press ⌘-W. By default, WordPerfect does not display the overlay while the insertion point is in the document window. With the overlay out of the way, you can edit more easily. Use the Environment dialog box, which is explained in Chapter 15, "Customizing WordPerfect," to turn on the Display Overlay option so that you can see your overlay while you edit your document.

To delete the overlay from your document, place the insertion point on the page containing the overlay. Then choose Remove from the Overlay submenu in the Tools menu.

Watermarks

A *watermark*, which you can use to create insignias or logos, is a graphic layer placed *under* the text. A watermark does not blacken out text; instead, the text in your document overwrites the graphic objects in a watermark.

Because of the similarities watermarks have to headers and footers, Chapter 4, "Formatting a Document," covers the mechanics of using

Part II

Refining Documents

watermarks. To open a watermark editing window, choose Watermark from the Tools menu and then choose New. In the New Watermark dialog box, click OK. You can use all the editing features described in this chapter to create your watermark.

Like a header or footer, a defined watermark appears on every page of your document until you turn the watermark off. After you close the watermark editing window, you must use Print Preview to view your watermark on-screen (see fig. 11.3).

Fig. 11.3
Print Preview of a page containing a watermark.

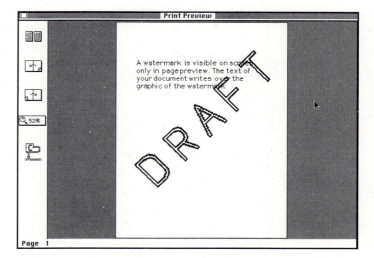

Watermarks and overlays are full-page graphics. Figure boxes, on the other hand, are big enough to surround only the drawing contained in the box. Figure boxes and document text share space in your document window. An overlay lays over the layer that contains the figure box and document text. Watermarks lay beneath the text layer.

Using the Graphics Tools

n the graphics window, you can use a variety of tools to edit and create your graphics. You can get into the graphics window in one of the following ways:

Chapter 11
Using the Drawing Window

- From the Tools menu, choose Graphic and then New.
- Click the small Graphic icon directly above the vertical scroll bar. (To return to your document from the Graphics window, click the same location, which now contains the WordPerfect icon.)
- Press ⌘-F1.

The tool palette appears in the graphics window (see fig. 11.4). You use some tools to create objects and other tools to modify existing objects. In addition, some editing tools, such as the Rectangle and Oval tools, are available only in the graphics (drawing) window.

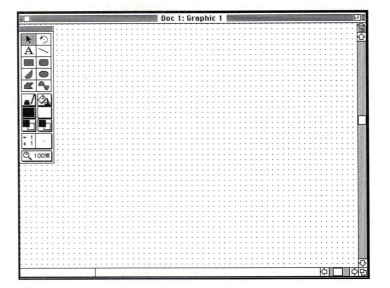

Fig. 11.4
The graphics window.

Click a tool to select it; the tool becomes gray. When you finish creating or modifying your object, click elsewhere on the page. The selected tool reverts to the pointer. To draw several objects with the same tool, double-click the tool to select it. The selected tool changes to reverse video. When you double-click a tool, you must select another tool before the mouse pointer changes.

The tools on the tool palette, shown in figure 11.5, are explained briefly in table 11.1. You can find more in-depth explanation of these tools in the following sections.

Part II

Refining Documents

Fig. 11.5
The tool palette.

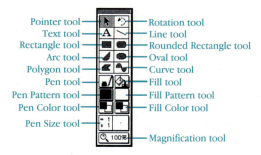

After you create a draw object but before you click someplace else on the page, handles appear around the object. These handles indicate the selected objects, which you can move, resize, and otherwise edit. For more information on selecting and editing graphic objects, see "Editing a Graphic" later in this chapter.

The Pointer Tool

With the default Pointer tool, you can select an object by clicking it, move an object by dragging it, and resize an object by dragging the sizing handles. Whenever you click outside the object, any other tool that you're using reverts to the pointer.

The Rotation Tool

The Rotation tool enables you rotate one or more objects around a handle. You can rotate any object in your graphics window, even text objects.

To rotate objects, follow these steps:

1. Select the object to be rotated and then click the Rotation tool. The pointer turns into a cross hair.

2. Place the cross hair over any handle and click. (This process is known as *grabbing a handle*.) Drag the handle to rotate the object; then release the button.

   The object rotates around the opposite handle as you drag the handle around the screen. When you release the mouse button, the object is redrawn in its rotated position.

Chapter 11
Using the Drawing Window

Table 11.1.
The Tool Palette

Tool	Function
Pointer	Used to select, move, and size objects (the default tool)
Rotation	Used to rotate one or more objects around a handle
Text	Used to add text to your graphics
Line	Used to draw vertical, horizontal, or angled lines
Rectangle	Used to draw rectangles and squares
Rounded Rectangle	Used to draw squares and rectangles with rounded corners
Arc	Used to draw any of the four types of arcs: wedge, closed wedge, chord, and closed chord
Oval	Used to draw circles and ovals
Polygon	Used to draw multisided objects
Curve	Used to draw Bézier curves
Pen	Used to draw borders around objects
Fill	Used to add a pattern to draw objects or graphics text boxes
Pen Pattern	Used to change the border pattern for your objects
Pen Color	Used to choose colors for the foreground and background around the edges of objects
Fill Color	Used to add color to the foreground and the background of objects
Pen Size	Used to change the thickness of the lines in line drawings
Zoom	Used to increase or decrease the magnification of the display

Part II

Refining Documents

> **Tip**
> Rotating objects with the Rotation tool is only as accurate as the mouse and your hand. If you must rotate to a precise angle, use the Rotate command in the Arrange menu.

Because single-clicking a tool accesses that tool only until you click again, you may find double-clicking the Rotation tool useful unless you know exactly where you want to place the object. By double-clicking the tool, you can adjust the location of the object without clicking the tool a second time.

To rotate more than one object, select all objects to be rotated; then grab a handle of a selected object and drag. Although only one object seems to be rotating, you see that the other selected objects rotate after you release the mouse button.

> **Tip**
> If your computer is low on memory, colors may disappear when you rotate imported graphics or text objects. To conserve memory, the colors do not appear on-screen even though the color codes remain. The colors reappear if you free up memory on your computer or open the file with more memory.

The Text Tool

You use the Text tool to add text to your graphics. Follow these steps:

1. Click the Text tool and then click the drawing pad. Drag the mouse pointer until the box is approximately the size you want.

2. The insertion point appears inside the box to enable you to type text. Type text inside the box.

    If you don't drag the mouse pointer to create a box, WordPerfect creates a very small box (a few letters wide). You can resize the box later, of course, but dragging a box initially is more efficient.

3. After you type the text, click outside the box to revert from the Text tool to the pointer; then click the box to select it. Grab a handle and drag to resize the box (see fig. 11.6). Your text appears in a rectangular graphic object.

The Line Tool

By using the Line tool, you can draw straight vertical, horizontal, or angled lines. To draw a line, follow these steps:

1. Select the Line tool.

2. Move the cross hair to the location in the drawing window where the line should begin; then click.

3. Drag the mouse pointer to the location where the line should end and release the mouse button.

    WordPerfect draws your line, using the mouse click as the beginning point and the release of the mouse button as the ending point.

Chapter 11
Using the Drawing Window

Fig. 11.6
Resizing a graphics text box after entering text.

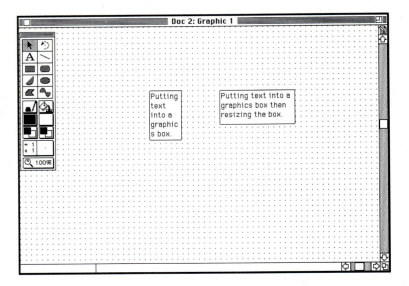

To ensure that a line you draw is exactly vertical, horizontal, or at a 45-degree angle, hold down the Shift key while you drag the mouse pointer to draw your line. Release the Shift key after you release the mouse button. Using the Shift-drag procedure, you can create vertical, horizontal, or 45-degree lines. To draw a line at another angle, don't use the Shift key. Instead, drag your line to the appropriate angle.

> **Tip**
> If you choose Show Coordinates from the Layout menu, the precise angle of the line you are drawing appears (as degrees from horizontal) on the status bar.

The Rectangle Tool

By using the Rectangle tool, you can draw rectangles and squares. To draw a rectangle, follow these steps:

1. Select the Rectangle tool.

2. Place the mouse pointer where the rectangle should begin and press the mouse button; then drag the pointer until the rectangle is the appropriate size.

    To draw a square, hold down the Shift key as you drag.

3. Release the mouse button. WordPerfect draws a rectangle in the editing window.

Handles remain around the rectangle. To change the size of the rectangle, drag a handle.

Part II
Refining Documents

The Rounded Rectangle Tool

The Rounded Rectangle tool draws squares and rectangles with rounded corners. You create rounded rectangles the same way you create rectangles (see the preceding section).

You can change how round the corners of a rounded rectangle are. The default corner radius is 0.125 inch. To change the radius, follow these steps:

1. Choose Rounded Corners from the Layout menu. The Rounded Corners dialog box appears (see fig. 11.7).

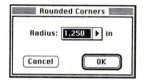

Fig. 11.7
The Rounded Corners dialog box.

2. Type a new radius into the Radius text box.

    The smallest acceptable number is 0.02 inch, which creates boxes with nearly square corners. A radius of about 2.0 inches (or larger) creates circles and ovals. Figure 11.8 shows the effect of various radius sizes.

3. Click OK to return to the drawing pad.

This procedure changes the corner radius for any new objects you draw. To change the corner radius of existing rounded rectangles, select the rectangles before you choose Rounded Corners from the Layout menu.

The Arc Tool

You use the Arc tool to draw any of the four types of arcs (curved lines), which are one-quarter of an oval. As with any of the shape creation tools, you draw an arc by selecting the tool in the tool palette and then clicking and dragging the shape in the drawing window.

The four types of arcs available are wedge (the default), closed wedge, chord, and closed chord (see fig. 11.9). The arcs in figure 11.9 were filled by using the Fill tool (described later in this chapter) so that you can see the shape of the open arcs more clearly.

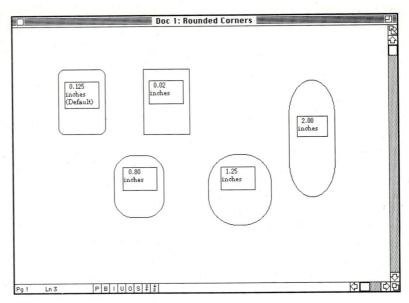

Fig. 11.8
Various radius sizes on rounded rectangles.

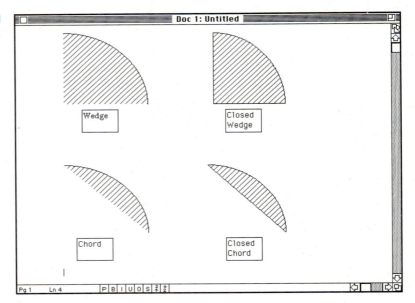

Fig. 11.9
The four types of arcs.

Part II

Refining Documents

To change arc types, you must access the Arc Type dialog box (see fig. 11.10). From the graphics editing window, choose Arc Type from the Layout menu. *Note:* In figure 11.10, the ⌘ key is held down to show extended key functions.

Fig. 11.10
Choosing an arc type.

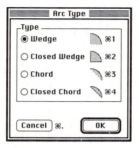

When you make an arc, the curve moves in a clockwise direction. To make a curve that extends from the 6 to the 9 on a clock face, you must start the arc in the 6 position and draw to the 9. If you start at the 9 position and draw to the 6, you actually get an arc extending from the 12 position to the 3 position.

Arcs do not print as smooth curves on non-PostScript printers—even on high-resolution printers such as the HP DeskWriter, an arc looks like a jagged paint image.

The Oval Tool

The Oval tool enables you draw circles and ovals. As with all graphics objects, you can rotate ovals by using the Rotation tool or by selecting the object and dragging a handle. If you hold down the Shift key while creating an oval, you create a circle (which to a mathematician is a special kind of an oval).

When you drag the cross hair to make a circle or oval, the beginning or end positions of the cross hair define the locations of two opposite handles of the object and do not touch the oval. If you draw a rectangle around the oval so that all four sides touch the oval, however, the beginning and end points of the cross hair appear in opposite corners of

Chapter 11
Using the Drawing Window

that rectangle. In figure 11.11, the upper object is actually the combination of an oval drawn on top of a rectangle to demonstrate this effect. The lower object is an oval still being drawn. The cross hair at the lower right shows where the lower right object handle will be.

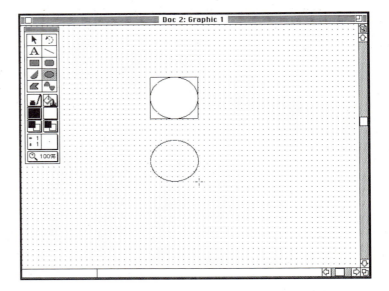

Fig. 11.11
Creating ovals with the Oval tool.

The Polygon Tool

With the Polygon tool, you can draw multisided objects such as triangles, trapezoids, parallelograms, and an irregular shape with consecutive straight lines. This tool works differently than many of the other tools, however, because you use a sequence of several click-and-drag motions to create a single polygon.

Follow these steps to create a polygon:

1. After selecting the Polygon tool, click the location where you want the object to begin; then move the pointer. Holding down the mouse button is not necessary.

    A straight line follows the cross hair. One end of the line is anchored to the point you clicked; the other end coincides with the cross hair location.

2. Click the location where you want the first line to end and the next line to begin.

Continue with this process until you complete the object.

3. To complete the polygon, click the cross hair over the first point you defined. WordPerfect closes the polygon by drawing a line from the last point to the first point.

You don't have to draw closed polygons. If you double-click at the end of any line segment, WordPerfect finishes the polygon without closing the figure, as shown in the top object of figure 11.12.

Fig. 11.12
Drawing polygons.

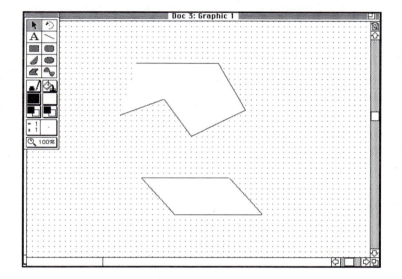

The Curve Tool

Although the Polygon tool works a little differently than the other tools, the Curve tool, which enables you to draw Bézier curves, is unlike any other tool and takes some getting used to.

A *Bézier curve* is a mathematically defined, nonuniform curve that is compatible with PostScript laser printers. In fact, Bézier curves define all PostScript font characters. Each curve segment requires four reference points: two *anchor points*, which determine where the curve segment begins and ends, and two *control points*, which establish the shape of each curve segment. Most curves are composed of a series of curves connected at anchor points—similar to the way polygon sides are connected at vertices. Knowing where to place the anchor and control points is the key to drawing the curves but takes some practice.

Chapter 11
Using the Drawing Window

Drawing Bézier curves also can be confusing because, as you drag a new control point, the shape of the previous curve segment adjusts to meet the tangency requirements defined by the new control point.

To draw a Bézier curve, follow these steps:

1. Click the Curve tool. You also can double-click to draw more than one curve segment without having to return to the tool palette.

2. To set the first anchor point, click and hold the mouse button at the location where the first curve should begin.

3. Drag to set the control point for the first curve segment. You see the control point on the opposite side of the anchor point.

    The direction that you drag sets the tangent for the first part of the curve. While you drag the first tangent, the anchor point, the cross hair, and the control point appear on-screen.

4. Release the mouse button. WordPerfect draws a curve between the anchor point and the location of the cross hair.

    This curve cannot pivot at the anchor point (thus the name) but must remain tangent to the line you dragged in step 3. The longer the tangent is, the longer the curve segment (or the bigger the loop) is when you place another anchor point.

5. Place the mouse pointer where the second anchor point should appear and click (see fig. 11.13). Be sure to keep the mouse button pressed if you intend to draw more segments.

Fig. 11.13
Drawing a Bézier curve.

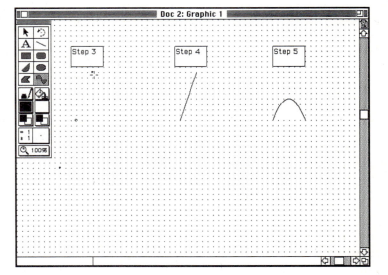

> **Tip**
> In general, you should not place anchor points at the peaks of loops. When an anchor point is placed at a loop apex, drawing a smooth loop is difficult.

When you press the mouse button, you define the location of the anchor point. To define the curve tangent at the new anchor point, you must drag the tangent line (to set a new control point) *before* you release the mouse button.

6. Repeat steps 2 through 5 to draw more curve segments.

7. To finish your curve, double-click the location where the last anchor point should be, holding the mouse button down on the second click; then drag the pointer to adjust the tangent of the curve as it approaches the last anchor point (that is, the end of your series of curve segments).

This combination of dragging at the end of a double-click is very foreign to many experienced Mac users and takes some getting used to. If you don't need to adjust the last tangent, double-click (normally) the location of the last anchor point. WordPerfect redraws the whole curve and displays a single set of handles for the composite group of curve segments.

You can edit a Bézier curve by double-clicking the curve with the Pointer tool. All the anchor points appear on the curve. Click an anchor point, and its control points appear. By dragging the control points, you can adjust the shape of the curve.

To master the Curve tool, try to create a Bézier curve copy of your signature. Although you certainly may find this feat initially frustrating, you will know how to draw almost any curve if you succeed. (Although the authors know this signature creation is possible, they haven't succeeded in creating their own signatures on-screen yet.)

The Pen Tool

The Pen tool, which is on by default, draws the edges (borders) around your objects. Borders do not appear around objects you create when the Pen tool is off (see fig. 11.14). You can turn borders on or off for selected objects by selecting the object and then selecting the Pen tool. To remove the box that surrounds a text object, for example, you unselect the Pen tool; the lines of the box disappear, and the text remains.

Click the Pen tool icon to toggle the Pen on or off. If you hold the mouse button down while the pointer is over the Pen tool, a pop-up menu appears with the options. An empty inkwell indicates that the border option is off; a full inkwell indicates that borders are on. If you do not select any object in the drawing window and turn off the Pen tool, the other drawing tools in the palette also change appearance, showing their respective shapes without the solid line around their perimeters.

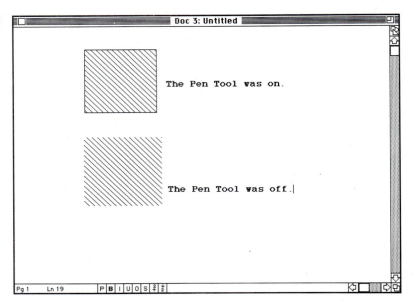

Fig. 11.14
Graphics boxes with Pen tool on and off.

The Fill Tool

The Fill tool is similar to the Pen tool, except that the Fill tool determines whether the interior of an object is filled with nothing (Fill Off) or with the fill pattern displayed in the Fill Pattern tool (Fill On), which is discussed in the next section.

As with the Pen tool, you can toggle the Fill tool by clicking the icon or by choosing Fill On or Fill Off from the pop-up menu attached to the tool icon. If you toggle the Fill tool on, the paint can in the icon represents "paint" being poured into the tray. If the Fill tool is off, an upright paint can and an empty tray appear in the tool.

The objects in figure 11.15 illustrate how the Fill tool works. By turning Fill off, you can see through the interior of objects; in the figure, the smaller vertical rectangle is visible through the larger rectangle's interior. If objects overlap with Fill on, on the other hand, the fill pattern of the top object blocks objects beneath it. In figure 11.15, for example, the oval blocks the right portion of the horizontal rectangle.

Part II

Refining Documents

Fig. 11.15
Objects created with the Fill tool on and off.

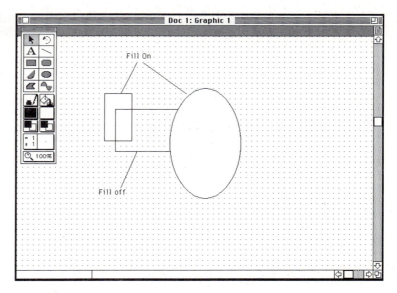

For all kinds of graphic objects except text, you must turn on the Fill tool, the Pen tool, or both. (If both tools are off, you create invisible objects.) Because the text in a text object is neither fill nor pen, you can turn both tools off and still see the text. The text labels in figure 11.15, for example, are text objects with Pen and Fill off.

The Pen Pattern and Fill Pattern Tools

The Pen and Fill Pattern tools enable you to choose patterns for objects. Each tool presents you with a pop-up palette containing 64 patterns—both palettes contain the same patterns—from which you can choose the pen or fill patterns (see fig. 11.16). Choose the appropriate pattern for the tool you are changing.

The default pattern for the Pen Pattern tool is black, and the default for the Fill Pattern tool is white. By choosing another pattern from the palettes, you can customize the appearance of your objects to distinguish them from one another (see fig. 11.17) or to create stylish objects (see fig. 11.18).

Chapter 11
Using the Drawing Window

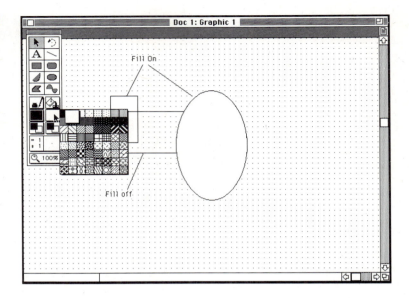

Fig. 11.16
The Fill Pattern tool pop-up palette.

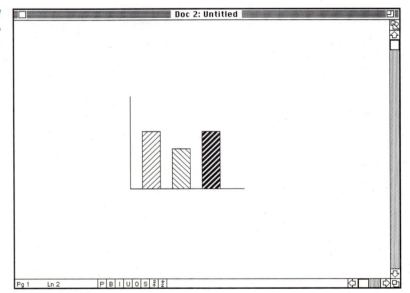

Fig. 11.17
Using fill patterns to differentiate objects.

Part II

Refining Documents

Fig. 11.18
Rectangles created with a fancy pen pattern.

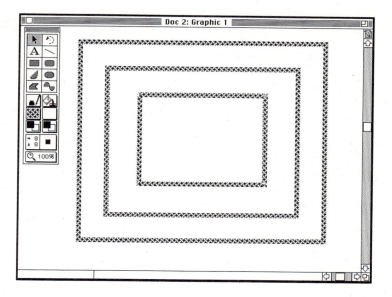

The bars in the graph shown in figure 11.17 are rectangles filled with different patterns. To change the pattern of a single object, follow these steps:

1. Select an object by clicking it.

2. Choose a new pattern from the Fill Pattern tool pop-up palette. WordPerfect changes the fill of the object to match the selected pattern.

To use a specific pattern for all new objects you create, make sure that no objects in the drawing window are selected, and then choose a new pattern from the palette.

The rectangles in figure 11.18 use a pattern that resembles a woven bamboo and a wide pen size, which is covered in the section on the Pen Size tool, later in this chapter. To change a pen pattern, follow these steps:

1. Select the objects. (To change the pen pattern of new objects only, do not select any object in the graphics window.)

2. Select a new pattern from the Pen Pattern tool pop-up palette. WordPerfect changes the fill pattern of your selected objects and displays the new pattern in the Pen tool icon.

Chapter 11
Using the Drawing Window

The Pen and Fill tools display the active pattern for any single selected object; if no objects are selected, these tools display the default pattern. If you select objects that use different pen or fill patterns, the Pen Pattern icon displays solid black, and the Fill Pattern icon displays solid white.

You can change any of the 64 patterns displayed in the pop-up palettes to create your own pattern. See "Editing Patterns and Colors" later in this chapter for more information.

The Pen and Fill Color Tools

You use the Pen and Fill Color tool icons to access the color pop-up palettes. With these tools, you choose the foreground and background colors of an object. You can see the current color choices in the overlapping squares that appear in the tool icons.

If you think in terms of text, the text on a page appears in black, which is the foreground color. The page itself, which is usually white, contains the background color. For fill and pen patterns, you must extend this type of reasoning to understand the difference between the foreground and background of a pen or a fill pattern. As you look at the patterns in figures 11.17 and 11.18, you may notice that part of the pattern is black and part is white. Black is the foreground color, and white is the background color.

For any pattern you see in WordPerfect's drawing window, you can change the background color (the white sections of the pattern) or the foreground color (the black sections). In addition, you can adjust the foreground and background colors independently for each pen and fill pattern.

You can change the default colors for all new objects by choosing a color from one color palette while no objects are selected in the drawing window. You also can change the colors of any single object or group of objects by selecting one or more objects before changing a color.

When you choose a foreground or background color from the pop-up palette, you must be careful where you place the pointer when you press the mouse button because each color tool icon controls two color palettes: one for foreground and one for background. WordPerfect changes the color or the pattern of the selected object and also displays the color choice in the section of the color tool icon to which it applies (see fig. 11.19).

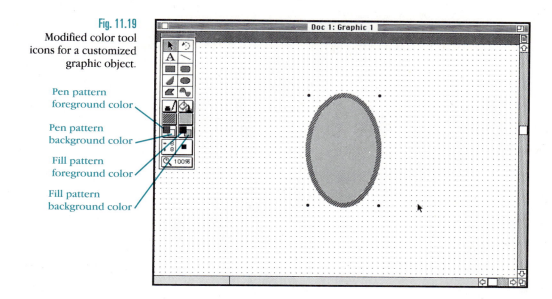

Fig. 11.19
Modified color tool icons for a customized graphic object.

Pen pattern foreground color

Pen pattern background color

Fill pattern foreground color

Fill pattern background color

Each color pop-up palette provides 256 color choices for pattern colors. If you don't like any of these colors, you can use the Macintosh system color wheel to choose from the 16 million colors available. See "Editing Patterns and Colors" later in the chapter for more information.

The Pen Size Tool

With the Pen Size tool, you can change the thickness of the lines in your line drawings. The default thickness is one point (one pixel) thick. You can change the width and height of the line thickness from one to eight points.

The left portion of the Pen Size tool shows the current pen thickness; the upper number shows the pen width, and the lower number shows the height. To change the thickness, click the Pen Size tool to access the Pen Size pop-up palette and drag the mouse pointer to the appropriate thickness. Notice that the numbers change on the tool (see fig. 11.20).

You also can change pen size by choosing Pen Size from the Layout menu. Enter the appropriate width and height in the width and height text boxes in the Pen Size dialog box. To change the units of measure from points to inches, centimeters, picas, cicéros, or didots, click pts (points) to call up the Units pop-up list.

Chapter 11
Using the Drawing Window

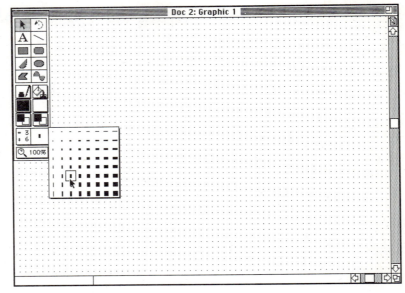

Fig. 11.20
Selecting a different pen thickness.

Figure 11.21 shows a polygon created with a tall, narrow pen. While you learn the graphics tools, you may want to leave the pen the same size height as width to simplify the appearance of your graphics.

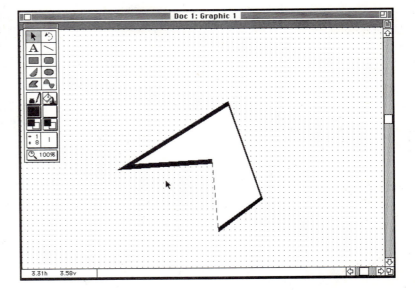

Fig. 11.21
A polygon created with a tall, narrow pen.

Part II

Refining Documents

The Zoom Tool

With the Zoom tool, you can increase or decrease the magnification of the display. Using this tool, you can examine a portion of a drawing more closely or see all of a graphic that doesn't fit on-screen.

To select a magnification, click the magnifying glass to display the Zoom pop-up list, which contains several predefined magnifications from which you can choose. To specify a magnification other than the predefined magnifications, choose Other; then type a value between 25 and 800 percent in the text box in the View dialog box. Click OK to complete the magnification change. See Chapter 6, "Printing a Document," for more information on using the Zoom tool.

Using the Grid

In the preceding examples that show the drawing window, you have been looking at a feature of the WordPerfect Graphics Editor that you may not have been aware of—the grid. Each of the dots in the drawing window is a *grid point*, the intersection of vertical and horizontal guide lines for drawing.

Using the grid display, which appears only in the graphics window and does not appear in the printed document, is like placing a piece of graph paper under your drawing so that you can draw objects easier. In addition to the visual aid grid points provide, the Grid Snap feature provides a mechanical means that can help you size and align objects.

You can find grid display features on the Layout menu. If you do not want the grid to show, choose Hide Grid. You also can turn on or turn off pointer coordinates from the Layout menu. The box at the left end of the status bar of the graphics window displays the pointer coordinates (refer to fig. 11.21). These coordinates indicate the horizontal and vertical distances of the pointer tip from the left and top edges of the graphics window page.

Changing the Grid

You can change the size and units of measure of the grid, the display color, and the heaviness of the grid lines. To change these features, choose Grid Options. The Grid Options dialog box appears.

Chapter 11
Using the Drawing Window

Changing the Grid Size

The first feature in the Grid Options dialog box is Grid Size. The default size is 9 points. To change the size of the grid, type a new number into the Grid Size text box. Because the box is highlighted when you open the Grid Options dialog box, you do not need to click it.

You can set the grid size as large as 5 inches, but sizes larger than 1 inch aren't much help in visual alignment and can even hinder drawing if you have Grid Snap on. You can set grid size as low as 0.0138 inch (1 point), but that size does nothing but paint your screen black with grid points. Grid sizes between 1/16th inch (0.063 inch) and 1/2 inch are most helpful.

You also can change the units of measure by clicking pts (points) to the right of the Grid Size text box and picking a new unit from a pop-up list. If you change just the units of measure, the number in the Grid Size box adjusts to the new units so that the grid size remains the same. If you change from points to inches, for example, the number changes from 9 to 0.125; the appearance of the grid remains the same.

Changing the Grid Color and Lines

The default display color for the grid is black. Click the color box and choose another color from the pop-up color palette.

Grid lines can be dotted or solid, as shown in figure 11.22. Three grades of dotted lines exist: light, medium, and heavy. Light dotting is the default feature. Experiment with color and lines to see what you like best. Remember that grid lines are just guides and that solid objects hide the grid lines.

> **Tip**
> Using a lighter grid color can give you the advantage of the lines and is less distracting than a darker grid color.

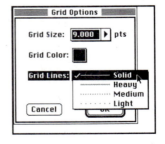

Fig. 11.22
Choosing a grid line from the Grid Lines pop-up menu.

Using the Grid Snap Feature

For precision in drawing objects, you can use the Grid Snap feature. When Grid Snap is on, lines begin and end at the nearest grid point. WordPerfect resizes all other drawing objects so that the handles of each object lie on a grid point. When you move an object while Grid Snap is on, the object moves horizontally and vertically in distances equal to a multiple of the grid spacing.

To use Grid Snap, set the grid size small enough to permit some placement flexibility; however, be careful not to make telling which grid line an object is resting on difficult. When you turn Grid Snap off, lines begin and end at the location of the pointer when you press and release the mouse button. You can change Grid Snap On (the default setting) by choosing the Grid Snap feature in the Layout menu.

To change the Grid Snap feature for just one object, hold down the Control key while you draw, resize, or move the object. By holding down the Control key, you turn Grid Snap on if it is off and turn it off if it is on, but only as long as you hold down the Control key. (**Note:** This procedure is one of the few defined uses you find for the Control key. If you have a Macintosh Plus keyboard, you don't even have a Control key.)

The Grid Snap feature is independent of the Show Grid feature. If Grid Snap is on, the objects still snap to the hidden grid.

> **Tip**
>
> With the Grid Snap feature, WordPerfect includes only the available option in the Layout menu so that you can toggle the option on and off. If the Grid Snap feature is on, for example, WordPerfect displays Grid Snap Off on the menu. If you choose Grid Snap Off to remove the grid, WordPerfect displays the Grid Snap On command.

Editing a Graphic

ordPerfect provides numerous editing features that you can use to enhance and modify the graphics you create. You can copy an object, for example, and then flip or rotate the object to create a mirror image. You can add colors and patterns to objects, and you can change these patterns and colors to create the intended appearance.

You edit graphics in the drawing window. Because graphics remain in the graphics window until you transfer them to your document, you can edit newly created objects by selecting them and applying the appropriate editing option. To edit a graphic that you already placed in a document, however, you must enter the Graphics Editor by using one of the following techniques:

- While editing in your document window, choose Graphics from the Tools menu; then choose Edit from the Graphics submenu. Type the number of the graphic box into the Find Graphic

Number text box in the Edit Graphic dialog box. (If you click the graphic before you choose the Graphics command, the correct number appears in the Graphic Number box.) Then choose Edit Content from the Edit Graphic dialog box; WordPerfect places the selected graphic on the drawing pad for editing.

- Double-click the graphic that you want to edit; WordPerfect moves the graphic directly to the drawing pad.

After you finish editing the graphic, you can return to the document in several ways: by clicking the document icon at the top of the vertical scroll bar, by clicking the drawing window close box, by choosing Close Graphic from the File menu, or by pressing ⌘-W.

> **Tip**
> If you label your graphic as a text box and don't enter text or a caption in the box, you may have to use the first method because no draw object or frame appears on-screen, and you may have trouble finding the box.

Selecting Objects to Edit

You can edit only selected objects. After you create a draw object, handles appear around the object. These handles remain on the newly created object until you click someplace else on the page. If you deselect an object (click somewhere else), you click the object again to select it; and the handles reappear. To select a text object—that is, a graphic object that contains text—you must click the object after you create it.

You now can use any editing feature on the selected object; for example, you can rotate, fill, or resize the object. Moving an object is the simplest editing operation: drag the object to its new location. To delete an object, select it and press Delete.

WordPerfect does not limit you to editing only one object. You also can select several objects to be edited simultaneously. To select more than one object, hold down the Shift key while you click the objects. Handles appear around all selected objects, which you then can edit as a unit. If you select three of four objects, you can rotate these objects simultaneously by issuing the Rotate command once, for example.

Grouping Objects

Sometimes you may create a drawing that consists of several separate objects but want to treat the objects as a single unit. Times may occur, for example, when you decide to rotate or resize a single object that really consists of several carefully placed objects. By defining the collection of objects as a group, you can reposition them simultaneously.

To define several objects as a group, follow these steps:

1. Select all the objects to be grouped (see fig. 11.23).

Part II
Refining Documents

Fig. 11.23
Selecting objects to group.

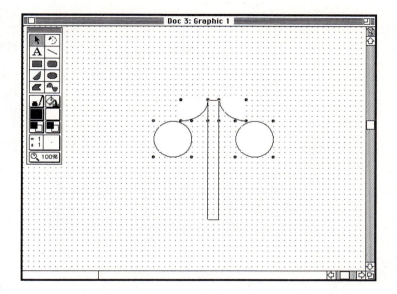

2. Choose Group from the Arrange menu. The individual handles disappear, and four handles appear around the entire grouping (see fig. 11.24).

Fig. 11.24
A grouped object.

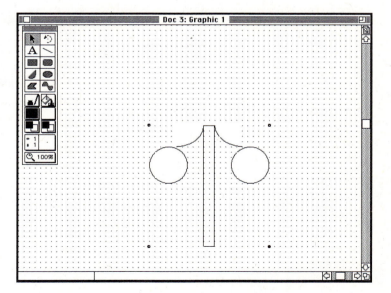

Chapter 11
Using the Drawing Window

You now can edit the drawing as a group. By grouping the objects, you click and drag the object with one motion instead of selecting and dragging each component separately. You no longer can edit only one component of the group, however, unless you ungroup the objects.

To ungroup a set of objects, follow these steps:

1. Select the grouped object.//
2. Choose Ungroup from the Arrange menu. Handles appear around each object in the selected group. You now can edit individual objects.

Duplicating and Replicating an Object

After you create an object, you can duplicate or replicate it. Although duplicating and replicating may sound like the same function, replicating provides several additional options. Using the Duplicate command, you can make a copy of a selected object (or objects). Using the Replicate command, you can make several copies at a time, change the size and color of the objects, and rotate replicated objects.

Duplicating Objects

To create a copy of an object, you use the Duplicate command. To duplicate one or more objects, follow these steps:

1. Select the object to be duplicated.
2. Choose Duplicate from the Edit menu. A copy of the selected object appears offset on top of the original (see fig. 11.25).
3. You can drag the copy to a new location.

Replicating Objects

To make more than one copy of selected objects, use the Replicate rather than the Duplicate command. To replicate objects, follow these steps:

1. Select the object to be replicated.
2. Choose Replicate from the Arrange menu. The Replicate dialog box appears (see fig. 11.26).

Part II
Refining Documents

Fig. 11.25
Duplicated objects on top of the original objects.

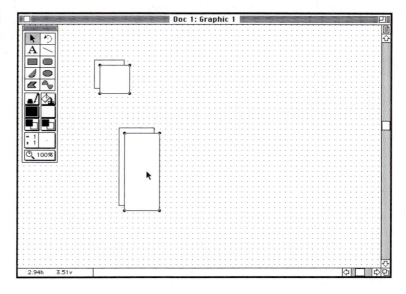

Fig. 11.26
The Replicate dialog box.

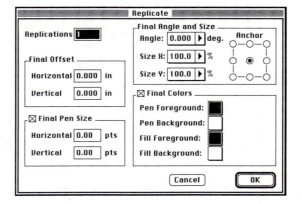

3. Choose the appropriate options, which are explained in the following list, and click OK or press Return. WordPerfect draws the multiple copies according to the options you choose.

The options in the Replicate dialog box are as follows:

■ *Replications.* In this text box, type the appropriate number of copies of the selected object.

Chapter 11
Using the Drawing Window

- *Final Offset.* This option places the last replicated object at the specified distance from the original. The intermediate objects are placed at even intervals between the first and the last objects.

    Suppose that you want 4 copies and type 1.5 inches in the Horizontal text box and 1 inch in the Vertical text box. You end up with 5 objects (four plus the original), with the fifth object 1.5 inches over and 1 inch down from the first (see fig. 11.27).

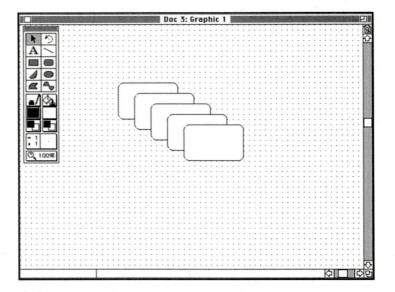

Fig. 11.27
A replicated object.

    To change the unit of measure from inches, click in to access the Units pop-up list; then choose another unit of measurement.

- *Final Pen Size.* This option enables you to grade the pen size (as described in the "The Pen Size Tool" section earlier) of your replicated objects. Start out, for example, with a pen size of 1 point for width and 1 point for height. Choose a final pen size of 6 points for width (Horizontal) and 3 points for height (Vertical). When you replicate the objects, the objects have progressively thicker borders (see fig. 11.28).

- *Final Angle and Size.* With this option, you can rotate an object around a specified point. You also can change the size of replicated objects. In both cases, the numbers that you specify are the final placement and size. The object shown in figure 11.29, for example, was created from a large circle by specifying a 270 degree angle, an X size of 50 percent, a Y size of 50 percent, and the right center as the anchor.

Fig. 11.28
Adjusting the pen size of replicated objects.

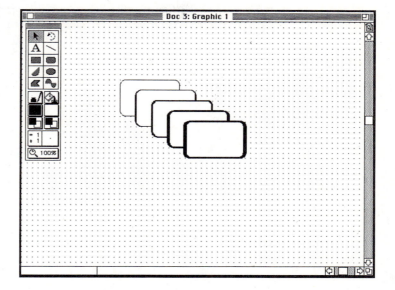

Fig. 11.29
An object created by choosing Final Angle and Size options.

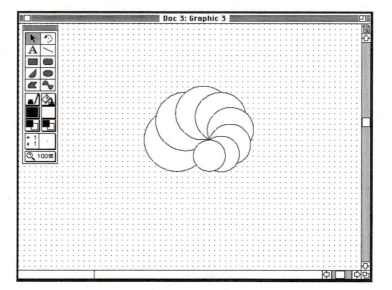

Chapter 11
Using the Drawing Window

■ *Final Colors.* This option enables you to change the pen and fill colors of the replicated objects. The colors are graded from your starting color (the color of the original object) to the color you choose in the Final Colors box. To see pen foreground and background or fill foreground and background change, you must choose pen and fill patterns in the tools palette. The color palettes in the Final Colors section give you a choice of 256 colors, but you can edit each choice by using the Macintosh system color wheel, from which you can choose from among more than 16 million colors.

Flipping an Object

The Flip commands on the Arrange menu enable you to rotate an object around its vertical or horizontal axis. To create symmetrical drawings, for example, you can duplicate an object and then flip and position the duplicated portion (see fig. 11.30).

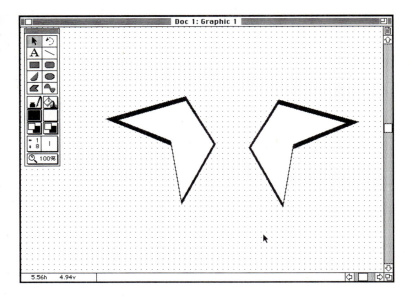

Fig. 11.30
An object and its horizontally flipped duplicate.

To flip an object, follow these steps:

1. Select the object.

Part II
Refining Documents

2. Choose Flip Horizontal or Flip Vertical from the Arrange menu. Flip Horizontal flips an object around its vertical axis. Flip Vertical flips the object around its horizontal axis.

   WordPerfect flips the object according to your specifications.

3. Position the object by dragging it; then click away from the object to deselect it.

Editing Patterns and Colors

Suppose that you created an object but want a particular pattern with just the right shade of mauve or puce in it, and the available choices don't include the shade or pattern you want. WordPerfect enables you to create your own colors and patterns.

Editing Colors

Several features in editing colors have not been detailed here, partly because of the difficulty of showing color changes in black-and-white print. To edit a color, double-click any color icon or palette square and experiment with the color wheel (assuming you have a color-capable Macintosh).

To edit a color, follow these steps:

1. Choose Colors from the Edit menu. The Color Palette dialog box appears (see fig. 11.31).

Fig. 11.31
The Color Palette dialog box.

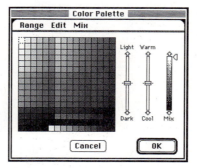

2. Click the color to be changed. White dotted lines appear around it.

Chapter 11
Using the Drawing Window

3. Edit the selected color by using the control bars on the Color Palette dialog box. Drag the indicators up and down on the control bars and watch the effects on your selected color.

    You can change the hue and saturation of the color with the Warm/Cool scroll bar and the Light/Dark scroll bar.

    You also can mix the selected color with another color. To choose a mix color, hold down the Option key and click the color to be mixed with the selected color. The Mix control bar changes to the mix color. As you drag the indicator down the Mix bar, the program adds the color in increasing amounts to the originally selected color. Only the small square that you originally selected on the palette changes color.

    If you decide to return to the original colors in the palette, choose Revert from the Edit menu at the top of the Color Palette dialog box.

4. After you finish editing colors, click OK or press Return. Any changes that you made appear in the Color palettes in the Tools palette, but only for that session in WordPerfect. When you close that file, the colors in the color palette revert to default settings.

Editing the palette makes the new colors available only for future color changes. After a color has been applied to an object, the color is retained by the object even if the palette is edited.

Editing Patterns

The patterns contained in the Pen and Fill Pattern tool pop-up palettes are the patterns defined by Apple as standard patterns. Because Apple's taste in patterns doesn't necessarily match yours, you can edit the patterns to suit your preferences.

To edit a pattern, follow these steps:

1. Choose Patterns from the Edit menu. The Pattern Edit dialog box appears (see fig. 11.32).

2. Click the pattern on the palette that you want to edit.

3. Click any location within the editing box to change black to white or white to black (see fig. 11.33).

    The block under the pattern palette shows you what your pattern looks like on-screen. Clicking in the Pattern Edit dialog box is the only bit-map (or paint-type) editing you can do in WordPerfect.

Figure 11.33 shows the white box (solid white pattern edited to contain a black heart).

Fig. 11.32
The Pattern Edit dialog box.

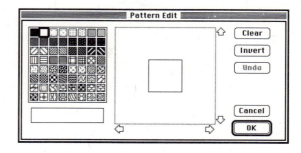

Fig. 11.33
A customized heart-shaped pattern.

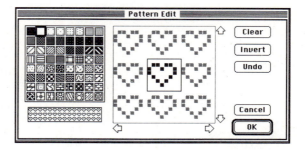

Other editing features in the dialog box are Clear, Invert, and Undo, which are described in the following:

- *Clear.* Removes all dots from the edit box, changing the pattern to white.

- *Invert.* Reverses the colors—black to white, white to black (see fig. 11.34).

Fig. 11.34
The Invert button reverses the colors.

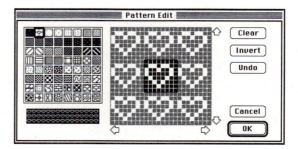

Chapter 11
Using the Drawing Window

- *Undo.* Cancels your most recent change to the pattern. If you undo something and then change your mind, you can reapply the change by clicking Undo again.

4. Click OK to exit the Pattern Edit dialog box and to save your changes. Click Cancel to exit the box without saving your changes.

Changing Graphic Options

Chapter 9, "Using Columns and Text Boxes," discusses using the Graphic Options dialog box with text boxes. Only the features different for graphic boxes are covered in detail here, namely Box Size, Graphic Size, and Graphic Offset.

To open the Graphic Options dialog box, follow these steps:

1. Click the graphic in your document.

2. Choose Graphic from the Tools menu; then choose Options from the Graphic submenu. The Graphic Options dialog box appears (see fig. 11.35).

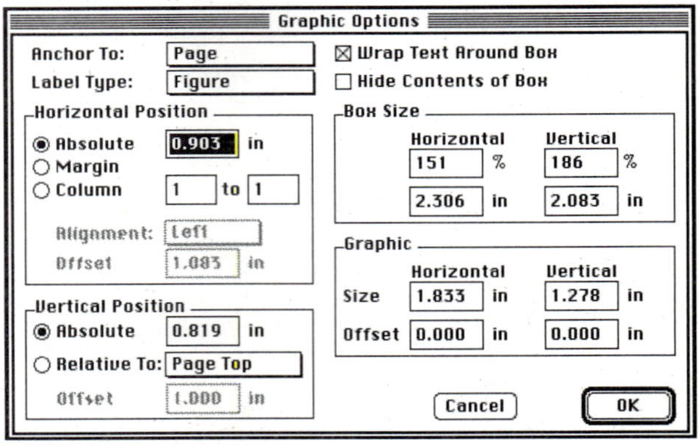

Fig. 11.35
The Graphic Options dialog box.

Like text boxes, the default anchor is as a character, although the default label type for graphic boxes is Figure. You can change the label type to Text, Table, or User. The Horizontal Position, Vertical Position, Wrap Text Around Box, and Hide Contents of Box options function the same way for graphic boxes as they function for text boxes. All these options

Part II

Refining Documents

pertain to the arrangement of a figure box on a page in your document. See Chapter 9 for more details on these box options.

Box Size

You use the Box Size options for graphics boxes the same way you use these options for text boxes, but the percentage boxes within this region of the dialog box have particular applications for graphics.

The box starts out at 100 percent in the horizontal and the vertical positions. If you use a bit-mapped graphic that was imported from another program, you can improve output on a laser printer by reducing the size of the image to a multiple of 24 percent. Reducing the size improves the image because the screen displays 72 dots per inch, but the laser printer prints 300 dots per inch. (Twenty-four percent of 300 is 72.) By reducing the image to 24, 48, 72, or 96 percent, you can improve the resolution of the graphic.

Although you don't have to choose a particular scaling factor for graphics created in WordPerfect because WordPerfect graphics are draw images, you may want to scale a figure box by a specific amount to get it to fit on a page better. In this case, you can use the figure box handles in your document window; however, entering values in the Box Size text boxes of the Graphic Options dialog box gives you more precise control over the box scaling or final size.

Graphic

The Graphic section of the Graphic Options dialog box is enabled only if you are working on a selected figure (not text) box. With this feature, you can change the size of the objects within the graphic box without changing the size of the box, and you can move the graphic object within the box.

The Size feature changes the size of the object(s) in the graphic box. Type numbers to change the graphic size. If you type numbers that make the graphic larger than the box size, part of the graphic is hidden. Zeros in any of the boxes means that particular feature is turned off.

You can use the Offset feature to crop objects within a graphics box. Suppose that you created a graph or illustration that you want to keep for use elsewhere. In a particular box, however, you want to show only part of the object. By offsetting the object in the graphic box, you can crop the picture to show just what you want (see fig. 11.36).

Fig. 11.36
Cropping a graphic object.

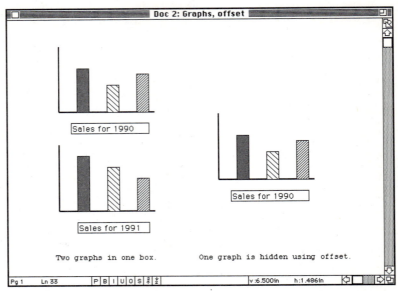

Unlike the Box Size option earlier, the precise control of entering numbers in the dialog box may get in the way of completing a cropping task quickly. To crop a figure box from the document window, follow these steps:

1. Click the graphic to be cropped. The sizing handles appear.

2. Hold the Option key down while you drag the box handle to create the cropped box size.

3. Also with the Option key pressed, place the pointer over the box contents (the pointer becomes a hand) and drag the contents of the figure box around until the part of the graphic you want to see is visible in the resized box.

By following these steps, you can monitor your cropping process visually rather than by making several trips to the Graphic Options dialog box.

Importing Graphics from Other Programs

y using the Clipboard or the Insert command, you can take an object that you have created in another program and insert it into a drawing window or directly into your document. An imported

Part II
Refining Documents

graphic placed directly into a document is not converted to a WordPerfect graphic but is displayed in the document. An object imported into a graphic window is converted to a WordPerfect graphic.

During the conversion, WordPerfect tries to separate the image into simpler object components to make editing easier. If the separation is not possible, the entire graphic is treated as one object.

WordPerfect can import several types of graphic images. The most frequent type of images you may import from other Macintosh applications are PICT and EPS (Encapsulated PostScript) images. The PICT format is a standard Macintosh drawing image format. Nearly all Mac graphics packages can save an image in PICT format. The higher-powered graphics and illustration packages, such as Adobe Illustrator, save images in EPS format. You can import EPS images into WordPerfect. You also can edit them if you're willing to work directly on the PostScript language commands, a subject that is well beyond the scope of this book.

Besides PICT and EPS graphics, WordPerfect can import several types of bit-mapped graphic (paint) images: MacPaint (another standard Mac format), GIF, PCX (a common DOS paint file format), and TIFF (a format common for digitally stored photographs). Remember that you cannot edit a bit-mapped image in WordPerfect, but you can insert these images into your document and print them.

To insert an entire graphics file in your document, follow these steps:

1. Place the insertion point in your document where you want the graphic to appear, or open a drawing window.

2. Choose Insert from the File menu. The Insert dialog box appears.

3. Set the Format pop-up menu in the dialog box to Graphics. The file list in the dialog box now shows only folders and graphics files.

4. From the list, choose the file of the image to be inserted and click Insert or press Return. WordPerfect closes the dialog box, imports the graphic, and places it at the insertion point in the document or in the center of the drawing window.

If you are running a graphics program and WordPerfect on your Mac, you can use the Clipboard to move a graphic to WordPerfect. In your graphics program, select the objects you want to move to WordPerfect, copy them (press ⌘-C), switch to WordPerfect, and paste them (press ⌘-V) into your document at the insertion point.

Chapter 11
Using the Drawing Window

Chapter Summary

This chapter covered the basics for creating graphics. You learned how to use the tools in the tool palette and move, duplicate, and rotate objects. You also learned how to paste graphics from other software programs.

Although you cannot equal the sophistication of dedicated illustration software packages, with the tools and features found in the graphics window, you can create graphs, line drawings, or intermediate-level illustrations.

Part II

Refining Documents

PART III
Using Advanced Features

Includes

Merging Documents

Sorting Text

Using Macros

Customizing WordPerfect

Taking Advantage of System 7

CHAPTER 12

Merging Documents

The Merge feature enables you to create large numbers of repetitive documents quickly and easily. Suppose, for example, that your company wants to send out a promotional letter to 200 potential clients. You create the letter once, and combine it with an address file that you created. With a little added effort, you even can personalize each letter. The result is 200 letters, each addressed to a specific person or company.

A merge normally requires both a primary file and a secondary file. The *primary file* is a document, such as a form letter or a contract, that you use repeatedly. The *secondary file* contains information, such as an address or data list, that WordPerfect inserts into the primary file.

The primary file contains formatting commands that act as placeholders, indicating to WordPerfect where information from the secondary file should be inserted. Within your primary file, you also can add a placeholder that enables you to type text from the keyboard. Using this technique, you can add personalized entries to a document that you don't need—or want—in a secondary file.

In this chapter, you merge a form letter and a list of names. When you finish this chapter, you will be able to do the following:

- Create a *primary file*—such as a form letter—with placeholders for variable information

- Create a *secondary file*, such as an address file

- Merge secondary and primary files
- Add codes to primary and secondary files for custom tasks
- Merge to a file or the printer

Although this chapter uses the example of a form letter and an address file, don't let that limit your creativity. You can merge files to create mailing labels, complete contracts, fill in schedules, or perform almost any other task that requires you to combine variable information with fixed information. You can even do a merge using only a primary file and input from the keyboard, prompting the user with customized messages to tell them what to do.

Understanding Merge Codes

WordPerfect provides several merge codes that you use to create your primary and secondary files. These codes appear in the Merge dialog box (see fig. 12.1). You access this dialog box choosing Merge from the Tools menu or pressing ⌘-Shift-M. You use the Merge dialog box to create primary and secondary files and to merge a document.

Fig. 12.1
The Merge dialog box.

The Merge dialog box has a close box in the upper left corner, indicating that this box is a *modeless* dialog box. Modeless dialog boxes remain open as you work, enabling you to move back and forth between the dialog box and the document window.

The list of codes is as follows:

- *Start Merge.* After you complete your primary and secondary files, you choose this command to begin the merge process.

- *Hide Merge Code.* Double-clicking this command replaces merge codes with a symbol (see fig. 12.2). Double-clicking again restores the codes.

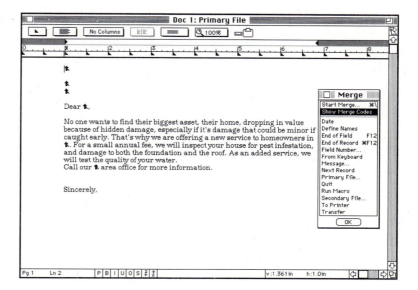

Fig. 12.2
Replacing merge codes with symbols.

- *Date.* Use this command to insert a date code in your primary file. When you merge the files, WordPerfect inserts the current date in the format you selected in the Date/Time dialog box.

- *Define Names.* With this option, you can assign a name to a field rather than a number. Using this option, you can call the first field *Name* instead of *Field 1*, for example.

- *End of Field.* In the secondary file, you use this code to signal the end of a unit of information, such as a name or complete address.

- *End of Record.* A record is one or more fields that you want grouped together—name, address, and salutation, for example. You insert an End of Record code at the end of the group.

- *Field Number.* When you choose this option, a dialog box appears in which you designate the field to be inserted into your primary file.

- *From Keyboard.* This option enables you to enter text from the keyboard into a merging file. When the computer encounters a From Keyboard code, it pauses for the input. After you add text, double-click End of Field in the Merge dialog box to continue the merge.

- *Message.* You use this option to insert messages into your primary or secondary files. You use messages as prompts or explanations for a merge in progress.

- *Next Record.* You use this code in the primary file to advance the secondary file to the next record. In most routine merges, however, adding this code is not necessary.

- *Primary File.* To change primary files during merge, insert a Primary File code. The merge continues with a new primary file, but the secondary file remains the same. To send one letter to people on the first half of a list and another letter to people on the second half of the list, for example, you use this option. Halfway through the secondary file, you add a Primary File code and type in the name of the new file.

- *Quit.* To merge only part of a primary or secondary file, enter a Quit code at the location where the merge process should end. If you want to use the entire file in the future, make sure you remove the code.

- *Run Macro.* You can add this code to a primary or a secondary file. When you choose Run Macro, a dialog box appears, and you choose the appropriate macro from the list of macros in your private library.

- *Secondary File.* Inserting a Secondary File code enables you to change secondary files in a merge while continuing with the same primary file. When you insert this message at the end of a secondary file, for example, the merge continues on the same form letter but uses a new list of names.

- *To Printer.* To send your merged document directly to the printer without saving it on disk first, insert the To Printer code at the end of the primary file. When WordPerfect encounters a To Printer code, it sends everything that has been merged up to that point directly to the printer. When you merge a large number of documents and letters, for example, you can use this code to save valuable disk space.

- *Transfer.* This option is an advanced feature that enables you to create, within a primary file, a second secondary file that contains duplicate field names. Merge codes for the new secondary file are enclosed between two transfer codes in the primary file.

Part III

Using Advanced Features

Creating a Secondary File

A merge must have a primary file that contains merge codes, including codes for fields. Secondary files consist of records that contain one or more fields. When you merge documents, the program inserts the data from the fields in the secondary file into the primary file at the appropriate merge codes. Because creating a primary file is dependent on knowing which secondary file field contains the data, creating the secondary file first is usually easier.

Although a secondary file can be a list of any information to be inserted into a document, one of the most common secondary files is an address list. In this lesson, you create an address list that you can merge with a form letter.

To begin your secondary file, follow these steps:

1. Open a new document window; then choose Merge from the Tools menu or press ⌘-Shift-M. The Merge dialog box appears in your document window.

2. Type *Adam Tamari* and click End of Field in the Merge dialog box or press F12. The name *Adam Tamari* becomes the first field in your first record, and the `<End of Field>` code appears after Adam Tamari (see fig. 12.3).

Fig. 12.3
The first field in your secondary document.

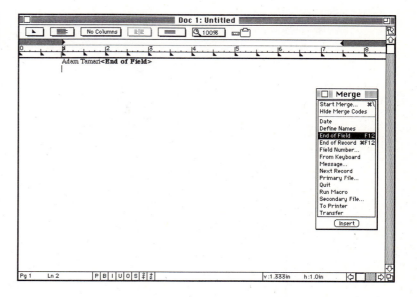

Chapter 12
Merging Documents

3. Type the following address, pressing Return between lines:

   2713 Oak St.
   Centerline, PA 17003

   Note: Be sure to press Return—do not choose End of Field—between lines of a multiline field; otherwise, WordPerfect inserts the End of Field code and divides the address.

4. Click End of Field from the Merge dialog box. The address is the second field in the secondary file.

5. To personalize the letter, enter a name to be used in a salutation into a field. Type *Mr. Tamari*; then Click End of Field.

6. To use the city name in the form letter, type *Centerline* and click End of Field.

7. Because people on this list are referred to an area office, you must enter the office into the record. Type *Centerline*, then click End of Field to complete the information for this record.

   You have five fields in your record. Although you cannot see the field numbers in your document, the fields are numbered consecutively from Field 1 through Field 5.

8. Double click End of Record or press ⌘-F12. Your secondary document should resemble the document shown in figure 12.4.

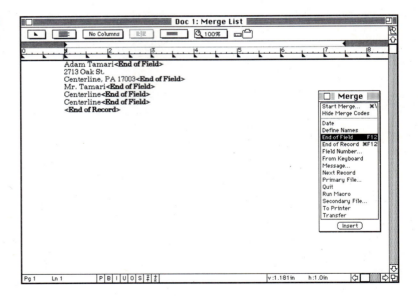

Fig. 12.4
A complete record.

Part III

Using Advanced Features

For practical purposes, you use a merge to create several documents that differ only in respect to the variable information. To add more records, you follow the same procedure as outlined in the preceding steps, and you do not put extra blank lines between records. Figure 12.5 shows a typical secondary file that contains several records.

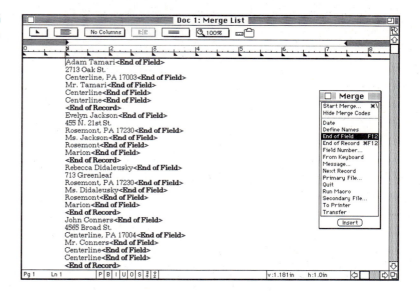

Fig. 12.5
A typical secondary file.

When you complete your secondary file, save it and close the secondary file window. The Merge dialog box, which you use to create your primary file, remains open.

You can add or delete records from your secondary file. If you delete a record, however, make sure that you delete the entire record. When you add records, make sure they contain the same number of fields as the other records in the file.

You may find remembering what field contains which type of information cumbersome. You can avoid having to remember field numbers by naming the fields. You can call the field that contains the name *Name* and the field that contains the address *Address*, for example.

To define field names, follow these steps:

1. Open a new document window. If the Merge dialog box is not open already, choose Merge from the Tools menu. The Merge dialog box appears.

Tip

If you add unalphabetized records to the beginning or end of an alphabetized list, use the Sort command. WordPerfect inserts the new records in the correct location. For more information on sorting files, see Chapter 13.

Chapter 12
Merging Documents

2. Click Define Names; then click Insert at the bottom of the dialog box. WordPerfect inserts a Define Names code into your file (see fig. 12.6).

Fig. 12.6
The Define Names code.

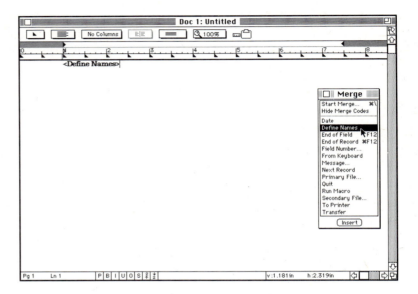

3. Type the name of your first field; for this example, type *Name* because the name is the first field entered. Press Return to indicate the end of that field name.

4. Type the name of your second field. For the example, type *Address*; then press Return.

5. Type the name of the third field. For the example, type *Salutation*; then press Return.

6. After you name all fields, double-click End of Record. WordPerfect inserts the <End of Record> code in the secondary file (see fig. 12.7).

Now you can enter text into your secondary file as described in the earlier steps. Do not put a blank line between the definition and the first record. After you define names and enter records, your secondary file should resemble the file shown in figure 12.8. When you create your primary file, you use the assigned field name rather than the field number. This process is covered in more detail in the next section, "Creating a Primary File."

Part III

Using Advanced Features

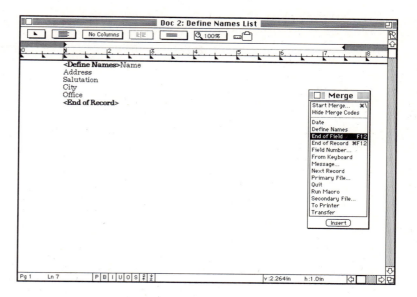

Fig. 12.7
Naming Fields.

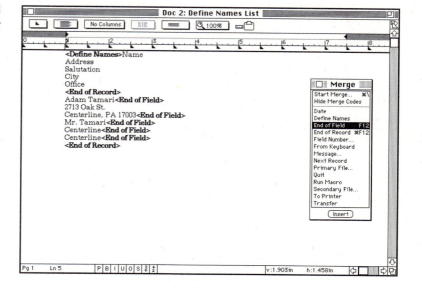

Fig. 12.8
Defining names in your secondary file.

Chapter 12
Merging Documents

Creating a Primary File

The primary file is your main document, such as a form letter or a contract. This file contains a body of text that does not change and codes that act as placeholders for variable information—name or address, for example—or give instructions. In this section, you create a simple form letter to merge with the secondary file that you created earlier.

Follow these steps to create a primary file:

1. Open a new document window.

2. If you closed the Merge dialog box when you completed your secondary file, select Merge from the Tools menu or press ⌘-Shift-M.

3. Press Return twice. (If you are using letterhead stationery, allow room for the letterhead).

4. Double-click Date in the Merge dialog box to enter a date formatting code (<Date>). The date formatting code inserts the current date when you merge your document.

5. Press Return twice; then double-click Field Number. The Merge Field Number dialog box appears (see fig. 12.9).

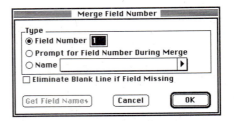

Fig. 12.9
The Merge Field Number dialog box.

6. Field Number 1, which is the name entry in your secondary file, is selected. Click OK to insert the <Field:1> code in your document (see fig. 12.10).

7. Press Return to move to the next line; then click Field Number to access the Merge Field Number dialog box again.

8. Type *2* into the Field Number box and click OK to insert the <Field:2> code into the primary file. You have entered the codes for name (Field 1) and address (Field 2) from your secondary file.

9. Press Return twice and type *Dear*, followed by a space.

Part III
Using Advanced Features

Fig. 12.10
Inserting the date code and the first field number code.

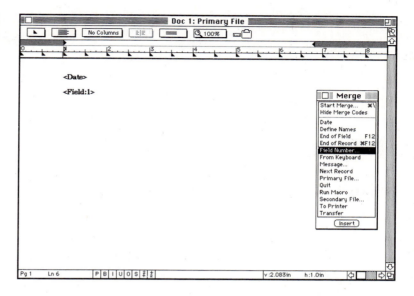

10. Click Field Number and type *3* in the Merge Field Number dialog box.

    WordPerfect inserts the <Field:3> code, which is the salutation from your secondary file, into the primary file.

11. Type a comma (,) after the field code.

12. Press Return twice; then type the following:

    > No one wants to find their biggest asset, their home, dropping in value because of hidden damage, especially if it's damage that could be minor when caught early. That's why we are offering a new service to homeowners in

13. A variable—the city name—goes into the body of the letter. Click Field Number, type *4* in the Merge Field Number dialog box, and click OK.

    WordPerfect inserts the <Field:4> code into the primary file.

14. Type a period (.) after the code; then type the following:

    > For a small annual fee, we will inspect your house for pest infestation and damage to both the foundation and the roof. As an added service, we will test the quality of your water.
    >
    > Call our

Chapter 12
Merging Documents

15. Click Field Number again and type 5 in the Merge Field Number dialog box; then press the space bar and type the following:

    area office for more information.

16. Press Return twice and type *Sincerely*, to complete your primary file (see fig. 12.11).

Fig. 12.11
The complete primary file.

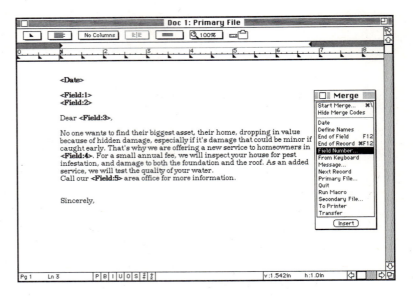

If you assigned names to your fields, as explained earlier, you would enter the field names instead of the field numbers into the primary file; as a result, your file would resemble the file shown in figure 12.12.

Performing the Merge

After you create a primary and a secondary file, you can merge the files together to create a third file. This process is *merging to a file*. Before you merge your files, however, you must save the primary and the secondary files.

WordPerfect merges files from the hard disk, not an open file. If you make changes to the primary or secondary file and do not save the changes before you merge the files, the merge document does not contain the appropriate information.

Part III
Using Advanced Features

Fig. 12.12
A primary file with field names.

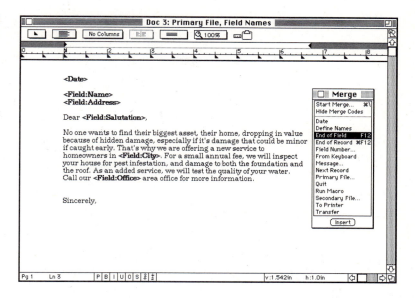

To merge the files, follow these steps:

1. Open a new document window.

2. If you closed the Merge dialog box, select Merge from the Tools menu to reopen it.

3. Click Start Merge. The button at the bottom of the dialog box changes from Insert to OK. Click OK. Alternatively, double-click Start Merge.

   The Open Primary dialog box, which contains a directory, appears (see fig. 12.13).

Fig. 12.13
The Open Primary dialog box.

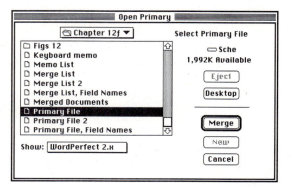

Chapter 12
Merging Documents

4. Click the primary file you want to open; then click Merge. Alternatively, double-click the file name.

    The Open Secondary dialog box appears (see fig. 12.14).

Fig. 12.14
The Open Secondary File dialog box.

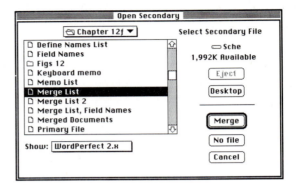

5. Select the appropriate secondary file; then click Merge. Alternatively, double-click the file name.

    The merge begins. After WordPerfect completes the merge, the merged document appears on-screen.

6. Check the merge file to be sure that it looks as you expect; then save or print the file.

Merging without a Secondary File

You can create a primary file with no field numbers in the file by entering From Keyboard codes or Keyboard Message codes where variable information should be inserted. If you have standard forms or contracts for which it is impractical to put the variable information into a secondary file, you may decide to merge without a secondary file. When you use From Keyboard or Keyboard Message codes, the user must enter the variable information into each document.

You initiate a merge without a secondary file the same way that you initiate a merge with a secondary file. After you select the primary file, the Open Secondary dialog box appears. Instead of selecting a secondary file, however, click No File; then click Merge. The merge begins, and when the computer encounters a keyboard code, WordPerfect prompts you to enter information from the keyboard.

Inserting Messages

The person writing the primary and secondary files may not be the same person who performs the merge. Sometimes you must give instructions or display a message that lets the user know the progress of the merge or indicates what information she must add from the keyboard. You place these instructions into messages that can be inserted wherever necessary in the document; in other words, you use message codes that elicit user response in place of merge codes.

You can include several types of messages in primary and secondary files. Although you can use all message types in primary files, you cannot use keyboard response or field number messages in secondary files. The types of messages are listed in the following:

- *User message.* A user message appears when a merge is in progress. In a long merge, you can use the message to let the user know how the merge is progressing; however, in a short merge, a user message may not be displayed a sufficient amount of time for a user to read.

- *Keyboard response message.* To insert text during a merge, you can add a keyboard response message to the primary file. The merge pauses when it reaches this message so that data can be input from the keyboard. In addition, a message box appears at the bottom of the screen. You can use this message box to prompt the user for the appropriate text to enter into the document. The user then must select the End of Field code to continue the merge.

- *Macro message.* A macro message pauses the merge to enable the user to choose a macro. The Run Macro dialog box appears. You can add a message, which appears in the upper right corner of the dialog box, to indicate which macro to select. Clicking Cancel in the Run Macro dialog box stops the merge (see fig. 12.15).

Fig. 12.15
Choosing a macro during a merge.

- *Primary file message.* A primary file message pauses the merge and displays the Directory dialog box, which enables the user to select a new primary file. You can add a message, which appears in the upper right corner of the dialog box, to help the user select the correct file. You use this option, for example, to send one letter to the people on the first part of your address list and another letter to the people on the remainder of the list.

- *Secondary file message.* A secondary file message stops a merge so that the user can select a new secondary file. Like other message insertions, you can add a prompt to help the user select the appropriate secondary file.

- *Field number message.* When you create a primary file, you may not know which field numbers to insert into the primary document because the information in field numbers can vary in different secondary files. By inserting a field number message into the primary file, you can help the user select the appropriate field number at the time of the merge.

  In some secondary files, for example, your salutation may be Field 2; in other files, the salutation may be Field 3. Rather than specify a particular field, you can insert a field number message that says, "Insert appropriate Field Number for salutation."

Although several of the message codes listed have the same function as codes that you add from the Merge dialog box, one significant difference does exist. When you add a code from the Merge dialog box, you must specify a particular change—a specific file, for example—that is fixed to your primary or secondary file.

When you add a Message code, however, the user can choose a change at the time of the merge. If you add a secondary file *code*, for example, you must specify the name of the new file. When you put in a secondary file *message*, the user chooses the new file while the merge is in progress. By using messages instead of codes, the merge is not restricted to specific address lists.

Suppose, for example, that you regularly update a report. Some of the information that goes into the report is stored in macros, but the macro used for any given report depends on the current quarter of the year. By inserting a macro message code rather a macro code, you can choose the correct macro for that particular report.

To insert a message, follow these steps:

1. Click Message in the Merge dialog box; then click Insert. The Merge Message dialog box appears (see fig. 12.16). User **Message is** the default message type.

Part III

Using Advanced Features

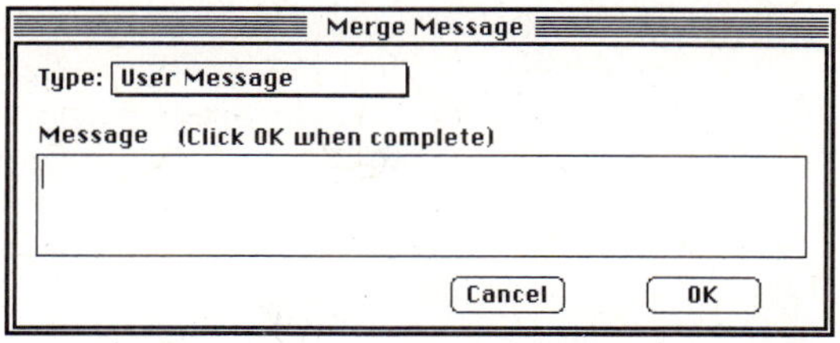

Fig. 12.16
The Merge Message dialog box.

2. To select another type of message, open the Type pop-up menu in the Merge Message dialog box and choose a different message type (see fig. 12.17).

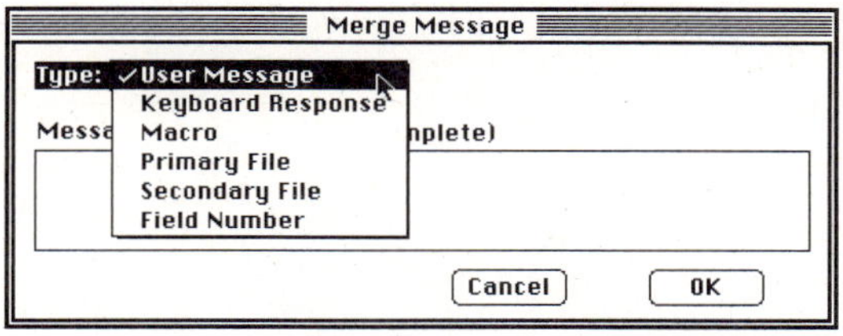

Fig. 12.17
The Type pop-up menu in the Merge Message dialog box.

3. Type the message that you want the user to see during the merge; then click OK. WordPerfect inserts a message code into your document (see fig. 12.18).

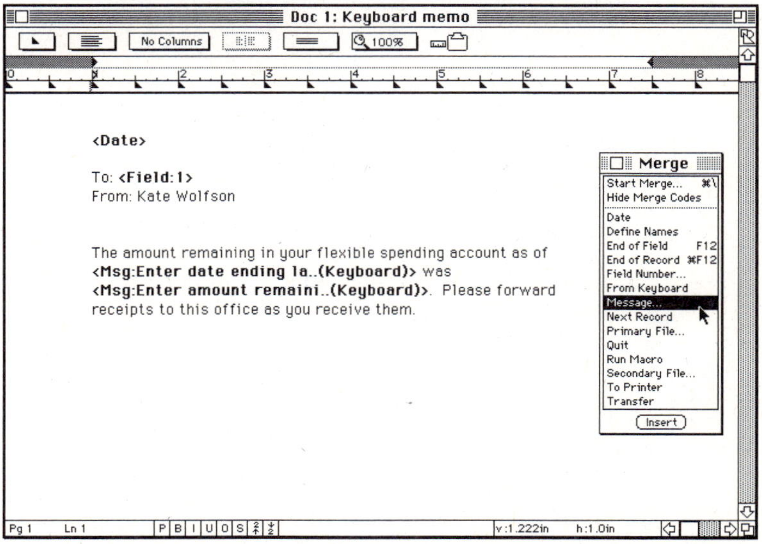

Fig. 12.18
A primary file with a keyboard response message code.

Chapter 12
Merging Documents

When you merge the file, your message appears while the merge searches the message code in the document. If you entered a user message code, the message appears while the merge continues. The other message codes require input from the user. The merge pauses when it reaches the code, displays the message, and waits for input from the user (see fig. 12.19). To continue the merge, double-click End of Field in the Merge dialog box.

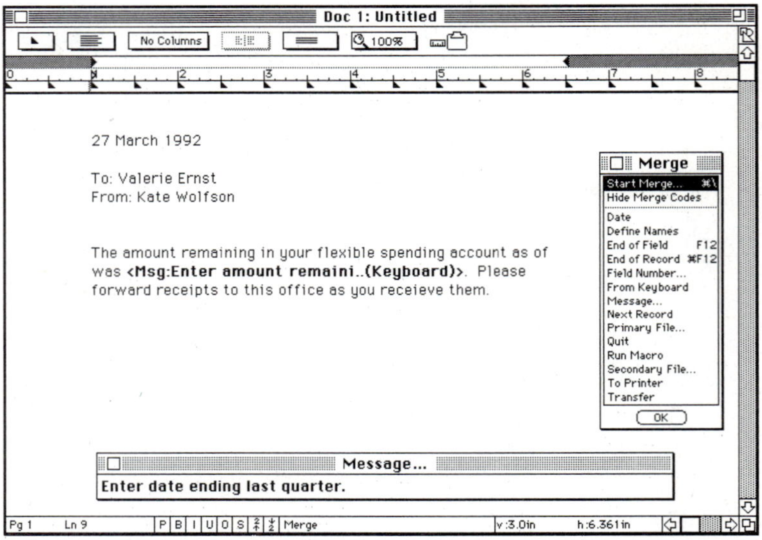

Fig. 12.19
A keyboard response message.

> **Tip**
>
> When you send files directly to the printer, the merged files don't appear on-screen. If you have not merged a particular file before, you may want to do a mini-merge to the screen before sending a thousand files to the printer so that you can make sure you didn't make any mistakes. Place a Quit code (from the Merge dialog box) in front of the Print code at the end of the primary file; then run the merge. The Quit code stops the merge and displays the merged document on-screen. When you are satisfied that the document is correct, remove the Quit code and merge to the printer.

Merging to the Printer

If you intend to print a large number of merged files, but you lack adequate disk space to merge to a file, you can merge directly to the printer. By placing a printer code at the end of your primary document, files are sent to the printer as they are merged.

To send a merge to the printer, follow these steps:

1. Place the insertion point at the end of the primary file.

2. If the Merge dialog box is not open, choose Merge from the Tools menu.

3. Click To Printer from the Merge dialog box; then click Insert. Alternatively, double-click To Printer. WordPerfect inserts the <Print> code at the end of the primary file (see fig. 12.20).

Part III

Using Advanced Features

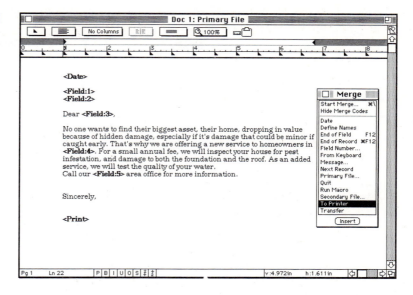

Fig. 12.20
Adding a Print code to the primary file.

When you merge files, WordPerfect sends everything that is merged up to the point of the print code to the printer. The merged data is not saved to disk or in the current document.

Chapter Summary

In this chapter, you learned to use the Merge feature to combine variable information with standard forms by creating two files: primary and secondary. You learned how to insert field and record codes that act as placeholders for variable information, and you learned how to place the variable information in a secondary file.

This chapter also included information on customizing the merge process. You learned to add special codes to the primary or secondary file, for example, and you learned how to change files during the merge process and add variable information to the merging file. In addition, you learned to add messages to show the progress of the merge or to prompt the user for input. Finally, you learned how to save disk space by sending merged files to the printer.

Chapter 12
Merging Documents

CHAPTER 13

Sorting Text

The Sort feature enables you to sort almost any kind of text that can be logically grouped. Using multiple sort keys, you can sort simple lists, tabbed text, merge records, paragraphs, and even multiple paragraph sections in a document. In addition, a filtering function enables you to specify selection rules so that you can sort a selection and retain only those pieces that conform to your filtering specifications. This chapter guides you through the terminology used by WordPerfect to describe its sorting features and helps you accomplish several typical sort operations.

Understanding Sort Options

WordPerfect provides two major categories of sorts. You can sort whole files or selected text in a document window. In either case, you can insert the sorted text into your document or save the text to a separate file. You use the same methods to perform both types of sort operations.

The different options available in the Sort feature are easier to use if you are familiar with the terminology WordPerfect uses to describe this operation. The basic strategy is to select *items* (the text to be kept together during the Sort), to specify the *sort keys* (the parts of the items that determine the item order), and to instruct WordPerfect where to write the results of the sort.

Sort Items

The first step in sorting text is to decide what information WordPerfect should keep together. In the case of the address list shown in figure 13.1, the logical units are the company name and address.

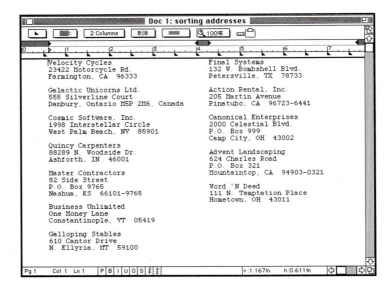

Fig. 13.1
An address list for sorting.

WordPerfect sorts three types of text groups, referred to as *items*: zones, groups, and merge records. The ending character (number of carriage returns) or merge code determines the type of item.

A *zone* is any text ending in one carriage return. Each line in the addresses listed in figure 13.1, for example, is a zone. A *group*, which is text ending in two carriage returns, can contain any number of zones. Because two carriage returns separate companies in figure 13.1, each company and its address comprise one group.

Merge records are collections of fields in a merge secondary file—discussed in Chapter 12, "Merging Documents"—ending with an <End of Record> code. The Sort feature handles merge record and group items similarly. The major difference is that a group contains only text and the merge record contains field and record codes in addition to text.

Part III

Using Advanced Features

Sort Keys

When you define the sort keys, you tell the program what information to use to determine the order of the sort. WordPerfect takes the information in the sort keys and rearranges the items according to the key order. (WordPerfect does not rearrange the information in an item, however.) To arrange the list shown in figure 13.1 alphabetically by company name, for example, you specify the company name as the sort key.

Although any word in an item can be a *sort key*, you must be able to describe the position—first, last, or third word after the second tab in the third line, for example—of the word in the item. You can sort the addresses in figure 13.1, for example, by company name (the first word on the first line of each address), by ZIP code (the last word), or by state (the next to last word). Consider, though, the address for Galactic Unicorns Ltd. The last word in this address is a country name, not a ZIP code.

When you sort text, a few problems can arise when you specify a sort key that isn't the first word on a line. After you specify one or more keys, however, the sorting operation itself is easy to accomplish.

Sorting a List

You can sort a list in several ways. You can sort the address list in figure 13.1 according to the information you consider to be most important. The simplest sort is alphabetizing the list by company name. You may want an alphabetized list so that you easily can find a company's address. If you have a large list of addresses that you want to sort by state before alphabetizing, you can use the multiple key sort to accomplish the task. If you use an address list to print a mailing label set, you may want to sort the addresses by ZIP code to take advantage of lower postage rates. Regardless of the type of information being sorted and regardless of the criteria you specify, the general procedure for sorting, explained in the following, remains the same:

1. Choose the material to be sorted by selecting text or choosing a file.

2. Specify the sort keys.

3. Specify the type of sort (alphabetic or numeric) and order (ascending or descending).

4. Choose a destination for the sorted material by replacing the selected material or creating a new file.

5. Initiate the sort.

The next two sections enable you to practice basic sorting techniques by using the address list shown in figure 13.1 as the example. If you already have an address list on which to practice, make sure that the addresses are separated from each other by a blank line, which defines the address as a group for sorting.

Sorting an Address List by Company Name

To sort any list by a single criterion only—company name, for example—you perform a *single key sort*. The key can be any part of a zone, group, or merge record. As long as only one item determines the order of the sorted material, the sort is single keyed.

To create an alphabetized list of the companies, follow these steps:

1. Make the address list the active window.

2. Choose Select All from the Edit menu or press ⌘-A to select all the addresses in the file.

3. Choose Sort from the Tools menu (see fig. 13.2). The Sort dialog box appears.

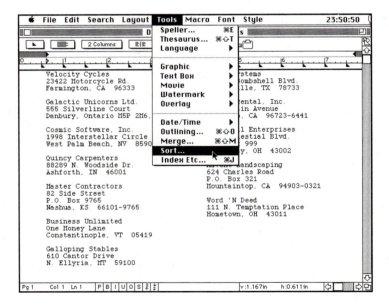

Fig. 13.2
The Tools Menu.

4. Choose Group from the Items pop-up menu (see fig. 13.3). By choosing Group, you indicate that WordPerfect should keep the whole address—everything between the Hard Returns—together.

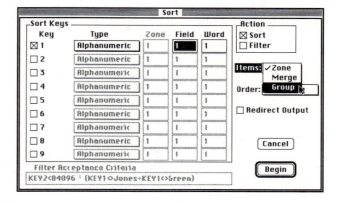

Fig. 13.3
Choosing Group from the Item pop-up menu.

5. Ensure that the settings in your dialog box are the same as those shown in figure 13.4.

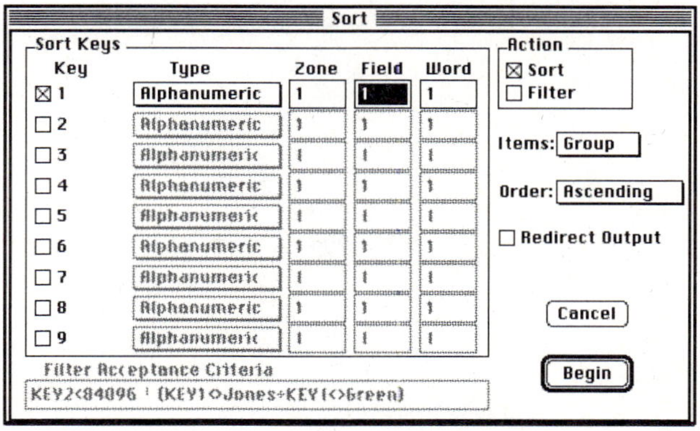

Fig. 13.4
The appropriate settings in the Sort dialog box.

When the Sort dialog box appears, an X appears in the Key 1 check box. For a single key sort, leave the rest of the key check boxes unchecked.

The default key type is Alphanumeric, as shown in the Type pop-up menu. Alphanumeric means that WordPerfect considers letters

Chapter 13
Sorting Data

and numbers in the sort (with letters preceding numbers in the sorted list). The other choice, Numeric, considers only numbers in the sort.

The Zone, Field, and Word default settings are *1*. You use these values to specify the precise key—such as the first word of the first field (before any tab characters) of the first zone (line) of a group. For the address list, this key is the first word of the company name.

The Ascending choice in the Order pop-up menu indicates that WordPerfect sorts the names from *A* to *Z*. The X appearing in the Sort check box indicates that you intend to perform a sort, and the unchecked Filter box indicates that WordPerfect should include all selected addresses in the output. So that the sorted list replaces the unsorted list in the open document, make sure that the Redirect Output box is not checked.

6. Click Begin or press Return to sort the list.

The address list, sorted alphabetically by company name, is shown in figure 13.5.

Fig. 13.5
The address list sorted by company name.

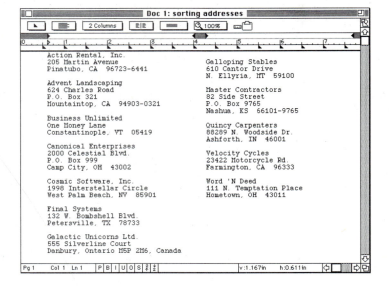

Part III

Using Advanced Features

Sorting Addresses by State and Company Name

The single key sort that you performed in the preceding steps is the simplest kind of sort. Although a list alphabetized by name can help you find information, you also may want information sorted by additional criteria. By specifying additional keys in the Sort dialog box, you can gain more control over the order of a sorted list. Suppose, for example, that you want the addresses sorted by state and, within each state, the addresses should be arranged alphabetically by name. You can specify the state as the first sort key and the name as the second sort key.

To print a list that is sorted by state and that has company names alphabetized within each state's list, you define two sort keys. The order of keys is important because WordPerfect sorts the list first by Key 1. If any of the groups have identical words as their first key, then the subgroup having the same Key 1 is sorted according to Key 2, and so on.

To sort the list by state first and then company name, the first key you define is the state name. Because some of the city names contain three words and others contain only one word, you may think that indicating to the program the location of the state name is difficult. Fortunately, WordPerfect provides another way to define keys: counting backward in zones, fields, and words by using negative numbers in the Sort Keys boxes. A zone with a value of -1, for example, uses the last zone in a group as part of the key definition.

To create the two key sorted list, follow these steps:

1. Make the address list the active window and choose Select All from the Edit menu. Alternatively, type ⌘-A.

2. Choose Sort from the Tools menu. The Sort dialog box appears.

3. Be sure the Items pop-up menu is set to Group. As in the previous example, the Key 1 box is active when you enter the Sort dialog box, and unless you changed the sort type to Numeric, Alphanumeric is the current sort type.

4. Double-click the Zone box of Sort key 1, and type *-1* to indicate that the state is in the last line of each address.

5. Press Tab twice to select the Sort key word box and type *-2* to indicate that the state is the next to last word in the zone indicated previously.

    You do not enter a value in the Field box because there are no tabs in the address (zone) to split the zone into fields. Key 1 specifies that the state is the first key; now you must sort the companies alphabetically within each state.

Chapter 13
Sorting Data

6. Click the Key 2 check box or type ⌘-2 to activate the second sort key, which enables you to sort the addresses by name within each state.

7. Leave the Zone, Field, and Word boxes of Key 2 set to 1, as shown in figure 13.6. (You used the same setting to sort the list by company name in the first example.)

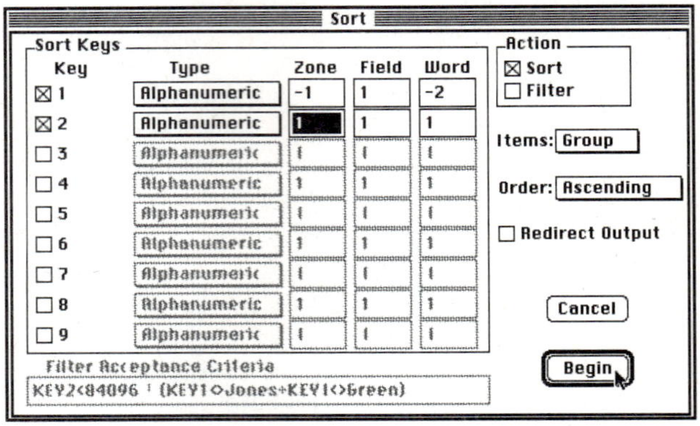

Fig. 13.6
The Sort dialog box for sorting addresses by state and company name.

8. Click Begin or press Return to initiate the Sort.

The sorted output should resemble figure 13.7.

Fig. 13.7
Addresses sorted by state and company name.

Part III
Using Advanced Features

Notice that the Canadian address appears at the top of the sorted list. The next to the last word in the last line (Key 1) of this address is *2M6*. In a long list of text items, some surprises are likely to arise as a result of a Sort. These surprises are not mistakes in sorting, just limitations in the ability to describe all keys by word position. Be sure to look over your results to make sure they reflect your intentions for the sort.

Sorting Tabbed Text

In addition to lists with groups separated by two Hard Returns, you may also have lists in which each line of text stands by itself, and you want to sort the information by an item appearing within the line. Generally, if you're sorting single lines of text (zones), the information is separated internally with tab characters. If you create a table using tab settings and then enter something similar to the following, for example, you create *tab delimited text*:

Catalogue number   [Tab]*Description* [tab]*Price*

In the tab delimited text, Tab characters mark the end of sections within a line. WordPerfect calls these sections *fields*. Figure 13.8 shows an address list similar to the list in figure 13.1; however, the address list in figure 13.8 has been converted to tab delimited text. If you use information exported from a database file, you are likely to encounter tab delimited text because database management programs frequently export data to word processors in tab delimited form.

Fig. 13.8
Addresses as tabbed text.

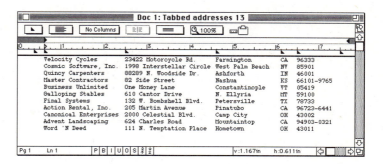

The main difference in sorting tabbed text in zones compared to sorting groups (as in the previous sections) is a greater reliance on using fields to specify sort keys. Because all the information you want is in a single zone, using fields in sort keys makes sorting easier.

Chapter 13
Sorting Data

To perform the state and company name sort on this list of addresses, follow these steps:

1. Choose Select All from the Edit menu or press ⌘-A to select all the addresses.

2. Choose Sort from the Tools menu. The Sort dialog box appears.

3. Set the Items pop-up menu to Zone. When you choose Zone, the Sort Keys Zone column goes gray because only one line (zone) per item exists in this sort.

4. Type *-2* in the Sort Keys Field box of Key 1. Unlike the addresses in the grouped list (refer to fig. 13.1), the state names in the tab delimited list now occupy a field of their own. (Because only one address line exists between the company name and the city name in this particular list, you also can enter *4* in the Sort Key Field box of Key 1.)

5. Click the Key 2 box or type ⌘-2 to activate the second key.

6. Make sure the Field and Word values of Key 2 are set to 1 (see fig. 13.9). Key 2 now specifies the first word of the first field, which is the company name in this example.

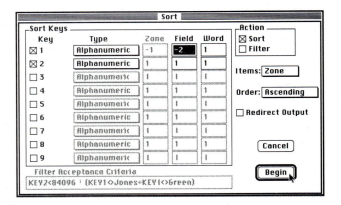

Fig. 13.9
The Sort dialog box for sorting tabbed text.

7. Click Begin or press Return to start the Sort. WordPerfect sorts the tab delimited text first by state and then by company (see fig. 13.10).

Part III

Using Advanced Features

Fig. 13.10
Results of sorting tabbed text.

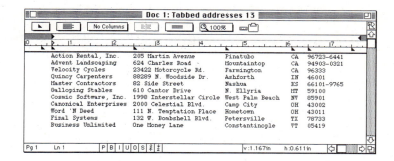

Sorting Addresses by ZIP Code

All the sorting examples shown thus far have illustrated how to sort words using the Alphanumeric sort keys. Times may occur, however, when you must use numbers instead of words as sort keys. Consider the numbers 1, 2, and 100, for example. An ascending order alphanumeric sort orders these numbers as 1, 100, and 2 because, just as all names beginning with *A* precede any names beginning with *B* in a alphabetized list, all numbers starting with *1* precede any numbers beginning with *2* in an alphanumeric sort. To produce a more standard numeric order (1, 2, 100, for example), you must use numeric keys in the Sort dialog box.

You can use numeric keys to sort tabbed text or grouped text. The strategy for defining the Zone, Field, and Word in the Sort dialog box is the same as described in the previous examples. The only difference, of course, is specifying the appropriate sort key in the Type pop-up menu.

To sort the addresses by ZIP code by using a numeric key, follow these steps:

1. Select all the tabbed addresses and choose Sort from the Tools menu. The Sort dialog box appears.

2. Choose Zone from the Items pop-up menu. Addresses are separated by a single Hard Return (zone marker) only; therefore, you want each zone to be the whole sort item.

3. Choose Numeric from the Key 1 Type pop-up menu. This setting tells WordPerfect to sort with the key as a number.

4. Set the Key 1 Field to *-1* and Word to *1* (see fig. 13.11). The ZIP code starts at the first "word" of the last field in each zone.

Chapter 13
Sorting Data

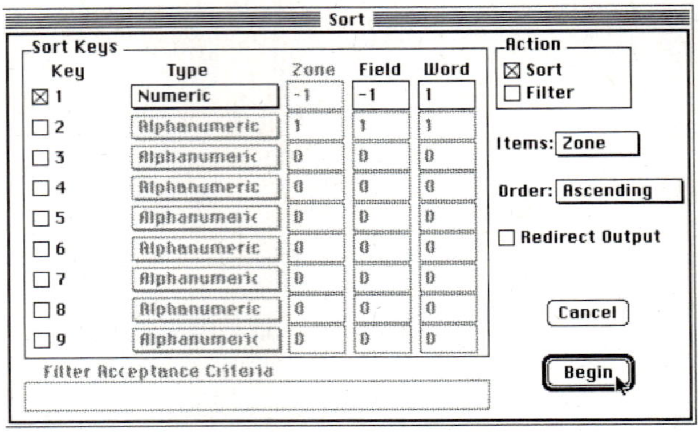

Fig. 13.11
Sorting ZIP codes numerically.

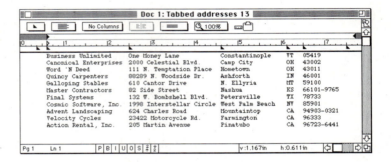

5. Click Begin or press Return to start the Sort.

WordPerfect sorts the tab delimited text by ZIP code (see fig. 13.12).

Fig. 13.12
Addresses sorted by ZIP code.

Sorting Merge Secondary Files

Sorting merge secondary files is similar to sorting groups. Merge secondary files, explained in Chapter 12, "Merging Documents," hold the data lists for a merge operation. Although a merge record—like a group—can have a variable number of zones, a merge record has a fixed number of fields. An <End of Field> flag marks the fields in a merge record (see fig. 13.13).

Part III
Using Advanced Features

Fig. 13.13
A merge secondary file for sorting.

Because a merge record field can have multiple lines ending in carriage returns (zones), the Field and Zone boxes change places in the Sort Keys area of the Sort dialog box (see fig. 13.14). Although Field and Zone boxes are transposed, you use the same techniques learned earlier to specify keys. In this case, you pick the field, then the zone within that field, and then specify the key word within the zone.

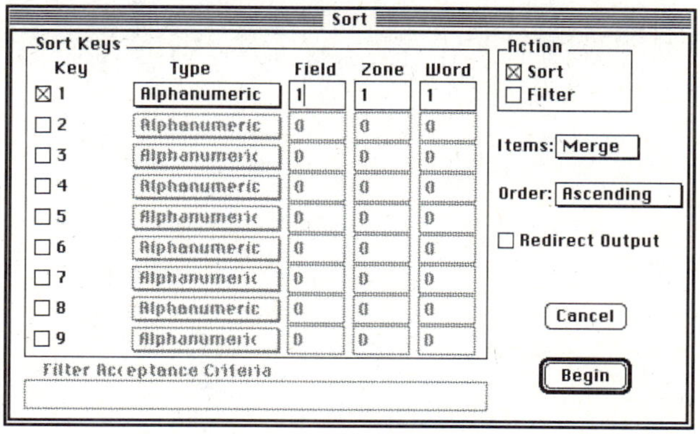

Fig. 13.14
The transposed Field and Zone boxes in the Sort dialog box.

Chapter 13
Sorting Data

Merge secondary files frequently contain address lists very similar to those used as sorting examples earlier in this chapter. You sort a merge secondary file to put the merge records in an appropriate order. For an address list, for example, you may decide to sort by ZIP code so that you can save money on postage. Also, if you make additions to any list, adding the new information anywhere in the list and then sorting the list is faster than searching for the right place to enter the new text.

Using Files for Sort Input and Output

WordPerfect enables you to use different documents for sort input and output. You can sort an entire file without opening it in a normal document window and insert the sorted text in an open document window or in a new file that you store directly to disk. The Redirect Output check box in the Sort dialog box controls the output phase of the sort. And the input phase is controlled by whether or not you select text. If you don't select text, WordPerfect assumes that you want to sort a whole file from disk rather than selected text.

When you are familiar with a list, opening the list file before starting a sort on that file is unnecessary. If you intend to sort a portion of a file and don't want the unsorted list rearranged, you can send the results of the sort operation to an output file. You even can sort a closed file and send the results to another file without displaying the results in an open document.

To sort a file without opening it and to put the sort results into the currently active document (empty or not), follow these steps:

1. Make sure no text is selected in the current document, and place the insertion point where the sorted list should begin.

2. Choose Sort from the Tools menu. A Sort dialog box containing a file list appears (see fig. 13.15). Because you didn't select text, WordPerfect assumes that you intend to sort an entire file.

3. From this Sort dialog box, select the file containing the list to be sorted.

4. Click Sort or press Return.

5. Set the options in the main Sort dialog box as discussed in the earlier examples. Be sure that Redirect Output is not checked; otherwise, WordPerfect stores the output in a file on disk instead of inserting the output into the active document.

Part III

Using Advanced Features

Fig. 13.15
Selecting a file to sort.

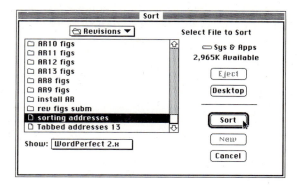

6. Click Begin or press Return to start the Sort.

   After the file is sorted, WordPerfect inserts the sorted list into the current document, starting at the location of the insertion point.

   To store the results of a sort in a file on disk rather than in the current document, you follow the preceding steps except that you activate the Redirect Output option by clicking the check box or pressing ⌘-R in the Sort dialog box so that an X appears in the check box. When the Save Sort Output dialog box appears, as shown in figure 13.16, you enter a file name and click Save or press Return. WordPerfect stores the sorted list in the file you named. After the sort is finished, WordPerfect returns you to the document that was active when you selected Sort from the Tools menu.

Fig. 13.16
The Save Sort Output dialog box.

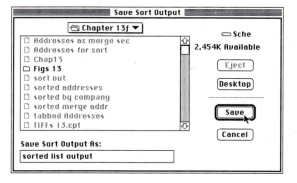

The file WordPerfect creates from a redirect sort output is a normal WordPerfect document. You can open and edit the sort output using standard WordPerfect techniques.

Chapter 13
Sorting Data

Using Filters

Although you can sort a section of a file by selecting a portion of the file before you specify sort keys, WordPerfect provides a more convenient way of selecting parts of a bigger list. The filtering function in the Sort dialog box enables you to tell the program to keep only the items containing specific words in the key locations. Text filtering captures specified items and enables others to pass through, just as a physical filter captures solids and enables liquids to pass through.

Setting Filter Keys and Criteria

Although you set filter keys the same way you set sort keys, you must give WordPerfect additional information to accomplish a filtering operation. The extra information is the *filter acceptance criteria*. The program locates the keys and compares the keys to the criteria to determine whether the program keeps or discards the item.

The Filter Acceptance Criteria section of the Sort dialog box describes the information to be collected in one place. To find only companies located in California or all people with last names that begin with *J*, for example, you use a filter to remove the zones, groups, or records that don't fit the specified description.

A filtering operation is similar to sorting except that you also must specify the filter acceptance criteria. The general steps you use to carry out filtering operations are listed in the following:

1. Select the text or choose a file that contains the text to be filtered.

2. Set the sort keys to define where the filter should attempt to match the criteria.

3. Check the Filter check box in the Action section of the Sort dialog box.

4. Specify the criteria for filtering in the Filter Acceptance Criteria text box.

5. Choose the destination of the filter by selecting or deselecting the Redirect Output check box.

6. Click the Begin button in the Sort dialog box.

To enable you to practice setting filter keys and criteria, this section provides an opportunity to filter the address list with which you have been working. To filter the company name file shown earlier to find only the companies in Ohio, for example, follow these steps:

Part III
Using Advanced Features

1. Open a new file to accept the filter output; then choose Sort from the Tools menu. The Sort dialog box containing a file list appears (refer to fig. 13.15).

2. Select the file containing the addresses and click Sort. Alternatively, you can double-click the file name or select the file name and press Return. The Sort dialog box with the sort key definitions appears.

3. Set the Items pop-up menu to Group.

4. If the Sort check box in the Action area of the Sort dialog box is checked, click the box or press ⌘-S so that the X disappears.

5. Activate Filter by clicking the check box or typing ⌘-F so that an X appears in the Filter box.

6. Define Key 1 with the following settings to specify the last line in each group, first field, next to last word:

Type	Alphanumeric
Zone	-1
Field	1
Word	-2

   The abbreviated state name is now defined as Key 1.

7. Select any text in the Filter Acceptance Criteria box and press Del.

8. Type *key1=ob*, as shown in figure 13.17. This criterion tells WordPerfect to look at Key 1 (the state abbreviation) and find all the items containing *ob* in that key location. *Note:* Filter keys are not sensitive to case.

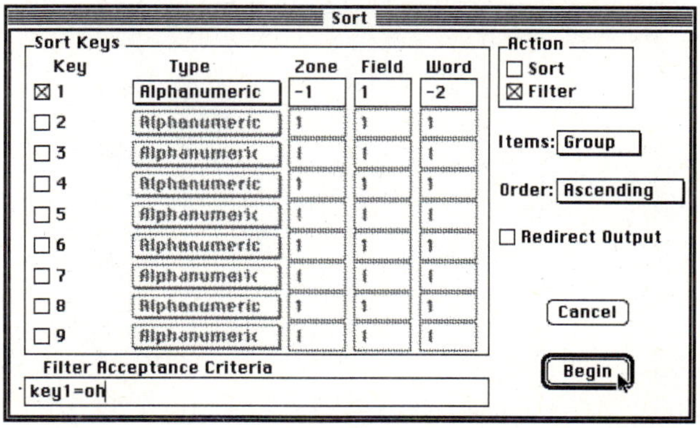

Fig. 13.17
The Sort dialog box set to filter the address file.

Chapter 13
Sorting Data

9. Click Begin or press Return to start the filtering operation.

   The names and addresses of the two companies containing Ohio addresses (Canonical Enterprises and Word 'N Deed) appear in the current document (see fig. 13.18).

Fig. 13.18
Companies filtered from an address file.

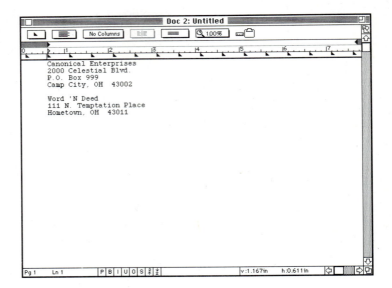

 If, in this example, some entries in the address file contained the word *Ohio* rather than the abbreviation *oh*, the filter—which looks for *oh*—would not pick the addresses containing *Ohio*. Filter acceptance criteria are not capable of matching partial words.

Understanding Filter Operators

In the last section you used a *filter operator*, perhaps without realizing it. The equal sign (=) in the Filter Acceptance Criteria expression was an operator that told the program how to compare the key to the text you typed after the operator. Eight filter operators exist. The most common operators used for filtering text are = (equal) and < > (not equal). If the key and the criterion don't match exactly (except for upper- and lowercase and character attributes), they are not equal. The comparison operators are shown in table 13.1.

Part III

Using Advanced Features

Table 13.1
Comparison Operators

Operator	Function
=	equal
<>	not equal
<	less than
>	greater than
<=	less than or equal
>=	greater than or equal to

These operators work as you probably expect them to work, especially in a numeric sort. For an alphanumeric sort, however, the comparison operators still work, but you must consider the letters at the beginning of the alphabet as *lower* in value than letters at the end of the alphabet. Remember, too, that longer words have a higher value than shorter words beginning with the same letters; for example, *Oh* is less than *Ohio* in WordPerfect's filtering scheme.

In addition to the six comparison operators, two Boolean operators, * (and) and + (or), also exist. These operators enable you to exclude some items that pass one filter criteria but not another (the * operator) or include some additional items that meet any one of several criteria (the + operator).

Using Multiple Filter Criteria

You can string together many filter acceptance criteria to make the entire expression complex enough to accomplish just about any filtering operation. The criteria expression does not have to fit in the short box in the Sort dialog box; the text scrolls to accommodate the criteria you add.

To practice a simple example of multiple filter criteria, set the criteria to collect names and addresses for companies in more than one state. To add Ohio and California, for example, you type *key1=oh+key1=ca* in the criteria box. These criteria tell WordPerfect to accept addresses for companies in Ohio (OH) and California (CA). Figure 13.19 shows the names and addresses captured with this filter.

Chapter 13
Sorting Data

Fig. 13.19
Addresses collected using multiple filter acceptance criteria.

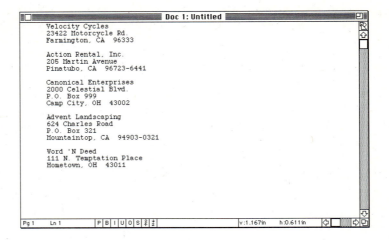

The method in which you enter the criteria is important. If you typed *key1=oh+ca*, the program beeps and displays an error alert (see fig. 13.20). Even though you are using multiple criteria on the same key, you must reenter the key designator (key1, key5, etc.) and the operator for each criterion.

Fig. 13.20
The filter syntax error alert.

Using KeyG to Search a Sort Item

All keys you specify in the Sort dialog box refer to one word in the same location in each sort item. To bypass the limitations in filtering that this one-key-one-word structure imposes in some filtering operations, WordPerfect provides an additional filter key—KeyG. *KeyG* compares the text assigned to it with every word in each sort item. To find all the companies that have *software* or *carpenters* in their name or address, for example, follow these steps:

1. Open a new document window and choose Sort from the Tools menu. The Sort dialog box containing the file list appears.

2. Select the file containing the address list and click Sort. The Sort dialog box containing the sort keys appears.

Part III
Using Advanced Features

3. Make sure that the Items pop-up menu is set to Group.
4. Delete all the text in the Filter Acceptance Criteria box and type *keyg=software+keyg=carpenters* in the box.
5. Click Begin or press Return to start filtering the address list.

The names and addresses of Cosmic Software, Inc. and Quincy Carpenters appear in your new document because a word in each of their names matches one of the KeyG specifications.

Combining Sorting and Filtering

You don't have to sort or filter individually; you can combine the two operations. Keys can be specified for sorting, filtering, or both. As an example of sorting and filtering, you can produce a partial list of addresses sorted by state and company name by combining two of the previous examples.

To produce a list of Ohio and California businesses sorted by state and company name, for example, follow these steps:

1. Open a new document window and click Sort from the Tools menu. The Sort dialog box containing the file list appears.
2. Select the file containing the complete address list and click Sort or press Return. The Sort dialog box with the sort keys appears.
3. Set the Items pop-up menu in the Sort dialog box to Group.
4. Make sure both Filter and Sort are checked in the Action box.
5. To specify the state as the first Sort key, enter the following settings for Key 1 in the Sort Keys section of the dialog box:

Type	Alphanumeric
Zone	*-1*
Field	*1*
Word	*-2*

6. To specify the company name as the second sort key, enter the following settings for Key 2:

Type	Alphanumeric
Zone	*1*

Chapter 13
Sorting Data

Field	*1*
Word	*1*

7. Delete all text in the Filter Acceptance Criteria box and type *key1=ob+key1=ca* in the box.

8. Click Begin or press Return to begin the sort and filter operation.

   Instead of the list shown in figure 13.20, you get a sorted and filtered list in a single operation (see fig. 13.21).

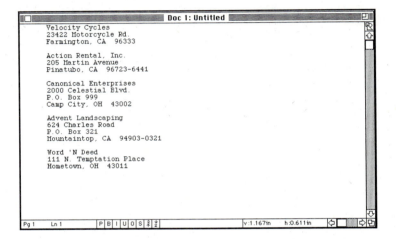

Fig. 13.21
The results of a combined sorting and filtering operation.

Chapter Summary

WordPerfect's sorting and filtering capabilities enable it to handle tasks that formerly required a database. If you have been using a list manager or flat file database to manage your mailing lists and other contact information, you may be able to do these tasks completely in WordPerfect.

This chapter examined how to sort a long list of items (lines, paragraphs, groups of paragraphs, and merge secondary files) and how to use filtering to pick and choose items from the list, based on the selection rules you specify. This chapter also discussed the sorting and filtering operations that you can perform by using a current document or by using input and output files.

Part III

Using Advanced Features

CHAPTER 14

Using Macros

Macros are computer programs that store collections of commands and keystrokes. By using macros, you can run WordPerfect through recorded sequences without retyping sometimes complex sequences of keystrokes. In addition, macros can save you the effort of repetitive work.

WordPerfect enables you to take advantage of its macro capabilities in several ways: you can use the predefined macros, edit existing macros, and even create your own macros. You use WordPerfect's installed macros by choosing the macros from a menu. To create your own macro, you simply turn on the macro recorder, perform the task, and turn off the recorder. Your new macro is ready for use with a single keystroke.

As you get more comfortable with recording and using macros, you may want to change an existing macro. WordPerfect's Macro Editor enables you to change existing macros easily. The Editor also has a very powerful syntax checker to tell you line by line whether the command you entered is valid. You even can use the Macro Editor to build complex macros that—with a few keystrokes or mouse clicks—create whole documents and pause for user input.

This chapter takes you through the first three stages of using macros with WordPerfect: running a predefined macro, recording a macro, and editing a macro to extend its usefulness. After reading this chapter, you will be able to create, use, and change macros that can save you time and effort as you create and edit documents.

Using the Predefined Macros

WordPerfect 2.1 contains 50 predefined macros, 11 of which are installed automatically in your system's Private Library when you install WordPerfect. These 11 macros are available from the Macro menu (see fig. 14.1). You can find the other 39 macros in the Macros file, which you access through the Documentation folder inside the WordPerfect 2.1 folder that is created by the installer routine. If you did a custom install and your hard disk doesn't contain the Macros file, the file is on the WordPerfect 3 distribution disk. (See Appendix A for more information on installing WordPerfect.)

Fig. 14.1
The Macro menu containing the installed macros.

Table 14.1 lists the automatically installed macros and their functions.

Running a Predefined Macro

Some macros included with WordPerfect show off the special features of the program. To run a predefined macro that enables you to create graphics, for example, follow these steps:

1. Choose New from the File menu or press ⌘-N to open a new document.

2. Choose Circular Text from the Macro menu. The Circular Text dialog box appears.

3. Type *Happy Birthday* in the Circular Text text box (see fig. 14.2).

Fig. 14.2
The Circular Text dialog box.

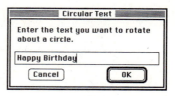

4. Click OK or press Return. The macro opens a graphic editing window and draws the circular text (see fig. 14.3).

5. Choose Close Graphic from the File menu, press ⌘-W, or click the Document icon at the top of the scroll bar to close the editing window.

WordPerfect inserts the circular text graphic at the location of the insertion point in the document.

Table 14.1
Automatically Installed Macros

Macro Name	Function
Change Attribute	Changes a text attribute (such as italic) to another attribute (such as underline) from the insertion point to the end of the document
Circular Text	Prompts user for text and then creates a graphic that wraps the text around a circle
Collate	Prints collated copies of a document
Drop Cap	Converts the first character of a paragraph into a drop cap
Envelopes	Automates the printing of a No. 10 business envelope, using selected text for the envelope address
Fancy Page Border	Creates a page border in the graphic overlay of the document page containing the insertion point
Footnotes <-> Endnotes	Converts the footnotes in the current document into endnotes, or converts endnotes into footnotes
Hanging Indent	Resets left-margin and first-line indent to create hanging indents
Memo	Creates a simple memorandum form
Pull Quote	Moves selected text to a bordered text box and adds quotation marks
Table	Creates a table based on number of rows and columns specified by the user

Chapter 14
Using Macros

Fig. 14.3
An example of circular text.

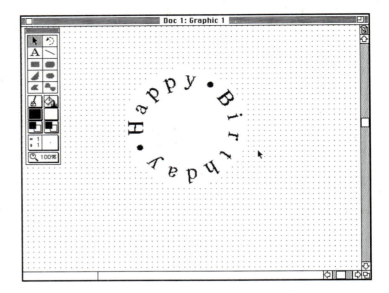

WordPerfect enables you to use the keyboard rather than the mouse to start the macro. If you are more familiar with or prefer using keyboard techniques to run a macro, follow these steps:

1. With any document window active and the insertion point located where you want the circular text graphic to appear, press ⌘-Shift-X. Alternatively, if you have an extended keyboard, press F9.

    The Run Macro dialog box appears.

2. Type *ci*. The macro list scrolls down, and Circular Text is highlighted (see fig. 14.4).

Fig. 14.4
The Run Macro dialog box.

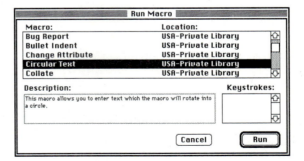

Part III
Using Advanced Features

If you start typing the name of a macro in the Run Macro dialog box, WordPerfect selects the first macro that matches what you type. In this example, typing *ci* (the beginning of *circular*) enables WordPerfect to select the Circular Text macro name from the list in the dialog box.

Notice that a description of the macro also appears in the Description box of the Run Macro dialog box. The descriptions of the predefined WordPerfect macros explain the function of the highlighted macro.

3. Press Return to run the selected macro. The Circular Text dialog box appears.

4. Enter your message: then press Return or click OK. WordPerfect draws the circular text.

5. Press ⌘-W to return to the document layer to continue editing your document.

Installing Predefined Macros

You can use the Librarian to install additional predefined macros from WordPerfect's Macros document file. The Macros file, which resides in the Documentation folder inside the WordPerfect 2.1 folder on your hard disk, contains the macros and their descriptions. Macro descriptions also are available in the Librarian dialog box while the installation macro is running.

To install additional predefined macros, follow these steps:

1. Open the Macros file by double-clicking its icon in the Finder or by choosing Open from WordPerfect's File menu.

    After the document opens, WordPerfect displays descriptions of the 50 macros contained in the file. Figure 14.5 shows the document window with the descriptions of the first few macros. You can read through the list by using the scroll bar, or if you prefer a hard copy of the list, you can print the document.

2. Choose Librarian from the File menu. The Librarian dialog box appears.

3. Set the Resource pop-up menu in the Librarian dialog box to Macros (see fig. 14.6).

    The box at the right shows the macros contained in WordPerfect's Macros document. The box at the left lists macros installed in your Private Library.

> **Tip**
> To scroll successfully through the list in the Run Macro dialog box, you must type smoothly. If you pause as you type, the program searches for a macro that starts with the character you type after the pause. You can type as much as you need to scroll to the appropriate macro. To reduce the amount of typing necessary, however, you can assign short, unique names to your macros; you also can assign keystroke commands to frequently used macros.

Fig. 14.5
The Macros document window.

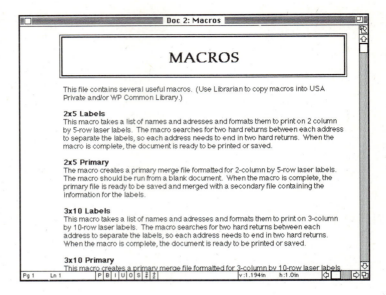

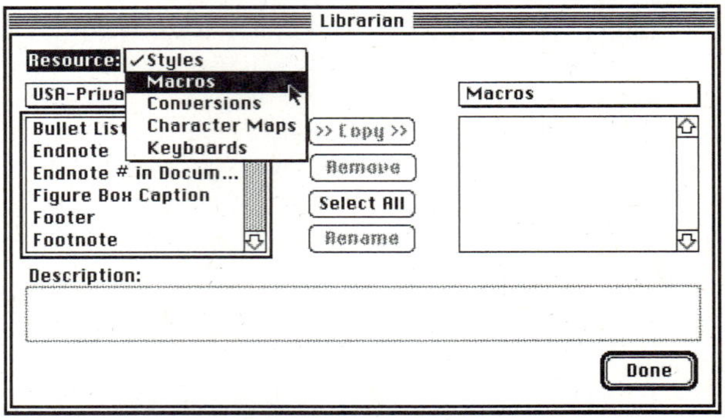

Fig. 14.6
Choosing Macros from the Librarian Resource pop-up menu.

> **Tip**
>
> If you have enough space on your hard disk, you can copy all the macros at one time by clicking the Select All button or pressing ⌘-A and clicking Copy. By installing all the macros, going through the installation process again is not necessary.

4. Press Tab or click the list under Macros to make the scroll box on the right side of the dialog box active. (A boldface border appears around the active list.)

5. Select a macro name from the Macros list. The description for the selected macro appears at the bottom of the dialog box (see fig. 14.7).

6. Click Copy or press ⌘-K. WordPerfect copies the selected macro into your Private Library.

Part III

Using Advanced Features

Fig. 14.7
Reading a macro description in the Librarian dialog box.

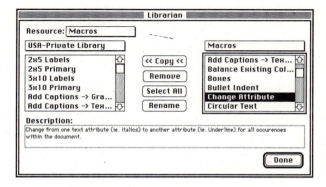

7. Click the Done button or press Return to close the Librarian dialog box.

WordPerfect installs macro descriptions with the macros so that you can read the descriptions in the Run Macro and Edit Macro dialog boxes. (The Edit Macro dialog box is covered later in this chapter.) See Chapter 15, "Customizing WordPerfect," for a complete explanation of using the Librarian to manage macros and other resources.

Recording Macros

Although the predefined macros do many interesting and useful things, they cannot handle all the repetitive tasks you may want automated. WordPerfect enables you to create your own macros. The easiest way to create a new macro is to record your actions as you perform a task. After you record a macro, you can run the macro to perform the task whenever you choose.

Creating a macro while you perform a task is as easy as starting the recorder, naming the macro, entering the appropriate keystrokes, and stopping the recorder. The following sections provide typical examples that enable you to practice creating a macro.

Creating a Macro To Enter Repetitive Text

You can create a macro that enters repetitive text, such as the closing of a business letter which may include not only the formal closing, but also a standard final paragraph. To create a macro that inserts the final paragraph and letter closing, follow these steps:

1. Starting in an open document window, choose Record from the Macro menu or press ⌘-F9. The New Macro dialog box appears.

2. Type *Letter Closing* in the Name text box of the New Macro dialog box.

3. Press Tab or click the Description text box; then type a description of the macro (see fig. 14.8).

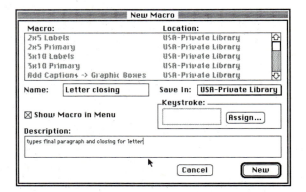

Fig. 14.8
The New Macro dialog box.

4. If Show Macro in Menu is deselected, click the check box so that an X appears. By activating this option, your macro appears in the Macro menu.

5. Click the New button or press Return to record your macro. The New Macro dialog box closes, leaving the macro recorder on and returning you to the document window.

6. Type the following paragraph and closing:

    We are pleased that you have decided to distribute the Wonderful Widget. We are looking forward to a bright future for both of our companies.

    Sincerely,

    A. W. Wonder
    President

    Be sure to include the carriage returns and tabs so that your text has the appropriate spacing.

7. To complete your macro, choose Stop Recording from the Macro menu or press ⌘-F9. A message box asks whether you want to save the changes to your macro.

Tip
Be sure to give your macro a description. A description can jog your memory when you look for the macro later, thus saving you the trouble of checking the Macro Editor or running the macro to see what task it performs.

Part III
Using Advanced Features

Fig. 14.9
A message indicating that you must use the keyboard while recording a macro.

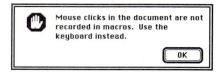

Tip

If you try to select text with the mouse while you record a macro, an error message appears (see fig. 14.9). Because a macro cannot record mouse clicks, you must use the Del and arrow keys to remove text and navigate through the document.

8. Click the Yes button or press Return to save the changes to your macro.

To use this paragraph and closing macro, choose Letter Closing from the Macro menu. WordPerfect enters the paragraph and closing at the insertion point.

Converting Tabbed Text to Merge Records

In the first macro you recorded, you entered text from the keyboard. Such macros are equivalent to the glossary functions in other word processors. A *glossary* stores text and character attributes of frequently used passages (sometimes called *boilerplate*) that you can insert in any document by using a single command.

WordPerfect's macro recorder goes much further, however, than recording just text keystrokes. You can record in a macro almost anything you can do from the keyboard or in a dialog box or menu. You can program into a macro almost any WordPerfect command or function. You can set margins, open files, search for and replace text with something new, and use any of the other 200-plus commands available in WordPerfect.

In Chapter 13, "Sorting Data," you sorted a tab-delimited address file. You normally use tab-delimited files to transfer information from a database program to a form that WordPerfect can use. If you are creating a merge document that uses a list of addresses, for instance, you must put the address list into a merge secondary file format by converting tab characters to End of Field markers and Hard Returns to End of Record markers. Although this task can be overwhelmingly time-consuming if done manually, you can create a macro. (For more information on creating secondary files, refer to Chapter 12, "Merging Documents.")

To create a macro that converts the tabbed text file to a merge secondary file, follow these steps:

1. If you don't have an extended keyboard and are using the numeric keypad to enter numbers, turn off the NumLock function by pressing Shift-Clear. (The Clear key is above the 7 key on the numeric keypad.)

Chapter 14
Using Macros

2. To make the address list the active document, click the window if the file is open. If the file is not open, open the file.

3. Because you will make substantial changes to the address list file, make a backup copy of the file.

4. Choose Record from the Macro menu or press ⌘-F9 on an extended keyboard. The New Macro dialog box appears.

5. Type the macro name and description in the appropriate text boxes of the New Macro dialog box.

6. Make sure the Show Macro in Menu box is checked and leave the Save In pop-up menu set to USA-Private Library so that you can access the macro in WordPerfect, regardless of whether the file is open.

7. Click the New button or press Return to record the macro.

8. Place the insertion point at the beginning of the file by pressing Home on an extended keyboard or by pressing Gold-Gold-↑.

   The Gold key is keypad 7 or keypad 5, unless you redefined the Gold key. See Chapter 15, "Customizing WordPerfect," for more information about redefining keys.

9. Press ⌘-F or choose Find/Change from the Search menu. The Find Forward or Find Backward dialog box appears.

10. If the Find Backward dialog box appears, choose Forward from the Direction menu of the current dialog box. The Find Forward dialog box appears.

11. In the Find Forward dialog box, choose Text Only from the Match menu, as shown in figure 14.10. Also from this dialog box, choose Case and Text Only from the Affect menu, and choose Select Match from the Action menu.

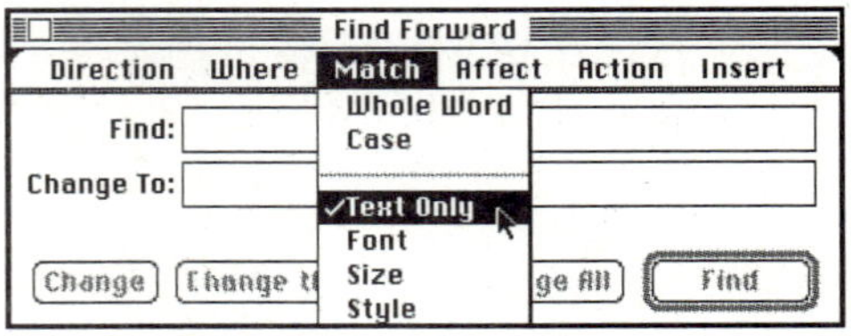

Fig. 14.10
Choosing options in the Find Forward dialog box.

These settings tell WordPerfect how to perform the Find/Change operation. See Chapter 3, "Editing a Document," for a full description of the options in this dialog box.

Part III
Using Advanced Features

12. Select Hard Return from the Insert menu in the Find Forward dialog box.

13. Press Tab to move the insertion point to the Change To text box.

14. Choose End of Field from the Insert menu in the dialog box.

15. Choose Hard Return, then End of Record, then Hard Return from the Insert menu. (Be sure to choose the End of Field and End of Record items from the Insert menu rather than type the words.)

    The Find dialog box, which should resemble the dialog box shown in figure 14.11, is prepared to change each Hard Return in the tabbed address list to an End of Record merge code.

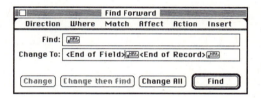

Fig. 14.11
Converting carriage returns to End of Record sequences.

16. Click the Change All button so that WordPerfect makes the End of Record substitutions for all occurrences.

17. Click the close box or press ⌘-W to close the dialog box.

You return to the address list document, which looks messy because you have completed only half of the conversion. To complete the macro, follow these steps:

1. Press Home or Gold-Gold-↑.

2. Press ⌘-F or choose Find/Change from the Search menu. The Find dialog box, in which you specify the next replacement operation (End of Field for Tab), appears.

3. Because the special Hard Return character in the Find box is selected, choose Tab from the Insert menu on the dialog box menu bar to replace the Hard Return with the special tab character.

4. Press Tab to move to the Change To text box. Leave the text in the Change To text box selected and choose End of Field from the Insert menu. WordPerfect replaces the text in the Change To text box with the special End of Field code.

5. Click the Change All button. WordPerfect replaces all tab characters in your address list with an End of Field merge code.

6. Close the Find dialog box by clicking the close box or pressing ⌘-W.

7. Choose Save As from the File menu. The Save As dialog box appears.

8. Click the Invoke Dialog check box, as shown in figure 14.12. When you activate the Invoke Dialog option, the macro recorder doesn't record the name you give the file. Instead, it includes a command that displays the dialog box so that the user can name the converted text file each time the macro is run.

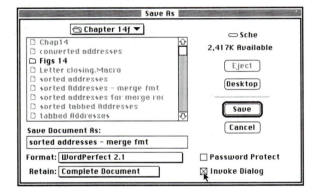

Fig. 14.12
Setting the Invoke Dialog option.

9. Enter a new name for the current file. By giving a new name to the current file, you retain the original file.

10. Click the Save button or press Return to save the file.

11. To view the recorded macro, as shown in figure 14.13, select the macro name from the bottom of the main Edit menu or click the window that appears almost totally hidden by your document window. Click the document window to return to the address list.

12. Choose Stop Recording from the Macro menu or press ⌘-F9 to close your macro. Alternatively, if the window containing the macro commands is in front of the document window, you can stop recording by clicking the close box of the macro window or pressing ⌘-W.

13. When the message asking whether you want to save the changes appears, click Yes or press Return to store the macro in your Private Library.

Tip

By including Save As in the macro, you can be ensured that WordPerfect saves the results of your conversion to a new file. Saving the original file is always a good idea in case you make a mistake with the conversion. The Save As operation enables you to keep the original by renaming the converted file.

Part III

Using Advanced Features

Fig. 14.13
The macro commands for converting tabbed text to merge records.

Now anytime you want to convert a tab delimited text file to a merge secondary file, you can open the text file and choose the appropriate macro from the Macro menu.

Remember that WordPerfect requires that merge secondary files contain the same number of fields in each record. If you don't have the same number of tab characters between each pair of hard carriage returns in your file or if you have stray Hard Returns, this macro produces an invalid secondary file. Most database exports include an extra tab to "save space" for an empty field, but be careful to check for these extra tabs the first time you convert a file.

Editing a Macro

The original version of WordPerfect for the Macintosh enabled you to create but not edit macros. If you made a mistake as you recorded your macro, you had to start over. Now WordPerfect includes a powerful Macro Editor that enables you to make corrections, add programming commands, or create a macro from scratch by typing commands into an empty macro window. You can edit a macro as you record or after you save the macro.

Chapter 14
Using Macros

Preparing to Edit a Macro

The beginning of the macro editing process is similar to the beginning of recording a new macro. To edit an existing macro, follow these steps:

1. Choose Edit from the Macro menu or press Shift-F9 on an extended keyboard. The Edit Macro dialog box appears.

2. Scroll through the macro list and single-click the macro to be edited (see fig. 14.14). The description of the macro you selected appears in the Description text box.

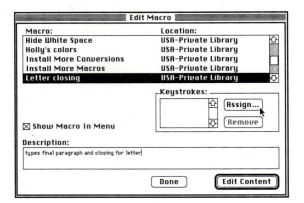

Fig. 14.14
The Edit Macro dialog box.

If you assigned a keystroke command to the macro, the keystroke definition appears in the Keystrokes list box. In the Edit Macro dialog box, you can change the assigned keystrokes, change the description of the macro, or determine whether the macro should appear in the Macro menu. (You can assign keystrokes to a macro by using the New Macro or Edit Macro dialog box or by choosing the Keyboards command from the Preferences submenu on the File menu. See Chapter 15 for more on the Keyboards command.)

Excluding a Macro from the Macro Menu

As mentioned earlier, WordPerfect assumes that any macro you record should appear in the Macro menu. After you record several macros or install all the macros WordPerfect supplies, however, the Macro menu can get unmanageably long.

To simplify the menu, select the macros to be excluded from the menu and click the Show Macro in Menu box so that the X disappears.

Part III
Using Advanced Features

Although no longer appearing in the Macro menu, these macros do remain available in your Private Library, and you can run the macros by using the Run Macro dialog box or issuing an assigned keystroke command.

To run a macro that doesn't appear in the main Macro menu, follow these steps:

1. Choose Run from the Macro menu.

2. Double-click the macro you want to run. Alternatively, select the macro and click the Run button or press Return.

Defining a Macro Keystroke

When you use a macro frequently, choosing a macro from the Macro menu can become tedious. By assigning a keystroke to a macro, however, you can run the macro by typing the appropriate keystroke.

To assign a keystroke to a macro, follow these steps:

1. In the Edit Macro dialog box, select the macro to which you intend to assign a keystroke.

2. Click the Assign button or press ⌘-A. The Assign Keystroke dialog box appears.

3. In the Keystroke text box, type the keystroke to be assigned to the macro.

   If you enter a keystroke that is assigned to some other function, the computer beeps, and the other function or character appears in the Assigned text box (see fig. 14.15).

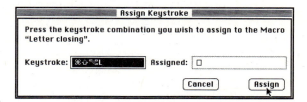

Fig. 14.15
The Assign Keystroke dialog box.

You can assign any keystroke—even a normal text character—to the macro. If you assign only a text character to a macro, however, the macro activates every time you type that character. Be sure to use one of the accepted modifier keys—Command (⌘), Option, or Gold—with any regular or shifted text character. (You cannot use the Control key in keystroke commands.)

Chapter 14
Using Macros

4. After you enter the keystroke commands, click the Assign button. The keystroke appears in the list space to the left of the Assign button in the Edit Macro dialog box.

If you activated the Extra Menu ⌘ Keys option in the Environment dialog box, the assigned keystroke also appears next to the macro name on the Macro menu (see fig. 14.16). See Chapter 15, "Customizing WordPerfect," for more information about the Environment dialog box and assigning keystroke commands.

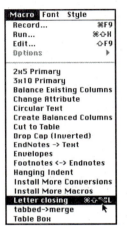

Fig. 14.16
An assigned keystroke command on the Macro menu.

Modifying the Macro Description

While the Edit Macro dialog box is open, you can change the macro description by clicking the Description text box and adding text. You also can use the mouse to select, cut, copy, and paste text in the Description text box. A complete but concise description of a macro can help you keep track of your macro functions.

Using the Macro Editor Window

After you choose the appropriate options in the Edit Macro dialog box, you can edit the macro. WordPerfect's Macro Editor, which you enter by clicking the Edit Content button in the Edit Macro dialog box, provides several features that make editing easier. Commands appear in boldface type after you press Return or move the insertion point to a different

Part III
Using Advanced Features

line. The Editor checks your commands and parameters to determine whether they are legal and underlines any errors. In addition, a message appears at the bottom of the window.

To edit a macro, you must be able to understand the parameters and commands. For an example of macro commands and parameters, open the Letter Closing macro that you created earlier in the chapter by following these steps:

1. Open the Edit Macro dialog box by choosing Edit from the Macro menu or pressing Shift-F9 on an extended keyboard.

2. In the Edit Macro dialog box, select the Letter Closing macro; then click the Edit Content button or press Return. The Macro Editor window containing the Letter Closing macro appears (see fig. 14.17).

Fig. 14.17
The Letter Closing macro commands in the Macro Editor window.

The *macro commands* appear in boldface at the beginning of each line. The macro processor considers the Hard Return and Tab characters as commands. The *parameters* appear between the parentheses. Macro parameters are usually in plain (not boldface) text, although a few special parameters appear in boldface type. Notice that the only parameters you have in this macro are the words you typed as you recorded the macro.

Chapter 14
Using Macros

Changing a Recorded Macro

Making changes to a macro is easy in the Macro Editor. To change the name of the product in the letter's final paragraph, for example, follow these steps:

1. Select the words in the Macro Editor window. (You use the same selection techniques to edit a macro that you use to edit any WordPerfect document.)

2. Type the new product name.

The Type( ) macro command can hold only 255 characters between the parentheses. When you record a macro that contains a great deal of text, WordPerfect creates several Type( ) commands in the macro definition—similar to word wrapping. If you add text within the Macro Editor window, you must do the text splitting yourself by typing *)*, entering a carriage return, and then typing *Type(* whenever a text segment approaches 255 characters.

3. To close the Editor window, click the window's close box, choose Stop Recording from the Macro menu, or press ⌘-F9 or ⌘-W. A message box asking whether you want to save the changes appears.

4. Click the Yes button or press Return to save the changes you made to the macro.

You also can edit commands in the Macro Editor. (*Commands* are words at the beginning of a line, that the Macro Editor recognizes.) Almost every command available in WordPerfect is also available as a macro command. Type a new command and press Return; if the command changes to boldface type, the command is valid.

Using On-Line Help

WordPerfect provides several ways to get help when you use the Macro Editor. When you make an error as you type a command or its parameters in the Macro Editor window, WordPerfect underlines the error (no boldface style appears), and the message `Error: Unrecognized Command` appears at the bottom of the window (see fig. 14.18). Although this error message isn't tremendously helpful, it does indicate that you must correct the command and not a parameter.

Part III
Using Advanced Features

Fig. 14.18
An error message in the Macro Editor.

When an Unrecognized Command error message appears, you can get help from the on-line Help file. By using the Help command in the Apple menu (introduced in Chapter 1, "Quick Start: Creating a Business Letter"), you can look up a command without leaving your computer.

To explore the macro help in the Help file, follow these steps:

1. Choose Help from the Apple menu or press ⌘-?. The Help dialog box appears.

2. Choose Macro Commands from the pop-up menu in the upper left corner of the Help dialog box (see fig. 14.19).

Fig. 14.19
Getting help for macro commands.

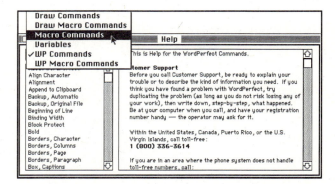

Chapter 14

Using Macros

3. To get help on a specific command, type the first few letters of the command. For help on the Hard Return command, for example, type *ha*. The Help file scrolls to a command that starts with the letters you typed and displays information on the command.

   You also can scroll through the list and choose a command by using the usual (but slower) mouse-clicking methods.

One potentially confusing aspect of the on-line Help file is that four sections deal with macros: Draw Macro Commands, Macro Commands, Variables, and WP Macro Commands (refer to fig. 14.19). You must choose the correct section from the pop-up menu before you can find a command and its help text in the rest of the Help dialog box. These options are explained briefly in the following:

- *Macro Commands.* Commands that you can use in graphics or text-based macros

- *WP Macro Commands.* Commands that you use only in the word processing part of WordPerfect

- *Draw Commands.* Commands available only in the draw layer of the program

- *Variables.* Contains a list of variables you can use in your macros. (Variables are covered later in this chapter.)

Determining whether a variable is available in text or graphics macros only or in both types of macros can be difficult; therefore, you may have to look in a couple of places for help on a specific command.

When you find a command in the Help file, WordPerfect displays the correct format of the command and an explanation of the command's parameters. Although the parameter lists of some of the commands can get fairly long, finding the data on-line is usually faster than paging through the macro manual (for which you must pay extra).

Editing a Macro Being Recorded

While you record a macro, you can switch to the Macro Editor. If the Macro Editor window is active for editing—that is, the Macro Editor window is the front window—the macro recorder pauses to enable you to edit. Whenever the Macro Editor window is active, you can edit commands. To go back and forth between editing a macro and recording, click the appropriate window or use the window list at the bottom of the Edit menu.

When you finish editing in the Macro Editor window, be sure to move the insertion point to the end of the macro before you return to your document to record more commands. If you leave the insertion point in the middle of the Macro Editor window, WordPerfect inserts any additional macro commands at the location of the insertion point in the Macro Editor window.

Using the Macro Options Menu

When you record or edit a macro, the Options submenu, accessed through the Macro menu, becomes active (see fig. 14.20). This submenu provides file-handling capabilities for macros and two types of pause-and-continue control.

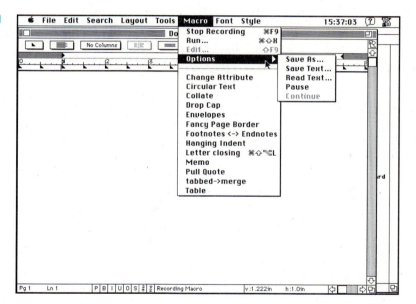

Fig. 14.20
The Options submenu.

The Save As Option

When you choose Save As from the Options submenu, the Save Macro As dialog box appears. This dialog box is essentially the same as the New Macro dialog box discussed earlier in the chapter (refer to fig. 14.8). You can use the Save Macro As dialog box to create a new macro by slightly modifying a previously saved macro.

Chapter 14
Using Macros

To create a slightly modified macro, follow these steps:

1. Choose Edit from the Macro menu or press Shift-F9 on an extended keyboard. The Edit Macro dialog box appears.

2. Select the macro you want to use as the model for the new macro and click Edit Contents to open the Macro Editor.

3. Change the macro as necessary.

4. Choose Save As from the Options submenu of the Macro menu. The Save Macro As dialog box appears.

5. Name the edited macro, change the description as necessary, and assign a new keystroke.

   Because the keystroke assigned to the original macro does not appear in the Keystroke section of the Macro Save As dialog box, you don't need to worry about conflicts in assignments.

6. Click the Save button or press Return. WordPerfect saves the new macro in your Private Library.

Macro Text Files

You can use text files to keep separate copies of your macros. You also can use text files to avoid using the Librarian to manage the task of sharing macros with other users. As you record or edit a macro, you can choose Save Text from the Options submenu under the Macro menu. The Save File dialog box appears (see fig. 14.21). The program suggests a file name in the Save Text of Macro As text box, but you can change the name. Click Save to save the text file.

Fig. 14.21
The Save File dialog box.

In addition to saving macro commands as text, you can import text into a Macro Editor window. The capability to convert plain text to a macro is a convenient way to acquire macros from other users. If someone posts the text of a macro on an electronic bulletin board, for example, you can copy the text and paste it into a WordPerfect macro window. No file transfer or Librarian use is required.

To insert the contents of a text file into a macro, follow these steps:

1. Choose Record from the Macro menu. The New Macro dialog box appears.

2. Name and describe the macro. Then click New to open a new macro.

3. Choose Read Text from the Options submenu of the Macro menu. An Open File dialog box appears.

4. Select the text file containing macro commands as text and click the Open button.

   WordPerfect places the text in the Macro Editor window.

The program shows you only text-type files in the Read Text Open File dialog box. Because the Macro Editor can read only text files, WordPerfect doesn't display word-processing documents or other types of files. If you open a text file that wasn't created as a macro text file, errors appear in the Macro Editor window. By using the Macro ending (.Macro) suggested by the program when you save macros as text, you can avoid opening the wrong text files.

The Pause/Resume Toggle

The Pause command on the Macro Options menu temporarily stops the macro recorder from recording more commands. If you intend to keep the Macro Editor open but don't want additional commands recorded while you edit something in the normal document window, for example, use the Pause command. After you choose Pause from the Macro Options menu, the option changes to Resume. Choose Resume to restart the macro recorder.

If you edited the macro commands while the recorder was paused, remember to put the insertion point at the bottom of the Macro Editor window. To edit macro commands instead of the contents of your main document window with the macro recorder paused, make the Macro Editor the front window; you don't have to choose Pause.

The Continue Command

Continue, the last command in the Macro Options menu, usually is dimmed. When a macro contains a Pause Until (*key*) command, the

Continue command in the Options submenu becomes active while the internal macro pause is in effect. Choose Continue to override the pause programmed into the macro. The Continue command is useful if you forget the key for which the Pause Until option is waiting.

You must type a Pause Until command directly into a macro window; the command cannot be recorded. With Pause Until, you can do an unlimited amount of editing in a document before continuing with macro execution. You can create a macro, for example, that types the heading and closing of a letter with a Pause Until in the middle. The macro then types the beginning of your letter, waits for you to enter the body of text, and then types the closing after you press the specified key that cancels the Pause Until command. (Don't confuse the macro recorder Pause command with the Pause Until command issued by a running macro.)

Creating Macros with Programmable Commands

Creating macros to play back the same sequence of events enables you to automate many repetitive tasks in WordPerfect. The capability to have macros adjust their output, based on user input or document properties, makes the macros more flexible. WordPerfect offers these extra capabilities in its *programmable macro commands*, which are accessible only through the Macro Editor.

> **Tip**
> Record as much of a macro as you can to reduce the amount of typing necessary and to save the trouble of remembering the order and type of parameters a command uses.

The programmable macro commands make up a full programming language with a nearly unlimited range of possibilities. Of course, the possibilities become available only after you know the language well. You can increase gradually the power of your macros as you learn the commands, however. This section introduces a few of the several dozen programmable commands. (WordPerfect sells the *Macro Reference* manual separately. You can order the manual directly from WordPerfect Corporation.)

Using Variables in Macros

One feature of any programming language is the availability of *variables*. You can think of variables as packets of information. You can put information into the variables, or you can read a variable to find out what it contains. Several types of variables that can hold macro command parameters or text to be inserted in your document exist. Unlike general programming languages, WordPerfect macro variables have fixed names, and you must remember what information you store in any given variable.

Part III
Using Advanced Features

Read/Write Variables

You can read and edit Read/Write variables, which you use to store text or numbers to use later to affect macro output. WordPerfect provides three types of read/write variables—document, global, and local—which are explained in the following:

- *Document.* WordPerfect saves these variables with a document. You must use a macro to set their values, but after the values are set, the same or another macro can read the values when the document is open. Ten document variables—DocVar0 through DocVar9—are available in each document.

- *Global.* These variables retain their values as long as WordPerfect remains open. After you assign a value to these variables, any macro you run during the session can read the variables. You also can assign a new value to any global variable with any macro. Fifty global variables are available—GlobalVar00 through GlobalVar49.

- *Local.* WordPerfect remembers these variables only while the macro that assigns their values is still running. When a macro ends, the values of any local variables used in that macro are gone. Fifty local variables are available—Var00 through Var49.

When you use variables in your macros, be sure not to insert spaces within the names. In addition, be sure to use a leading zero for local and global variables under 10—for example, Var02, not Var2. Don't replace the zero with the letter O.

The 110 read/write variables provide plenty of "memory" for complex macro functions. If you want a macro to ask the user for a name to insert in various places in the document, for instance, WordPerfect stores that name in a variable.

Read-Only Variables

WordPerfect controls the values stored in read-only variables. These variables contain information, such as the length of the top margin, the current page number, whether color is available on the Mac you're using, and more than 100 other attributes of your system and the document being edited.

You can change something in the document that may result in a change to the read-only variable, but you cannot use a macro command to assign a value directly to the variable. A list of the read-only variables is included in the *WordPerfect for Macintosh Reference Manual* and the on-line Help file under Variables (refer to fig. 14.19).

As an example of using read-only variables, you can create a macro that prints the current page of a document. The Print dialog box of WordPerfect Version 1.0.x contains this option; Version 2.1 does not. To create the macro that enables you to print the current page of a document, follow these steps:

1. From any document window, choose Record from the Macro menu. The New Macro dialog box appears.

2. Name the macro Print Page, give the macro a description, and—if you intend to use the macro often—assign a keystroke.

3. Click the New button or press Return to start recording the macro.

4. Choose Print from the File menu or press ⌘-P.

5. Press Tab and type *1* in the From text box; press Tab again and type *1* in the To text box. Your Print dialog box should resemble the dialog box shown in figure 14.22.

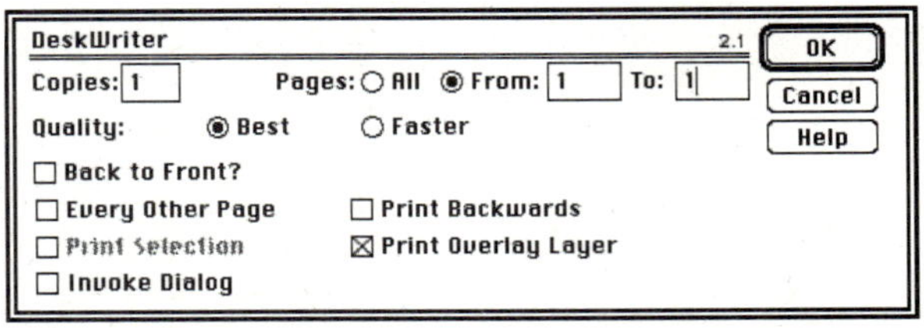

Fig. 14.22
Creating the print page macro.

6. Click OK or press Return. WordPerfect prints the first page of your document.

    You must print the page as you create the macro because WordPerfect doesn't save the dialog box settings to the Macro Editor window until you leave the dialog box with something other than a Cancel command.

7. To bring the Macro Editor window to the front, click the window or choose the window from the list at the bottom of the Edit menu. You now can see and edit the macro commands you just recorded.

8. Select the first *1* in the Print Options parameter list and type *physicalpage* (do not put a space between the words). PhysicalPage is the name of a WordPerfect read-only variable.

9. Replace the next *1* in the dialog box with the same variable name (*physicalpage*).

Part III
Using Advanced Features

10. Move the insertion point below the two commands by clicking the appropriate location in the Macro Editor window or using the arrow keys. Your Macro Editor window should resemble the window shown in figure 14.23.

Fig. 14.23
The Print Page macro.

11. Close the Macro Editor window. When the message asking whether you want to save the changes appears, click Yes or press Return.

You now have a macro that, when invoked, prints the page containing the insertion point.

The PhysicalPage variable stores the number of the current page without regard to any page number resets you may include in the file. The page number that appears on the status bar in the lower left of the document window reflects logical page number; therefore, using the status bar to fill in boxes within the Print dialog box so that you can print the current page is not always possible. If, for example, you open a new document and use the Page Format dialog box to set the page number to 5 (because the first four pages are in another file and will be printed separately), the status bar indicates you are on (logical) page 5. At the same time, you are on the first (physical) page of the new document.

The reason you use the macro recorder instead of typing the two macro commands directly into the Macro Editor window is that by recording the macro you must know only which parameters represent the first and last pages of the print range. You don't have to figure out how many parameters the Print Options command has or how the parameters are spelled; the recorder puts all this information in the macro definition for you. You also don't have to worry about including the necessary supporting commands. (Supporting commands, which aren't necessary here, can be confusing, especially in macros using Find/Change.)

Operators

Variables are not of much use if you can only read a read-only variable or store a value in another variable. WordPerfect provides a set of operators that enable you to calculate new values and store the result to a variable. You also can perform math functions (addition, subtraction, multiplication, division, and modulo), compare text or numerical values (equal, not equal, less than, greater than, Boolean *and*, and Boolean *or*), and perform alphanumeric concatenation (join).

To use the operators to write a value to any variable, you use the Assign command:

>**Assign(Var03**; **Var01+Var02)**

or

>**Assign(Var10**; **TopMargin+10)**

The first statement adds the values of Var01 and Var02 and stores the result in Var03. The second statement determines the top margin, adds 10 to the margin value, and stores the result in Var10. (In macros, margins are measured only in points. A *point* equals 1/72nd of an inch.)

Another major use of variables and operators is in conditional expressions:

>**If(Var03<10)**
>>**Type**(one thing)
>
>**Else**
>>**Type**(something else)
>
>**End If**

Here, a macro is looking at the value of Var03 and doing one of two things depending on the value of Var03. If Var03 is less than 10, WordPerfect enters the words *one thing* in the active document. If Var03 is not less than 10, WordPerfect enters the words *something else* in the document.

Including User Input

Another aspect of flexibility in macro use is the capability of creating a macro that asks the user for information. In creating a macro that formats an inter-office memo, for example, you can include a section that asks for the author's name, gives the user the opportunity to type a paragraph in an otherwise very structured document, or asks the user for the number of copies to print at the end of the macro run.

These tasks, and many more, are possible in WordPerfect macros. A macro can ask for user input in three ways: the Get commands, the Prompt command, and the Menu command, each of which provide advantages for certain tasks.

The Get Commands

Seven Get commands are available: Get Character, Get Integer, Get Key, Get Measure, Get Number, Get String, and Get Text. The Circular Text dialog box discussed at the beginning of the chapter (refer to fig. 14.2) resulted from the following command in the Circular Text macro:

> **Get String (Var00**;50;"Circular Text";"Enter the text you want to rotate about a circle.")

The Get commands enable you to exert a great deal of control over the type of input that the program can accept from the user. Because Get Integer accepts only integers (no letters or decimals) from the user, you can control the input to accept only integers between 1 and 100, for example. As part of the Get Integer command, you program the range of numbers you want to accept. If you enter a number outside that range, an error alert box appears and offers you the chance to enter a number within the range. (Because all Get commands store their results in a variable, user input must be shorter than 255 characters long.)

The Prompt Command

The Prompt command enables you do almost anything in the active document until a specified condition is met. You can use this command, for example, to enter long passages of text that don't fit in a variable slot. If you run the Install More Macros macro, for example, the dialog box shown in figure 14.24 appears.

Fig. 14.24
The Install Macros dialog box.

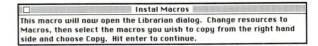

This dialog box is the result of the following sequence in the macro:

> **Prompt** ((**ScreenSizeH**-482)/2;250;"Instal Macros";"This macro will now open the Librarian dialog. Change resources to Macros, then select the macros you wish to copy from the right hand side and choose Copy. Hit enter to continue.")
>
> **Pause Until (#Enter#)**
>
> **Librarian Dialog**
>
> **End Prompt**

Until you press the Enter key on the numeric keypad, the macro is in suspended animation. You can do any editing you like without affecting the rest of the macro. When you press Enter, the macro resumes execution with the command that follows the pause—in this case, the macro opens the Librarian dialog box.

The Menu Command

The Menu command enables you to present a short list of options during execution of the macro. The macro user selects one option, and the macro handles its internal processing based on the menu response. The Install More Conversions macro provides an example of the menu command. The following lines produce the menu shown in figure 14.25:

> **Menu** (Var01;"Have you copied the private library onto your hard disk?";{"Yes";"No"})

Fig. 14.25
The menu from the Install More Conversions macro.

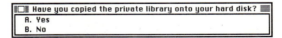

The macro user chooses an option from the menu by clicking the option or typing the letter next to the option. The macro issuing the Menu command must contain a section of commands pertaining to each of the options presented in the menu.

Adding Loops to Macros

Repetition is one task that computer programs do very well. One of the original reasons for using macros was to automate frequently used single tasks. By using loops in a macro, you can further automate tasks that require several repetitions of the same task within a main task.

You can make the macro processor loop through a series of commands in at least five ways: For, For Each, Go, Repeat, and While. In the following example, you use only one of these methods to do a multiple search-and-replace operation many times in the same file.

Earlier in the chapter you converted a tab-delimited text file into a merge record list. At the time, you were reminded that merge records must have the same number of fields in each record. This condition is easy to meet in many tabbed-text files but is more difficult to control in more general list files.

Figure 14.26 shows an address list to be converted to merge records. Some addresses in the list contain an extra line that must be handled properly during conversion in order to merge records successfully. Advent Landscaping and Master Contractors each have four lines in their address. The other addresses have only three lines.

Fig. 14.26
An irregular address list for conversion to merge records.

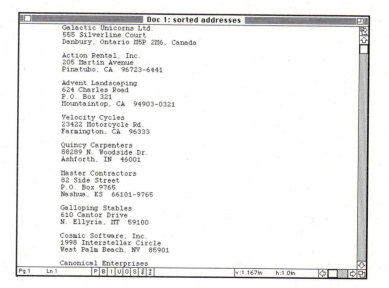

Chapter 14

Using Macros

The general strategy for creating the macro is to use the macro recorder to record the conversion of one record and then use the Macro Editor to add the looping control.

The macro breaks the addresses into two fields: the company name and the address. Only the strategy of the recording step is presented here (rather than the step-by-step instructions for creating the macro), followed by a detailed description of how to add the looping commands.

Each company name occupies one line. Starting at the top of the page, find the first carriage return (the Return following the first company name) and convert the Return to an End of Field code. After converting the first carriage return, find the double carriage return at the end of the first address and convert those returns to the sequence of codes for an End-of-Record marker. To extend this strategy, you can search backwards from the End of Record and separate the city, state, and ZIP code line from the rest of the address.

The macro that results from the single address conversion to a merge record is shown in figure 14.27.

Fig. 14.27
The macro to convert a single address to a merge record.

In figure 14.27, notice that some of the information recorded about Find/Change dialog box settings is unnecessary. Including the Font, Size, and Language parameters is unnecessary, for example, because you are searching and replacing text only. Some information also is repetitive.

Although rearranging the macro to remove redundant and unnecessary information can speed up the macro execution slightly, leaving the extra information in the macro is better, in case you later need the information.

To add the looping control, follow these steps:

1. Click the end of the first line in the macro and press Return to create a blank line for a new macro command.

2. Type *repeat*; then move the insertion point to the end of the macro by clicking or using the arrow keys. The Repeat command is one of the looping commands that enables you to repeat a group of commands.

3. Type *until(findstatusflag=0)* and press Return. (The Macro Editor takes care of uppercase letters in commands and variables.)

   The Until command signifies the end of a Repeat loop. FindStatusFlag is a read-only variable that is set to 1 if a Find command finds the specified text. The variable equals 0 if the Find operation fails. The Repeat/Until structure repeats all the steps between the Repeat and Until commands until one of the Find commands fails to find its target text.

4. Delete the two lines that say Abort When Not Found. The new last line of the macro takes care of situations in which nothing is found by one of the Find operations (that is, when the macro reaches the end of the file). You want the macro to end normally, not abort, at the end of the file.

   You also can enter the last line of the macro as *Until(!FindStatusFlag)*, where the ! is the Not operator.

You must include a test of FindStatusFlag or leave the Abort When Not Found commands in place when you use Find in a macro. Without one of these two tests, the macro proceeds merrily on its way even when no match is found for the Find text.

5. Close the Macro Editor window by clicking its close box and save the changes to the macro by clicking Yes when WordPerfect asks whether you want to save changes.

If you run the macro on the original address list (or delete the merge codes from the file containing the single converted record produced while recording the macro), you get a converted address list with two fields per record (see fig. 14.28).

Chapter 14
Using Macros

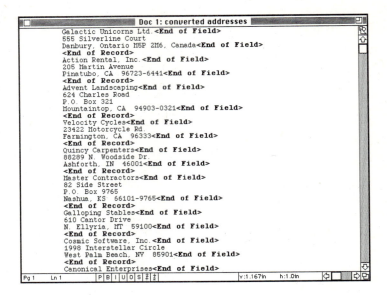

Fig. 14.28
The converted address list.

Nesting and Chaining Macros

Nesting and chaining are two more ways to control macro command execution. After a nested macro executes, the macro processor returns to the macro that started the nested macro and picks up the original macro sequence immediately following the call to the nested macro. **Run**(*macro name*) is the command that creates a nested macro structure.

When you create and execute a chained macro structure, the macro processor finishes with one macro and jumps to the chained macro, with no further connection to the original macro (unless the second macro chains back to the first). **Chain**(*macro name*) is the command that creates a chained macro. To use a chained structure, make sure that no Return or End Macro command is in the macro file. These two commands override a Chain command.

Nesting and chaining were extremely useful in Version 1 of WordPerfect for the Macintosh. Before the introduction of the Macro Editor, the capability to record a small section of a task, make sure the section worked, and then chain or nest the section to other macros was useful. With the introduction of the Macro Editor, the necessity of compartmentalizing a small segment of a macro is no longer necessary.

After you create or obtain several basic macros for your particular tasks, you may consider nesting and chaining as a way to manage the structure of your macros. As you learn about macros, however, you may find that being able to look in a single Macro Editor window at all the commands you use is more helpful.

As in other computer programming, you can create macros to use in more than one macro and then nest these macros whenever you need them—much like creating a subroutine that can be "called" from anywhere in the program.

Creating Graphics Macros

You create graphics macros the same way you create text-based graphics macros, except that you record these macros in the draw window. Your macros can combine graphics macros and "regular" macros; WordPerfect considers text or graphics macros to be simply a list of commands to execute.

To create a graphics macro, follow these steps:

1. From the draw window, turn on the macro recorder.
2. Draw whatever shapes you desire.
3. Stop recording and save the macro.

Because the parameter lists of the draw macro commands are more tedious to type than most of the text macro commands (see fig. 14.29), you should record as much as possible of your graphics macros.

Fig. 14.29
A graphics macro and its output.

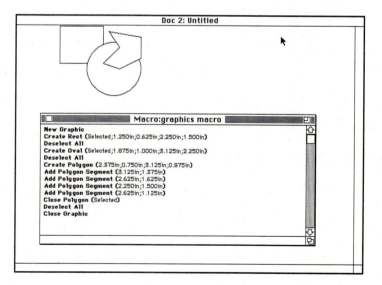

Chapter 14
Using Macros

Chapter Summary

WordPerfect's macro feature, which is a complete programming language that contains variables, operators, and conditional structures, is easy to use because you can record a macro as you perform the tasks.

The Macro Editor enables you to change any of the commands you record or type into the editor window. The Editor even checks each command you type to see whether the command is legal, that is, contains the proper number and type of parameters. Using the Macro Editor enables you to extend the power of macros beyond simple recorded procedures.

Recording macros saves time by reducing the typing required and by limiting the number of command definitions you must remember or look up. For a more extensive look at complete macro examples, use the Macro Editor to peruse some of the 50 macros WordPerfect includes with the program.

Part III
Using Advanced Features

CHAPTER 15

Customizing WordPerfect

The other chapters of this book have shown you how to choose options and commands to customize the settings of specific documents and to override defaults in specific sets of circumstances. In this chapter, you learn to set up the program to do things *all the time* so that choosing options from dialog boxes to alter settings or remembering commands to get the same results every time is not necessary.

Whether you turned here because of an earlier reference or arrived here as you progressed through the book, you probably have an idea of what features you want to customize. This chapter explains how to customize WordPerfect so that, instead of adjusting your work patterns to fit the program's standard settings, you can make WordPerfect fit your work style.

After you complete this chapter, you will be able to understand the differences between preferences and style elements and change the preferences to suit your work habits. You also will be able to change and save settings in the Normal style and use the Librarian to add, change, or remove resources from a WordPerfect document and the Private and Common libraries.

Differentiating Preferences and Styles

One potentially confusing distinction in WordPerfect Version 2.1 is the difference between a preference and style elements (formatting styles, as discussed in Chapter 8, and character attribute styles, such as boldface, italic, and so on). Because Version 1.0 didn't have styles, all settings saved with the program were referred to as *defaults*. In fact, WordPerfect has applied the term *defaults* to what now are *preferences*, which is the appropriate Apple term for these application features.

With the inclusion of styles in Versions 2.0 and 2.1, the distinction is made between functions that affect the appearance of the printed document (*styles*) and the settings that affect only the on-screen appearance or function (*preferences*). The location of document and dialog windows on-screen, for example, affects only how you interact with the program. Because they have no effect on the final document appearance, these settings are called *preferences*. Any formatting command, however, affects the appearance of the printed document; consequently, formatting commands are *style* elements.

To see the difference between a style element and a preference, you can look at the codes window. To view the codes window, choose Show Codes from the Edit menu or press ⌘-Shift-K or Option-F2. The codes window, which displays WordPerfect's internal formatting codes, opens at the bottom of the current document window (see fig. 15.1).

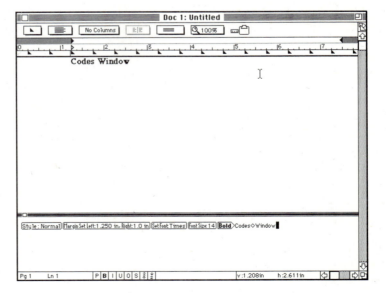

Fig. 15.1
The codes window.

Part III

Using Advanced Features

Compare what appears in the main document window at the top of the screen with the contents in the codes window. Anything that appears as a code is a style element, not a preference.

Notice that the codes shown in figure 15.1 include margins, font name, font size, and text style. All these items are *style elements*. Notice also, however, that no Show Ruler code appears. Whether you choose to display the ruler or not, no code concerning the visibility of the ruler is stored in the document. Your preference for showing or hiding the ruler is stored by WordPerfect in the USA-2.1 Preferences file.

The distinction between a preference and a style element can get a bit murky for some features. The custom date/time format, for example, is stored as a preference; however, if you use the Auto Update command, the program also inserts in a document a code that defines the date format.

Setting Preferences

The largest group of options saved in the Preferences file is accessed by choosing Preferences from the File menu (see fig. 15.2). The Preferences submenu enables you to set environment options, default folder locations, and the settings associated with keyboard layout.

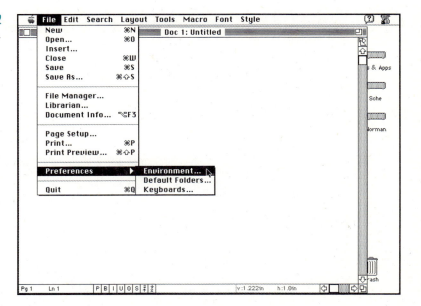

Fig. 15.2
The Preferences submenu.

Chapter 15
Customizing WordPerfect

Environment

Most references made to this chapter refer to settings in the Environment dialog box, which controls several options. This section explains most of the options in detail; however, the language-specific options are mentioned only briefly. To access the Environment dialog box, shown in figure 15.3, choose Environment from the Preferences submenu in the File menu.

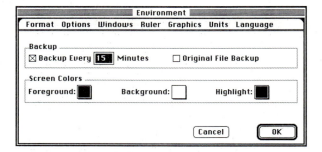

Fig. 15.3
The Environment dialog box.

Tip
If you have the ruler displayed in your document window, the fastest way to open the Environment dialog box is to double-click a number on the ruler.

The Environment dialog box consists of two sections that contain options which control automatic backups of files and on-screen colors. This dialog box also contains seven pull-down menus that help you to customize various features of WordPerfect.

Automatic Backups

The first option in the Environment dialog box is Backup, which automatically backs up open documents at timed intervals. You should not turn off this option. The first time you lose an important document that you're working on—because of a power failure, for example—you will be glad the backup exists. The timed backup feature is *not* a substitute for regularly saving your documents, however.

WordPerfect Corporation has set the program to make a backup copy of your document every five minutes. If the slight delay that occurs while the program does a backup bothers you, you can increase the time between backups; however, because WordPerfect remembers the keystrokes you enter during the backup, you don't lose anything if you type as the program saves a backup. The program also waits for a pause in your typing before it starts a backup so that your work is not disturbed by a backup operation.

If you have the automatic backup option activated and a power failure occurs (and the program was running long enough to perform a backup), one of two dialog boxes appears the next time you start WordPerfect.

If the Temporary Files Exist alert box appears, you can recover the automatic backup versions by clicking No or pressing Return, unless you are running WordPerfect from a file server on a network (see fig. 15.4). WordPerfect uses temporary files to store parts of a document you are editing. These files, which are not normal document files, are deleted when you quit WordPerfect.

Fig. 15.4
The Temporary Files Exist alert box.

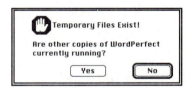

If the WordPerfect Backup Files Exist alert box appears, you can recover the automatic backup versions by clicking Open or pressing Return (see fig. 15.5). Backup files are copies of all open documents kept by WordPerfect on disk as you work. Backup files are deleted when you close a document window.

Fig. 15.5
The WordPerfect Backup Files Exist alert box.

Tip
Decide immediately whether to keep the retrieved backup files or return to the previous copy on disk. If you leave the window open for a while, you may lose track of what changes you made to which version.

WordPerfect opens all the backup files for the previous session in untitled windows. To keep the backup copies, you must save them. If you don't need the retrieved files, close the untitled window and click No in the Save Changes alert box.

If you click Delete on the Backup Files Exist alert box, WordPerfect deletes, rather than opens, the backup files. Opening the backup files is always safer than clicking Delete, however, because you can check the contents of the retrieved files before you delete them.

If you click Cancel in the Backup Files Exist alert box, you postpone the decision about the old files until the next WordPerfect session. Although

Chapter 15
Customizing WordPerfect

the program starts, it doesn't delete or open the existing backup files. The next time you open WordPerfect, the Backup Files Exist alert box appears again.

If you are extremely cautious about saving revisions over an old copy of a document, you can set the Original File Backup in the Environment dialog box. When you save a file, Original File Backup causes WordPerfect to rename the old version by adding *Backup* to the file name. The program then writes a new copy of the current file with the current name.

Screen Colors

The other main block in the Environment dialog box is the section on setting screen colors. *Foreground* color is the on-screen color of text. *Background* color is the color of the window behind the text. *Highlight* color is the color of the background when you select text. The program internally controls the color of selected text.

> **Tip**
> Be sure to pick colors for text and background that are compatible. Text should be easy to read. Experiment with color selection to find the combination that works best for you.

To change the foreground, background, or highlight color, click the square of the color you want to change and choose a new color from the pop-up palette that appears. Like a text pop-up menu, the color you choose from the palette fills the square next to Foreground, Background, and Highlight options. You also can double-click a color square to access the Mac color wheel from which you can choose a custom color. See your Macintosh documentation for a complete discussion of the color wheel.

After you choose a color, click OK in the Environment dialog box to accept the setting changes and return to your document. To cancel the changes, choose Cancel. Notice that the Environment dialog box does not have a close box. You must click OK or Cancel to return to the document window.

> **Tip**
> Screen colors are an extremely personal choice. If you have eyestrain problems from long hours at the computer, try resetting your screen colors. One possible combination is pale yellow (almost white) text on a royal blue background.

You can control the rest of the Environment options from pull-down menus on the dialog box. If you pull down any of the menus, you can see the active options (a check mark appears beside active options). To turn on an option, choose the option in the menu. To turn off the option, select it from the menu again, and the check mark disappears.

The Format Menu

The options in the Format menu, shown in figure 15.6, control formatting. The first two options—Paragraph and Single Paragraph—determine where a formatting change (such as margin or tab setting change) takes place and how much of the document is affected after the change.

Part III
Using Advanced Features

Although you can select only one item at a time, you can switch between options while you edit a document.

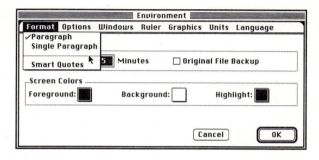

Fig. 15.6
The Environment dialog box Format menu.

Tip
Screen colors do not affect how a document prints. If you have a color printer and intend to print text in color, use the Character dialog box to set the text color for printing.

Paragraph mode is the most useful setting for formatting mode. If you choose Paragraph mode, formatting changes take effect at the beginning of the paragraph (or page, in the case of page-formatting options) that contains the insertion point. Changes affect all text following the insertion point until the program finds another code that changes the same feature to another value.

If the format mode is set to Paragraph, for example, and you change the left margin from 1 to 1.5 inches, then the left margin is reset for the paragraph holding the insertion point and all paragraphs following it until another margin change code is encountered. If you didn't change the margin anywhere later in the document, the most recent change affects text to the end of the document.

Single Paragraph mode works like Microsoft Word's formatting mode: changes affect only the current paragraph. To change several paragraphs at one time, you must select the paragraphs before you issue the formatting command.

The other Format menu option, Smart Quotes, determines whether typographers' quotation marks ('single' and "double") or straight quotation marks (shown on the key next to the Return key) appear. To insert the straight quotation marks representing foot and inch marks (for example, *he is 5'11" tall*), turn off the Smart Quotes feature. You also can toggle Smart Quotes by pressing Shift-F3 on an extended keyboard.

Chapter 15
Customizing WordPerfect

The Options Menu

The Options menu, shown in figure 15.7, holds four miscellaneous options: two that affect the window or menu displays and two that affect document files.

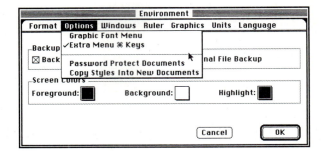

Fig. 15.7
The Environment Options menu.

The Graphic Font Menu and Extra Menu ⌘ Keys options control the appearance of menus. The Graphic Font Menu displays each available font in its own typeface (see fig. 15.8). This option also slows the display speed of the menu. After you become familiar with the fonts in your system, turn off this option so that the typefaces are not displayed.

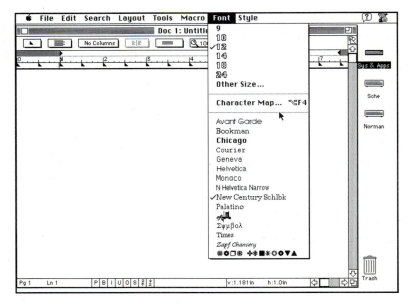

Fig. 15.8
The Font menu with styles displayed.

Part III

Using Advanced Features

The Extra Menu ⌘ Keys option causes WordPerfect to display more keyboard shortcuts in the menus (see fig. 15.9). By activating this option, you can learn the keyboard shortcuts more quickly; this option also does not slow the display of the menus. (You can use keyboard shortcuts whether you display the shortcuts or not.)

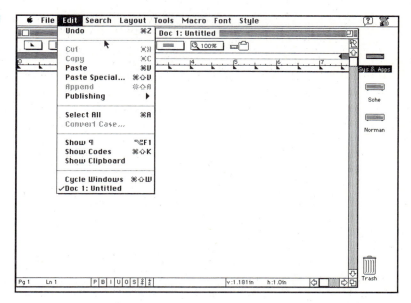

Fig. 15.9
The Edit menu with extra shortcut keys displayed.

If the Password Protect Documents option is checked, the first time you save a document, the Password dialog box, in which you assign a password to the document, appears. Turn this option on only if you want all your documents password protected. The Save As dialog box enables you to turn on password protection for individual files.

The Copy Styles Into New Documents option enables you to have all the default styles (Normal, Header, Footer, and so on) copied into every new document that you create. Turn this option on if you share files frequently with other users. See the discussion in Chapter 8, "Formatting with Styles," on the Update to Library command for more details. (Update to Library does for one file what Copy Styles Into New Document does for all new documents.)

Chapter 15
Customizing WordPerfect

The Windows Menu

The eight options on the Windows menu, shown in figure 15.10, affect the appearance of your document window. Two of the options, Show ¶ and Show Codes, also appear on the main Edit menu so that you can switch the features on and off without entering the Environment dialog box. You can access the other options only through the Environment dialog box Windows menu, however.

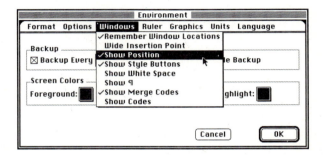

Fig. 15.10
The Environment dialog box Windows menu.

Among the most visible preference settings are those of the Show commands: Show ¶ (accessed from the Edit menu or by pressing Option-F1) and Show Codes (accessed from the Edit menu or by pressing ⌘-Shift-K or Option-F2).

Show ¶ makes invisible characters—returns, tab, spaces, indentations, and so forth—visible. Making the normally hidden characters visible can help you decipher some spacing problems; however, displaying these characters also creates a cluttered document on-screen. The Show Codes option enables you to see what WordPerfect is doing with formatting commands; however, the codes window, like the ruler, takes space away from the area available to view your document's contents.

When you choose the Show Position and Use Style Buttons options, WordPerfect adds information to the status bar of the document window (see fig. 15.11). The Use Style Buttons option adds the style buttons, which activate the Plain Text, Bold, Italic, Underline, Outline, Shadow, Superscript, and Subscript character formats. The Show Position box reports the location of the insertion point on the page. Because the various fonts and sizes are variable sizes, this box helps you judge how far the insertion point is from the bottom or left edge of the paper.

By choosing the Show White Space option, you make the blank space at the top and bottom of a page appear on-screen (see fig. 15.12). The space occupied by headers, footers, and notes is included in the blank space, but the headers and notes do not appear. The Show White Space option gives the on-screen document a more *WYSIWYG* ("what you see is what you get") appearance but doesn't accomplish much else. Screen space is usually too valuable to waste with extra blank space.

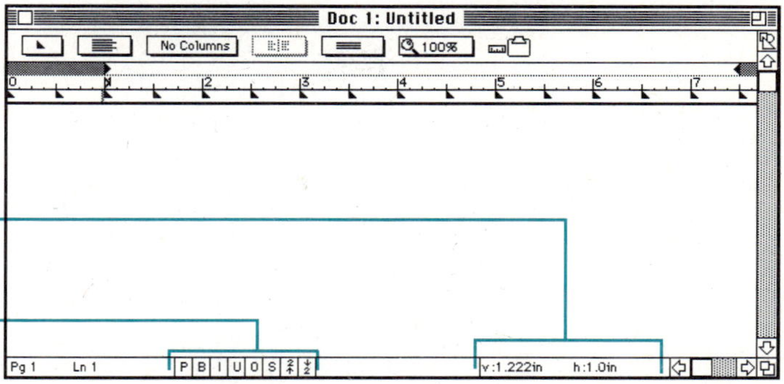

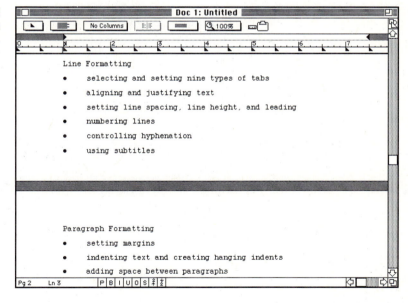

Fig. 15.11
Style Buttons and Show Position on the status bar.

Fig. 15.12
The effect of Show White Space at a page break.

The Wide Insertion Point option widens the insertion point so that you can see it more easily. The insertion point highlights the next text character (as though that character is selected) when this option is on. Because blank spaces in most Mac fonts are much narrower than other

Chapter 15
Customizing WordPerfect

characters, using the Wide Insertion Point takes some getting used to because the width of the insertion point varies quite a bit as you move through existing text.

The Remember Window Location option controls whether document window size and location are remembered when you save and close a file. Turn on this option if you want a document window to reappear in the same location the next time you access the window. Turn off the option if you want WordPerfect to calculate the appropriate size and location of any new window. You turn off this option mainly so that WordPerfect can stack and offset several open documents.

The Show Merge Codes option determines whether you see the <End of Field> and <End of Record> codes in your merge secondary files or the field names in a merge primary file. When the option is on, the codes or field names appear in your document window. When this option is off, only a boldfaced ↑ appears at the location of any type of merge code. See Chapter 12, "Merging Documents," for more information on merging.

The Ruler Menu

The options on the Environment dialog box Ruler menu affect the behavior of the ruler (see fig. 15.13). The first option, Show Ruler, determines whether WordPerfect displays the ruler when you open a document. The other two options, Snap to Grid in Ruler and Show Ruler Guides, help you align tab and margin settings with the ruler.

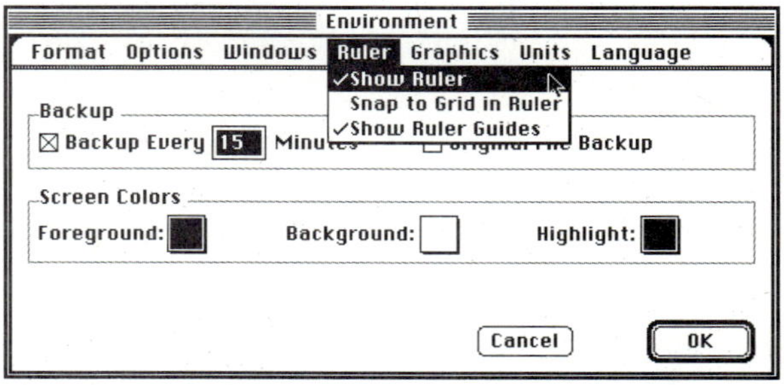

Fig. 15.13
The Environment dialog box Ruler menu.

The Show Ruler option displays the ruler at the top of each document window. You can change margins, tab settings, alignment, and so on much faster by using the ruler rather than pulling down a menu and choosing settings in a dialog box. The ruler takes screen space away from your document contents, however. Because you can show and hide the ruler by using the Layout menu or the ⌘-R keyboard command, you easily can override the Show Ruler setting in the Environment dialog box.

The Snap to Grid in Ruler option limits the location of tabs and margin and column markers to locations every 1/16 inch (assuming that inches is the default unit of measure). With this option on, setting consistent tab locations in different paragraphs is easier, but you have less flexibility in tab and margin placement.

Show Ruler Guides determines whether the vertical dotted lines dropping from the ruler during tab and margin setting operations appear. Because these lines can help you accomplish many alignment tasks, you should leave this option on unless you find the lines distracting.

The Graphics Menu

In Chapter 9, "Using Columns and Text Boxes," you learn how to anchor a text box by using the Graphic Options dialog box. You also can use the Environment dialog box's Graphics menu to anchor a text box (see fig. 15.14). The menu also offers options that determine whether to display figures and overlays in a document.

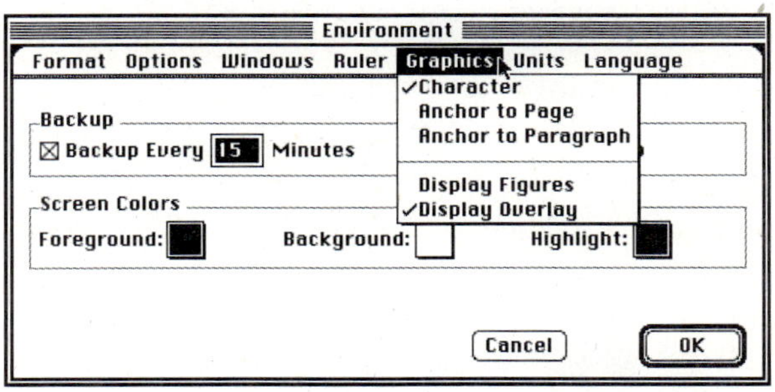

Fig. 15.14
The Graphics menu on the Environment dialog box.

You can use the Character, Anchor to Page, and Anchor to Paragraph options to place text boxes. (The initial setting is Character.) Because turning a character-anchored or paragraph-anchored box into a page-anchored box is so easy, you should choose Character or Paragraph.

A character-anchored box acts as a single character. A paragraph-anchored box moves up and down the page according to the location of the first line of the paragraph containing the box definition code. A page-anchored box stays at the same place on a page. Any character- or paragraph-anchored text box that you drag to a new location becomes a page-anchored text box automatically.

Two other options—Display Overlay and Display Figures—also appear on the Graphics menu. If a check mark appears beside the Display Overlay option, the overlays you created appear in your document. If you activate Display Figures, figures that you added to the document appear. When this option is not checked, however, only an empty graphic box appears in place of the figure. To see the figure associated with a box, you click the appropriate graphics box; the figure appears. When you begin editing again, the figure disappears.

The Display Overlay and Display Figures options affect only the on-screen appearance of the document. Regardless of whether you activate the options or not, the document prints according to the choices you make in the Print dialog box, which is discussed in Chapter 6, "Printing a Document."

The Units Menu

If you want the ruler and dialog boxes to measure distances in units other than inches, select another unit from the Units menu (see fig. 15.15). Two options on the menu, didots and cicéros, are European units of measure.

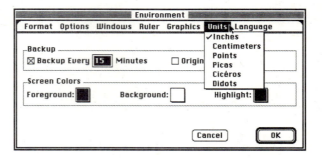

Fig. 15.15
The Units menu on the Environment dialog box.

> **Tip**
> Several dialog boxes hide a pop-up menu behind the units indicator (in, for example) so that you can change the measurement system for a single setting.

The Language Menu

Unless you have an additional language module available on your hard disk, leave the Language menu options set as shown in figure 15.16. If you use multiple languages and the initial settings of these options cause difficulties, see the section on Environment in the WordPerfect manual.

Part III
Using Advanced Features

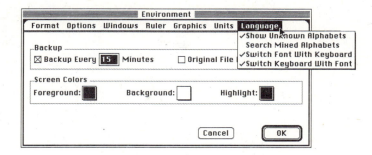

Fig. 15.16
The Environment dialog box Language menu.

Default Folders

The Default Folders option under Preferences in the File menu enables you to set the default location of documents, temporary and backup files, dictionary and thesaurus files, and—if you are connected to a network server—the Common Library. Of these options, only the Common Library must be set. The other options can use a default setting. If you are not connected to a network server, however, setting the Common Library location is not necessary.

When you choose Default Folders from the Preferences submenu, the Default Folders dialog box appears (see fig. 15.17). You use the same techniques to set any of the default folder paths.

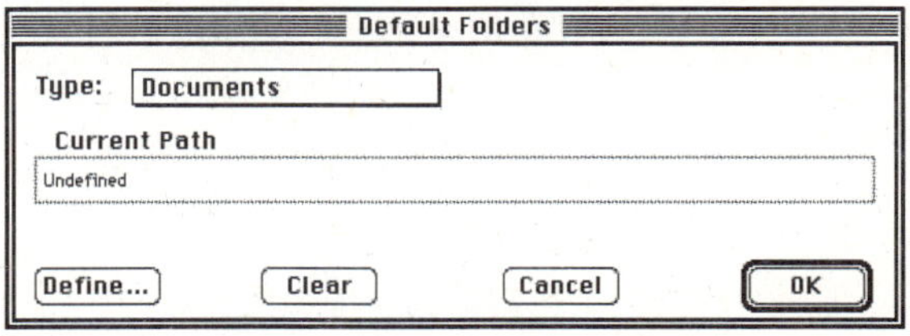

Fig. 15.17
The Default Folders dialog box.

To set one of the default folders, follow these steps:

1. Choose the type of folder from the Type pop-up menu, shown in figure 15.18. (Folder types are discussed later in the chapter.)

2. Click Define. The Get Path dialog box appears (see fig. 15.19).

3. Use the Macintosh file list navigation methods to find and open the folder in which you want to place the document files.

Chapter 15
Customizing WordPerfect

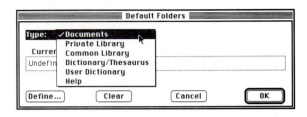

Fig. 15.18
Choosing a type of folder from the Type pop-up menu.

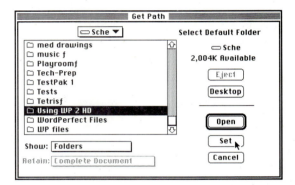

Fig. 15.19
The Get Path dialog box.

4. Click Set in the Get Path dialog box. The name of the set folder appears in the folder pop-up menu above the file list.

5. Click OK in the Default Folders dialog box.

The default folder settings are saved for future sessions.

The Default Document Folder

If you use the procedure described in the preceding steps and choose Documents from the Type pop-up menu, WordPerfect opens the specified folder whenever you choose Save As or Open from the File menu. To save all your documents in one place, you can choose the default documents folder. To save a document elsewhere, you always can move to a different folder before you click Save.

If you use several different folders for your documents, you should leave the default documents folder *undefined* so that WordPerfect uses the normal Macintosh file system default (the last folder you were in) as the folder that appears when the file dialog box opens. When you save a file to a particular folder, the program uses that folder until you specify another folder.

Part III

Using Advanced Features

If you set a folder previously and want to reset the default documents folder to undefined, follow these steps:

1. Choose Preferences from the File menu; then choose Default Folders from the Preferences submenu. The Default Folders dialog box appears.

2. Choose Documents from the Type pop-up menu.

3. Click Clear in the Default Folders dialog box. The setting in the Current Path text box is replaced by Undefined.

4. Click OK or press Return to save the changed path, close the dialog box, and return to your document.

The Dictionary/Thesaurus and Help Files Path

You can save the path to the spelling dictionary, thesaurus, user dictionary, and help files by setting the Default Folders Type pop-up menu to the appropriate choice and following the instructions given for setting the default folders for documents, explained in the "Default Folders" section earlier.

WordPerfect looks in the folder containing the WordPerfect application for these files when you choose Speller, Thesaurus, or Help from the main menus. If you move the application or the files, the program displays a dialog box that asks you to locate the dictionary, thesaurus, or help files. After you locate the file, click Open.

If you don't use the Default Folders command to set the path to those files, the next time you use one of these applications, you must specify the path again.

The Common Library and Private Library Folders

Using a Common Library is one way that a group of people on a network can maintain a single set of style and macro definitions. If your system is connected to a network file server, the network administrator must set up the Common Library on the server. Before you can use the standard setting routine to set the Common Library location, the network administrator also must set the access permission levels that enable you to use the file. (See the section on the Librarian later in this chapter for more information on libraries.)

The WordPerfect Installer automatically creates a Private Library file in the WordPerfect folder inside the Preferences folder in the System Folder

Chapter 15
Customizing WordPerfect

on your hard disk. If, for whatever reason, you want to store the Private Library elsewhere, use the Default Folders dialog box with the Type pop-up menu set to Private Library to define the path to your library file. (Refer to "The Default Document Folder" earlier in this chapter for specific steps in defining a path.)

Keyboards

The Keyboards option in the Preferences menu opens the Keyboard Management dialog box (see fig. 15.20). This dialog box enables you to change almost all the actions controlled by the keyboard.

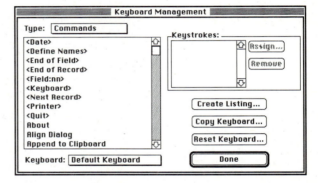

Fig. 15.20
The Keyboard Management dialog box.

Using the Keyboard Management dialog box, you can do any of the following:

- Redefine keys on the keyboard to insert any character into a document

- Add or change keyboard shortcuts for commands

- Assign a keyboard command to open the main pull-down menus or submenus

- Assign or change a keyboard command for styles or macros in the Private Library or current document

- Assign a keystroke that causes the program to insert the value of a variable into the document (used primarily in macros)

- Choose among several keyboard definitions stored in your Private Library

Using Another Keyboard Definition

> **Tip**
> You must use the Librarian to move the extra keyboard definitions into your Private Library. See the section on the Librarian later in this chapter for specific directions.

The changes listed in the preceding section apply to a specific keyboard definition. The keyboard definition that your editing affects appears in the Keyboard pop-up menu of the Keyboard Management dialog box.

When you install WordPerfect, only the Default Keyboard is created in your Private Library. WordPerfect also supplies two additional keyboards, shown in figure 15.21, as resources in the Keyboards file contained in the Documentation folder that is in your WordPerfect 2.1 folder (created by the Installer) or on one of the distribution disks.

Fig. 15.21
Choosing a keyboard definition.

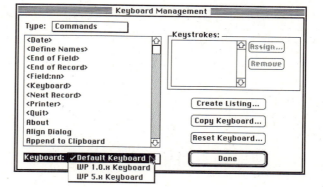

These extra keyboard definitions are approximations of the keyboard command definitions used by the 1.0 series of WordPerfect for the Macintosh and the 5.x series of DOS WordPerfect. If you are familiar with the keyboard commands of either program, you may want to install the extra resources and set the Keyboard pop-up menu in the Keyboard Management dialog box to your familiar program's keyboard. You then can use many keyboard commands of WordPerfect 2.1 for Macintosh without learning new keyboard commands.

Modifying Keyboard Definitions

You can change many types of keyboard commands by selecting an option from the Keyboard Management Type pop-up menu (see fig. 15.22). This section describes how to change a keyboard command. To activate the Select All command by pressing ⌘-Z rather than ⌘-A, for example, redefine the keyboard command for Select All.

Chapter 15
Customizing WordPerfect

Fig. 15.22
The Type pop-up menu in the Keyboard Management dialog box.

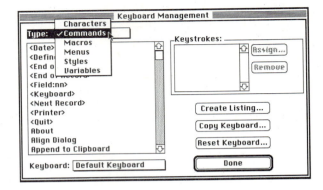

> **Tip**
> The characters assigned to ⌘-Option-*letter* keystrokes are usually the same as the characters assigned to Option-*letter* keystrokes in Macintosh fonts. You can use the ⌘-Option-*letter* keystroke combination without losing keyboard access to the character that appears in the Assign Keystroke dialog box.

To change a keyboard shortcut for a command, follow these steps:

1. If you have not done so already, from the File menu choose Preferences and then Keyboards. The Keyboard Management dialog box appears.

2. Choose a command from the scrollable list below the Type pop-up menu. (Command is the default type in the Type pop-up menu.) If you want to change a keyboard command for a character, macro, menu command, style, or macro variable, choose the appropriate item from the Type pop-up menu.

3. Click Assign or press ⌘-A to activate the Assign Keystroke dialog box (see fig. 15.23).

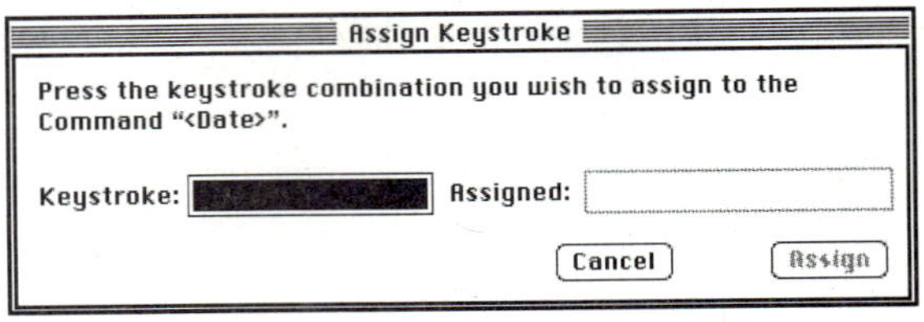

Fig. 15.23
The Assign Keystroke dialog box.

4. Type the keystroke combination you plan to assign to the command. You can press keys on your keyboard alone or in combination with Option, Shift, Command (⌘), ⌘-Shift, Option-Shift, or ⌘-Option.

   If the combination you enter already is assigned, the Macintosh beeps and displays the other command or character in the Assigned text box. You can try another combination or accept the one you just typed.

Part III
Using Advanced Features

You cannot use the Control key as a modifier key in a keyboard command—that is, WordPerfect sees the keystroke Control-A as just *A*.

5. After you enter an acceptable combination, click Assign. Your new definition replaces any existing definition for the keystroke combination.

6. Click Done or press Return in the Keyboard Management dialog box after you finish changing your keyboard definition.

WordPerfect enables you to use the ⌘, Option, and Shift keys (and their combinations) when you define keystroke combinations. You also can use the *Gold* key. The Gold key is defined as the numeric keypad 7 key or the numeric keypad 5 key, but you can assign an additional or different key to act as the Gold key. The Gold key is a convenient way of avoiding conflicts with any other Macintosh keyboard commands in the program.

The Character type in Keyboard Management is font specific. To redefine the normal character definitions (to create a Dvorak keyboard layout, for example), you must change all fonts in your system.

If you make changes to a keyboard and later decide to assign the default keyboard layout to the modified keyboard, follow these steps:

1. Click Reset Keyboard in the Keyboard Management dialog box, accessed through the Preferences submenu. The Reset Keyboard alert box appears (see fig. 15.24).

Fig. 15.24
The Reset Keyboard dialog box.

2. Click Overwrite. The keyboard definition for the keyboard set in the Keyboard pop-up menu is overwritten with the WordPerfect default keyboard definition.

This option gives you a way to recover the default layout if you change the default keyboard without making a copy of it.

Chapter 15
Customizing WordPerfect

Creating Your Own Keyboard Definitions

Besides the supplied keyboard definitions or slight changes of these keyboards, you can create your own keyboard definition. To create a new definition, you make changes to a copy of an existing definition.

You may want to experiment with different keyboard definitions while keeping a copy of your current definition. By creating a new definition, you can return to the old definition by choosing it from the Keyboard pop-up menu of the Keyboard Management dialog box.

To create your own keyboard definitions, follow these steps:

1. Choose Keyboards from the Preferences submenu in the File menu. The Keyboard Management dialog box appears.

2. Click Copy Keyboard. The New Keyboard dialog box appears.

3. Enter the name of the definition in the New Keyboard dialog box (see fig. 15.25). The name that WordPerfect presents is the name of the current keyboard preceded by Copy of.

Fig. 15.25
The New Keyboard dialog box.

4. Click OK.

5. Make changes to the new definition by using the Keyboard Management dialog box.

Printing a List of Keyboard Commands

Keeping track of the default keyboard commands is a difficult task. Keeping track of changes you make is even harder because no reference manual exists for your changes. WordPerfect, however, can create a list of the types of commands in the Keyboard Management dialog box. To print a list of all the keyboard commands, follow these steps:

1. Choose Keyboard from the Preferences submenu in the File menu to open the Keyboard Management dialog box.

2. Select a keyboard definition from the Type pop-up menu.
3. Click Create Listing. The Create Listing dialog box appears.
4. Enter a name in the Save Listing As text box (see fig. 15.26).

Fig. 15.26
The Create Listing dialog box.

5. Click Save or press Return. WordPerfect saves the listing as a text file with the name you gave it.
6. Click Done or press Return to close the Keyboard Management dialog box.
7. From the File menu, choose Open and open the file you created in step 4.
8. Choose Print from the File menu. WordPerfect prints the list of keyboard commands.

Setting a Custom Date and Time Format

WordPerfect enables you to define a format for the date that is inserted into a document when you use the Text Date/Time or Auto Update Date/Time commands. Although you usually access these commands through the Date/Time submenu of the Tools menu, you use the Date/Time Options dialog box to control the format these commands use.

To change the way WordPerfect formats a date in the date commands, follow these steps:

1. Choose Options from the Date/Time submenu in the Tools menu. The Date/Time Options dialog box appears (see fig. 15.27).
2. Press Delete to remove the date format that is in the Date box.

Fig. 15.27
The Date/Time Options dialog box.

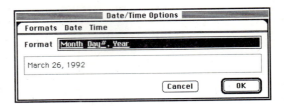

3. You can select a date format from the Formats menu, shown in figure 15.28, or you can create your own format by using the dialog box's Date and Time menus, shown in figures 15.29 and 15.30.

Fig. 15.28
The Format menu in the Date/Time Options dialog box.

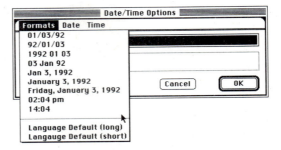

Fig. 15.29
The Date menu in the Date/Time Options dialog box.

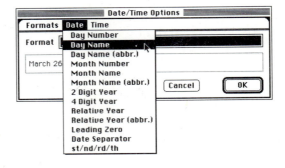

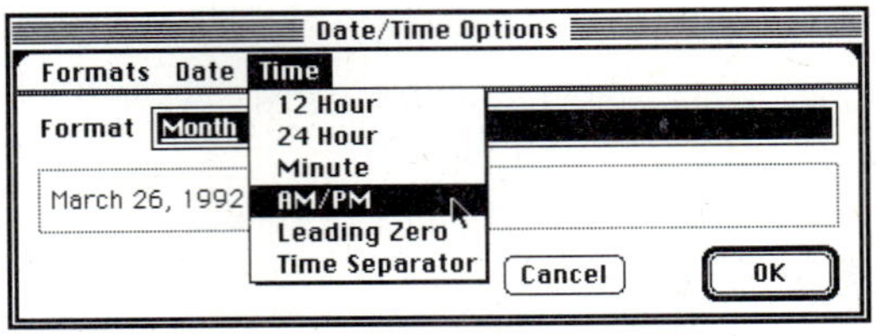

Fig. 15.30
The Time menu in the Date/Time Options dialog box.

Part III

Using Advanced Features

The options on the Date and Time menus offer a flexible environment for defining automatic date insertion. If you want all dates to appear as *this 3rd day of August, 1991*, for example, type *this* (include a space after the word), select Day Number from the Date menu, and then select st/nd/rd/th from the Date menu. Next, type *day of* (include spaces before and after the words) and then select Month Name from the Date menu. Finally, type a , (include a space after the comma) and select 4 Digit Year from the Date menu.

The Date/Time Options dialog box should resemble figure 15.31. When you use the Auto Update Date/Time or Text Date/Time commands, the program inserts the code or text for the expanded date format into your document.

Fig. 15.31
A modified date format.

4. Click OK or press Return. WordPerfect stores your Date/Time format in the USA-2.1 Preferences file and closes the dialog box.

After you define the Date/Time format, use the Text command from the Date/Time submenu under the Tools menu to insert the current date in your document at the insertion point. You can edit a Text date (change *29 March 1992* to *28 March 1992*, for example) after you enter the date.

To update the date automatically when you open the document, choose Auto Update from the Date/Time submenu of the Tools menu. This command inserts a code in your document that shows the date on your computer's clock, in the format you defined, at the insertion point.

Controlling the Normal Style

ordPerfect enables you to customize styles. With WordPerfect, you can modify the Normal style, which is especially important if you use styles or share files electronically with other people.

The Normal style is used in every document you create. Because WordPerfect uses the Normal style as a template for many of the other styles—footnote and endnotes, for example—you must understand how WordPerfect uses the Normal style.

Chapter 15
Customizing WordPerfect

The Normal style defines the font and font size, the line and page margins, tab settings, and so forth for your document. If you haven't modified the Normal style and you create a new document, the document uses 1-inch left and right margins, and the text you enter is 12-point Geneva type.

Modifying the Normal Style

Chapter 8, "Formatting with Styles," covers formatting styles, such as the Normal style. (Do not confuse formatting styles with text styles, such as boldface and italic.) The purpose of this section is to explain how to modify the Normal style and to point out some effects of modifying the Normal style.

Nearly all the styles installed by the WordPerfect Installer use the Normal style for font, font size, margin, and tab settings. If you use headers, footers, footnotes, or endnotes, you may want to change the Normal style settings. If you change the settings for these elements, you can change the Normal style so that reformatting each footnote you create is unnecessary.

Because the Normal style dictates that 12-point Geneva text is used, you must make two trips to the Font menu each time you open a new document if you plan to use 10-point Times type. Furthermore, you must make these trips to the Font menu every time you enter a header, footer, endnote, footnote, and so on because those items also start out as 12-point Geneva (the default Normal style settings for font and size). To avoid these tedious trips to the Font menu, you simply can change the Normal style.

To change the Normal style, follow these steps:

1. Choose Edit from the Styles submenu, which you access through the Layout menu. Alternatively, type Option-F10. The Edit Style dialog box appears.

2. Select Normal from the list of styles (see fig. 15.32).

3. Click Edit Content. The Private Library Style window appears at the bottom of the document window. You now can make *any* formatting changes—font, size, margins, borders, tab settings, and so forth—that should apply to all your documents.

4. From the main Font menu, select a font and font size for the customized Normal style.

Part III
Using Advanced Features

Fig. 15.32
The Edit Style dialog box.

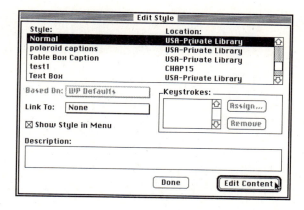

5. Set the appropriate margins and tabs; generally, these settings should be the ones you use most frequently.

   Figure 15.33 shows the Private Library Style window after the Normal style has been changed.

Fig. 15.33
The modified Normal style in the Private Library Style window.

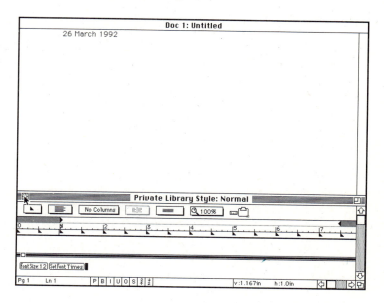

6. Click the close box of the Private Library Style window or press ⌘-W.

Chapter 15
Customizing WordPerfect

If you manually set the fonts in your documents, do not edit the Normal style after you enter text in your document; otherwise, you must reset each font setting. For the same reason, do not include font choices in other styles you use.

Using the Normal Style in Shared Documents

If you electronically share your documents with other users, install your Normal style in the document itself, using the Librarian (as described in the next section) or the Update to Library command in the Styles submenu from the Layout menu (refer to Chapter 8, "Formatting with Styles").

When WordPerfect opens a document, the program uses formatting styles that are installed in the document before looking in the Private Library for style definitions. Because all documents use a Normal style, you must install your Normal style description in a document file to ensure that WordPerfect formats the document as you intend. If you don't install the style in the document and share the file with someone who uses a Normal style that is defined differently than your Normal style, your file's formatting may be ruined when the file is opened on the other machine.

Similarly, to edit your own Normal style in the future, install the current Normal style in every document; otherwise, opening an old document after you change your Normal style may result in significant reformatting chores.

Using the Librarian

The WordPerfect Librarian utility resembles Apple's Font/DA Mover. You use the Librarian to copy, rename, or remove resource modules from documents, the Private Library, and the Common Library. The Librarian manages resources such as styles, macros, file conversion filters, keyboard definitions, and character maps. The capability to move these resources from one file to another gives you (and WordPerfect) a convenient way to transfer resources between files and users without modifying the main program.

If a set of styles, a keyboard definition, or a set of macros are developed for specific uses in your organization, you can distribute those resources in a single, small file so that other users can install these resources in their Private Library. (The Private Library file is installed in the Preferences folder inside your System Folder.)

If you and the users who need a copy of the resource are on a network, distributing resources is even easier: you copy the resources into the Common Library on the file server, and the other users can use the Default Folders dialog box to tell WordPerfect the location of the Common Library. See the section "Comparing the Private and Common Libraries" later in this chapter for more information on the libraries.

Understanding Librarian Resources

Most of the Librarian resources (styles, macros, keyboards, and conversion filters) have been mentioned earlier. Some considerations that can help you manage the resources more efficiently are discussed here.

Styles

When you create a new style, WordPerfect stores the style in the active document unless you indicate, in the Styles dialog box, that WordPerfect should store the style in the Private or Common Library. (For more information on creating and using styles, see Chapter 8, "Formatting with Styles.")

You should store a copy of a frequently used style in the Private Library. Keeping a frequently used set of formatting commands in a style in the library saves you from reentering all the formatting commands each time you need them. So that document formatting is not lost when you open the document on another machine, however, you should install all styles used in a document within the document itself before you or someone else edits a copy of the file on another Macintosh.

Macros

The default location for a macro is the Private Library. If you intend to give a copy of the macro to other users, however, you should install a macro in a document. The other users, then, can use the Librarian to copy the macro from the document to their own Private Libraries. For more information on creating macros, see Chapter 14, "Using Macros."

Chapter 15
Customizing WordPerfect

Character Maps

Although character maps aren't available yet, WordPerfect plans to release character maps, which provide more consistent special character translation when you transfer files between WordPerfect products on different brands of computers.

Conversion Filters

Beginning with Version 2.1, WordPerfect's default location for conversion filters is in a separate folder (Conversions) in the WordPerfect folder in the Preferences folder inside the System Folder of your hard disk. You can use the Librarian, however, to store conversion filters in your Private Library or in an individual file.

Almost the only time you must be concerned with conversion resources is when WordPerfect releases an updated conversion that is distributed separately from an update of the main program. The Installer program updates conversion filters when you install a new version of the program. The only reason to copy a conversion filter to a document is to transfer the conversion to a user who doesn't have a copy. (For more information about file conversion resources, see Chapter 7, "Managing Files and Documents.")

You can save some disk space if your system is connected to a network and the Common Library is installed on the server. WordPerfect looks in the Common Library for conversions (or any other resource) that the program cannot find in the active document or your Private Library.

Keyboards

As discussed earlier in this chapter, keyboard resources enable you to define several keyboard layouts for all WordPerfect commands in WordPerfect Version 2.1. You choose the keyboard layout used by the program in the Keyboards Management dialog box, which you access from the File menu by choosing Preferences and then Keyboards.

Comparing the Private and Common Libraries

WordPerfect provides three levels of resource storage. WordPerfect looks for resources first in the document to be edited. If the program doesn't find the resources in the document, it searches your Private Library. If the resource definitions still are not found, WordPerfect checks the

Common Library (if you have used the Default Folders dialog box to set the directory path for a Common Library).

Resources installed in a document control WordPerfect operation in preference to resources stored in either Library. By installing resources in a document, you can control your own Normal style (or any other style or resource) without worrying about the results of giving the document to other WordPerfect Mac users for further editing.

WordPerfect creates the Private Library file during installation. This library, stored in the Preferences folder of your computer's System Folder, can hold any Librarian resource you create or transfer. The Common Library, which is the same type of file as the Private Library, is normally installed on a file server so that every member of a group has access to the resources collected in the Common Library. By using the Common Library resource rather than a Private Library resource, you can maintain consistency among users' documents and save space on the users' hard disks.

You cannot choose directly to use a Common Library resource rather than a Private Library resource. If a resource of a particular name exists in your Private Library, WordPerfect uses the Private Library copy. To use a Common Library resource that has the same name as a resource in your Private Library, you must rename the resource in your Private Library, using the Librarian. You normally cannot rename resources in the Common Library. In fact, you should not change a Common Library resource because the change may surprise and annoy others who use the old resource from the Common Library.

Moving a Resource

Now that you know what kind of resources the Librarian manages, you should know how to use the Librarian dialog box to move resources. Moving a resource created by someone else is easier than redefining a style, keyboard definition, or macro on your own. The time saving is particularly evident for macros, although you also can transfer macros as text files (as described in Chapter 14, "Using Macros").

Another example of a tedious manual task that the Librarian simplifies installing a keyboard definition. WordPerfect for Macintosh has its own set of command key equivalents defined for many of the commands in the application (for example, ⌘-A for Select All). Many of these command key equivalents are very different from similar keyboard commands in DOS WordPerfect and from the commands in Version 1.0.x for the Mac.

Chapter 15
Customizing WordPerfect

Knowing that some of their current customers have memorized a set of keyboard commands, WordPerfect Corporation includes keyboard definitions for WordPerfect for Macintosh Version 2.1 that use the keyboard commands of WordPerfect 5.x (DOS) or 1.0.x (Macintosh). To use either keyboard definition, you must use the Librarian to move the definitions from a document named Keyboards (installed with your other WordPerfect 2.1 files).

To move these keyboard definitions from the Keyboards document to your Private Library, follow these steps:

1. Open the Keyboards file in the Documentation folder within your WordPerfect 2.1 folder, which the WordPerfect Installer created. If you did a custom install and did not install the documentation, the Keyboards file is on the disk WordPerfect 3. You can open the file on the distribution disk or copy the file to your hard disk and then open it from there.

2. Choose Librarian from the File menu. The Librarian dialog box appears.

3. Choose Keyboards from the Resources pop-up menu (see fig. 15.34).

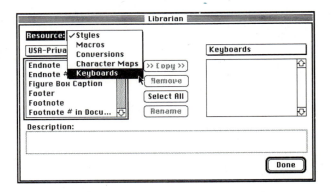

Fig. 15.34
Choosing a Resource option from the Librarian dialog box.

The list of keyboard definitions in the Private Library appears on the left. The list of keyboard definitions in the Keyboards document appears on the right.

4. Press Tab or click the resource list on the right side of the dialog box under Keyboards. Notice that the extra border appears around the list box (see fig. 15.35).

Fig. 15.35
An activated document resource list.

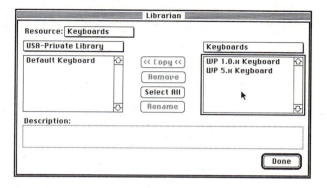

5. Click Select All. All resources—in this case, the two keyboard definitions—in the boldfaced bordered list are selected.

6. Click Copy to copy the selected resources into your Private Library.

7. After WordPerfect finishes copying the resources, click Done or press Return to leave the Librarian.

Now you can switch your keyboard layout to one of the newly installed definitions. From the File menu, choose Preferences and then Keyboards. When the Keyboard Management dialog box appears, choose the appropriate settings.

In addition to moving resources from a document to your Private Library, you also can copy resources from a Common Library to your Private Library. The most likely reason for copying a Common Library resource is to use the resource as a starting point for a slightly modified style, macro, or keyboard definition on your Mac. In general, you shouldn't copy resources from the Common Library unless you also rename them; otherwise, you defeat the purpose of the Common Library.

To copy a style from the Common Library to your Private Library, follow these steps:

1. With any document open, choose Librarian from the File menu. The Librarian dialog box appears.

2. Choose Styles from the Resource pop-up menu. The scrollable lists display the styles in the Private Library (left) and the open document (right).

3. Select Common Library from the file list pop-up menu on the right side of the dialog box (see fig. 15.36). The scrollable list at the right now shows the styles defined in the Common Library.

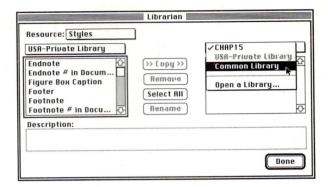

Fig. 15.36
Selecting the Common Library.

You can choose Common Library only if the Common Library is installed and you have used Default Folders (under Preferences in the File menu) to set the path to the Common Library. Otherwise, the Common Library option is dimmed.

4. Select the style you want to copy from the style list at the right.

5. Click Copy. The Librarian places a copy of the selected style in your Private Library.

6. Click Done or press Return to close the Librarian dialog box and return to your open document window.

One other option in the file list pop-up menu shown in figure 15.36 is worth mentioning. The Open a Library option enables you to choose and open any WordPerfect resource library. This option is useful if you plan to copy several resources from someone else's library. The other person can give you a copy of his Private Library; using the Librarian to copy resources individually to an intermediate file is not necessary. The Open a Library option also enables you to open the USA-Private Library easily on the distribution disk if you must reinstall resources from the original copy.

Deleting a Resource

To remove a resource from a document or a library, follow these steps:

1. With any document open, choose Librarian from the File menu. The Librarian dialog box appears.

2. From the Resource pop-up menu, choose a resource type.

Part III
Using Advanced Features

3. From the document or library list, choose the resource that you want to remove.

4. Click Remove. An alert box asking you to confirm the deletion appears.

5. Click OK. WordPerfect deletes the specified resource.

6. Click Done or press Return to close the Librarian dialog box.

Chapter Summary

In this chapter, you learned the difference between *preferences*, which control how the program presents on-screen information, and *style elements*, which affect the final appearance of a document. You also learned how to use the Librarian to control where WordPerfect gets its style, macro, keyboard, and file conversion definition information.

In addition, this chapter explained how to use the Date/Time Options dialog box to set or create almost any date format; how to edit keyboard definitions one command at a time, switch among predefined layouts, or create custom layouts to redefine how WordPerfect reacts to any keyboard command; and how to include additional on-screen information, such as style buttons, extra ⌘ keys for menus, and normally invisible characters like Tab and Return.

You learned how you can use the Librarian to install styles—especially the Normal style—into documents so that you can safely share files electronically with other WordPerfect Mac users. You learned not to include font selections in Style definitions if you change fonts manually in a document, and you learned how to include a font selection and other formatting information in your Normal style.

CHAPTER 16

Taking Advantage of System 7

In Apple's System 7 software, WordPerfect 2.1 offers you several new features: Balloon Help, Publish and Subscribe, and Quick-Time. Chapter 2, "An Overview of WordPerfect 2.1," explains how to access and use the Balloon Help feature. This chapter deals primarily with using Publish and Subscribe to create dynamic links between WordPerfect and other documents (from WordPerfect or other System 7-compatible applications). This chapter also discusses the use of QuickTime movies in WordPerfect documents. *Note:* To use the features discussed in this chapter, Apple System 7.0 or newer must be installed on your Macintosh.

Using Publish and Subscribe

The Mac has always provided the Cut, Copy, and Paste commands, which enable you to move information easily from one document or application to another. This method has one limitation, however, if you use these commands to update information; when you change the information in one place, you must search for the information in other files and manually change each occurrence. System 7 provides a way to link information dynamically so that changes in the information automatically apply to the linked information in other files.

Apple calls this dynamic linking *Publish and Subscribe*. After you select text or graphics in a document, you can create a *publisher* that sends the selected material to an *edition* file. You then can *subscribe* to the edition from the same document, from another document created by WordPerfect, or from another application that supports Publish and Subscribe. In WordPerfect, you also can subscribe to editions created in spreadsheet applications, graphics programs, or any other application that can create a publisher.

True to the publishing analogy, you cannot subscribe to information that hasn't been published. The publisher determines what information to include in an edition and controls when and under what conditions an edition is updated. The subscriber, on the other hand, controls when updated information in an edition should be used. The information flows in only one direction—from publisher through an edition to the subscriber. In System 7, an edition is a special kind of file, and publishers and subscribers are the parts of documents that share the edition information.

Consider, for instance, a project to develop class notes and a descriptive brochure for a WordPerfect training course. Suppose that you want to include a full-sized copy of the course schedule in the student handouts and a smaller version of the schedule in a brochure. The following example shows how, by typing the schedule once, you can create a publisher in the document that has the master schedule, subscribe to the schedule edition, and then format the subscriber to fit in the brochure.

Creating a Publisher

To do this exercise, you must create a schedule similar to the schedule shown in figure 16.1. To see some of the useful capabilities of Publish and Subscribe, be sure to use more than one text style—boldface and plain text, for instance. Also use a variety of indenting and text-alignment formatting options.

To create the schedule shown in figure 16.1, follow these steps:

1. In a new document window (or on a new line of text in an existing document), press ⌘-B to activate boldface text style.

2. Type *Overview*.

3. Press Shift-F5 (the Flush Right command) to align the remaining text with the right margin.

    If you don't have an extended keyboard, you must define another keystroke to access Flush Right. See Chapter 15, "Customizing

WordPerfect," for instructions on defining another keystroke. You also can use a Right Tab set at the right margin. See Chapter 4, "Formatting a Document," for more details.

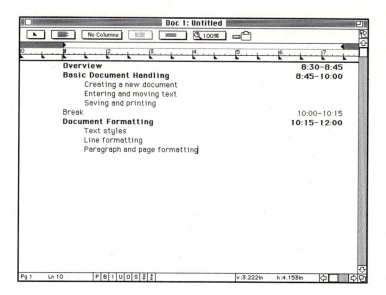

Fig. 16.1
A sample schedule.

4. Type *8:30-8:45* and press Return.

5. Complete the rest of the schedule by following the same procedure you used to enter the first line. To indent lines—as illustrated in lines 3 through 6, for example—press Tab.

Creating a single master schedule (the publisher) forces you to make changes in the same copy of the list, further aiding the process of organizing multiple copies. When you create a publisher for the schedule, you also can be assured that you have the most up-to-date copy of your schedule, which is particularly helpful if you use the schedule in several documents.

After you create the schedule, create a publisher by doing the following:

1. Select the material (text, graphic, or both) that you want to publish.

   You can create a publisher containing as little as a single character (a bit silly) or as big as an entire document (potentially confusing if the document is large). Select as much material as you need to make the publisher a logical, self-contained entity.

2. Choose Create Publisher from the Publishing submenu of the Edit menu. The Create Publisher dialog box appears (see fig. 16.2).

Fig. 16.2
The Create Publisher dialog box.

The dialog box contains a miniature image of the material to be saved in the edition, a scrolling file list from which you choose a folder to hold the edition, a name text box in which you name the edition, and the usual file control buttons.

> **Tip**
> You may want to keep your edition files in one folder to make them easier to find later.

3. Type a name for the edition in the Name of New Edition text box.

   Although WordPerfect suggests part of the name (`-Edition`, which appears in the name box when you open the dialog box), you can use any name. Leaving `-Edition` in the name can make finding the editions in the file list easier, however, when you later subscribe to the edition.

4. Click the Publish button or press Return. The program saves the edition file in the specified folder, the dialog box closes, and you return to the document with the publisher selected.

Creating a Subscriber

After you create an edition file (as described in the preceding section), you can create a brochure that contains a reduced copy of the schedule you placed in Publisher.

To create the brochure, you must prepare the brochure's layout in a new document and create a subscriber that accesses the edition material. Follow these steps:

1. Choose New from the File menu or press ⌘-N.

2. If you have not done so already, display the ruler by pressing ⌘-R or choosing Show Ruler from the Layout menu.

3. Create a text box by pressing ⌘-F2 or choosing New from the Text Box submenu in the Tools menu.

   Creating a text box now is unnecessary; however, by subscribing to the schedule within a box, you can simplify repositioning the schedule when you lay out the rest of the brochure. (Refer to Chapter 9, "Using Columns and Text Boxes," for more information on text boxes.)

4. Choose Subscribe To from the Publishing submenu in the Edit menu. The Subscribe To dialog box appears. Because the system remembers the most recent edition file worked on, the schedule edition is selected when this dialog box appears (see fig. 16.3).

Fig. 16.3
The Subscribe To dialog box.

   To subscribe to another edition, use the standard Macintosh file selection methods.

5. Click the Subscribe button or press Return. The dialog box closes, and the program inserts the contents of the edition in the text box you created.

Because the default dimensions of a new text box cannot display the entire edition, your text box may look odd (see fig. 16.4). Don't worry; all the information is still there. For information on resizing and manipulating text boxes, see Chapter 9, "Using Columns and Text Boxes."

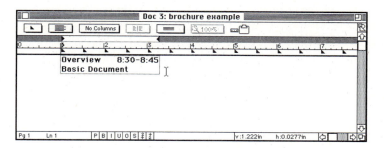

Fig. 16.4
The text box after you subscribe to the schedule edition.

Chapter 16
Taking Advantage of System 7

To complete the schedule subscriber, follow these steps:

1. If you are continuing immediately after the Subscribe To dialog box closes and inserts the edition in your text box (step 5 in the preceding steps), single-click inside the Text box to select the contents of the box.

   If you edited other information in your document after you created the subscriber, you must double-click the text box to select its contents.

2. From the Font menu, choose 9 to reduce the size of the text in the subscriber. If an edition contains more than one font size, and you want to keep a relative size difference on the modified subscriber, choose Other Size in the Font menu; then use the Relative Size pop-up menu to modify your subscriber. (See Chapter 4, "Formatting a Document," for more information on relative font sizes.)

3. Drag the right margin marker to 4.25 inches on the ruler.

4. Click once outside the text box; then click once inside the text box to display the text box sizing handles.

5. Drag the right center handle just beyond 4.25 inches on the ruler to make the text box big enough to display the edition of your schedule (see fig. 16.5).

Fig. 16.5
The reformatted schedule subscriber.

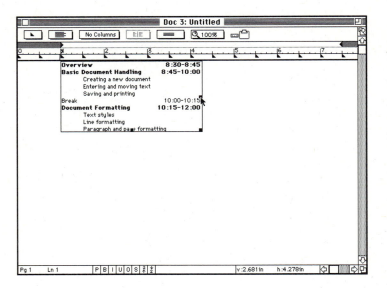

Part III

Using Advanced Features

Your publish and subscribe example is now complete. You can drag the subscriber text box, like any other text box, around the page in the brochure document.

To change the schedule, open the document containing the schedule publisher, edit the schedule as necessary, and then save the document. The changes you make in the publisher are transferred to the edition and to subscribers that are linked to the edition.

Make sure that the Send Editions publish option is set to On Save; otherwise, you must update an edition manually after editing a publisher. When the On Save option is active, you just save the document containing the publisher; the program automatically updates the editions.

Choosing a Subscriber Format

At the bottom of the Subscribe To dialog box, you can see a pop-up menu that offers a choice of formats for a subscriber (see fig. 16.6). The Subscription Format To Use pop-up menu determines, in part, the appearance of the edition in the subscriber.

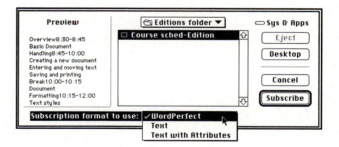

Fig. 16.6
The Subscription Format To Use pop-up menu.

In WordPerfect, the format choices are similar to the options found in the Retain pop-up menu in the Save As dialog box, discussed in Chapter 7, "Managing Files and Documents." The following list explains the subscription formats:

- *WordPerfect.* This format option retrieves all information in the edition file when you subscribe to a WordPerfect edition.

- *Text.* This option retrieves only text, not formatting or graphics. The Text option is useful if you want the subscriber to use the font and style settings that are active at the insertion point when you subscribe to the edition. By choosing Text, for example, you don't have to worry what font the publisher uses because the subscriber matches the font used at the location of the insertion point in the document.

- *Text with Attributes.* This option retrieves everything except graphics.

The subscriber format options also affect editions from other applications. The specific choices available may vary from application to application, but choices from spreadsheets can be particularly important. To subscribe to an edition of a range of cells from a Microsoft Excel file, for instance, you can choose between text and PICT files. If you format an Excel table (in Excel) so that the table is more readable, for example, subscribe to the edition as PICT. If you want only the data in the Excel publisher, use the Text format option.

If you choose the Text format option, you must do significant formatting of the subscriber. The Text option brings in the Excel data as text values separated by tab characters. Figure 16.7 shows the difference between the PICT and Text format options when you subscribe to an Excel publisher in WordPerfect.

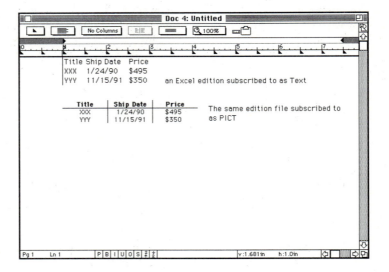

Fig. 16.7
The effects of format options on a Microsoft Excel edition.

Setting Publisher Options

According to Apple guidelines, whenever you save a document that contains a publisher, changes made to the publisher material are transferred from the publisher to the edition file. In WordPerfect 2.1, on the other hand, you must update documents manually. If you frequently go through several revision steps as you work on a document, you may not want an edition to be updated every time you save a file. Having too many interim edition updates increases the chances—especially if you share editions over a network—that someone may subscribe to an interim edition and not update the file to the final version.

Although the WordPerfect default publisher option requires that you update editions manually, you can change the default. To change the default so that a publisher updates editions when you save the document that contains the publisher, follow these steps:

1. In the document that contains the publisher, place the insertion point inside the publisher. If the publisher is a graphic, you can click the publisher once.

2. Choose Publisher Options from the Publishing submenu in the Edit menu. The Publisher Options dialog box appears (see fig. 16.8).

Fig. 16.8
The Publisher Options dialog box.

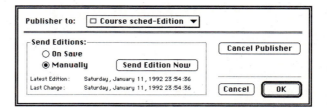

3. Click the On Save radio button to set the publisher for automatic edition updating.

4. Click OK or press Return.

Now, when you save the document containing the publisher, WordPerfect automatically updates the edition file.

To update an edition manually, follow these steps:

1. Choose Publisher Options from the Publishing submenu in the Edit menu. The Publisher Options dialog box appears.

2. Click Send Edition Now. The program transfers changes you made to the publisher to the edition file. Any subscribers linked to the editions display the new edition information, as well.

Setting Subscriber Options

When you first subscribe to an edition, the subscriber is set to accept updates from an edition whenever the publisher modifies the edition. If a document containing a subscriber isn't open when the subscriber's edition is updated, the actual change to the subscriber takes place the next time you open the document.

You may want to disable the automatic updating if, for example, you subscribe to numbers that change weekly, and you are still working on last week's report. In this situation, you can subscribe to the edition containing the numbers early in the week and turn off automatic updating. If the publisher corrects the numbers in midweek, you can retrieve the corrections without risking an automatic update.

To disable the automatic updating so that the subscriber is updated only by specific request, follow these steps:

1. Click somewhere in the subscriber to select it. (The Subscriber Options command is available only when the subscriber is selected.)

2. Choose Subscriber Options from the Publishing submenu in the Edit menu. The Subscriber Options dialog box appears (see fig. 16.9).

   Alternatively, double-click a subscriber. In this example, double-click twice—once to activate the text box and select the subscriber, and the second time to open the dialog box.

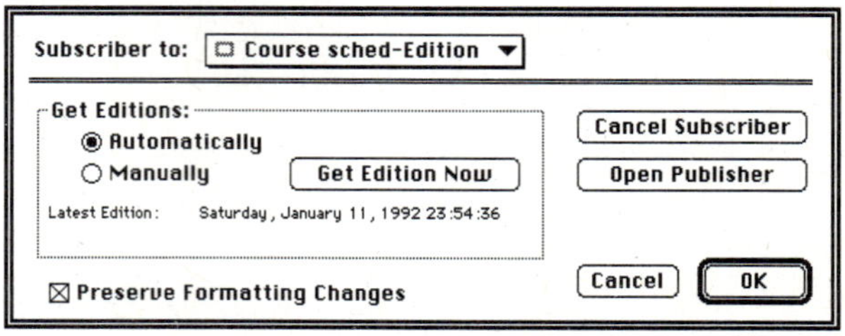

Fig. 16.9
The Subscriber Options dialog box.

3. Click the Manually radio button.
4. Click OK or press Return.

After you choose Manually, you must open the Subscriber Options dialog box and click the Get Edition Now button when you want the subscriber to retrieve the latest edition file.

The Preserve Formatting Changes check box in the Subscriber Options dialog box is important (refer to fig. 16.9). Preserve Formatting Changes enables the publisher to update the edition without losing formatting changes made to the subscriber. If you leave the Preserve Formatting Changes check box unchecked, you must redo the font and formatting changes on every update. Leave this check box checked unless you want to reformat subscribers.

The Open Publisher button on the Subscriber Options dialog box enables you to change a publisher without searching for the file on disk. Suppose that you notice a mistake in a subscriber in your current document. Rather than find the publisher by opening the other document from the File menu, you can access the publisher by following these steps:

1. Double-click the subscriber to open the Subscriber Options dialog box.

2. Click the Open Publisher button.

If you have enough available memory on your computer—even if you must open the publisher's application—System 7 takes you to the publisher document, with the publisher visible and available for editing.

Canceling a Publisher or a Subscriber

You can break the link between an edition and a publisher or a subscriber by clicking the Cancel Publisher or Cancel Subscriber buttons in the appropriate options dialog boxes (refer to figs. 16.8 and 16.9). The Cancel Subscriber option affects only the link to the edition file. The cancellation does not affect the edition file itself, the edition's publisher, and any other subscribers to the edition.

When you cancel a subscriber, WordPerfect doesn't delete the contents of the former subscriber from your document. In fact, after the subscriber is canceled, you can edit the material—something you couldn't do when the material was a subscriber.

Canceling a publisher directly affects only the link between the publisher and its edition file. When you cancel a publisher, however, all subscribers to the affected edition are linked to material that cannot change. Cancel a publisher only if you do not plan to update the information in any of the subscribers.

> **Tip**
> While the link to the edition file exists, you can change only some formatting features of the subscriber; you cannot edit the contents.

Chapter 16

Taking Advantage of System 7

Using Movies in Documents

Apple's QuickTime system extension enables you to include movies in your documents—heralding the arrival of a long-promised multimedia revolution. The prospect of having the capability to open an instructional document, click a graphic, and insert a video demonstration into the document text is exciting. Imagine receiving this book on disk instead of paper, with movie clips to demonstrate each step-by-step instruction.

Although extensive use of videos takes vast amounts of hard disk space and fast networks, you can experiment with QuickTime movies in WordPerfect. QuickTime is even newer than System 7 itself. If you have an early edition of System 7, you must install a copy of the QuickTime extension. WordPerfect provides a copy of QuickTime on the Version 2.1 distribution disks.

Inserting a Movie

Explaining how to make a QuickTime movie is beyond the scope of this book. Unless you have access to special hardware and software required to make a movie, you must work with existing movies that are formatted as computer files. You may be able to find a sample movie from users groups and on-line systems; WordPerfect supplies a sample movie (a rotating WordPerfect logo) with the rest of the Version 2.1 files.

> **Tip**
> Be careful about how many QuickTime movies you download from an on-line service. Movies are big files, and downloading can get expensive.

For now, most of the QuickTime format movies available are experiments in computer animation or experiments in converting home video to a digitized format. (Few movies last longer than 10 seconds.) Nonetheless, you may find some of these movies as more than QuickTime demonstrations. One available QuickTime movie that science teachers and students may be interested in including in a document shows a rotating segment of a DNA molecule.

After you have a copy of a movie on disk, you can insert the movie in a WordPerfect document by following these steps:

1. Place the insertion point where you want WordPerfect to insert the movie box.

2. Choose Insert from the Movie submenu of the Tools menu. The Insert dialog box appears, with the Show pop-up menu already set to Movies so that the file list in the dialog box shows the names of only movies and folders.

Part III

Using Advanced Features

If you choose Insert from the File menu instead, you must set the Show pop-up menu to All or Movies to see your movie in the file list. The Movies setting is much more convenient because you don't see extraneous files in the list. See Chapter 7, "Managing Files and Documents," for more information on the Show pop-up menu in the Insert and Open dialog boxes.

3. Select your movie from the Insert dialog box by using the normal file-list navigation techniques. (See Chapter 3, "Editing a Document," if you need more information on this step.)

4. Click Insert or press Return.

The movie appears in a figure box at the insertion point (see fig. 16.10).

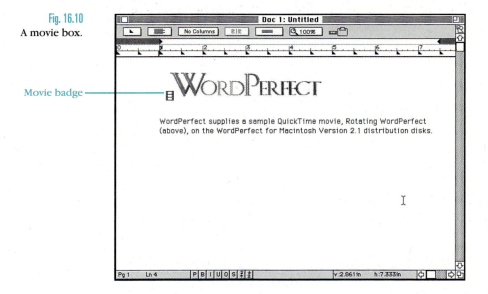

Fig. 16.10
A movie box.

Movie badge

Because movies are large files (several hundred kilobytes of disk space for a few seconds of video), WordPerfect inserts only a reference in your document to tell the program where to find the movie. Don't expect to be able to insert a movie, copy your document to a floppy, take the floppy down the hall, and watch the movie. Some networks, however, may allow this kind of viewing; talk to your network administrator for information on sharing QuickTime movies on a network.

Chapter 16
Taking Advantage of System 7

Playing a Movie

With the exception of the small *movie badge*—a filmstrip icon in the lower left corner of the movie box—nothing distinguishes a movie from a regular graphic (refer to fig. 16.10).

To play the movie, follow these steps:

1. Double-click the movie or click the movie badge.
2. Click the Play/Pause button on the movie control panel that appears (see fig. 16.11).

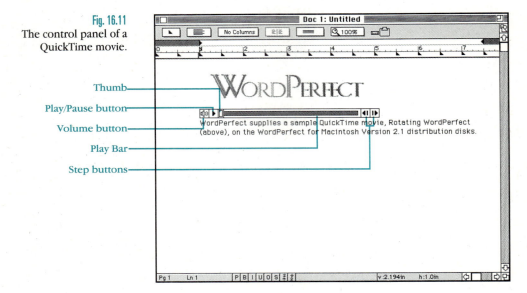

Fig. 16.11
The control panel of a QuickTime movie.

Thumb
Play/Pause button
Volume button
Play Bar
Step buttons

You can control the sound level, pause the movie, advance or rewind the movie one frame at a time, and manually select a movie frame by using the controls shown in figure 16.11. To stop a movie, click in the document outside the movie box.

Changing Movie Settings

In the Movie Settings dialog box, you can manage the image that appears in a document while a movie is inactive; you also can choose options that control movie playback. To view or change these options, follow these steps:

1. Click the movie once.
2. Choose Settings from the Movie submenu in the Tools menu. The Movie Settings dialog box appears (see fig. 16.12).

Fig. 16.12
The Movie Settings dialog box.

The following list briefly discusses each option in the Movie Settings dialog box. The best way to develop a feel for the effects of choosing these options is to experiment with different settings.

- *Playback pop-up menu.* This option enables you to choose between playing the movie once (Play Once) and playing the movie continuously until you stop it (Loop).

- *Direction pop-up menu.* This pop-up menu enables you to play the movie forward or backward.

- *Speed text box.* Although you can type any speed into the Speed box, the suggested range of 0.5-4.0 is the practical limit. The speed value is a ratio of the playback speed to the recording speed. At a speed of 1.0, for instance, the movie plays at the speed at which it was recorded. At 4.0, the movie plays four times faster than the recording speed.

- *Suppress This Badge check box.* If checked, the movie badge and movie control panel do not appear in the document. To start the movie after you suppress the badge, double-click the movie or choose Play from the Movie submenu in the Tools menu. You can pause a movie that has no badges displayed by clicking the movie once. To restart a movie, double-click it.

- *Original Poster, Original Size, and Replace Poster.* With these options, you can change the appearance of the poster in the document when the movie is not playing.

Tip
You can stop a movie anytime by clicking outside the movie.

Chapter 16
Taking Advantage of System 7

A *poster* is the frame of the movie that appears in the movie box when the movie is not selected or playing. Normally, the poster is set to the first frame of a movie. To use some other frame for the poster, do the following:

1. Click the appropriate movie; then choose Settings from the Movie submenu in the Tools menu. The Movie Settings dialog box appears.

2. By using the playback controls below the movie in the Movie Settings dialog box, choose the frame of the movie you want to become the new poster. Click the right step button, for example, to advance through the movie one frame at a time in the dialog box. Stop when you find the desired frame.

3. Click Replace Poster.

4. Click OK or press Return. The Movie Settings dialog box closes, and your document displays the new poster for the movie box.

After you choose a new poster, you can return to using the first frame as the poster by displaying the Movie Settings dialog box and clicking Original Poster.

WordPerfect enables you to resize a movie box by dragging the box handles. (See Chapter 9, "Using Columns and Text Boxes," for information on resizing boxes.) To return the movie to its original size and proportion, click Original Size in the Movie Settings dialog box.

Changing Frames, Captions, and Options

The Frame, Caption, and Options choices in the Movie submenu in the Tools menu are the same as the options for text and graphics boxes. See Chapter 9, "Using Columns and Text Boxes," and Chapter 11, "Using the Drawing Window," for more details on these menu commands. Frame and Caption are relatively self-explanatory. The Options command controls how and where a box is placed on the page.

Chapter Summary

In this chapter, you learned about two of the most visible enhancements that System 7 offers: QuickTime movies and Publish and Subscribe. You learned how to use Publish and Subscribe to make live links to data from other WordPerfect documents and documents from other applications. These links simplify maintaining accurate copies of changing data. You also learned how to include and manipulate QuickTime movies.

Part III

Using Advanced Features

Installing WordPerfect

Before you can use the application, you must install WordPerfect on your hard disk. WordPerfect and its associated files come on six 800K disks. WordPerfect includes a copy of the Apple Installer application and a script file, which make installing and starting WordPerfect easy. The Installer enables you to choose between an easy install or a customized install. The following sections explain how to accomplish either type of installation.

Preparation

Before you install WordPerfect, you should make backup copies of the distribution disks. Most computer users have experienced, at one time or another, a "mishap"—disk or system failure, for example—of some kind. A backup can make catastrophes of this sort less painful. If you don't copy the distribution disks, at least back up your hard disk after you complete installation so that you can reinstall the application from the original disks or your backup copy, if necessary.

WordPerfect now ships distribution disks without the write-protect tab in place, making accidental overwriting of a distribution disk or virus infections virtually impossible. Because you need the disks if you upgrade to a newer interim release at a local dealer (the dealer copies the new release onto your disks, erasing the older files), store the

distribution disks in a safe place after installation. You should store the disks out of direct sunlight, away from other sources of heat, and away from magnets.

The first step in the installation process is to view the Read Me file that WordPerfect includes on the installation disk. WordPerfect has made some changes to the installation process for Versions 2.0 and 2.1, so although you may not understand everything in the file, try to read the entire file at least once. Installation-specific information appears at the beginning of the Read Me file.

Follow these steps to see the Read Me file:

1. Insert the disk labeled Installer.
2. Double-click the Read Me file icon (see fig. A.1).

Fig. A.1
The Read Me file on the Installer disk.

3. Read through the file, using the scroll bar or arrow keys.

Easy Installation

The easiest way to get started with WordPerfect is to have the Installer do an "easy install." You need about 3,600K of hard disk space to hold the files installed by Easy Install. If you have less disk space available, you must customize the installation (see the next section) or remove some files from your disk to make space available.

The Installer puts most of the files in a folder named WordPerfect 2.1 on your hard disk. If a folder with that name doesn't exist already, the program creates the folder.

If you are installing a release newer than Version 2.1, the Installer replaces the old version with new version and arranges to have the old versions deleted the next time you start your computer. Although you can delete older versions manually before running the Installer, you run the risk of accidentally throwing away some of your own documents. Having the Installer clean up after installation is more convenient, but you need enough free disk space to hold both versions because the program doesn't delete the old version until you install the new version.

Appendix A

Installing WordPerfect

Follow these steps to perform an easy install:

1. Choose Quit from the File menu to close the application that displays the Read Me file.

2. Double-click the Installer application icon.

   After the Installer starts up, WordPerfect displays an initial screen (see fig. A.2).

Fig. A.2
The initial Installer screen.

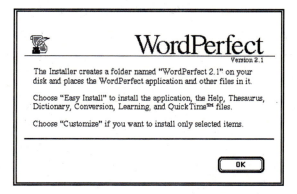

3. Click OK or press Return to continue the installation process.

   The Easy Install dialog box appears (see fig. A.3).

Fig. A.3
The Easy Install dialog box.

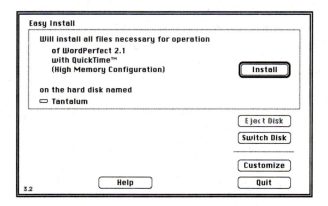

4. If you have more than one hard disk or a partition on your hard disk, click the Switch Disk button until the drive or partition that

Appendix A
Installing WordPerfect

should hold WordPerfect appears in the lower left corner of the dotted box in the Easy Install dialog box.

5. Now you can choose between Easy Install (click Install) or a customized installation (click Customize). The options available if you click Customize are discussed later in this appendix. For now, click Install or press Return to start the installation process.

As the installation progresses, WordPerfect displays a status dialog box that informs you of the progress of the installation (see fig. A.4).

Fig. A.4
The Installation Progress dialog box.

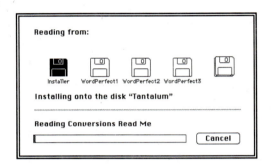

After the Installer finishes with each floppy disk, it ejects the disk and tells you which disk to insert next (see fig. A.5).

Fig. A.5
The Disk Swap alert box.

6. Insert the specified disk.

After each disk necessary to install the application and other files have been loaded, the Installer tells you to reinsert the Installation disk.

7. Insert the Installation disk.

In a few seconds, the Installer displays a message indicating that installation is complete (see fig. A.6).

Fig. A.6
The Installation Finished message box.

8. Click Quit or press Return to leave the Installer program.

9. Open the WordPerfect 2.1 folder on your hard disk and double-click the WordPerfect application icon (see fig. A.7). A dialog box in which you enter your name and registration number appears.

Fig. A.7
Starting WordPerfect by clicking its icon.

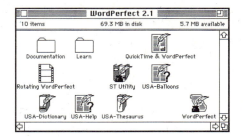

10. Type your name and WordPerfect registration number in the appropriate text boxes in the personalization dialog box (see fig. A.8). Use the Tab key to move between the two boxes in the dialog box; you also can use the mouse to select text to be changed.

Fig. A.8
The WordPerfect personalization dialog box.

Appendix A
Installing WordPerfect

> **Tip**
>
> If you have an antivirus utility running on your Macintosh, you may receive one or more warnings from the utility during installation. Because Apple created the Installer application to install system software, antivirus utilities think the application sometimes acts "strangely."
>
> Choose the option from the antivirus utility that enables the Installer to continue. WordPerfect recommends that you scan the distribution disks first, turn off the antivirus utility, install WordPerfect, and then turn the protection back on.

If an entry already appears in the Name text box, WordPerfect found the information in your Chooser resource (System 6) or the Sharing Setup control panel (System 7). You can change the information in the Chooser by selecting Chooser from the Apple menu. You can access the Sharing Setup panel by choosing Control Panels from the Apple menu and then double-clicking the Sharing Setup icon in the window that opens. See your system documentation for more information on the Chooser and Sharing Setup.

11. Click OK or press Return to exit the personalization dialog box. WordPerfect continues its launch process and presents you with a new, empty document window. You are now ready to use WordPerfect.

If you click Cancel in the personalization dialog box, the application finishes loading, and you still can use the program. Each time you start WordPerfect, however, the personalization dialog box reappears until you enter something in the boxes.

Although you don't have to enter your license number in the personalization dialog box, the number is handy if you need to call WordPerfect about upgrades or problems. (Your license number appears on a license certificate shipped with each copy of the program.) The information from the personalization dialog box appears in the About WordPerfect box (see fig. A.9), which you access by choosing About WordPerfect in the Apple menu while you run the program.

Fig. A.9
The About WordPerfect dialog box.

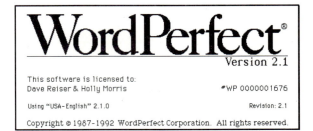

Custom Installation

To reduce the amount of disk space required by WordPerfect or to indicate which files to install and where to install them, you can use the Customize option in the Installer. You also can use the custom install feature to install additional files later.

Appendix A
Installing WordPerfect

To do a customized installation, follow these steps:

1. From the Easy Install dialog box, click the Customize button (refer to fig. A.3). The Custom Install dialog box appears (see fig. A.10).

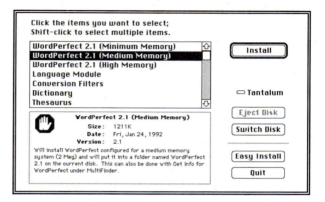

Fig. A.10
The Custom Install dialog box.

2. Use the Switch Disk button to change the hard disk or hard disk partition where the files are installed.

3. Select the files you want to install from the list in the Custom Install dialog box. If you select a single file in the list, a description of that file appears in the lower half of the dialog box (refer to fig. A.10). The choices listed in this dialog box are discussed immediately following these steps.

4. After you select all the files you plan to install, click Install or press Return to start the actual installation; then proceed from step 6 in the "Easy Installation" section of this appendix.

The first three choices in the dialog box file list refer to slightly different configurations of the main application. The only difference in configuration is the amount of memory the application reserves in MultiFinder when the application runs. Choose only one of the files, described in the following list, for installation:

- *Minimum Memory.* This configuration reserves 800K for WordPerfect. You cannot do any graphics with this limited amount of memory.

- *Medium Memory.* This configuration reserves 1,200K, which is a passable amount of memory. However, if you frequently work with big files or color graphics, you should have more memory.

Tip
You must use the Installer to install the WordPerfect application on your hard disk. However, you can drag all the files on the distribution disks from their respective floppy disk Finder windows to your hard disk. To retrieve only the Macros document on disk 3, using the Installer can take longer than copying the file.

Appendix A
Installing WordPerfect

■ *High Memory.* This configuration reserves 3,000K (probably overkill for most files, but more memory usually results in faster operation).

Fig. A.11
The Info window for the WordPerfect application.

> **Tip**
>
> To change the amount of memory WordPerfect reserves when you launch the application, click the WordPerfect icon in the Finder (refer to fig. A.7), choose Get Info from the File menu, and type a new number in the Current Size text box in the Info window (see fig. A.11).

If you choose more than one file from the Custom Install list by clicking additional names while holding down the Shift key, a list of the files selected appears in the file description box (see fig. A.12). To see all selected files, you must scroll through the list.

Fig. A.12
Selecting more than one file in the Custom Install dialog box.

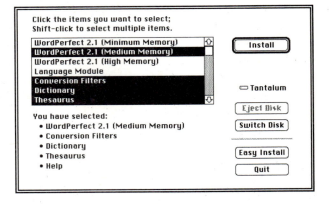

File Organization

esides the WordPerfect 2.1 folder, the Installer creates another folder named WordPerfect in the Preferences folder inside the System Folder of your hard disk. The Installer puts a folder called

Appendix A
Installing WordPerfect

Conversions and a file called USA-Private Library in this second WordPerfect folder. The Conversions folder contains all the file format conversion filters that enable WordPerfect to read files from other word processors. The Private Library contains a collection of definitions of styles, macros, and keystroke commands.

The first time you run WordPerfect, the program looks in the System/Preferences/WordPerfect folder for a file called USA-2.1 Preferences (see fig. A.13). If a USA-2.1 Preferences file does not exist, WordPerfect creates the file from internal information. The Preferences file keeps track of the preferences you set for various program features, such as whether the ruler is displayed when you open a new document. See Chapter 15, "Customizing WordPerfect," for more information about the Preferences file and its settings.

Fig. A.13
Auxiliary files created by the Installer and WordPerfect.

Tip
If you select one of the three configurations of the WordPerfect application for installation, don't choose the Language Module also. When the Installer installs the WordPerfect application, the Installer also merges the Language Module with the application. Choosing the Language Module in the Custom Install list results in an unnecessary copy of the Language Module to your hard disk.

WordPerfect must have the information in the Preferences and Private Library files to run. If you delete the files, WordPerfect can create new copies, but those copies do not contain any of the special information stored when you changed the preference settings, created macros or styles, or moved other resources into the Private Library.

Appendix A
Installing WordPerfect

Index

Symbols

* (asterisk)
   (and) operator, 435
   wild card, 173
+ (or) operator, 435
. (period) key (numeric keypad), 53
... (ellipsis), 40
   wild card, 173
< (less than) operator, 435
< = (less than or equal) operator, 435
< > (not equal) operator, 434
= (equal) operator, 434
> (greater than) operator, 435
> = (greater than or equal) operator, 435
? (question mark) wild card, 172
⌘ key, *see* Command key
⌘- – (Delete) keyboard shortcut, 183
⌘-= (Add) keyboard shortcut, 181
⌘-- (hyphen) (Soft Hyphen) keyboard shortcut, 132
⌘-? (Help) keyboard shortcut, 39, 42
⌘-← (beginning of line) keyboard shortcut, 46
⌘-→ (end of line) keyboard shortcut, 46
⌘-↑ keyboard shortcut
   move up folder levels, 222
   top of screen, 46
   view previous, 60
⌘-↓ (bottom of screen) keyboard shortcut, 46
⌘-A keyboard shortcut
   Assign Keystroke, 266, 453
   Clear All, 123
   Select All, 52
⌘-B (Bold) keyboard shortcut, 71-72

⌘-C (Copy) keyboard shortcut, 38, 66
⌘-Delete (Smart Delete) keyboard shortcut, 69
⌘-E keyboard shortcut
   Edit Style, 266
   Speller, 39
⌘-Esc (Repeat) keyboard shortcut, 47
⌘-F (Find/Change) keyboard shortcut, 76
⌘-F2 (Text Box) keyboard shortcut, 289
⌘-F3 (Copy Ruler) keyboard shortcut, 97
⌘-F5 (Left/Right Indent) keyboard shortcut, 138
⌘-F6 (Select Paragraph) keyboard shortcut, 52
⌘-F7 (Paragraph Border) keyboard shortcut, 157
⌘-F8 (first-line indent) keyboard shortcut, 138
⌘-F9 (Record Macro) keyboard shortcut, 39, 446
⌘-F10 (New Style) keyboard shortcut, 254
⌘-F11 (Table of Contents level 2) keyboard shortcut, 338
⌘-F12 (End of Record) keyboard shortcut, 402
⌘-F13 (Full Page view) keyboard shortcut, 96
⌘-F14 (Superscript) keyboard shortcut, 108
⌘-F15 (Subscript) keyboard shortcut, 107
⌘-G (Generate Index, Etc.) keyboard shortcut, 337
⌘-H keyboard shortcut
   Character, 101, 108
   List Headwords, 186
⌘-I (Italic) keyboard shortcut, 39, 72
⌘-J (Index, Etc.) keyboard shortcut, 332

⌘-K (Copy) keyboard shortcut, 444
⌘-L (Lowercase) keyboard shortcut, 113
⌘-M (Page Format) keyboard shortcut, 136
⌘-N keyboard shortcut
   New, 62
   Word Count, 185
⌘-O (Open) keyboard shortcut, 39, 59
⌘-P (Print) keyboard shortcut, 39, 211
⌘-Q (Quit) keyboard shortcut, 39, 54
⌘-R keyboard shortcut
   Redirect Output, 431
   Show Common Words, 181
   Show Ruler, 32, 93, 117
⌘-Return keyboard shortcut
   Advance Page, 32
   Hard Page Break, 142
⌘-S keyboard shortcut
   Save, 39, 53
   Show Style, 263
⌘-Shift (Codes Show/Hide) keyboard shortcut, 38
⌘-Shift-- (hyphen) (Nonbreaking Hyphen) keyboard shortcut, 133-134
⌘-Shift-? (Help) keyboard shortcut, 39
⌘-Shift-A (Append) keyboard shortcut, 68
⌘-Shift-B (Find Previous) keyboard shortcut, 38, 87
⌘-Shift-C keyboard shortcut
   Center Align, 38
   Center Page, 153
⌘-Shift-D (Date/Time) keyboard shortcut, 38
⌘-Shift-Esc (Repeat Count) keyboard shortcut, 47
⌘-Shift-G keyboard shortcut
   Go to Dialog, 38
   Go To, 50

⌘-Shift-H (Header/Footer) keyboard shortcut, 144
⌘-Shift-I keyboard shortcut
  Indent Paragraph, 138
  Indent, 39
⌘-Shift-J (Justify) keyboard shortcut, 125
⌘-Shift-K (Codes Show/Hide) keyboard shortcut, 73, 476
⌘-Shift-M (Merge) keyboard shortcut, 398
⌘-Shift-N (Find Next) keyboard shortcut, 38, 87
⌘-Shift-O (Outline) keyboard shortcut, 313
⌘-Shift-P (Print Preview) keyboard shortcut, 39, 204
⌘-Shift-Return (Column Break) keyboard shortcut, 277
⌘-Shift-S (Save As) keyboard shortcut, 39
⌘-Shift-T (Thesaurus) keyboard shortcut, 176
⌘-Shift-U (Select Sentence) keyboard shortcut, 52
⌘-Shift-W (Cycle Windows) keyboard shortcut, 38, 237
⌘-Shift-X (Run Macro) keyboard shortcut, 39, 442
⌘-Shift-Y (Select Paragraph) keyboard shortcut, 52
⌘-space bar (Hard Space) keyboard shortcut, 133
⌘-T (Plain Text) keyboard shortcut, 72, 107
⌘-U keyboard shortcut
  Underline, 72
  Uppercase, 113
⌘-V (Paste) keyboard shortcut, 39, 66-67
⌘-W (Close) keyboard shortcut, 38, 186
⌘-X (Cut) keyboard shortcut, 38, 64, 66
⌘-Y (Apply Style) keyboard shortcut, 259
⌘-Z (Undo) keyboard shortcut, 39, 53, 70

A

About WordPerfect (Apple menu) command, 532
About WordPerfect dialog box, 113, 532
absolute tabs, 122
accessing
  formatting features, 92
    with menus, 92-93
    with ruler, 93-97
  help, 10
  keyboard shortcuts with Extra Menu ⌘ Keys, 92
  menu commands, 38
    with keyboard, 38-39
    with mouse, 37
Action pull-down menu (Find dialog box), 84
addresses
  lists
    converting to secondary merge files, macro for, 469-471
    creating, 401-403
    sorting by ZIP codes, 427-428
Affect pull-down menu (Find dialog box), 82-84
aligning text, 23, 124-126
  with space bar, 200
anchor points, 367
anchoring text boxes
  as characters, 296
  to pages, 296-297
  to paragraphs, 297
and (*) operator, 435
antonyms, 177
Append (Edit menu) command, 68-69
appending text, 67-69
Apple LaserWriter Page Setup dialog box, 194-203
Apply (Styles submenu) command, 259
Apply Style dialog box, 259
Arc tool, 363-365
Arc Type (Layout menu) command, 365
Arc Type dialog box, 365
arcs, drawing, 363-365
arrow keys
  Gold key combinations, 48-49
  moving around documents, 46
Assign Keystroke dialog box, 263-264, 453-454, 494-495
asterisk (*) wild card, 173

attributes
  defining styles with existing, 254-257
  retaining when opening/inserting, 223-225
auto aided hyphenation, 132
Auto Update (Date/Time submenu) command, 499
automatic
  backups, 478-480
  hyphenation, 132
axes, rotating objects on, 386-387

B

background
  color, 480-481
  printing, 193
Backspace key, 44
backups
  automatic, 478-480
  before installing WordPerfect, 527
Balloon Help, 42
Bar tabs, 120-121
Bézier curves, 367-369
binding width, setting, 198-199
bit maps, 354
  importing, 393
bit-mapped
  fonts
    printing faster, 201
    smoothing graphics, 201
    smoothing text, 201
  graphics, precision alignment, 203
Block Protect (Page submenu) command, 152
boilerplate, 447
Bold (Style menu) command, 71-72
boldface text style, 71-72
Boolean operators, 435
borders
  around
    characters, 153-158
    columns, 283-287
    graphics, 369-370
    pages, 155-156
    paragraphs, 153-158
  filling, 158-159
  spacing, 159-160

Index

Borders (Layout menu) command, 155, 284
boxes, creating lists of, 345-346
breaks
   column, 277
   page, hard, 142
bulleted lists, 139
   creating, 265-267

C

Caption (Text Box submenu) command, 305-306
captions, text box
   adding to, 305-306
   changing positions, 308-309
Case Convert dialog box, 113
cells, 284
Center Line command, 126
Center Page (Page submenu) command, 153
center tabs, 118
centering text vertically, 153
chaining macros, 472-473
Character command
   Borders submenu, 157-158
   Layout menu, 101, 108, 112, 115
Character Border Style dialog box, 160
Character Format dialog box, 101, 108, 111-112, 115
Character Map (Font menu) command, 103-104
character maps, managing with Librarian, 504
characters
   adding borders, 153-154, 157-158
   anchoring text boxes as, 296
   endnote, 323-325
   formatting, 98
      changing case, 112-113
      changing font size, 100-101
      changing fonts, 98-99
      changing text styles, 105-107
      coloring text, 115
      extended characters, 103-104
      kerning text, 113-115
      redlining, 109-110
      setting relative point sizes, 101-103
      Small Caps text style, 112
      strikeouts, 109-110
      subscripts, 107-109
      superscripts, 107-109
      underlining, 111-112
Chooser (Apple menu) command, 190-191
Chooser dialog box, 190-191
chord arcs, 363-364
circles, drawing, 365-366
Circular Text (Macro menu) command, 440-441
Circular Text dialog box, 440-441
citations, 341
   editing full form definitions, 344
   marking, 341-343
clearing tabs, 19, 117, 124
Clipboard, 63
Close box (document window), 32
closed chord arcs, 363-364
closed wedge arcs, 363-364
codes
   for merging, 398-400
   finding, 88-89
   hidden, 73-74
   paired, 74
Color Palette dialog box, 387-388
colors
   adding to text, 115
   graphics
      editing, 387-388
      filling objects with, 374-375
      in grids, 378
   columns
      borders, 285
      filling text area, 287-288
   on-screen, 480-481
   printing in, 210
   text boxes
      filling with, 307-308
      frames, 307
Colors (Edit menu) command, 387-388
Column (Borders submenu) command, 284-289
Column Border Style dialog box, 283-289
Column Break (Columns submenu) command, 277
column breaks, 277
Column Format dialog box, 278-281
columns
   adding and adjusting, 277-281
   borders
      adding, 283-284
      designing, 284-287
   clearing in Thesaurus, 178
   extended, 283
   filling text area with colors or patterns, 287-288
   in text boxes, 294
   newspaper, 281-282
   parallel, 281-283
   spacing between borders and text, 288
   types, 276
Columns (Layout menu) command, 277
Command (⌘) key, 38, 41, 113
   displaying keyboard shortcuts for buttons, 222
   in dialog boxes, 61
Command mode, numeric keypad in, 48-49
command-key shortcuts, 41-42
   see also keyboard shortcuts
commands
   About WordPerfect (Apple menu), 532
   accessing
      with keyboard, 38-39
      with mouse, 37-38
   Append (Edit menu), 68-69
   Apply (Styles submenu), 259
   Arc Type (Layout menu), 365
   Auto Update (Date/Time submenu), 499
   Block Protect (Page submenu), 152
   Bold (Style menu), 71-72
   Borders (Layout menu), 155, 284
   Caption (Text Box submenu), 305-306
   Center Line, 126
   Center Page (Page submenu), 153

Character
  Borders submenu, 157-158
  Layout menu, 101, 108, 112, 115
Character Map (Font menu), 103-104
Chooser (Apple menu), 190-191
Circular Text (Macro menu), 440-441
Colors (Edit menu), 387-388
Column (Borders submenu), 284-289
Column Break (Columns submenu), 277
Columns (Layout menu), 277
Continue (Macro Options submenu), 461-462
Convert Case (Edit menu), 112-113
Copy (Edit menu), 62-65
Copy Ruler, 97
Create Publisher (Publishing submenu), 514
Cut (Edit menu), 22, 62-65
Cycle Windows (Edit menu), 237
Date/Time (Tools menu), 497
Default Folders (Preferences submenu), 489-492
direct menu, 39-40
Duplicate (Edit menu), 382
Edit
  Endnotes submenu, 322
  Footnotes submenu, 326-327
  Graphics submenu, 379-380
  Macro menu, 452-455
  Styles submenu, 260-264, 269, 500-501
  Text Box submenu, 291-292
Endnotes (Layout menu), 320
Envelopes (Macros menu), 212
Environment (Preferences submenu), 92-93, 98, 478-489

File Manager (File menu), 219-232
Find Code (Search menu), 88-89
Find Next (Search menu), 87
Find Previous (Search menu), 87
Find/Change (Search menu), 74-79
Flip Horizontal (Arrange menu), 387
Flip Vertical (Arrange menu), 387
Flush Right, 126
Footnotes (Layout menu), 326
for opening dialog boxes, 40
Format
  Columns submenu, 278-281
  Line submenu, 129
  Page submenu, 136
Frame (Text Box submenu), 306-309
Go To (Search menu), 50
Graphic (Tools menu), 358
Grid Options (Layout menu), 377-378
Grid Snap (Layout menu), 379
Group (Arrange menu), 381
Header/Footer (Layout menu), 144, 147
Help (Apple menu), 42
Hide Balloons (Balloon Help menu), 42
Hide Grid (Layout menu), 377
hierarchical menu, 40-41
in macros
  Get, 467
  Menu, 468
  Prompt, 467-468
Indent (Layout menu), 138
Index Etc. (Tools menu), 332-351
Insert (File menu), 393
Insert (Movie submenu), 522-523
Italic (Style menu), 72
Kerning (Line submenu), 114-115

Keyboards (Preferences submenu), 492-497
Language (Tools menu), 134-135, 173-174
Left/Right Indent (Layout menu), 138
Letter Closing (Macro menu), 447
Librarian (File menu), 271-272, 443, 506
Line (Layout menu), 114, 122, 129, 131
List Headwords (Thesaurus submenu), 186
Margin Release (Layout menu), 139
Merge (Tools menu), 398-400
Movie (Tools menu), 522
New
  Endnotes submenu, 320
  File menu, 62
  Footnotes submenu, 326
  Graphics submenu, 358
  Styles submenu, 254-258
  Text Box submenu, 289
Open (File menu), 59
Options
  Date/Time submenu, 497-499
  Endnotes submenu, 324-325
  Footnotes submenu, 328-330
  Graphic submenu, 390-392
  Macro menu, 459
  Text Box submenu, 294-304
Other Size (Font menu), 100, 113
Outline (Style menu), 105
Outlining (Tools menu), 313-319
Overlay (Tools menu), 355-356
Page
  Borders submenu, 155-156
  Layout menu, 136
Page Break (Layout menu), 142
Page Format (Layout menu), 141

Index

Page Setup (File menu), 193-203
Paragraph
  Borders submenu, 157
  Layout menu, 138
Paste (Edit menu), 22, 62-67
Patterns (Edit menu), 388-390
Pause (Macro Options submenu), 461
Pen Size (Layout menu), 375
Plain Text (Style menu), 72, 107
Preferences (File menu), 13-14, 33, 92, 477
Print (File menu), 27, 208-211
Print Preview (File menu), 204-207
programmable macro, 462-473
Publisher Options (Publishing submenu), 519-520
Publishing (Edit menu), 514
Quit (File menu), 27-28, 54
Record (Macro menu), 446
Redline (Style menu), 110
Remove
  Style menu, 110
  Styles submenu, 268
Replicate (Arrange menu), 382-386
Resume (Macro Options submenu), 461
Rotate (Arrange menu), 361
Rounded Corners (Layout menu), 363
Save (File menu), 23-24, 53
Save As (Macro Options submenu), 459-460
Save Text (Macro Options submenu), 460-461
Select All (Edit menu), 52
Set Language (Language submenu), 173-174
Settings (Movie submenu), 525-526
Shadow (Style menu), 105
Show ¶ (Edit menu), 44-45
Show Balloons (Balloon Help menu), 42
Show Codes (Edit menu), 73, 476

Show Common (Speller menu), 181
Show Coordinates (Layout menu), 362
Show Ruler (Layout menu), 32, 93, 117
Sort (Tools menu), 420-438
Speller (Tools menu), 25-26, 163-165
Stop Recording (Macro menu), 446
Strikeout (Style menu), 110
Style (Endnotes submenu), 325
Styles (Layout menu), 254
Subscribe To (Publishing submenu), 515-518
Subscriber Options (Publishing submenu), 520-521
Subscript (Style menu), 107
Subtitle (Language submenu), 134-135
Superscript (Style menu), 108
Tabs (Line submenu), 122
Text, 16-17
Text (Date/Time submenu), 499
Text Box (Tools menu), 289
Thesaurus (Tools menu), 176-179
Underline (Style menu), 17-18, 72
Undo (Edit menu), 53, 70
Ungroup (Arrange menu), 382
Update (Styles submenu), 265
Watermark (Tools menu), 148-149, 357
Word Count (Thesaurus submenu), 185
WordPerfect Help (Balloon Help menu), 43
Common Library
  comparing with Private Library, 504-505
  copying resources to Private Library, 507-508
  folder, 491-492
  styles, 253
compressed files, 246
concordances, 334-335

Continue (Macro Options submenu) command, 461-462
control points, 367
conversion filters, 239-240
  managing with Librarian, 504
Convert Case (Edit menu) command, 112-113
converting files, 239
  conversion filters, 239-240
  exporting files
    compressed, 246
    in other formats, 242-244
    stationary, 246
    text files, 245
  importing files, 240-242
  RTF format, 240
  XTND conversion utility, 240
Copy (Edit menu) command, 62-65
Copy Ruler command, 97
Copy Ruler icon, 97
copying
  Common Library resources to Private Library, 507-508
  documents, 69
  graphics objects multiple times, 382-386
  ruler, 97
  text, 63-65
cover pages, printing, 209
Create Listing dialog box, 497
Create Publisher (Publishing submenu) command, 514
Create Publisher dialog box, 514
creating documents, 12-13, 44-45, 62
criteria
  filter acceptance, 432-434
  multiple, 435-436
cropping objects within graphics boxes, 391-392
cross-references
  counting in thesaurus files, 185-186
  creating, 347-349
  generating, 350-351
  marking targets, 349-350
Curve tool, 367-369
Custom Install dialog box, 533-534

Cut (Edit menu) command, 22, 62-65
cutting and pasting text, 22, 63-67
Cycle Windows (Edit menu) command, 237

D

Date/Time (Tools menu) command, 497
Date/Time Options dialog box, 497-499
dates, setting format preferences, 497-499
decimal tabs, 119
Default Folders (Preferences submenu) command, 489-492
Default Folders dialog box, 489-492
defaults, 476
   styles, 250-251
Delete key, 44, 53
deleting
   endnotes, 323
   folders, 229
   footnotes, 327-328
   hidden codes, 74
   overlays, 356
   records from secondary files, 403
   resources, 508-509
   styles from documents, 271-272
   text, 21-22, 53
     selected, 69
   styles, 72, 268
   words from existing dictionaries, 183
dialog boxes
   About WordPerfect, 113, 532
   Apply Style, 259
   Arc Type, 365
   Assign Keystroke, 263-264, 453-454, 494-495
   Case Convert, 113
   Character Border Style, 160
   Character Format, 101, 108, 111-112, 115
   Chooser, 190-191
   Circular Text, 440-441

Color Palette, 387-388
Column Border Style, 283-289
Column Format, 278-281
command-key shortcuts, 41-42
Create Listing, 497
Create Publisher, 514
Custom Install, 533-534
Date/Time Options, 497-499
Default Folders, 489-492
Discontinue Header/Footer, 147
Document Info, 228
Easy Install, 529-530
Edit Graphic, 380
Edit Macro, 452-455
Edit Note, 322, 326-327
Edit Style, 260-501
Edit Text Box, 291-292
Endnote Options, 324-325
Environment, 14, 34, 93, 98, 116-117, 136, 478-489
File Info, 227
File Manager, 219-232
Find, 75-87
Find Code, 88
Find Forware, 77
Folder Info, 230
Footnote Options, 328-330
Get Path, 489-490
Go To, 50
Graphic Options, 295-304, 390-392
Grid Options, 377-378
Header/Footer, 145-147
Help, 11-12, 42-44
holding down Command (⌘) key, 61
Index, Table of Contents, Etc., 332-351
Input Conversion Format, 241-242
Insert, 393
Installation Progress, 530
Kerning, 114
Keyboard Management, 492-497
keyboard shortcuts, 113
Librarian, 271-272, 443-444, 506-509
Line Format, 41, 127-133
menu commands for opening, 40

Merge, 398-400
Merge Field Number, 406
Merge Message, 412-413
modeless, 398
Movie Settings, 524-526
New Folder, 229
New Header/Footer, 144-145
New Keyboard, 496
New Macro, 446
New Style, 254-258
Open, 59-62
Open Primary, 409-410
Open Secondary, 410
Other Font Sizes, 100-103
Outlining, 313-319
Page Border Style, 155-156
Page Format, 137, 140-144, 152
Page Setup, 193-204
Paragraph Format, 138-140
Pattern Edit, 388-390
Pen Size, 375
Position Hyphen, 132
Print, 27, 208-211
Publisher Options, 519-520
Redline/Strikeout, 110
Relative Sizes, 101-102
Repeat, 47
Replicate, 382-386
Rounded Corners, 363
Run Macro, 442-443
Save As, 26, 54
Save File, 460-461
Save Macro As, 459-460
Set Language, 174
Set Repeat Count, 47
Sort, 420-438
Speller, 25, 162-168, 171-175
Subscribe To, 515-518
Subscriber Options, 520-521
Subtitles, 134-136
Superscript/Subscript Options, 108-109
Suppress Format, 150-151
Tab, 122-123
Text Box Frame, 306-309
Text Type, 245
Thesaurus, 176-179
Update Style, 265
View, 94-96
Watermark Options, 149

Word Search, 231-232
WordPerfect personalization, 531
dictionaries
   counting words in, 186
   creating, 183-184
   existing
      adding words, 179-182
      deleting words, 183
   setting paths, 491
   user, 162
      adding words, 167-168
direct menu commands, 39-40
Direction pull-down menu (Find dialog box), 79-80
Discontinue Header/Footer dialog box, 147
Document Info dialog box, 228
document
   read/write variables, 463
   styles, 252
   windows, 31-33
      insertion point, 36
      scroll bars, 36
      status bar, 32-36
documents
   columns, adding and adjusting, 277-281
   copying, 69
   creating, 12-13, 44-45, 62
   deleting
      styles, 271-272
      text, 53
   editing, 20
      aligning text, 23
      cutting and pasting text, 22
      inserting/deleting text, 21-22
      selecting text, 21
   finding codes, 88-89
   flipping, 202
   information on, 228
   inserting text, 51
   movies in, 522-526
   moving
      resources to Private Library, 505-507
      within, 45-50
   multiple, 233
      arranging windows on-screen, 233-235
      combining, 238-239
      switching between, 237

   opening, 58
      from Finder, 58
      from within WordPerfect, 59
      multiple documents, 62
      second copy, 235-237
   previewing, 204-207
   printing, 27, 211
      current page, macro for, 464-465
      part of, 208-209
   retaining attributes, 223-225
   saving, 23-24, 53-54
   selecting text, 51-52
   setting
      paths, 490-491
      preferences, 483
      tabs, 19-20
   shared, Normal style in, 502
   spell-checking, 25-26, 163-165
   stationary, 246
   typing text into, 15-19
   undoing last action, 70
dpi (dots per inch), 208
dragging the Size box technique, 32
draw graphics, 354
drive partitions, 222
drop shadows, 61
Duplicate (Edit menu) command, 382
duplicate words, spell-checking for, 166
duplicating graphics objects, 382

E

Easy Install dialog box, 529-530
Edit command
   Endnotes submenu, 322
   Footnotes submenu, 326-327
   Graphics submenu, 379-380
   Macro menu, 452-455
   Styles submenu, 260-264, 269, 500-501
   Text Box submenu, 291-292
Edit Graphic dialog box, 380
Edit Macro dialog box, 452-455
edit mode for text boxes, 291-292

Edit Note dialog box, 322, 326-327
Edit Style dialog box, 260-264, 269, 500-501
Edit Text Box dialog box, 291-292
editing
   Bézier curves, 369
   captions, 306
   documents, 20-23
   endnotes, 321-322
   existing dictionaries, 179-182
   footnotes, 326-327
   graphics, 379-380
      colors, 387-388
      patterns, 388-390
   macros, 451-459
   outlines, 319
   styles, 260-262
   tables of authorities citation full form definitions, 344
   text boxes, 291-292
edition files, 512
ellipsis (...), 40
   wild card, 173
End key, 48
Endnote Options dialog box, 324-325
Endnote Style Definition window, 325
endnotes
   changing options, 323-325
   creating, 320-321
   deleting, 323
   editing, 321-322
   viewing, 322
Endnotes (Layout menu) command, 320
enhanced status bar, 35
Enter key, 44
envelopes
   paper sizes, 196
   printing, 211-212
      center-fed with no return address, 212
      center-fed with return address, 213-214
      edge-fed with return address, 215
Envelopes (Macros menu) command, 212
Envelopes macro, 212

Environment (Preferences submenu) command, 92-93, 98, 478-489
Environment dialog box, 14, 34, 93, 98, 116-117, 136, 478
   Backup, 478-480
   Format menu, 480-481
   Graphics menu, 487-488
   Language menu, 488-489
   Options menu, 482-483
   Ruler menu, 486-487
   screen colors, 480-481
   Units menu, 488
   Windows menu, 484-486
EPS (Encapsulated PostScript) images, importing, 393
equal (=) operator, 434
exiting WordPerfect, 27-28, 54-55
exporting files, *see* converting files
extended
   characters, 103-104
   columns, 276-277, 283
Extra Menu ⌘ Keys option, 92

F

F1 (Undo) keyboard shortcut, 39, 70
F2 (Cut) keyboard shortcut, 38, 64
F3 (Copy) keyboard shortcut, 38, 65
F4 (Paste) keyboard shortcut, 39, 67
F5 (Indent) keyboard shortcut, 39, 138
F6 (Select Sentence) keyboard shortcut, 52
F7 (Character Border) keyboard shortcut, 157
F9 (Run Macro) keyboard shortcut, 39, 442
F10 (Apply Style) keyboard shortcut, 259
F11 (Table of Contents level 1) keyboard shortcut, 338
F13 (100 Percent view) keyboard shortcut, 96
F14 (Redline) keyboard shortcut, 110

F15 (Strikeout) keyboard shortcut, 110
field names, defining for secondary merge files, 403-404
figure boxes, 355
   creating lists of, 345-346
   labeling boxes as, 298-299
File Info dialog box, 227
file lists
   controlling, 61-62
   navigating, 60-61
File Manager (File menu) command, 219-232
File Manager dialog box, 219-220
   file list, 220-222
   File menu, 225-228
   Folder menu, 225, 228-230
   Retain menu, 223-225
   Search menu, 225, 230-232
   Show menu, 222-223
files
   combining multiple, 238-239
   compressed, 246
   converting, 239-246
   edition, 512
   finding in File Manager file list, 220
   hierarchies, 221
   information on, 227
   input and output for sorting, 430-431
   Macros, 440
   merging to, 408-410
   opening from file lists, 221
   organizing at WordPerfect installation, 534-535
   PostScript, printing to, 210
   primary merge, 397, 406-409
   Read Me, 528
   RTF (Rich Text Format), 240
   secondary merge, 397, 401-404
   stationary, 246
   WordPerfect 2.x, viewing, 222-223
Fill Color tool, 374-375
Fill Pattern tool, 371-374
Fill tool, 370-371
filling with colors or patterns
   borders, 158-159
   columns, 287-288

   graphics objects, 370-375
   text boxes, 307-308
filtering and sorting, 437-438
filters, 432
   acceptance criteria, 432-434
   multiple, 435-436
   KeyG key, 436-437
   keys, 432-434
   operators, 434-435
Find Code (Search menu) command, 88-89
Find Code dialog box, 88
Find dialog box, 75-79
   Action menu, 84
   Affect menu, 82-84
   Direction menu, 79-80
   Insert menu, 85-87
   Match menu, 81-82
   Where menu, 80-81
Find Forward dialog box, 77
Find Next (Search menu) command, 87
Find Previous (Search menu) command, 87
Find/Change (Search menu) command, 74-79
Finder, opening documents, 58
finding and changing, *see* searching and replacing
first-line indents, 137-138
Flip Horizontal (Arrange menu) command, 387
Flip Vertical (Arrange menu) command, 387
flipping
   documents, 202
   graphics objects, 386-387
Flush Right command, 126
Folder Info dialog box, 230
folders
   Common and Private Library, 491-492
   creating, 228-229
   default
     document, 490-491
     setting, 489-490
   deleting, 229
   information on, 230
   nested, 223
   opening, 221
   renaming, 229
   viewing, 222-223
Font menu, 98-100

fonts
    bit-mapped, printing, 201
    changing for characters,
        98-99
    downloading extra, 203
    size
        changing for characters,
            100-101
        setting relative point sizes,
            101-103
    substituting, 200
footers, adding, 144-147
Footnote Options dialog box,
    328-330
footnotes
    changing options, 328
    creating, 325-326
    deleting, 327-328
    editing, 326-327
    labels, 329
    positioning, 330
    spacing, 329-330
Footnotes (Layout menu)
    command, 326
foreground color, 480-481
Format command
    Columns submenu, 278-281
    Line submenu, 129
    Page submenu, 136
formatting
    accessing features, 92-97
    borders
        filling, 158-159
        spacing, 159-160
    characters, 98
        adding borders, 153-154,
            157-158
        changing case, 112-113
        changing font size,
            100-101
        changing fonts, 98-99
        changing text styles,
            105-107
        coloring text, 115
        extended, 103-104
        kerning text, 113-115
        redlining, 109-110
        setting relative point sizes,
            101-103
        Small Caps text style, 112
        strikeouts, 109-110
        subscripts, 107-109
        superscripts, 107-109
        underlining, 111-112

date and time preferences,
    497-499
default styles, retaining
    when exporting, 272-273
defining styles with existing,
    256-258
indexes, 335-336
lines of text, 116-117
    clearing tabs, 124
    hyphenating, 131-134
    justifying, 124-126
    numbering lines, 129-131
    setting line spacing/height/
        leading, 127-129
    setting tabs, 117-124
    subtitles, 134-136
manual, retaining when
    applying styles, 273-274
pages, 140
    adding borders, 153-156
    adding headers/footers,
        144-147
    adding page numbers,
        142-144
    centering text
        vertically, 153
    eliminating widows/
        orphans, 151-152
    inserting hard page
        breaks, 142
    setting top/bottom
        margins, 140-142
    suppressing page
        formatting elements,
        150-151
    watermarks, 148-150
paragraphs, 136
    adding borders, 153-154,
        157-158
    adding space between
        paragraphs, 140
    indenting text, 137-139
    setting margins, 136-137
preferences, 480-481
subscribers, 517-518
tables
    of authorities sections, 343
    of contents, 338-339
    with styles, 249-250
see also converting files
fractional character widths, 199
Frame (Text Box submenu)
    command, 306-309
frames for text boxes, 306-307

G

generated lists
    creating, 330-331
    cross-references, 347-351
    custom, 345-347
    indexes, 331-337
    of boxes, 345-346
    tables
        of authorities, 341-345
        of contents, 337-341
generic language, setting,
    173-174
Get commands in macros, 467
Get Path dialog box, 489-490
global read/write variables, 463
glossaries, 447
Go To (Search menu)
    command, 50
Go To dialog box, 50
Gold keys, 48-49, 264
grabbing handles, 359
Graphic (Tools menu)
    command, 358
Graphic icon (document
    window), 32
Graphic Options dialog box,
    295-304, 390-392
graphics
    arcs, 363-365
    Bézier curves, 367-369
    bit-mapped (paint), 354
        precision alignment, 203
    borders around, 369-370
    draw, 354
    editing, 379-380
        colors, 387-388
        patterns, 388-390
    figure boxes, 355
    grids, 377-379
    importing, 392-393
    lines, 361-362
        changing thickness,
            375-376
    macros, 473
    objects
        duplicating, 382
        filling with colors, 374-375
        filling with patterns,
            370-374
        flipping, 386-387
        grouping, 380-382
        multiple copies, 382-386

rotating, 359-361
selecting, 359
selecting to edit, 380
ovals and circles, 365-366
overlays, 355-356
printing, 210
polygons, 366-367
rectangles and squares, 362
rounded, 363
setting preferences, 487-488
smoothing on bit-mapped
fonts, 201
text, adding, 361
tool palette, *see* tool palette
watermarks, 356-357
zooming, 377
graphics boxes
cropping objects, 391-392
resizing, 391
and moving objects in, 391
see also text boxes
greater than (>) operator, 435
greater than or equal (> =)
operator, 435
Grid Options (Layout menu)
command, 377-378
Grid Options dialog box,
377-378
grid points, 377
Grid Snap (Layout menu)
command, 379
grids in graphics windows, 377
changing colors and
lines, 378
resizing, 378
snapping to, 379
Group (Arrange menu)
command, 381
grouping graphics objects,
380-382
groups, sorting, 418
gutters, 277

H

handles
grabbing, 359
resizing text boxes with,
292-293
hanging indents, 138-139
hard
disks, drive partitions, 222
page breaks, inserting, 142
spaces, 133

Header/Footer (Layout menu)
command, 144, 147
Header/Footer dialog box,
145-147
headers, adding, 144-147
headwords, 176
counting and creating list
of, 185-186
help, 10, 42-44
accessing, 10
describing Page Setup
options, 204
files, setting paths, 491
for macros, 456-458
Help (Apple menu)
command, 42
Help dialog box, 11-12, 42-44
Help key, 42
hidden codes, 73-74
Hide Balloons (Balloon Help
menu) command, 42
Hide Grid (Layout menu)
command, 377
hiding
graphics grids, 377
text box contents, 304
hierarchical menu commands,
40-41
hierarchies of files, 221
highlight color, 480-481
Home key, 48
horizontal positioning of text
boxes, 299-301
hyphenating, 131-134
hyphens
nonbreaking, 133
soft, 132-133

I-J

icons
Copy Ruler, 97
Graphic (document
window), 32
importing
files, *see* converting files
graphics, 392-393
Indent (Layout menu)
command, 138
indenting text, 137-139
first-line, 137-138
hanging, 138-139
paragraph, 138

Index Etc. (Tools menu)
command, 332-351
Index, Table of Contents, Etc.
dialog box, 332-351
indexes, 331
defining formats, 335-336
generating, 336-337
marking entries, 332-335
Input Conversion Format dialog
box, 241-242
input files for sorting, 430-431
Insert command
File menu, 393
Movie submenu, 522-523
Insert dialog box, 393
Insert pull-down menu (Find
dialog box), 85-87
inserting
hard page breaks, 142
soft hyphens, 132
text, 21-22, 51
insertion point, 36
Installation Progress dialog
box, 530
installing
predefined macros, 443-445
WordPerfect, 527-535
inverting images, 202
Italic (Style menu)
command, 72
italic text style, 71-72

justifying text, *see* aligning text

K

kerning, 91, 113-115
Kerning (Line submenu)
command, 114-115
Kerning dialog box, 114
Keyboard Management dialog
box, 492-497
keyboard shortcuts, 38-39
⌘- – (Delete), 183
⌘-= (Add), 181
⌘-- (hyphen) (Soft
Hyphen), 132
⌘-? (Help), 39, 42
⌘-← (beginning of
line), 46
⌘-→ (end of line), 46

⌘-↑
  move up folder levels, 222
  top of screen, 46
  view previous, 60
⌘-↓ (bottom of screen), 46
⌘-A
  Assign Keystroke, 266, 453
  Clear All, 123
  Select All, 52
⌘-B (Bold), 71-72
⌘-C (Copy), 38, 66
⌘-Delete (Smart Delete), 69
⌘-E
  Edit Style, 266
  Speller, 39
⌘-Esc (Repeat), 47
⌘-F (Find/Change), 76
⌘-F2 (Text Box), 289
⌘-F3 (Copy Ruler), 97
⌘-F5 (Left/Right
  Indent), 138
⌘-F6 (Select Paragraph), 52
⌘-F7 (Paragraph
  Border), 157
⌘-F8 (first-line indent), 138
⌘-F9 (Record Macro),
  39, 446
⌘-F10 (New Style), 254
⌘-F11 (Table of Contents
  level 2), 338
⌘-F12 (End of Record), 402
⌘-F13 (Full Page view), 96
⌘-F14 (Superscript), 108
⌘-F15 (Subscript), 107
⌘-G (Generate Index,
  Etc.), 337
⌘-H
  Character, 101, 108
  List Headwords, 186
⌘-I (Italic), 39, 72
⌘-J (Index, Etc.), 332
⌘-K (Copy), 444
⌘-L (Lowercase), 113
⌘-M (Page Format), 136
⌘-N
  New, 62
  Word Count, 185
⌘-O (Open), 39, 59
⌘-P (Print), 39, 211
⌘-Q (Quit), 39, 54
⌘-R
  Redirect Output, 431
  Show Common
    Words, 181

Show Ruler, 32, 93, 117
⌘-Return
  Advance Page, 32
  Hard Page Break, 142
⌘-S
  Save, 39, 53
  Show Style, 263
⌘-Shift (Codes Show/
    Hide), 38
⌘-Shift-- (hyphen)
    (Nonbreaking Hyphen),
    133-134
⌘-Shift-? (Help), 39
⌘-Shift-A (Append), 68
⌘-Shift-B (Find Previous),
  38, 87
⌘-Shift-C
  Center Align, 38
  Center Page, 153
⌘-Shift-D (Date/Time), 38
⌘-Shift-Esc (Repeat
    Count), 47
⌘-Shift-G
  Go to Dialog, 38
  Go To, 50
⌘-Shift-H (Header/
    Footer), 144
⌘-Shift-I
  Indent Paragraph, 138
  Indent, 39
⌘-Shift-J (Justify), 125
⌘-Shift-K (Codes Show/
    Hide), 73, 476
⌘-Shift-M (Merge), 398
⌘-Shift-N (Find Next),
  38, 87
⌘-Shift-O (Outline), 313
⌘-Shift-P (Print Preview),
  39, 204
⌘-Shift-Return (Column
    Break), 277
⌘-Shift-S (Save As), 39
⌘-Shift-T (Thesaurus), 176
⌘-Shift-U (Select
    Sentence), 52
⌘-Shift-W (Cycle Windows),
  38, 237
⌘-Shift-X (Run Macro),
  39, 442
⌘-Shift-Y (Select
    Paragraph), 52
⌘-space bar (Hard
    Space), 133
⌘-T (Plain Text), 72, 107

⌘-U
  Underline, 72
  Uppercase, 113
⌘-V (Paste), 39, 66-67
⌘-W (Close), 38, 186
⌘-X (Cut), 38, 64, 66
⌘-Y (Apply Style), 259
⌘-Z (Undo), 39, 53, 70
accessing with Extra Menu
    ⌘ Keys, 92
assigning to
  macros, 453-454
  styles, 263-264
changing for commands,
    493-495
dialog boxes, 113
F1 (Undo), 39, 70
F2 (Cut), 38, 64
F3 (Copy), 38, 65
F4 (Paste), 39, 67
F5 (Indent), 39, 138
F6 (Select Sentence), 52
F7 (Character Border), 157
F9 (Run Macro), 39, 442
F10 (Apply Style), 259
F11 (Table of Contents
    level 1), 338
F13 (100 Percent view), 96
F14 (Redline), 110
F15 (Strikeout), 110
insertion point
    movements, 49
Option-; (Match Multiple
    Characters), 173
Option- ← (left one
    word), 46
Option- → (right one
    word), 46
Option-F1 (Codes Show/
    Hide), 45
Option-F2 (Codes Show/
    Hide), 38, 73, 476
Option-F4 (Character
    Map), 103
Option-F5 (Page
    Format), 136
Option-F7 (Page
    Border), 155
Option-F10 (Edit Style), 260
Option-F11 (Generate
    Index, Etc.), 337
Option-F13 (Go To), 50
Option-Shift- → (select
    word and punctuation/
    spaces), 69

Index

Shift-Clear (Num Lock), 39, 48
Shift-Esc (Num Lock), 39
Shift-F7 (Column Border), 284
Shift-F9 (Edit Macro), 452
Shift-F10 (Update Style), 265
Shift-F14 (Character Format Small Caps), 112
Shift-F15 (Character Format), 111
Shift-Tab
  Margin Release, 139
  Outline levels, 312
keyboards
  accessing menu commands, 38-39
  changing keyboard commands, 493-495
  definitions, 493
    creating, 496
  managing with Librarian, 504
  printing commands lists, 496-497
  selecting text, 52
  setting preferences, 492
Keyboards (Preferences submenu) command, 492-497
KeyG filter key, 436-437
keys
  . (period) (numeric keypad), 53
  Command (⌘), 41, 61, 113
  Delete (or Backspace), 44, 53
  End, 48
  filter, 432-434
  Gold, 48, 264
  Help, 42
  Home, 48
  KeyG filter, 436-437
  numeric, 427-428
  Page Down, 48
  Page Up, 48
  Return (or Enter), 32, 44, 312
  sort, 419
  Tab, 44, 312

L

labels, footnote, 329
landscape orientation, 196-197
Language (Tools menu) command, 134-135, 173-174
languages
  alternate, 174-175
  generic, 173-174
  setting preferences, 488-489
Layout menu, 37
leader tabs, 120
leading, 127-129
left
  margins, setting, 136-137
  tabs, 19
Left/Right Indent (Layout menu) command, 138
Legal outlining style, 316-318
less than (<) operator, 435
less than or equal (<=) operator, 435
Letter Closing (Macro menu) command, 447
Librarian (File menu) command, 271-272, 443, 506-509
Librarian dialog box, 271-272, 443-444, 506-509
Librarian utility, 502-503
  resources
    deleting, 508-509
    levels of storage, 504-505
    moving, 505-508
    types, 503-504
Line (Layout menu) command, 114, 122, 129, 131
Line Format dialog box, 41, 127-133
Line tool, 361-362
lines
  changing thickness, 375-376
  drawing, 361-362
  in graphics grids, 378
lines of text
  formatting, 116-117
    clearing tabs, 124
    hyphenating, 131-134
    justifying, 124-126
    numbering, 129-131
    setting spacing/height/leading, 127-129
    setting tabs, 117-124
    subtitles, 134-136

linking styles, 268-269
List Headwords (Thesaurus menu) command, 186
lists
  File Manager file list, 220-222
  sorting, 419-420
  see also generated lists
local read/write variables, 463
loops in macros, 469-471

M

Macro Editor, 454-459
Macro menu, excluding macros from, 452-453
macros, 439
  assigning keystrokes to, 453-454
  converting text to, 460-461
  creating by modifying macros, 459-460
  describing, 454
  editing, 451-452
    after recording, 456
    while recording, 458-459
  Envelopes, 212
  excluding from Macro menu, 452-453
  graphics, 473
  loops, 469-471
  managing with Librarian, 503
  nesting and chaining, 472-473
  on-line help for, 456-458
  pausing
    during recording, 461
    while running, 461-462
  predefined, 440-441
    installing, 443-445
    running, 440-443
  programmable commands, 462-473
  recording, 445
    for converting tabbed text to secondary merge files, 447-451
    for entering repetitive text, 445-447
  saving as text files, 460
  user input, 467-468
  variables, 462

read-only, 463-466
read/write, 463
with operators, 466
Macros file, 440
Margin Release (Layout menu) command, 139
margins
anchoring text boxes to, 299-300
binding width, 198-199
in text boxes, 293
reducing or enlarging, 196
setting
left/right margins, 136-137
top/bottom page margins, 140-142
Match pull-down menu (Find dialog box), 81-82
memos, macro for creating, 445-447
Menu command in macros, 468
menus
accessing
commands, 37-39
formatting features, 92-93
Action (Find dialog box), 84
Affect (Find dialog box), 82-84
appearance preferences, 482-483
Direction (Find dialog box), 79-80
Font, 98-100
Insert (Find dialog box), 85-87
Layout, 37
Match (Find dialog box), 81-82
pop-up, 40, 61
pull-down, 61
Relative Size, 103
ruler, 94
Style, 40
Where (Find dialog box), 80-81
Zoom, 94-96
Merge (Tools menu) command, 398-400
Merge dialog box, 398-400
Merge Field Number dialog box, 406
Merge Message dialog box, 412-413

merge records, *see* secondary merge files
merging
codes for, 398-400
messages for, 411-414
primary files for, 406-409
secondary files for, 401-404
to files, 408-410
to printers, 414-415
without secondary files, 410
messages, inserting in merges, 411-414
modeless dialog boxes, 398
modes
Command, numeric keypad in, 48-49
edit, 291-292
Typeover, 53
mouse
accessing menu commands, 37-38
insertion point, 36
selecting text, 51-52
Movie (Tools menu) command, 522
movie badges, 524
Movie Settings dialog box, 524-526
movies in documents
changing settings, 524-526
frames and captions, 526
inserting, 522-523
playing, 524
moving
around documents, 45
with arrow keys, 46
with Go To command, 50
with keyboard, 48
with numeric keypad, 48-49
with Repeat feature, 46-47
with scroll bars, 45-46
objects within graphics boxes, 391
resources, 505-508
text boxes, 304-305
through file lists, 60-61
MultiFinder, 58
multiple
documents, 233-239
opening, 62
filter acceptance criteria, 435-436
key sorts, 423-425

N

nested
folders, 223
macros, 472-473
searches, partial, 232
networks
printers, 190-191
zones, 191
New command
Endnotes submenu, 320
File menu, 62
Footnotes submenu, 326
Graphics submenu, 358
Styles submenu, 254-258
Text Box submenu, 289
New Folder dialog box, 229
New Header/Footer dialog box, 144-145
New Keyboard dialog box, 496
New Macro dialog box, 446
New Style dialog box, 254-258
newspaper columns, 276, 281-282
nonbreaking hyphens, 133
Normal style, 250
modifying, 499-502
not equal (<>) operator, 434
numbering
lines, 129-131
pages, 142-144
numbers
endnote, 323-325
outline, 313-315
spell-checking words with, 165-166
numeric
keypad, moving around documents, 48-49
keys, sorting by, 427-428

O

objects
duplicating, 382
flipping, 386-387
grouping, 380-382
in graphics boxes
cropping, 391-392
resizing and moving, 391
multiple copies, 382-386
rotating, 359-361

selecting, 359
   to edit, 380
   zooming, 377
on-line help for macros, 456-458
Open (File menu) command, 59
Open dialog box, 59-60
   file lists, 60-62
   Retain pop-up menu, 62
   Show pop-up menu, 61
Open Primary dialog box, 409-410
Open Secondary dialog box, 410
opening
   documents, 58
   creating new documents, 62
   from Finder, 58
   from within WordPerfect, 59
   multiple, 62
   files or folders, 221
operators
   Boolean, 435
   filter, 434-435
   in macros, 466
Option-; (Match Multiple Characters) keyboard shortcut, 173
Option-← (left one word) keyboard shortcut, 46
Option-→ (right one word) keyboard shortcut, 46
Option-F1 (Codes Show/Hide) keyboard shortcut, 45
Option-F2 (Codes Show/Hide) keyboard shortcut, 38, 73, 476
Option-F4 (Character Map) keyboard shortcut, 103
Option-F5 (Page Format) keyboard shortcut, 136
Option-F7 (Page Border) keyboard shortcut, 155
Option-F10 (Edit Style) keyboard shortcut, 260
Option-F11 (Generate Index, Etc.) keyboard shortcut, 337
Option-F13 (Go To) keyboard shortcut, 50
Option-Shift-→ (select word and punctuation/spaces) keyboard shortcut, 69
Options command
   Date/Time submenu, 497-499

Endnotes submenu, 324-325
Footnotes submenu, 328-330
Graphic submenu, 390-392
Macro menu, 459
Text Box submenu, 294-304
or (+) operator, 435
orientation, 196-197
orphans, 151-152
Other Font Sizes dialog box, 100-103
Other Size (Font menu) command, 100, 113
Outline (Style menu) command, 105
Outline outlining style, 316-317
outlines
   creating, 312-313
   customizing, 318-319
   editing, 319
   numbering, 313-315
   styles, 315-316
Outlining (Tools menu) command, 313-319
Outlining dialog box, 313-319
output files for sorting, 430-431
Oval tool, 365-366
ovals, drawing, 365-366
Overlay (Tools menu) command, 355-356
overlays, 355-356
   printing, 210

P

Page command
   Borders submenu, 155-156
   Layout menu, 136
Page Border Style dialog box, 155-156
Page Break (Layout menu) command, 142
Page Down key, 48
Page Format (Layout menu) command, 141
Page Format dialog box, 137, 140-144, 152
Page Setup (File menu) command, 193-203
Page Setup dialog box, 193-194
   adding options, 197
   Apple LaserWriter, 194

Binding Width option, 198-199
Fractional Character Widths option, 199
help, 204
Options option, 201-203
paper sizes option, 195-196
Printer Effects option, 200-201
Reduce or Enlarge option, 196-197
Page Up key, 48
pages
   adding borders, 153-156
   anchoring text boxes to, 296-297
   formatting, 140
   adding headers/footers, 144-147
   adding page numbers, 142-144
   centering text vertically, 153
   eliminating widows/ orphans, 151-152
   inserting hard page breaks, 142
   setting top/bottom margins, 140-142
   suppressing page formatting elements, 150-151
   watermarks, 148-150
   positioning footnotes, 330
   printing
     cover, 209
     current, macro for, 464-465
paint graphics, *see* bit maps
paired codes, 74
paper
   printing on both sides of, 210
   selecting sources, 209
   setting sizes for printers, 195-196
Paragraph command
   Borders submenu, 157
   Layout menu, 138
Paragraph Format dialog box, 138-140
paragraph indents, 138
Paragraph outlining style, 316-317

Index

paragraphs
    adding borders, 153-154, 157-158
    anchoring text boxes to, 297
    formatting, 136
        adding space between paragraphs, 140
        indenting text, 137-139
        setting margins, 136-137
parallel columns, 276, 281-283
password protection, 483
Paste (Edit menu) command, 22, 62-67
pasting
    ruler, 97
    text, *see* cutting and pasting text
paths, setting, 490-491
Pattern Edit dialog box, 388-390
patterns
    columns
        borders, 285
        filling text area, 287-288
    graphics
        editing, 388-390
        filling objects with, 370-374
    text boxes
        filling with, 307-308
        frames, 307
Patterns (Edit menu) command, 388-390
Pause (Macro Options submenu) command, 461
Pen Color tool, 374-375
Pen Pattern tool, 371-374
Pen Size (Layout menu) command, 375
Pen Size dialog box, 375
Pen Size tool, 375-376
Pen tool, 369-370
period (.) key (numeric keypad), 53
phonetic spelling suggestions, 166-167
PICT images, importing, 393
pixels, 199
Plain Text (Style menu) command, 72, 107
Pointer tool, 359
Polygon tool, 366-367
polygons, drawing, 366-367
pop-up menus, 40, 61

portrait orientation, 196-197
Position Hyphen dialog box, 132
posters, 526
PostScript files, printing to, 210
precedence of style definitions, 252
predefined macros, 440-441
    installing, 443-445
    running, 440-443
preferences
    automatic backup, 478-480
    comparing to styles, 476-477
    document, 483
    format, 480-481
    graphics, 487-488
    languages, 488-489
    measurement units, 488
    menu appearance, 482-483
    ruler, 486-487
    screen colors, 480-481
    setting, 477
    window appearance, 484-486
Preferences (File menu) command, 13-14, 33, 92, 477
previewing documents, 204-207
primary merge files, 397
    creating, 406-409
Print (File menu) command, 27, 208-211
print area, expanding, 203
Print dialog box, 27, 208-211
Print Preview (File menu) command, 204-207
printers
    binding width, 198-199
    choosing, 189-193
    fonts
        downloading extra, 203
        printing bit-mapped faster, 201
        smoothing graphics on bit-mapped, 201
        smoothing text on bit-mapped, 201
        substituting, 200
    fractional character widths, 199
    merging to, 414-415
    orientation, 196-197
    page setups, 193-194

paper
    sizes, 195-196
    sources, 209
    reducing or enlarging printing and margins, 196
printing
    background (spooling), 193
    bit-mapped fonts faster, 201
    cover pages, 209
    documents, 27, 211
        current page, macro for, 464-465
        part of, 208-209
    enhancing speed or quality, 200-201
    envelopes, 211-215
    from Print Preview screen, 207
    graphic overlays, 210
    in colors, 210
    keyboard commands lists, 496-497
    multiple copies, 209
    on both sides of paper, 210
    reducing or enlarging, 196
    reverse order, 211
    to PostScript files, 210
Private Library
    comparing with Common Library, 504-505
    copying Common Library resources to, 507-508
    folder, 491-492
    moving document resources to, 505-507
    styles, 252
        deleting styles from, 271-272
programmable macro commands, 462-473
Prompt command in macros, 467-468
Publish and Subscribe, 511-512
    publishers
        canceling, 521
        creating, 512-514
        setting options, 519-520
    subscribers
        canceling, 521
        creating, 514-517
        formatting, 517-518
        setting options, 520-521
Publisher Options (Publishing submenu) command, 519-520

Publisher Options dialog box, 519-520
Publishing (Edit menu) command, 514
pull-down menus, 61
pulling down menus, 34

Q

question mark (?) wild card, 172
QuickTime system extension, 522-526
Quit (File menu) command, 27-28, 54

R

Read Me file, 528
read-only variables, 463-466
read/write variables, 463
Record (Macro menu) command, 446
recording macros, 445-447
records, deleting from secondary files, 403
Rectangle tool, 362
rectangles
    drawing, 362
    rounded, 363
Redline (Style menu) command, 110
Redline/Strikeout dialog box, 110
redlining, 109-110
reference words, 176
Relative Size pop-up menu, 103
Relative Sizes dialog box, 101-102
relative tabs, 121-122
Remove command
    Style menu, 110
    Styles submenu, 268
Repeat dialog box, 47
Repeat feature, 46-47
Replicate (Arrange menu) command, 382-386
Replicate dialog box, 382-386
resizing
    graphics boxes, 391
    objects in, 391
    graphics grids, 378

Show Codes window, 74
    text boxes, 292-293, 304
resources
    deleting, 508-509
    moving, 505-508
    storage levels, 504-505
    types, 503-504
Resume (Macro Options submenu) command, 461
Return key, 32, 44
    outline level 1, 312
reverse order printing, 211
right
    margins, setting, 136-137
    tabs, 119
Rotate (Arrange menu) command, 361
Rotation tool, 359, 361
Rounded Corners (Layout menu) command, 363
Rounded Corners dialog box, 363
Rounded Rectangle tool, 363
rows, column, 277
RTF (Rich Text Format) files, 240
ruler, 32
    accessing formatting features, 93-97
    Alignment pop-up menu, 124-125
    copying and pasting, 97
    creating columns, 278
    displaying, 16
    setting preferences, 486-487
    Tab Type pop-up menu, 117-122
Run Macro dialog box, 442-443

S

Save (File menu) command, 23-24, 53
Save As (Macro Options submenu) command, 459-460
Save As dialog box, 26, 54
Save File dialog box, 460-461
Save Macro As dialog box, 459-460
Save Text (Macro Options submenu) command, 460-461

saving
    documents, 23-24, 53-54
    macros as text files, 460
    not saving changes, 55
screen colors, 480-481
scroll bars, 12, 36
    moving around documents, 45-46
scrolling Show Codes window, 74
SCSI (Small Computer System Interface) printers, 190
search histories, 177-178
searching
    and replacing, 74-79
        next or previous occurrence of words/phrases, 87
    for files in File Manager file list, 220
    sort items, 436-437
    without opening each file, 230-232
secondary merge files, 397
    converting address lists to, macro for, 469-471
    converting tabbed text to, macro for, 447-451
    creating, 401-404
    merging without, 410
    sorting, 418, 428-430
sections, 341
Select All (Edit menu) command, 52
selecting text, 21, 51-52
serial printers, 190-192
Set Language (Language submenu) command, 173-174
Set Language dialog box, 174
Set Repeat Count dialog box, 47
sets of columns, 277
Settings (Movie submenu) command, 525-526
Shadow (Style menu) command, 105
Shift key, 52
Shift-Clear (Num Lock) keyboard shortcut, 39, 48
Shift-Esc (Num Lock) keyboard shortcut, 39
Shift-F7 (Column Border) keyboard shortcut, 284
Shift-F9 (Edit Macro) keyboard shortcut, 452

Shift-F10 (Update Style) keyboard shortcut, 265
Shift-F14 (Character Format Small Caps) keyboard shortcut, 112
Shift-F15 (Character Format) keyboard shortcut, 111
Shift-Tab keyboard shortcut
 Margin Release, 139
 Outline levels, 312
Show ¶ (Edit menu) command, 44-45
Show Balloons (Balloon Help menu) command, 42
Show Codes (Edit menu) command, 73, 476
Show Codes window
 resizing, 74
 scrolling, 74
Show Common (Speller menu) command, 181
Show Coordinates (Layout menu) command, 362
Show Position feature, 13
Show Ruler (Layout menu) command, 32, 93, 117
single key sorts, 420-422
Size box (document window), 32
size of fonts
 changing, 100-101
 setting relative point size, 101-103
Small Caps text style, 112
smart delete feature, 69
snapping to grids, 379
soft hyphens, 132
Sort (Tools menu) command, 420-438
Sort dialog box, 420-438
sorting
 and filtering, 437-438
 by number, 427-428
 categories of, 417
 defining sort keys, 419
 input and output files for, 430-431
 items, 418
 lists, 419-420
 multiple key, 423-425
 secondary merge files, 428-430
 single key, 420-422
 tabbed text, 425-427

space bar, aligning text with, 200
spaces, hard, 133
spacing
 between and above footnotes, 329-330
 between column borders and text, 288
 between paragraphs, 140
 for borders, 159-160
 in and around text boxes, 308-309
Speller, 25-26, 161-162
 checking documents
  entire, 163
  from insertion point to end, 164-165
  part, 164
 checking words
  duplicates, 166
  with numbers, 165-166
 languages
  alternate, 174-175
  generic, ignoring, 173-174
 looking up words, 171
 practicing with, 168-171
 replacing misspelled words, 167
 running, 167
 selecting text, 162
 skipping words, 168
 suggested alternate spellings, 166-167
 user dictionaries, adding words, 167-168
 wild cards with, 171-173
Speller (Tools menu) command, 25-26, 163-165
Speller dialog box, 25
 Add option, 168
 Check Duplicate Words option, 166
 Check menu, 163
 Check Selection option, 164
 Check Suggest Phonetics option, 167
 Check To End option, 162, 165
 Check Words With Numbers option, 165-166
 Dictionary menu, 175
 Insert Match Multiple Characters option, 173
 Insert Match One Character option, 172

 Look Up option, 171
 Replace option, 167
 Skip Always option, 168
 Skip Once option, 168
spooling, 193
squares
 drawing, 362
 rounded, 363
ST Utility application, 168, 179
 creating dictionaries, 183-184
 counting words in dictionaries, 186
 existing dictionaries
  adding words, 179-182
  deleting words, 183
 with thesaurus files, 185-186
starting WordPerfect, 10, 30-31
stationary documents, 246
status bar, 13-15, 32-36
Stop Recording (Macro menu) command, 446
Strikeout (Style menu) command, 110
strikeouts, 109-110
Style (Endnotes submenu) command, 325
style buttons, 34-35
style definition window, 261-267
Style menu, 40
styles
 adding to Styles submenu, 262-263
 applying, 258-259
 assigning keyboard shortcuts to, 263-264
 basing on other styles, 270-271
 Common Library, 253
 comparing to preferences, 476-477
 copying into new documents, 483
 default, 250-251
  retaining formatting when exporting, 272-273
 defining, 251
  from existing text, 253-258
 deleting, 271-272
 document, 252
 editing, 260-262
 formatting with, 249-250
 linking, 268-269

Index

553

managing with
    Librarian, 503
  Normal, 250, 499-502
  precedence, 252
  Private Library, 252
  removing from text, 268
  retaining manual formatting
    when applying, 273-274
  text
    changing, 70-72, 105-107
    deleting, 72
    updating, 265
    using text in definitions,
      265-267
Styles (Layout menu)
  command, 254
subdocuments, 80
subgroups, 176
Subscribe To (Publishing
  submenu) command,
  515-518
Subscribe To dialog box,
  515-518
Subscriber Options (Publishing
  submenu) command,
  520-521
Subscriber Options dialog box,
  520-521
subscribers
  canceling, 521
  creating, 514-517
  formatting, 517-518
  setting options, 520-521
Subscript (Style menu)
  command, 107
subscripts, 107-109
Subtitle (Language submenu)
  command, 134-135
Subtitles dialog box, 134-136
Superscript (Style menu)
  command, 108
Superscript/Subscript Options
  dialog box, 108-109
superscripts, 107-109
Suppress Format dialog box,
  150-151
synonyms, 177
System 7
  Balloon Help, 42
  Publish and Subscribe,
    511-521
  QuickTime system
    extension, 522-526

T

tab delimited text, 425
Tab key, 44
  outline levels, 312
tables
  boxes
    creating lists of, 345-346
    labeling as, 298-299
  of authorities
    creating, 341
    defining section
      formats, 343
    editing citation full form
      definitions, 344
    generating, 345
    marking citations, 341-343
  of contents
    creating, 337
    defining formats, 338-339
    generating, 341
tabs
  absolute, 122
  Bar, 120-121
  center, 118
  clearing, 19, 117, 124
  decimal, 119
  left, 19
  leader, 120
  relative, 121-122
  right, 119
  setting, 19-20, 117-124
Tabs (Line submenu)
  command, 122
Tabs dialog box, 122-123
targets, 348
  marking, 349-350
templates, envelope, 213-215
text
  adding to graphics, 361
  aligning, 23
    with space bar, 200
  appending, 67-69
  boldface, 71-72
  centering vertically, 153
  coloring, 115
  converting to macros,
    460-461
  copying, 63-65
  cutting, 22, 63-65
  defining styles from,
    253-258
  deleting, 21-22, 53
    selected, 69

entering in text boxes, 290
hidden codes, 73-74
indenting, 137-139
inserting, 21-22, 51
italic, 71-72
kerning, 113-115
lines of, formatting, 116-117
  clearing tabs, 124
  hyphenating, 131-134
  justifying, 124-126
  numbering lines, 129-131
  setting line spacing/height/
    leading, 127-129
  setting tabs, 117-124
  subtitles, 134-136
pasting, 22, 63-67
removing styles from, 268
repetitive, macros for
  entering, 445-447
searching for and replacing,
  74-79
  next or previous
    occurrence, 87
selecting, 21, 51-52
  to spell-check, 162
smoothing on bit-mapped
  fonts, 201
spacing between footnotes
  and, 329-330
styles
  changing, 70-71, 105-107
  deleting, 72
tabbed
  converting to secondary
    merge files, macro for,
    447-451
  sorting, 425-427
typing
  into documents, 15-19
  over in Typeover mode, 53
underline, 71-72
using in style definitions,
  265-267
wrapping around text
  boxes, 302-303
Text (Date/Time submenu)
  command, 499
Text Box (Tools menu)
  command, 289
Text Box Frame dialog box,
  306-309
text boxes
  anchoring
    as characters, 296

to pages, 296-297
to paragraphs, 297
captions
  adding, 305-306
  changing positions, 308-309
columns, 294
creating, 289-290
  lists of, 345-346
editing, 291-292
entering text, 290
filling with colors or patterns, 307-308
frames, 306-307
functions of, 294-296
hiding contents, 304
labeling, 298-299
margins, 293
moving, 304-305
positioning
  horizontally, 299-301
  vertically, 301-302
resizing
  by changing dimensions, 304
  with handles, 292-293
spacing in and around, 308-309
wrapping text around, 302-303
Text command, 16-17
text files
  exporting, 245
  saving macros as, 460
Text tool, 361
Text Type dialog box, 245
thesaurus, 161, 175
  adding nondocument words to documents, 178-179
  clearing columns, 178
  counting and creating list of headwords, 185-186
  looking up synonyms and antonyms, 177
  looking up words, 175-176
  search histories, 177-178
  setting paths, 491
Thesaurus (Tools menu) command, 176-179
Thesaurus dialog box, 176-179
times, setting format preferences, 497-499
Title bar (document window), 31

tool palette, graphics, 357-360
  Arc tool, 363-365
  Curve tool, 367-369
  Fill Color tool, 374-375
  Fill Pattern tool, 371-374
  Fill tool, 370-371
  Line tool, 361-362
  Oval tool, 365-366
  Pen Color tool, 374-375
  Pen Pattern tool, 371-374
  Pen Size tool, 375-376
  Pen tool, 369-370
  Pointer tool, 359
  Polygon tool, 366-367
  Rectangle tool, 362
  Rotation tool, 359-361
  Rounded Rectangle tool, 363
  Text tool, 361
  Zoom tool, 377
triangles, drawing, 366-367
Typeover mode, 53

U

Underline (Style menu) command, 17-18, 72
underline text style, 71-72
underlining, 111-112
Undo (Edit menu) command, 53, 70
Ungroup (Arrange menu) command, 382
units of measure, setting preferences, 488
Update (Styles submenu) command, 265
Update Style dialog box, 265
user
  dictionaries, 162
    adding words, 167-168
    setting paths, 491
  input in macros, 467-468
user-defined boxes
  creating lists of, 345-346
  labeling, 298-299
utilities
  Librarian, 502-509
  ST Utility, 168, 179-186
  XTND conversion, 240

V

variables in macros, 462
  read-only, 463-466
  read/write, 463
  with operators, 466
vertical
  centering of text, 153
  positioning of text boxes, 301-302
View dialog box, 94-96

W

Watermark (Tools menu) command, 148-149, 357
Watermark Options dialog box, 149
watermarks, 148-150, 356-357
wedge arcs, 363-364
Where pull-down menu (Find dialog box), 80-81
widows, 151-152
wild cards, 86
  spell-checking with, 171-173
windows
  appearance preferences, 484-486
  document, 31-33
    insertion point, 36
    scroll bars, 36
    status bar, 32-36
  endnote, 321-322
  Endnote Style Definition, 325
  footnote, 326
  Macro Editor, 454-459
  multiple
    arranging on-screen, 233-235
    for single documents, 235-237
    switching between, 237
  Show Codes
    resizing, 74
    scrolling, 74
  style definition, 261-262, 265-267
Word Count (Thesaurus menu) command, 185
Word Search dialog box, 231-232

word wrapping, 15-19
WordPerfect
   exiting, 54-55
   installing
     custom installs, 532-535
     easy installs, 528-532
     organizing files, 534-535
     preparation, 527-528
   opening documents from within, 59
   quitting, 27-28
   starting, 10, 30-31
WordPerfect Help (Balloon Help menu) command, 43
WordPerfect personalization dialog box, 531
words
   looking up
     in Speller, 171
     in Thesaurus, 175-179
   reference, 176
   replacing misspelled, 167
   spell-checking
     duplicates, 166
     with numbers, 165-166
wrapping text, 15-19
   around text boxes, 302-303

X-Z

XTND conversion utility, 240

ZIP codes, sorting by, 427-428
zones
   network, 191
   sorting, 418
Zoom box (document window), 32
Zoom pop-up menu, 94-96
Zoom tool, 377
zooming graphics, 377

Index

Free Catalog!

Mail us this registration form today, and we'll send you a free catalog featuring Que's complete line of best-selling books.

Name of Book _____

Name _____

Title _____

Phone ( ) _____

Company _____

Address _____

City _____

State _____ ZIP _____

Please check the appropriate answers:

1. Where did you buy your Que book?
   - ☐ Bookstore (name: _____)
   - ☐ Computer store (name: _____)
   - ☐ Catalog (name: _____)
   - ☐ Direct from Que
   - ☐ Other: _____

2. How many computer books do you buy a year?
   - ☐ 1 or less
   - ☐ 2-5
   - ☐ 6-10
   - ☐ More than 10

3. How many Que books do you own?
   - ☐ 1
   - ☐ 2-5
   - ☐ 6-10
   - ☐ More than 10

4. How long have you been using this software?
   - ☐ Less than 6 months
   - ☐ 6 months to 1 year
   - ☐ 1-3 years
   - ☐ More than 3 years

5. What influenced your purchase of this Que book?
   - ☐ Personal recommendation
   - ☐ Advertisement
   - ☐ In-store display
   - ☐ Price
   - ☐ Que catalog
   - ☐ Que mailing
   - ☐ Que's reputation
   - ☐ Other: _____

6. How would you rate the overall content of the book?
   - ☐ Very good
   - ☐ Good
   - ☐ Satisfactory
   - ☐ Poor

7. What do you like *best* about this Que book?
   _____
   _____
   _____

8. What do you like *least* about this Que book?
   _____
   _____
   _____

9. Did you buy this book with your personal funds?
   ☐ Yes   ☐ No

10. Please feel free to list any other comments you may have about this Que book.
    _____
    _____
    _____
    _____

Order Your Que Books Today!

Name _____

Title _____

Company _____

City _____

State _____ ZIP _____

Phone No. ( ) _____

Method of Payment:

Check ☐   (Please enclose in envelope.)

Charge My: VISA ☐   MasterCard ☐   American Express ☐

Charge # _____

Expiration Date _____

Order No.	Title	Qty.	Price	Total

You can **FAX** your order to **1-317-573-2583**. Or call **1-800-428-5331, ext. ORDR** to order direct.

Please add $2.50 per title for shipping and handling.

Subtotal _____

Shipping & Handling _____

Total _____

BUSINESS REPLY MAIL	
First Class Permit No. 9918 Indianapolis, IN	

Postage will be paid by addressee

11711 N. College
Carmel, IN 46032

NO POSTAGE
NECESSARY
IF MAILED
IN THE
UNITED STATES

BUSINESS REPLY MAIL
First Class Permit No. 9918   Indianapolis, IN

Postage will be paid by addressee

11711 N. College
Carmel, IN 46032

NO POSTAGE
NECESSARY
IF MAILED
IN THE
UNITED STATES